Leveraging ChatGPT and Artificial Intelligence for Effective Customer Engagement

Rohit Bansal
Department of Management Studies, Vaish College of Engineering, Rohtak, India

Abdul Hafaz Ngah
Faculty of Business Economics and Social Development Universiti Malaysia Terenganu, Malaysia

Aziza Chakir
FSJES AC, Hassan II University, Casablanca, Morocco

Nishita Pruthi
Maharshi Dayanand University, India

A volume in the Advances in Business Information Systems and Analytics (ABISA) Book Series

IGI Global
PUBLISHER of TIMELY KNOWLEDGE

Published in the United States of America by
IGI Global
Business Science Reference (an imprint of IGI Global)
701 E. Chocolate Avenue
Hershey PA, USA 17033
Tel: 717-533-8845
Fax: 717-533-8661
E-mail: cust@igi-global.com
Web site: http://www.igi-global.com

Library of Congress Cataloging-in-Publication Data

Names: Bansal, Rohit, 1982- editor. | Ngah, Abdul Hafaz, 1973- editor. | Chakir, Aziza, 1984- editor. | Pruthi, Nishita, 1997- editor.
Title: Leveraging ChatGPT and artificial intelligence for effective customer engagement / edited by Rohit Bansal, Abdul Hafaz Ngah, Aziza Chakir, Nishita Pruthi.
Description: Hershey, PA : Business Science Reference, [2024] | Includes bibliographical references and index. | Summary: "This book provides deeper understanding on the role of Artificial Intelligence powered ChatGPT in enhancing better customer engagement and gain competitive edge"-- Provided by publisher.
Identifiers: LCCN 2023040609 (print) | LCCN 2023040610 (ebook) | ISBN 9798369308158 (hardcover) | ISBN 9798369308165 (ebook)
Subjects: LCSH: Customer relations. | Marketing--Technological innovations. | Artificial intelligence. | ChatGPT.
Classification: LCC HF5415.5 .L4748 2024 (print) | LCC HF5415.5 (ebook) | DDC 658.8/12--dc23/eng/20240229
LC record available at https://lccn.loc.gov/2023040609
LC ebook record available at https://lccn.loc.gov/2023040610

This book is published in the IGI Global book series Advances in Business Information Systems and Analytics (ABISA) (ISSN: 2327-3275; eISSN: 2327-3283)

British Cataloguing in Publication Data
A Cataloguing in Publication record for this book is available from the British Library.
All work contributed to this book is new, previously-unpublished material.
The views expressed in this book are those of the authors, but not necessarily of the publisher.
For electronic access to this publication, please contact: eresources@igi-global.com.

Advances in Business Information Systems and Analytics (ABISA) Book Series

ISSN:2327-3275
EISSN:2327-3283

Editor-in-Chief: Madjid Tavana, La Salle University, USA

MISSION

The successful development and management of information systems and business analytics is crucial to the success of an organization. New technological developments and methods for data analysis have allowed organizations to not only improve their processes and allow for greater productivity, but have also provided businesses with a venue through which to cut costs, plan for the future, and maintain competitive advantage in the information age.

The **Advances in Business Information Systems and Analytics (ABISA) Book Series** aims to present diverse and timely research in the development, deployment, and management of business information systems and business analytics for continued organizational development and improved business value.

COVERAGE

- Data Management
- Strategic Information Systems
- Business Process Management
- Algorithms
- Business Decision Making
- Information Logistics
- Legal information systems
- Business Systems Engineering
- Decision Support Systems
- Data Analytics

IGI Global is currently accepting manuscripts for publication within this series. To submit a proposal for a volume in this series, please contact our Acquisition Editors at Acquisitions@igi-global.com or visit: http://www.igi-global.com/publish/.

The Advances in Business Information Systems and Analytics (ABISA) Book Series (ISSN 2327-3275) is published by IGI Global, 701 E. Chocolate Avenue, Hershey, PA 17033-1240, USA, www.igi-global.com. This series is composed of titles available for purchase individually; each title is edited to be contextually exclusive from any other title within the series. For pricing and ordering information please visit http://www.igi-global.com/book-series/advances-business-information-systems-analytics/37155. Postmaster: Send all address changes to above address.

Titles in this Series

For a list of additional titles in this series, please visit:
http://www.igi-global.com/book-series/advances-business-information-systems-analytics/37155

Advancement in Business Analytics Tools for Higher Financial Performance
Reza Gharoie Ahangar (Lewis University, USA) and Mark Napier (Lewis University, USA)
Business Science Reference • © 2023 • 321pp • H/C (ISBN: 9781668483862) • US $250.00

Cases on Enhancing Business Sustainability Through Knowledge Management Systems
Meir Russ (University of Wisconsin-Green Bay, USA & Stellenbosch University, South Africa)
Business Science Reference • © 2023 • 366pp • H/C (ISBN: 9781668458594) • US $240.00

Streamlining Organizational Processes Through AI, IoT, Blockchain, and Virtual Environments
Marisol Hernández Hernández (Universidad Autónoma del Estado de México, Mexico)
Business Science Reference • © 2023 • 253pp • H/C (ISBN: 9781668486399) • US $250.00

Data-Driven Approaches for Effective Managerial Decision Making
Anubha (Jaipuria Institute of Management, Ghaziabad, India) and Himanshu Sharma (IILM Institute for Higher Education, New Delhi, India)
Business Science Reference • © 2023 • 336pp • H/C (ISBN: 9781668475683) • US $255.00

Handbook of Research on AI and Machine Learning Applications in Customer Support and Analytics
Md Shamim Hossain (Hajee Mohammad Danesh Science and Technology University, Bangladesh) Ree Chan Ho (Taylor's University, Malaysia) and Goran Trajkovski (Western Governors University, USA)
Business Science Reference • © 2023 • 423pp • H/C (ISBN: 9781668471050) • US $325.00

Building Secure Business Models Through Blockchain Technology Tactics, Methods, Limitations, and Performance
Shweta Dewangan (ICFAI University, Raipur, India) Sapna Singh Kshatri (Shri Shankaracharya Institute of Professional Management and Technology, India) Astha Bhanot (Princess Nourah Bint Abdulrahman University, Saudi Arabia) and Mushtaq Ahmed Shah (Lovely Professional University, India)
Business Science Reference • © 2023 • 283pp • H/C (ISBN: 9781668478080) • US $250.00

For an entire list of titles in this series, please visit:
http://www.igi-global.com/book-series/advances-business-information-systems-analytics/37155

IGI Global
PUBLISHER of TIMELY KNOWLEDGE

701 East Chocolate Avenue, Hershey, PA 17033, USA
Tel: 717-533-8845 x100 • Fax: 717-533-8661
E-Mail: cust@igi-global.com • www.igi-global.com

Table of Contents

Detailed Table of Contents

Digital transformation and artificial intelligence (AI) are closely linked as AI is often seen as one of the main drivers of digital transformation. Digital transformation involves implementing digital technologies to transform business processes, revenue models and customer relationships. AI, on the other hand, uses algorithms to learn, reason and make decisions based on data. By integrating AI into digital transformation processes, companies can improve their operational efficiency, their capacity for innovation and their competitiveness. For example, AI can be used to automate repetitive and time-consuming tasks. Artificial intelligence (AI) is a technology that can bring many benefits in many fields, but it also presents potential risks, so business managers must know how to use this technology well.

Nowadays, discussions in the academic world and the media have focused on the potential advantages and disadvantages of ChatGPT and its variations that employ generative artificial intelligence models on their potential impacts on the economy, democracy, society, and environment. It is yet unknown if these technologies lead to job growth or job displacement, or if they merely budge human labor by producing new knowledge and judgments that may be insignificant or practically irrelevant. With the release of ChatGPT, the market for generative AI tools has seen a surge in the development of more powerful and sophisticated tools. This "AI arms race" has widened the range of business applications and raised risks related to security, privacy, bias, and other ethical dilemmas. In light of these advancements, the study provides a range of viewpoints and potential lines of inquiry to further business studies in the field of generative AI.

ChatGPT is an artificial intelligence chatbot that can interact with users in a natural and engaging way. It can adapt to different conversational scenarios and provide detailed and relevant responses. ChatGPT is based on a large language model that has been fine-tuned using human feedback and reinforcement learning. In this chapter, the authors explore how ChatGPT can be used for customer engagement in various domains, such as e-commerce, education, entertainment, and health. The benefits and challenges of using ChatGPT as a customer service agent, a personal assistant, a tutor, a storyteller, and a health coach has been discussed. Some examples of ChatGPT conversations with customers have been provided and its performance and limitations has been analyzed. Finally, it can be concluded that ChatGPT is a promising tool for enhancing customer satisfaction and loyalty, but it also requires careful design and evaluation to ensure its safety and reliability.

Artificial intelligence-based chat generative pre-trained transformer (ChatGPT), and provides numerous ideas for future research in consumer studies and marketing in the context of ChatGPT. It is a revolutionary technology that uses advanced artificial intelligence techniques to generate natural language responses to a given prompt or input. It has been used across various fields, from natural language processing to customer service to content creation. Since its launch in late 2022, ChatGPT has generated significant debate surrounding its hallmarks, benefits, and potential pitfalls. ChatGPT can offer enhanced consumer engagement, improved customer service, personalization and shopping, social interaction and communication practice, and cost-effectiveness. The proposed chapter aims to explore howChatGPT can be used to optimize digital marketing campaigns and overall improved business strategies and customer engagement.

In the digital era, businesses strive to harness various advancements in the tech field to attain heightened levels of customer engagement and ensure the effectiveness of their marketing strategies. For instance, digital marketing has the capacity to utilize AI advancements to a significant extent. In particular, nowadays, digital marketers are leveraging a recent large language-model-based chatbot called "ChatGPT," which enables users to engage in human-like conversations and has unprecedented opportunities to reshape and revolutionize the ecosystem of digital marketing and customer engagement. In this regard, this chapter underscores the transformative potential of ChatGPT in the domain of digital marketing and its profound implications for augmenting customer engagement by reviewing and synthesizing existing literature. Moreover, it considers the ethical implications surrounding AI deployment. By synthesizing existing literature, this chapter provides a comprehensive overview of the current state of knowledge in this domain, guiding future research and practice.

This chapter explores the integration of ChatGPT and AI for customer engagement, emphasizing its transformative potential. It begins by introducing the theme and the significance of ChatGPT in revolutionizing customer service through AI advancements. Subsequently, it delves into practical applications, discussing how ChatGPT understands and addresses customer inquiries effectively, automates routine tasks, and offers personalized assistance. Ethical considerations in AI implementation are also addressed. Real-world case studies demonstrate successful ChatGPT implementations, offering insights and best practices for maximizing customer engagement. The chapter concludes by envisioning the future of AI-powered customer support, highlighting the importance of a balanced integration of AI and human agents for sustainable customer experiences and business growth.

Marketers are continuously looking for fresh, cutting-edge approaches to connect with their target consumers as businesses are becoming progressively more dependent on technology and digital platforms. ChatGPT, an AI-driven chatbot that employs natural language processing (NLP) to interact with users in a human-like manner, is one of their newest technologies. ChatGPT enables businesses to offer customized and immediate support to their audience by smoothly connecting with a variety of digital platforms. ChatGPT boosts client engagement by delivering a customized and captivating user interface owing to its capacity to grasp human-like discussions. It enables companies to have more meaningful contact with their clients, immediately resolving their issues and forging a solid brand-client bond. In this chapter, the role of ChatGPT in enhancing customer engagement and how it can help businesses in achieving their marketing goals is explored. This study is based on secondary sources, including books, publications, websites, reports, and more.

This chapter analyzes the transformative potential of ChatGPT, an AI-powered tool, in reshaping consumer experience across various industries. It provides an in-depth exploration of how ChatGPT, through its advanced capabilities in natural language processing and machine learning, can enhance consumer engagement, automate repetitive tasks, and deliver personalized responses to complex queries. The chapter also underscores the strategic role of ChatGPT in digital marketing and consumer support. The chapter analyzes ChatGPT-consumer Interaction (CCI), discussing the importance of CCI design patterns, prompt engineering and usability evaluation in creating effective and engaging consumer interactions, and provides a real-life case study. The chapter further discusses the opportunities that ChatGPT presents for businesses. It highlights how the tool can help organizations gain a competitive edge by providing faster, more accurate consumer service, and by leveraging consumer data to inform decision-making and create targeted marketing campaigns.

ChatGPT is a flexible platform with many uses. ChatGPT may improve teamwork or company growth. In terms of technical innovation and the ability it has to improve people's lives, ChatGPT is hard to beat. The majority of current applications of AI are focused on automating previously manual tasks. ChatGPT demonstrates, on the other hand, that AI may evolve into a helpful helper that picks up new skills via regular usage. This study reviews ChatGPT's contemporary usage in different areas and businesses and examines its role in cryptocurrency. We have merely tapped the surface of ChatGPT's economic possibilities for all sectors. From revolutionary content creation to improved customer experiences and targeted product suggestions, this conversational AI system may unleash growth strategies. Among the many applications of ChatGPT in the cryptocurrency trading industry are real-time market analysis, historical asset appraisal, and risk management. Investors and traders may rest comfortably knowing they have quick access to information regarding ChatGPT's history, giving them peace of mind.

Digital technology plays a vital role in the hospitality sector, which creates a strong relationship with customers and a practical experience. Adopting online digital marketing strategies and different platforms include social media marketing, content writing, SEO, PPC, email and online marketing. Earlier, hotel and restaurant owners only believed in word-of-mouth and print advertising to attract customers. But nowadays, digital media has become the first choice to attract guests; it is more engaging content, and builds a solid connection with online platforms. Through online digital marketing, the hotel industry can target different demographics and connect with guests worldwide. Digital marketing gives customers memorable experiences while staying in hotels, dining at a restaurant, and attending mega-events. Customers always see the reviews, comments, and ratings of the hotels/restaurants on the social platform, and customers decide to visit the hotel/restaurant where digital networks play an essential role in promotional activities in the hospitality sector.

The hospitality industry is experiencing a paradigm shift with the integration of cutting-edge technologies, and one such innovation is chatGPT (generative pre-trained transformer). This book chapter examines how chatGPT can revolutionize the hospitality industry and empower aspiring hoteliers. Through the use of chatGPT, hotels may provide 24/7 support to visitors by answering questions, making recommendations for nearby attractions, and expediting reservation requests. The virtual assistant's capacity to comprehend natural language and respond to it improves visitor experiences and develops a sense of comfort and happiness. Additionally, ChatGPT helps hoteliers acquire insightful data from customer conversations, enabling data-driven decision-making and customized service offers. As a result of the language model's capacity to perceive and interpret sentiment, future problems can be identified, allowing hoteliers to proactively resolve guest concerns and guarantee visitor loyalty.

recommendations for teachers, administrators, and policymakers of higher education.

Preface

ChatGPT is a powerful AI-powered text-based artificial intelligence tool that can revolutionize customer engagement and content creation for businesses. With ChatGPT, businesses can automate repetitive tasks, improve customer engagement, and respond to complex search queries with accuracy and efficiency. ChatGPT utilizes data science to enhance chatbot conversations, making them more natural and engaging for customers. By leveraging machine learning techniques such as natural language processing and sentiment analysis, ChatGPT's chatbots can understand customer intent, personalize responses, and anticipate their need. Artificial intelligence (AI) is already transforming the way businesses operate and interact with their customers. One particularly impactful application is generative AI, which can generate content such as blog posts, social media posts, product descriptions, and imagery. ChatGPT is one such generative AI tool. It leverages a combination of deep neural networks and natural language processing algorithms to create engaging content quickly and efficiently. AI tools also enable greater collaboration by providing shared platforms for teams to work together more effectively. Through natural language processing (NLP) applications such as virtual assistants and chatbots, teams can communicate with customers more efficiently while improving overall productivity levels across the organization. Chatgpt can also help businesses provide faster and more accurate customer service by automating certain activities, such as responding to emails. This reduces the time it takes for customers to get the information they need while also improving overall customer satisfaction. AI's ability to identify customer trends and patterns can assist in decision-making regarding marketing initiatives and product development efforts. Leveraging this data helps businesses better understand their customers' needs and create targeted campaigns that boost engagement and customer retention rates.

Accordingly, the book title: Leveraging ChatGPT and Artificial Intelligence for Effective Customer Engagement, is self-explanatory. The book contains seventeen chapters that attempt to mirror the major areas of research on the topic and thus offer valuable findings to practitioners and readers.

Chapter one assesses the various direct and indirect, economic, human, social and individual risks that lie behind the promises of AI. Chapter two assembles perspectives and research directions on ChatGPT in the context of business and decision-making while taking into account the innovative and disruptive powers of generative AI, as well as its favorable and unfavorable effects. Chapter three benefits and challenges of using ChatGPT as a customer service agent, a personal assistant, a tutor, a storyteller, and a health coach. It highlights that that ChatGPT is a promising tool for enhancing customer satisfaction and loyalty, but it also requires careful design and evaluation to ensure its safety and reliability. Chapter four explores how ChatGPT can be used to optimize digital marketing campaigns and overall improve business strategies and customer engagement. Chapter five underscores the transformative potential of ChatGPT in the domain of digital marketing and its profound implications for augmenting customer engagement by reviewing and synthesizing existing literature. Moreover, it considers the ethical implications surrounding AI deployment. Chapter six envisions the future of AI-powered customer support, and highlights the importance of a balanced integration of AI and human agents for sustainable customer experiences and business growth. Chapter seven investigates how ChatGPT might assist organizations in attaining their marketing objectives and what function it plays in boosting customer engagement. Chapter eight analyzes ChatGPT-consumer Interaction (CCI), discusses the importance of CCI design patterns, prompts engineering and usability evaluation in creating effective and engaging consumer interactions, and provides a real-life case study. The chapter further discusses the opportunities that ChatGPT presents for businesses. It highlights how the tool can help organizations gain a competitive edge by providing faster, more accurate consumer service, and by leveraging consumer data to inform decision-making and create targeted marketing campaigns. Chapter nine highlights the role of ChatGPT in the cryptocurrency industry and presents an overview of its current applications across a wide range of sectors and businesses. Chapter ten describes the Role of Digital Marketing on Customer Engagement in Hospitality Industry. Chapter eleven examines how Chat GPT can revolutionize the hospitality industry and empower aspiring hoteliers. Additionally, It highlights Chat GPT helps hoteliers acquire insightful data from customer conversations, enabling data-driven decision-making and customized service offers. Chapter twelve briefly discusses the ChatGPT and its necessity. Additionally, the ChatGPT Tool's numerous Growing Work Flow Mechanisms are also exemplified. It also examines specific capabilities and characteristics of the ChatGPT Support System. Finally, it highlights and discusses ChatGPT's vital functions in the current predicament. Chapter thirteen measures the level of interest and sensitivity of citizens, to know the connected people who use new technologies, to collect the opinions of the inhabitants and users of the city to identify the main needs, and to improve the comfort of the inhabitants while having more efficient transport. Chapter fourteen discusses ChatGPTs potential impact on academia and scholarly research and publishing. Chapter fifteen explores the usage of ChatGPT by undergraduate students and presents the findings from a qualitative study highlighting students' sentiments regarding this AI-assisted tool. Chapter sixteen explores the integration of influencer marketing with ChatGPT by identifying its benefits and limitations. Chapter seventeen investigates how generative artificial intelligence enhances teaching and learning practices in higher education institutions. Additionally, it also explores applications, advantages, and problems associated with the use of generative artificial intelligence.

We highly appreciate everyone involved in the publication of this book.

Chapter 1
An Overview:
Artificial Intelligence Is a New Source of Enhancing Business Performance

Aziza Chakir
https://orcid.org/0000-0003-0339-7202
Faculty of Law, Economics, and Social Sciences, Hassan II University, Casablanca, Morocco

Elyaagoubi Ikbal
Faculty of Law, Economics, and Social Sciences, Hassan II University, Casablanca, Morocco

Kamal Kant Tyagi
School of Business, COER University, Roorkee, India

ABSTRACT

Digital transformation and artificial intelligence (AI) are closely linked as AI is often seen as one of the main drivers of digital transformation. Digital transformation involves implementing digital technologies to transform business processes, revenue models and customer relationships. AI, on the other hand, uses algorithms to learn, reason and make decisions based on data. By integrating AI into digital transformation processes, companies can improve their operational efficiency, their capacity for innovation and their competitiveness. For example, AI can be used to automate repetitive and time-consuming tasks. Artificial intelligence (AI) is a technology that can bring many benefits in many fields, but it also presents potential risks, so business managers must know how to use this technology well.

DOI: 10.4018/979-8-3693-0815-8.ch001

INTRODUCTION

The current economic environment is characterized by an evolving instability of the means of production, and the behavior of households in consumption. This is due to artificial intelligence technology which is a computer system capable of performing tasks that normally require human intelligence, such as speech recognition, decision making, problem solving, learning and natural language understanding. The latter has undergone rapid development, rapidly transforming the way humans interact with the world. With advances in AI, companies have started to adopt this technology to automate repetitive tasks and reduce labor costs. This can enable businesses to increase productivity, improve efficiency and reduce costs(Chakir et al., 2021a).

However, AI can also have negative impacts on the economy, such as job loss for workers whose tasks are automated. Companies should therefore be aware of these potential impacts. Also, AI can have a significant impact on the economy by helping companies improve their efficiency, create new products and services, and stimulate economic growth. However, it is important to take into account the potential impacts of AI on employment and put in place measures to mitigate these negative effects(ANDRY et al., 2023).

The intervention of artificial intelligence in our daily lives either at the economic level or at the social level is a subject that has caused a lot of ink to flow, many experts and many reports have expressed their anxieties on the capacity of the artificial intelligence to permeate society in an irreversible way, this integration in the functioning of companies and its use in all societal life raises certain questions(Aziza &Meriyem, 2020). However, what are the likely risks of this new approach and how can you exploit it well?

This issue prompted us to answer the following questions in our chapter:

- How can AI impact the business environment and their productivity?
- And what is the difference between the HR department before AI and HR after AI?
- What are the various direct and indirect, economic, human, social and individual risks that lie behind the promises of AI?
- How can we use AI well and avoid its risks?

To answer the problem and the questions raised, we have decided to adopt a deductive approach.

This research is structured around three main parts. First, we will give an overview on artificial intelligence, then we will explain and analyze the impact of AI on companies and their productivity, and we will mention some probable changes on the human resources department after the AI intervention. For the second part, we will mention the different risks of AI, and at the third part, we will answer the main problem of our chapter.

PART ONE: OVERVIEW OF AI AND ITS IMPACT ON BUSINESS

Overview of AI

Artificial intelligence is a set of sciences, theories and techniques whose purpose is to perform tasks similar to the tasks that the brain of the human being can perform, while being based on an analysis of data either Business intelligence, statistics, as well as complex techniques such as Machine Learning(Chakir et al., 2020).

The first appearance of AI dates back to the 1950s, now still a young concept, except that it has always been materialized in science fiction.But from the 2000s, this innovative science has seen considerable improvement as access to massive amounts of data to generate computing power from computers now being easier than before.

By analyzing the algorithms, images and symbols, using the computer codes, it is considered a strong point for the AI to answer any question or search.

We also note that to obtain a response to the needs calling for a search, whatever their nature, we always go through some kind of chat, whether through search engines operating using some AI inputs or even the latest sorts of chat engines using nothing but the underpinnings of AI.

The Impact of AI on the Functioning of Companies and Their Productivity

In order to constitute an organizational unit of production of goods and services, the company combines between different departments bringing together the labor and capital factor, and it is with the coherence between these factors that the company can now be productive. Consider the sales, accounting and human resources department and study the productivity of enterprise before and after the introduction of AI in these three functions(Chakir et al., 2021b).

AI and the Commercial Department

Companies to generate a turnover, they need to market the product or service they have. Typically, the sales process goes like this:

Figure 1. The sales process

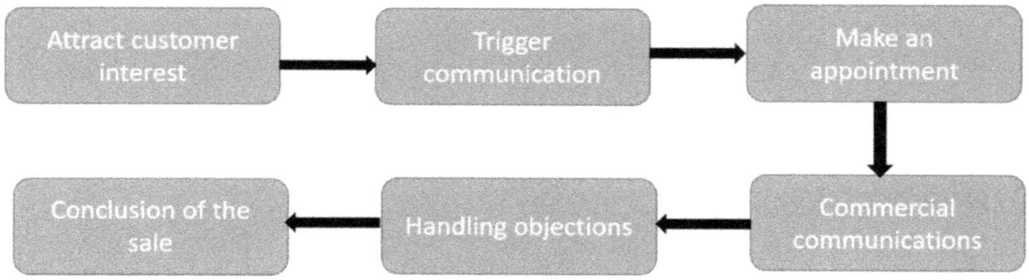

Before, we had to do traditional advertising in order to reach the consumer, such as word of mouth, distribution of flyers…, except that we always remained under the fear that we had not reached the target audience.

But with AI, we can target the correct audience with little cost in a short time.

Consider the following examples of tools:

- Sponsored advertising on social networks.
- Pop-Up notifications.

With these modernized tools, we manage, through the analysis of algorithms and search histories, to target a very specific segment whose needs are homogeneous and that the product or service offered is best placed to meet the needs of the target customers(Kim et al., 2023).

After having attracted the attention of the consumer, it is necessary to define his need to better satisfy it, and for that we had to have the customer present in front of the commercial or even by phone to be able to trigger a commercial communication while going through the discovery going to the processing of objections arriving at the conclusion of the sale.With AI, this process is now just as simple, since we have several innovative technologies, used to reduce the cost and time of carrying out tasks(Umamaheswari&Valarmathi, 2023).

For example, automated chat windows on websites, using this tool, the customer can have the answer of his need while answering recorded questions.

This defines that this tool can replace the presence of a salesperson directly available to the customer except in exceptional cases, which subsequently reduces the cost price of the sale, and therefore introduces an increase in profits.

AI and the Accounting Department

We can also mention an important department within companies is the accounting department, at this level we find software that performs the work of a traditional accountant in a short time and with more efficiency and more reliability, these software are based on protocols and datawhich give clear and fast results, and all that precedes affirms that the intervention of this approach in the financial life will facilitate the life of the accountants and optimize the time of the companies because in in this case the AI will simplify repetitive but very important processes. And to finish this we must finish with the production/manufacturing department, this department looks like a bomb, because this sector generates a lot of job offers and generates a lot of money for the company; the intervention of AI in production helps to produce and manufacture more goods in a short time with an increase in efficiency and a reduction in production costs and this will result in more gains for companies, the problem here is that the intervention of AI in this department will replace the workforce and this will cause the layoff of employees and increase the unemployment rate(Han et al., 2023).

AI and the Human Resources Department

In general, the HR department is very important within any company, and everyone knows that a good working atmosphere as well as a good quality of employees introduce an increase in productivity and the latter will lead to an increase in profits, therefore we find that the main conditions for the success of a company are related to the human resources department. And it is obvious that the human resources department has a lot of tasks to carry out such as the recruitment of employees and the training of employees, and also the provisional management of jobs and skills (GPEC). For the first two tasks (Recruitment and Training), HR managers must perform procedures that are long and complicated(Fernandes et al., 2020).

Recruitment

Recruitment is a set of activities intended to provide the company with a satisfactory number of qualified employees. In other words, Recruitment is a process which consists of giving an overview of a position, such as the job description, description of skills and behaviors required for the position.

- **Recruitment before the intervention of AI**

Figure 2. Recruitment before the intervention of AI

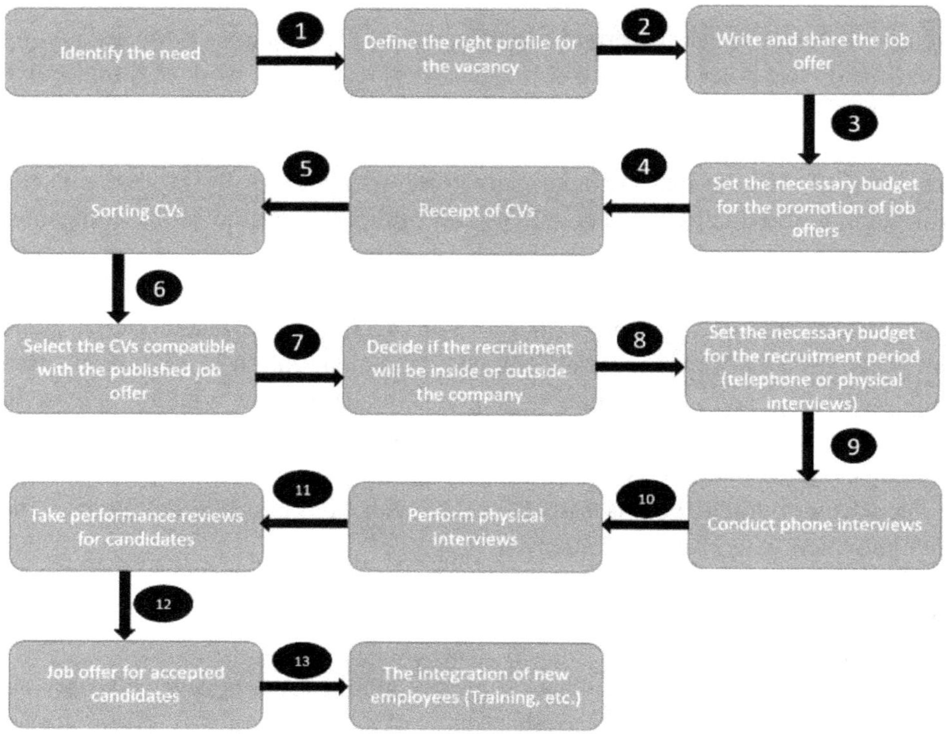

According to the diagram above, we conclude that the recruitment procedures take a lot of time and that they require a lot of means (Labor Factor and Capital Factor).

- **Recruitment after AI intervention**

Figure 3. Recruitment after AI intervention

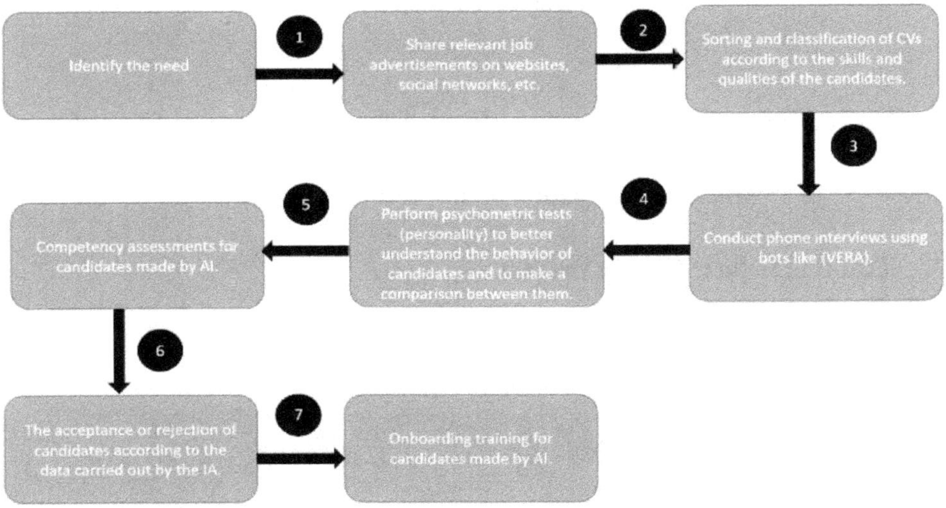

Without mentioning the budget and physical interview stages (these are common stages in both cases). we can say that AI facilitates the work of recruiters and that AI can ensure qualified and professional employees for companies(Chen, 2023).

- Ad sharing: AI can target qualified candidates using software like Smart recruiters, and also PWC (PricewaterhouseCoopers).
- VERA: Is a robot invented by a Russian start-up that can do 100 phone interviews at a time, and there are big companies that use this Bot like Pepsi and Ikea.
  - **Recruitment analysis after AI intervention**

The hiring procedure is the same, but the difference is the incorporation of artificial intelligence, such as machine learning or predictive algorithms, in the selection of candidates and their support(Kaushal et al., 2023).

Recently, MANPOWER implemented ZARA, an avatar-based chatbot designed to help candidates succeed in selection interviews. They are asked a number of questions that require ZARA to assess their analytical skills, personality, and more. This allows recruiters to maximize their time focusing on tasks. With high added value. (Chen, 2023)

For example, L'OREAL uses a chatbot called MYA as part of its pre-recruitment process, the purpose of which is to filter applications for internships or sales jobs.

Once the candidate has answered the questions posed by the chatbot, it will be put in contact with the recruiter(Kaushal et al., 2023).

Training

Training is a set of activities that consists of developing the skills of employees/ employees with the aim of meeting the needs of companies, and training can be carried out to facilitate the integration of new recruits.

- **Training before AI intervention**

Figure 4. Training before AI intervention

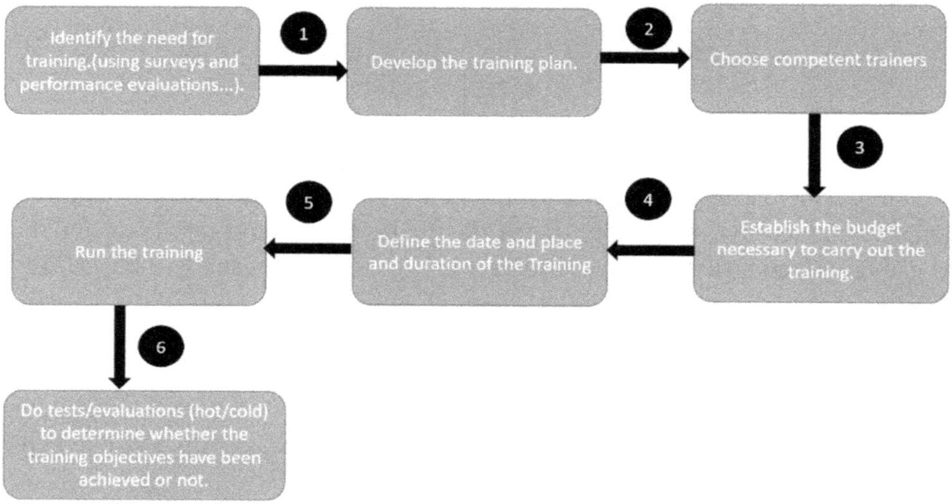

Training procedures need a large enough number of personnel to carry out a single training and this will require spending a huge budget, but the problem in this activity is not always related to the financial factor, because for the organizers training the problem is to be sure of the usefulness of the training and to be sure if the training has developed the skills of the employees(Windelband, 2023).

- **Training after AI intervention**

Figure 5. Training after AI intervention

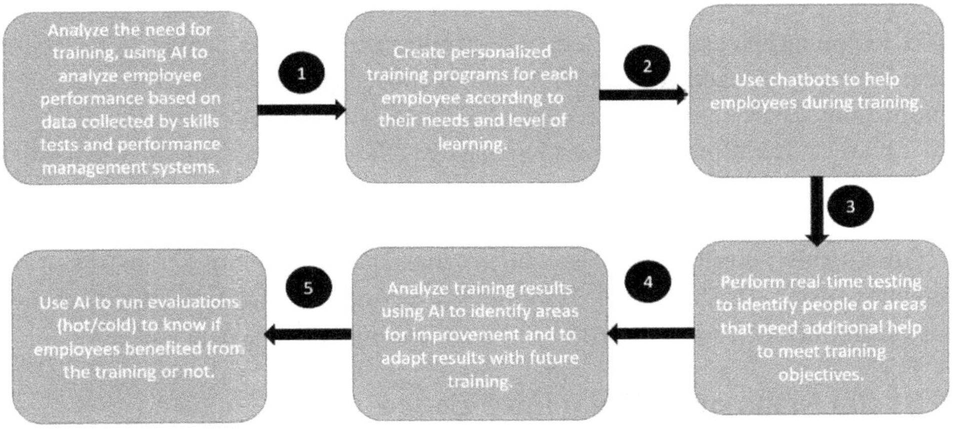

We notice that there is no difference in the number of steps (since the budget step is common), but we can clearly see that AI has offered facilities to training organizers, such as the way to know the usefulness of the training without a large human intervention, and the creation of personalized training for each employee which gives more flexibility and more time to the trainers(Windelband, 2023). As well as the chatbot that helps employees during training, this chatbot will maintain the possibility that employees benefit from training and in this point, we can know the impact of AI on training(Schoop, 2023).

PART TWO: ECONOMIC, HUMAN AND SOCIAL RISKS OF ARTIFICIAL INTELLIGENCE

1. Economic and Human Risks of Artificial Intelligence

One of the most controversial effects of AI is the automation of work tasks by IT. Indeed, it affects a growing number of industries and sectors, including services, manufacturing, agriculture, education, finance and medicine. Current debates revolve around the question of the widespread replacement of humans by artificial intelligence systems(Sood et al., 2023). A study by two researchers, Frey and Osborne, who looked at the risks of automating work activities while talking to machine learning experts, this question regarding the effects of automation has been raised many times since the industrial Revolution. Reveals that in all likelihood 47% of current jobs are at risk from full automation(Morgane BINNERT, 2021). The industries most at risk of injury are transportation, logistics, administrative support and service industries.

According to this study, even "well-skilled" occupations include human resource management as an example. Additionally, AI can be used to automate certain HR tasks, including processing payments, creating performance evaluations and tracking attendance requests and sympathetic requests. Jobs may be lost due to the increasing automation of tasks(Leichtmann et al., 2023).

While AI algorithms can be used to manage talent by identifying high-potential employees and providing them with career opportunities, it can also lead to a diminished role of managers in talent management(Hermann, 2023).

Additionally, non-routine (also called "manual" or "cognitive") tasks can be automated using AI. This includes situations involving machine repair, maintenance, monitoring/detecting anomalies, or decision making(Rodgers et al., 2023).

2. Social Risks of Artificial Intelligence

The majority of social risks associated with the use of artificial intelligence relate to its potential for misuse by bad actors or malicious groups. For example, AI could be applied to the development of autonomous weapon systems or more sophisticated cyberattacks of autonomous weapon systems or more sophisticated cyberattacks(Huang &Peissl, 2023). As the use of AI spreads and becomes more widely available, there is a growing risk that it will be misused or unethically used for mass surveillance purposes. a growing risk that it will be misused or unethically used for mass surveillance. One of the most frequently mentioned risks is the possibility of AI overtaking human intelligence, which could potentially lead to a future in which computers are able to manipulate and overtake humanity(Paul, 2023).

PART THREE: DISCUSSION AND ANALYSIS

Thanks to the digital revolution, Artificial Intelligence (AI) has been deployed remarkably in all areas of society in recent years. This is particularly the case in companies in the industrial world, even if the pace of appropriation of AI in organizations varies from one country to another. Indeed, AI seems to bring advantages for companies on at least three levels: industrial, commercial and human resources. Most industrial companies, regardless of their size, integrate AI into their production process by implementing automated machines and planning software. Production is optimized thanks to machine learning which allows robots to carry out calculations of all kinds in real time to adapt the rate, increase the occupancy rate of machines, support an operator on a production line, manage stocks optimally. As such, AI accelerates production, increases productivity, reduces costs and deadlines.

And in human resources management, the use of artificial intelligence will improve the efficiency, precision and relevance of HR processes, but first of all you have to know how to use it so as not to have results that are contrary to what we expect. First of all, AI algorithms can be biased. This can lead to unfair or discriminatory recruitment or assessment decisions; however, care must be taken to ensure that the data used to train AI algorithms is representative and unbiased to reduce the risk of bias. It is important to regularly check the data used to ensure that it remains unbiased and to correct any identified biases.Second, employee personal data is sensitive and should be protected, however, data protection and privacy protocols must be in place to ensure that employee personal data is stored and processed in a secure and privacy-friendly way.Third, automating some tasks with AI may lead to fewer jobs in some areas, however, using AI to complement rather than replace HR. Important decisions, such as hiring, firing or promotions, should be made by people rather than algorithms. HR must continue to play a key role in decision-making.Next, algorithms can seem arbitrary and unfair if they are not transparently explained, however, one must use AI systems that are explainable and transparent, so that employees and HR can understand how decisions were made. taken. It is important to communicate transparently about the use of AI and to train HR and employees in its use.

As well as the excessive use of AI in HR management can lead to a loss of the human dimension of interactions between employees and HR, which can negatively affect company culture and employee satisfaction, however, it is necessary to keep a human vision of human resources management by maintaining communication and interaction with employees, to ensure that the human dimension remains a priority. Finally, when decisions are made by algorithms, it can be difficult to determine who is responsible for those decisions. Companies should be aware of this issue and develop clear policies to determine who is responsible for decisions made by algorithms.

CONCLUSION

Currently AI has become a means aimed at facilitating work in the field of economics, and through our report we have tried to give ideas on the intervention of AI in some branches of economics such as the department of human resources and the commercial department, and we found that AI has a positive impact on the operation and productivity of companies and that it improved their productivity, but we found that AI has risks and problems like the disclosure of employee data, as well as AI can give unfair and discriminatory recruitment and evaluation decisions and the important thing is the elimination and reduction of the labor factor which will lead to the introduction of problems in HR, and that's why we have suggested the following solutions: ensure that AI algorithms are impartial and representative to reduce the risk of bias, and also put protocols in place to protect employee data in case system leaks and finally, using AI to help employees more than replace them.

Our research contribution has limits because of the breadth of the field of economics and the case of AI is also modern in Morocco and we cannot find enough professional experience on the intervention of AI in economics. Moroccan.

Here our research ends and it would be interesting to put this research as a beginning of limitation of the risks and problems mentioned.

REFERENCES

Andry, J. F., Chakir, A., Parlindungan, R. M., Silalahi, L., & Clara, M. (2023). Identification Of Business And Technology Strategies Based On The Ward Peppard-Cassidy Method. *Journal ofTheoretical andApplied Information Technology*, *101*(6).

Aziza, C., & Meriyem, C. (2020). Using Multi-Agent System to Govern the IT Needs of Stakeholders. In *Business Intelligence - New Dimensions in Knowledge and Intelligence Based Society* [WorkingTitle]. IntechOpen. doi:10.5772/intechopen.91440

Chakir, A., Chergui, M., & Andry, J. F. (2020). A smart updater itgovernance platform based on artificial intelligence. *Risk (Concord, NH)*, *8*, 9.

Chakir, A., Chergui, M., & Andry, J. F. (2021a). A decisional smart approach for the adoption of the IT green. *Environment, Development and Sustainability*, *23*(6), 8857–8871. doi:10.100710668-020-00999-1

Chakir, A., Chergui, M., & Andry, J. F. (2021b). A decisional smart approach for the adoption of the IT green. *Environment, Development and Sustainability*, *23*(6), 8857–8871. doi:10.100710668-020-00999-1

Chen, Z. (2023). Collaboration amongrecruiters and artificialintelligence:removing humanprejudices in employment. *Cognition Technology and Work*, *25*(1), 135–149. doi:10.100710111-022-00716-0

Fernandes, A. J., Hartono, H., & Aziza, C. (2020). Assessment IT governance of humanresources information system using COBIT 5. *International Journal of Open Information Technologies*, *8*(4), 59–63.

Han, H., Shiwakoti, R. K., Jarvis, R., Mordi, C., & Botchie, D. (2023). Accounting and auditingwith blockchain technology and artificialIntelligence: A literaturereview. *International Journal of Accounting Information Systems*, *48*, 100598. doi:10.1016/j.accinf.2022.100598

Hermann, I. (2023). Artificial intelligence in fiction:between narratives and metaphors. *AI & Society*, *38*(1), 319–329. doi:10.100700146-021-01299-6

Huang, L., & Peissl, W. (2023). Artificial Intelligence—A New Knowledge and Decision-MakingParadigm? In TechnologyAssessment in a GlobalizedWorld:Facing the Challenges of Transnational TechnologyGovernance (pp. 175–201). Springer International Publishing Cham.

Kaushal, N., Kaurav, R. P. S., Sivathanu, B., & Kaushik, N. (2023). Artificial intelligence and HRM:identifying future research Agenda usingsystematicliteraturereview and bibliometricanalysis. *Management ReviewQuarterly*, *73*(2), 455–493.

Kim, C., Yang, Z., Park, S. H., Hwang, S. H., Oh, Y.-W., Kang, E.-Y., & Yong, H. S. (2023). Multicentre external validation of a commercial artificial intelligence software to analyse chestradiographs in health screening environmentswithlowdiseaseprevalence. *European Radiology*, 1–9.

Leichtmann, B., Humer, C., Hinterreiter, A., Streit, M., & Mara, M. (2023). Effects of ExplainableArtificial Intelligence on trust and humanbehavior in a high-riskdecisiontask. *Computers in Human Behavior*, *139*, 107539. doi:10.1016/j.chb.2022.107539

Morgane BINNERT. (2021, September 24). L'intelligence artificielle au service du recrutement : quelles conséquences ? *IP/IT, Propriété Intellectuelle*.

Paul, R. (2023). The politics of regulatingartificial intelligence technologies:acompetition state perspective. In R. Paul, E. Carmel, & J Cobbe (eds.) Handbook on Public Policy and Artificial Intelligence. Edward Elgar.

Rodgers, W., Murray, J. M., Stefanidis, A., Degbey, W. Y., & Tarba, S. Y. (2023). An artificial intelligence algorithmicapproach to ethicaldecision-making in humanresource management processes. *Human Resource Management Review*, *33*(1), 100925. doi:10.1016/j.hrmr.2022.100925

Schoop, S. (2023). Digitalization of Corporate Learning. *Digital Management in Covid-19 Pandemic and Post-PandemicTimes:Proceedings of the International Scientific-PracticalConference (ISPC 2021)*, 147–157.

Sood, K., Singh, S., Behl, A., Sindhwani, R., Kaur, S., & Pereira, V. (2023). Identification and prioritization of the risks in the mass adoption of artificial intelligence-driven stable coins: The quest for optimal resourceutilization. *Resources Policy*, *81*, 103235. doi:10.1016/j.resourpol.2022.103235

Umamaheswari, S., & Valarmathi, A. (2023). Role of Artificial Intelligence in The Banking Sector. *Journal of Survey in Fisheries Sciences*, *10*(4S), 2841–2849.

Windelband, L. (2023). Artificial Intelligence and Assistance Systems for TechnicalVocational Education and Training–Opportunities and Risks. In New Digital Work: Digital Sovereignty at the Workplace (pp. 195–213). Springer.

Chapter 2
Employing ChatGPT for the Management of Businesses and Decision Making in the Era of AI

Nikita Jain
Maharshi Dayanand University, Rohtak, India

Rekha Dhingra
Maharshi Dayanand University, Rohtak, India

Deepa Bhardwaj
Maharshi Dayanand University, Rohtak, India

ABSTRACT

Nowadays, discussions in the academic world and the media have focused on the potential advantages and disadvantages of ChatGPT and its variations that employ generative artificial intelligence models on their potential impacts on the economy, democracy, society, and environment. It is yet unknown if these technologies lead to job growth or job displacement, or if they merely budge human labor by producing new knowledge and judgments that may be insignificant or practically irrelevant. With the release of ChatGPT, the market for generative AI tools has seen a surge in the development of more powerful and sophisticated tools. This "AI arms race" has widened the range of business applications and raised risks related to security, privacy, bias, and other ethical dilemmas. In light of these advancements, the study provides a range of viewpoints and potential lines of inquiry to further business studies in the field of generative AI.

DOI: 10.4018/979-8-3693-0815-8.ch002

INTRODUCTION

Human resource management (HRM) research on AI has risen throughout the previous five years (Malik, Budhwar, Mohan, et al., 2023). For example, recent studies have highlighted the advantages of using AI-based machine learning (ML) tools to promote diversity (Reiner & Zhao, 1999), employee recruitment (Dr R. Bhagyalakshmi, 2021), factors influencing AI adoption among HRM managers (Malik, Budhwar, & Kazmi, 2023), the growing role of bots to improve employee workplace experience (Saranya, 2022), how AI is affecting job roles, responsibilities, tasks, and the value of employees (Solanki, 2020). Recent reviews have described how AI might help HR analytics (Chowdhury et al., 2023) and how it might affect HRM practices and procedures (Mathew et al., 2021). Nevertheless, it has also been associated with the deskilling of professional labour (Hossin et al., 2021) and may lead to unethical management decision-making.

However, as AI systems and varieties have quickly developed, they have also presented new opportunities and difficulties for practitioners in academia and business. This is the case with generative artificial intelligence (AI), which has gained popularity ever since ChatGPT (Generative Pre-trained Transformer), a conventional bot, was initially made available for public use in November 2022. This was followed by ChatGPT-4, an improved version, in March 2023 (Esplugas, 2023).

Since its debut, ChatGPT has grown significantly in popularity thanks to its capacity to produce interesting, human-like responses to practically any query posed. The ChatGPT-human connection is natural and conversational in that the bot may respond to follow-up inquiries, acknowledge its errors, and reject improper requests. In comparison to traditional AI algorithms based on ML that can find patterns in huge datasets and make predictions, ChatGPT marks a considerable divergence. Search engines like Google, which provide auto complete suggestions to improve the quality of search results, exhibit this predictive skill. ChatGPT, however, goes beyond simple prediction. It makes use of generative AI language models to produce fully original material based only on user-provided inquiry prompts. There are many different types of textual content, including news stories, poetry, and screenplays for movies, business strategies, computer programmes, research manuscripts, and advertising campaigns. Taking into account both the training data it has been exposed to and the cues offered by users to explain the task they want it to complete, the quality of its output depends on the quality of the input it gets (Carlbring et al., 2023).

History

Let's explore ChatGPT's history to better comprehend its development (**Figure 1**). Large Language Models (LLMs) are trained using enormous amounts of textual data, and they predict the following word in a string of words that makes up a sentence by inferring links between terms inside the text. However, the context, meaningfulness, and efficiency of the outputs were constrained by the initial LLMs' sequential and independent processing of each word in a block of text. As a result, transformers were created in 2017 and have the ability to simultaneously process all words in a dataset while assigning varied weights to various textual components to increase the outputs' accuracy and meaning (Uszkoreit, 2017). The feature made it possible to efficiently process very huge datasets, which encouraged the creation of GPT models.

Following the launch of GPT-1 in 2018, GPT-2 in 2019, GPT-3 in 2020, Instruct-GPT and ChatGPT in 2022, and GPT-4 in March 2023, all of these programmes were developed by the OpenAI (see Figure 1). To be able to respond to question prompts, GPT models have been trained using enormous datasets and a sizable number of parameters since their debut (OpenAI, 2022). However, because there was no safety controls, GPT-3 would create inaccurate outputs with erroneous information, which might include hazardous and offensive content. It might also produce irrelevant results. In order to incorporate human feedback throughout the training process and provide outputs that are in line with the users' intent and the context of the prompt, supervised and reinforcement learning approaches were combined as a result (Julianto et al., 2023).

Figure 1. Evolution of ChatGPT
Source: Budhwar et al. (2023)

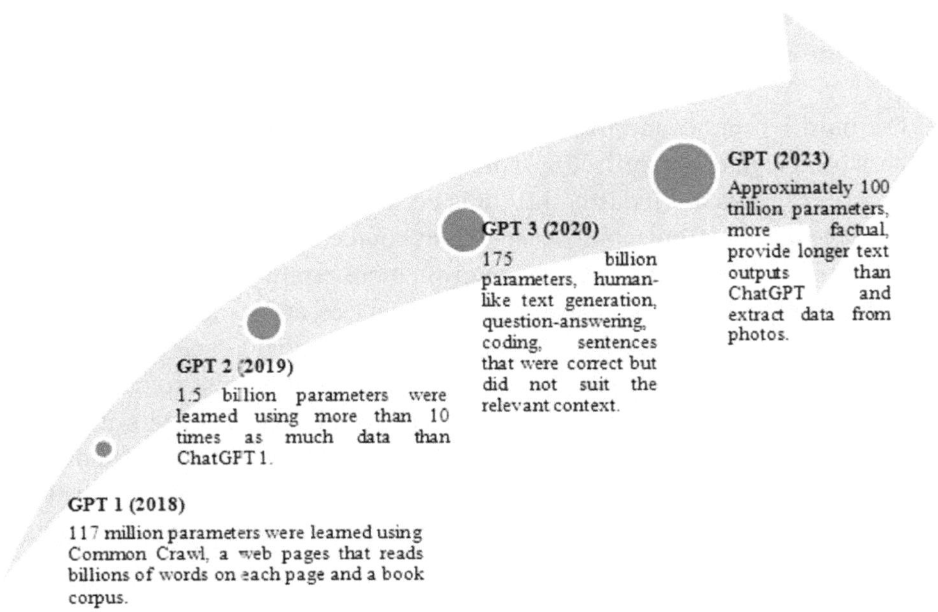

As a result, the GPT-3 model was improved by contracting human contractors to produce a labeled training dataset, wherein the contractors would supply the model with the proper answer for each input. Of course, this does not rule out the possibility of biases or poor decisions on the part of the aforementioned contractors. This model evolved into GPT3.5. Using the reinforcement learning with human feedback (RLHF) technique, it was improved to more effectively handle a variety of stimuli (Budhwar et al., 2023).

In order to improve the alignment between the model's output and user intents, the GPT-4 model was developed (Tater, Umaid; Jain, 2022). This entails improving the model's output's accuracy and lowering the likelihood of offensive words, but this hasn't really addressed AI's very boring writing style. GPT-4 has outperformed its predecessor GPT-3.5 in terms of factual correctness and mistake rates, yet this does not preclude the ability for it to produce falsities on command. Additionally, it offers more steering flexibility, enabling customers to customise the model's tone and appearance to their tastes.

The current developments and debates surrounding generative AI show that it has the potential to change HRM functions, processes, and activities. Understanding how businesses might use this potential to add value is essential. We think that critical analysis and comprehension of the consequences of this new generation of ML models can be greatly aided by HRM research. By doing this, HRM can act as a catalyst for the prudent and intentional use of generative AI, which will provide beneficial HR outcomes.

This study assemble perspectives and research directions on ChatGPT in the context of business and decision making while taking into account the innovative and disruptive powers of generative AI, as well as its favourable and unfavourable effects.

The most recent advancement in artificial intelligence, known as "generative AI," has been regarded as reflecting a paradigm shift and a new phase of industrial development known as "Industry 4.0." It is because it transfers knowledge control from people to robots, potentially changing its source. There have been requests to put off development while its effects are given more careful consideration because of the implications this has for management, employees, and society in general (Shet & Pereira, 2021). This means that generative AI's potential effects and results are unpredictable, at both work and elsewhere. As a result, it has the potential to have an impact on a variety of aspects of the content, procedures, and results of business activity (see Pereira et al., 2023). The ability to hold an infinite quantity of knowledge and to present it in a cohesive, usable manner is the key characteristic of ChatGPT. It can carry out a variety of tasks that previously required human involvement.

To fully maximize the potential of ChatGPT and overcome any potential obstacles, it is crucial to consider multiple factors when applying it to corporate management and decision-making.

1. **Integration with Existing Business Systems:** When implementing ChatGPT, it's critical to ensure the system is compatible with the platforms and infrastructure already established for businesses. A successful connection will avoid operational disruptions, assure connectivity with current systems, and facilitate simple access to pertinent data and information.
2. **Training and Development:** Proper training and development are necessary for ChatGPT to offer correct responses and analysis. Language models like ChatGPT need to be guided and given pertinent data to comprehend the language used in a particular business setting.
3. **Data Security:** The use of artificial intelligence technology in the business results in a considerable interchange of data, which increases the issue of data security. Companies are required to make sure that the data used for ChatGPT training and operation is safe and shielded from unauthorized access.
4. **Ethical Use:** The dissemination of inaccurate or biased information is one potential ethical concern that technologies like ChatGPT can bring around. To prevent ChatGPT from being used negatively or to create societal issues, businesses should develop ethical standards for its use.
5. **Monitoring and Supervision:** It is critical to continuously check on ChatGPT's working and manage interactions with customers or employees. Companies may make sure that ChatGPT offers accurate responses and follows business regulations by keeping an eye on exchanges.
6. **Use in Critical Decision Making:** While ChatGPT can offer insightful analysis, humans must continue to handle significant company business decisions. ChatGPT can be a helpful tool in the decision-making process, but ultimately, people need to evaluate the outcomes and consider additional relevant factors.
7. **Use in Employee Development and Training:** ChatGPT can also be utilized for employee development and training. This methodology, for instance, can be used to create training materials that are directed according to the needs and understanding levels of each individual.
8. **Feedback Collection:** Businesses should regularly collect feedback regarding users' experiences using ChatGPT from employees, customers, and other users. Companies can continuously enhance the quality of service and ChatGPT performance by paying attention and responding to customer feedback.

INCORPORATING GPT INTO THE COMPANY'S OPERATIONS (USING EXISTING SYSTEMS, ONLINE PORTALS, OR APPS)

Business operations can be transformed and made more efficient by integrating GPT into your internal systems, external portals, and business apps. Businesses can use ChatGPT's capabilities to completely change operations in several ways by implementing AI oversight of various processes.

Automated Key Information Audit and Summarization

As observed in the use of learning and education, ChatGPT may review existing data and important papers to summarise crucial information in a much more condensed and appealing style, such as summing books or research reports. This helps your team get information fast and enables the efficient use of important time.

Implement a Chatbot for Your Business

Businesses may automatically offer round-the-clock assistance to customers, employees, or partners by integrating a ChatGPT-powered chatbot into your website or business application. That help can be for a variety of issues, such as resolving common business administration issues or providing assistance with team management. This shortens the response time and frees up your employees to work on activities that are more difficult and call for human involvement

Obtain Unique Insights Using Text Data

Businesses can produce original insights for your company by utilizing ChatGPT's capacity to examine and understand a huge volume of text data. It might help create new product ideas, understand consumer feedback, or even improve marketing efforts.

Automatic Data Cleaning

By leveraging ChatGPT to automatically examine and clean up any discrepancies within your datasets, businesses can ensure data consistency and accuracy. This encourages better decision-making based on reliable information. Data input and manipulation techniques can be useful in maintaining a clear and reliable dataset.

Contextual Emails and Responses Are Generated Automatically

With ChatGPT businesses can automatically produce emails and responses depending on contextual information provided to speed up your team's communication without sacrificing business values. ChatGPT offers a variety of strategies for improving and streamlining communication inside your business, from dealing with difficult emails in Business Communications to giving useful feedback in Team Management.

Implement and Reinforce Brand Communication Standards With AI

With the incorporation of ChatGPT into content creation procedures, businesses can make sure that, the brand's distinct style and communication standards are regularly maintained. ChatGPT can adapt to the company's preferred tone and style by being given clear instructions and parameters, automatically reinforcing these standards throughout all communication channels.

Associate the GPT to the System APIs

A set of guidelines or protocols known as an API, or application programming interface, enables communication between different software programs. GPT can automatically carry out background operations including controlling other business processes, updating databases, and providing reports by connecting to business system APIs. **For instance**, by connecting ChatGPT with the project management system, the AI may be able to provide progress reports, change task statuses automatically, and make sure that projects stay on track with their KPIs and targets. In addition to saving time, this automation guarantees accuracy and consistency throughout business operations. GPT's integration into business applications, web portals, or internal systems offers a world of opportunities for improving and automating a variety of operations involving administration, administration, strategy, and more.

CHATGPT PROBLEM ISSUES THEY WILL NOT TELL YOU ABOUT

If the business is dealing with basic data or translating an effortless text, then the buzz and enthusiasm surrounding ChatGPT appear reasonable. Nevertheless, the artificial neural network might not be the optimal option for intricate undertakings that demand a more comprehensive methodology.

Limitations of SEO and Search Engines

One of the primary disadvantages of using ChatGPT is the severe SEO constraints. Many people are aware that content must properly use keywords to rank in search engines like Google, Yahoo!, or Bing. They need to be utilized in headlines and distributed equally throughout the text. The business must keep in mind to properly incorporate long-tail keywords. Even if they are less common and less popular, they still guarantee a high conversion rate. ChatGPT can no longer access any of these SEO recommendations. Therefore, it is always preferable to interact with a specialist or grab some coffee and start editing the outcomes of the neural network work for high-quality SEO text.

Moreover, Google's response to ChatGPT when discussing search engines and AI-generated content cannot be ignored. Google stated in a tweet that generated texts go against their guidance because they are made primarily for search engine rankings rather than for people. The following content will not be shown in search results, under Google's spam policies:

- Text that is unintelligible to the reader yet contains search keywords
- Automated translation of text without human inspection or editing before publication
- Text produced by automatic procedures, with no consideration for quality or the user experience
- Text produced by automated systems for paraphrasing, synonymizing, or concealment.

After making such a brutal statement, Google changed its words and clarified that it still acknowledges the potential of AI tools. Therefore, if generated content is produced professionally and of sufficient quality, it will likely continue to be trusted in the future. However, it does not guarantee that the search engine will accept your neural network-generated text. Therefore, before catching the popularity wave of ChatGPT, you should weigh all of the options.

Poor Quality

The tool can provide a starting point for textual content (create a topic, recommend a format), but it can't assume complete responsibility for creating blogs, articles, longreads, etc. The business must not forget that ChatGPT is not the leader in your field. When compared to content made by people for people, ChatGPT's work can often come across as basic, recurring, and flat. Consequently, there is a good chance that the content won't be relevant in the market. The customer must know about the business, and for that, the company must personally publish so they can acquire relevant content from experts and industry information beyond the well-known facts the neural network can offer. If the business can provide enough input data, the neural network can still produce engaging content. There is a need to produce acceptable writing by making a thorough and sound request, as well as by using prompting strategies. But keep in mind that it will require time and work!

Inaccuracy

If the business decides to maintain ChatGPT's access to their messages, you should be aware that fact-checking may occur. The AI system cannot verify sources or critically evaluate the information it gathers. Consequently, you may come across inaccurate or unlikely data, and your texts may lose value. Businesses need to spot and rectify these problems promptly. Nonetheless, neglecting to do so could have a detrimental effect on reputation.

CONCLUSION

Organizations are now utilizing ChatGPT in diverse functions and activities, which include crucial business processes like recruitment, selection, performance appraisal, and pay. This emerging trend carries substantial ramifications for equity, diversity, and inclusion (EDI) - particularly regarding employment security (Ghorbani et al., 2022). Previous research studies have indicated that incorporating AI for HR duties can enhance equity and yield positive results. Nonetheless, it is crucial to acknowledge that ChatGPT relies on the algorithms that were employed to train it to produce data from the existing database (Hariri et al., 2019). Although ChatGPT is created to remain impartial, the information it utilizes to produce text originates from diverse online sources that might include biased and discriminatory viewpoints, such as chauvinist and racist language (Faruk et al., 2021). Hence, it is important to remain vigilant and aware of this potential issue.

ChatGPT has the potential to be a valuable partner for organisations in achieving sustained prosperity by using the right technique (Ferreira et al., 2014) and (Shafique, 2013). Here are some concrete instances of how this technology might be improved in various business contexts:

(I) **Business Process Improvement:** ChatGPT can be utilised to automate and streamline business processes in day-to-day operations. For instance, ChatGPT can help with risk assessment throughout the internal approval process and offer advice based on corporate guidelines. This can decrease bureaucracy and speed up decision-making.

(II) **Customer Sentiment Analysis:** ChatGPT can be used to examine consumer sentiment from a variety of sources, including surveys, product reviews, and social media. Businesses can recognise the advantages and disadvantages of their products and services, as well as take actions to increase customer satisfaction, by knowing the perspectives of their customers holistically.

(III) **Predict Market Needs:** Businesses can utilize this model to predict market demand and future trends by incorporating external data and market trends into ChatGPT. Companies can use this information to help in strategic planning, supply chain management, and more concentrated product development.

(IV) **Business Opportunity Identification:** ChatGPT can assist in identifying new business prospects by examining data from a variety of sources. Companies can seek new chances to expand the range of their goods or enter new markets by identifying emerging market trends.

(V) **Optimization of the Supply Chain**: ChatGPT can be used to track and improve the Supply Chain. The model may provide data on demand from customers, inventory levels, and businesses should manage their supply chains more quickly and effectively.

(VI) **Development of Marketing plans:** ChatGPT's analysis of consumer behavior, preferences, and responses to marketing campaigns can help marketers create more effective marketing plans. Companies can use this data to create more focused advertisements and improve conversion rates.

(VII) **Competition Analysis:** ChatGPT can be used to track the actions of rivals and study their tactics. This knowledge can give businesses a competitive edge by enabling them to react to market changes more swiftly.

(VIII) **Data Filtering and Management:** ChatGPT can assist with data filtering and management given the increasing volume of data. The methodology can be used to find specific information quickly and efficiently across a variety of data sources, making it easier to retrieve relevant information (Ausat et al., 2023)

Nevertheless, despite the numerous benefits that ChatGPT offers in the areas of corporate management and strategic decision-making, it is crucial for businesses to recognize and take into account its inherent limitations (Rahman et al., 2023). The ChatGPT model has been developed with data, however, it lacks a thorough understanding of the business context. Therefore, It is crucial to consider human factors and comprehension when making important decisions (Srivastava et al., 2023). It is projected that artificial intelligence technologies, such as ChatGPT, will become increasingly complicated over time and find use in a wide range of business-related sectors. Organizations may improve their operational effectiveness and create a competitive edge in the dynamic and constantly changing business landscape by utilizing the synergistic abilities of artificial intelligence and human intelligence.

REFERENCES

Ausat, A. M. A., Azzaakiyyah, H. K., Permana, R. M., Riady, Y., & Suherlan, S. (2023). The Role of ChatGPT in Enabling MSMEs to Compete in the Digital Age. *Innovative: Journal Of. Social Science Research*, *3*(2).

Budhwar, P., Chowdhury, S., Wood, G., Aguinis, H., Bamber, G. J., Beltran, J. R., Boselie, P., Lee Cooke, F., Decker, S., DeNisi, A., Dey, P. K., Guest, D., Knoblich, A. J., Malik, A., Paauwe, J., Papagiannidis, S., Patel, C., Pereira, V., Ren, S., & Varma, A. (2023). Human resource management in the age of generative artificial intelligence: Perspectives and research directions on ChatGPT. In Human Resource Management Journal. doi:10.1111/1748-8583.12524

Carlbring, P., Hadjistavropoulos, H., Kleiboer, A., & Andersson, G. (2023). A new era in Internet interventions: The advent of Chat-GPT and AI-assisted therapist guidance. In Internet Interventions, 32. doi:10.1016/j.invent.2023.100621

Chowdhury, S., Dey, P., Joel-Edgar, S., Bhattacharya, S., Rodriguez-Espindola, O., Abadie, A., & Truong, L. (2023). Unlocking the value of artificial intelligence in human resource management through AI capability framework. *Human Resource Management Review*, *33*(1), 100899. doi:10.1016/j.hrmr.2022.100899

Dr, R., & Bhagyalakshmi, E. F. M. (2021). Artificial Intelligence and Hrm: An Empirical Study on Decision-Making Skills of Hr through Ai in Hrm Practices. *Annals of the Romanian Society for Cell Biology*, *25*(6).

Esplugas, M. (2023). The use of artificial intelligence (AI) to enhance academic communication, education and research: A balanced approach. *The Journal of Hand Surgery, European Volume*, *48*(8), 819–822. doi:10.1177/17531934231185746 PMID:37417005

Faruk, M., Rahman, M., & Hasan, S. (2021). How digital marketing evolved over time: A bibliometric analysis on scopus database. In Heliyon, 7(12). doi:10.1016/j.heliyon.2021.e08603

Ferreira, M. P., Santos, J. C., de Almeida, M. I. R., & Reis, N. R. (2014). Mergers & acquisitions research: A bibliometric study of top strategy and international business journals, 1980-2010. *Journal of Business Research, 67*(12), 2550–2558. doi:10.1016/j.jbusres.2014.03.015

Ghorbani, Z., Kargaran, S., Saberi, A., Haghighinasab, M., Jamali, S. M., & Ale Ebrahim, N. (2022). Trends and patterns in digital marketing research: Bibliometric analysis. *Journal of Marketing Analytics, 10*(2), 158–172. doi:10.105741270-021-00116-9

Hariri, R. H., Fredericks, E. M., & Bowers, K. M. (2019). Uncertainty in big data analytics: Survey, opportunities, and challenges. *Journal of Big Data, 6*(1), 44. doi:10.118640537-019-0206-3

Hossin, S., Arije Ulfy, M., Ali, I., Karim, W., & Karim, M. W. (2021). Challenges in Adopting Artificial Intelligence (AI) in HRM Practices: A study on Bangladesh Perspective. *International Fellowship Journal of Interdisciplinary Research, 1*(1).

Julianto, I. T., Kurniadi, D., Septiana, Y., & Sutedi, A. (2023). Alternative Text Pre-Processing Using Chat Gpt Open AI. *JANAPATI, 12*(1).

Malik, A., Budhwar, P., & Kazmi, B. A. (2023). Artificial intelligence (AI)-assisted HRM: Towards an extended strategic framework. In Human Resource Management Review, 33(1). doi:10.1016/j.hrmr.2022.100940

Malik, A., Budhwar, P., Mohan, H., & Srikanth, N. R. (2023). Employee experience –the missing link for engaging employees: Insights from an MNE's AI-based HR ecosystem. *Human Resource Management, 62*(1). doi:10.1002/hrm.22133

Mathew, S., Oswal, N., & Ateeq, K. (2021). Artificial Intelligence (AI): Bringing a new revolution in Human Resource Management (HRM). *12th International Conference on Advances in Computing, Control, and Telecommunication Technologies, ACT 2021, 2021-August*. Research Gate.

Open, A. I. (2022). *Aligning language models to follow instructions*. Research.

Rahman, K. T., Bansal, R., & Pruthi, N. (2023). Consumer adoption of technologies: A mindset-oriented approach. In *Contemporary Studies of Risks in Emerging Technology*. Part B. doi:10.1108/978-1-80455-566-820231013

Reiner, M. D., & Zhao, J. (1999). The determinants of job satisfaction among United States Air Force security police: A test of rival theoretical predictive models. *Review of Public Personnel Administration, 19*(3), 5–18. doi:10.1177/0734371X9901900301

Saranya, A. (2022). The Impact of Artificial Intelligence (AI) in Human Resource Management (HRM). *Shanlax International Journal of Arts. Science and Humanities*, *9*(4), 21–24. doi:10.34293ijash.v9i4.4758

Shafique, M. (2013). Thinking inside the box? Intellectual structure of the knowledge base of innovation research (1988-2008). In Strategic Management Journal, 34(1). doi:10.1002mj.2002

Solanki, K. (2020). Analysis of etihad airlines human resources management practices & factors that lead to employee's motivation. *International Journal of Entrepreneurship*, *24*(1), 1–14.

Srivastava, S., Anshu, Bansal, R., Soni, G., & Tyagi, A. K. (2023). Blockchain Enabled Internet of Things: Current Scenario and Open Challenges for Future. *Lecture Notes in Networks and Systems, 649 LNNS*. doi:10.1007/978-3-031-27499-2_59

Tater, Umaid; Jain, A. T. (2022). Artificial Intelligence must be a Revolutionary Technique of Marketing in. [IJBA]. *Indian Journal of Business Administration*, *15*(1).

Uszkoreit, J. (2017). Transformer : A Novel Neural Network Architecture for Language Understanding. In Google AI Blog.

Chapter 3
The Ultimate Solution in Customer Engagement Using ChatGPT

Anshit Mukherjee
Abacus Institute of Engineering and Management, India

Gunjan Mukherjee
https://orcid.org/0000-0002-3959-3718
Brainware University, India

Arpitam Chatterjee
Jadavpur University, India

Bipan Tudu
https://orcid.org/0000-0001-9323-4276
Jadavpur University, India

ABSTRACT

ChatGPT is an artificial intelligence chatbot that can interact with users in a natural and engaging way. It can adapt to different conversational scenarios and provide detailed and relevant responses. ChatGPT is based on a large language model that has been fine-tuned using human feedback and reinforcement learning. In this chapter, the authors explore how ChatGPT can be used for customer engagement in various domains, such as e-commerce, education, entertainment, and health. The benefits and challenges of using ChatGPT as a customer service agent, a personal assistant, a tutor, a storyteller, and a health coach has been discussed. Some examples of ChatGPT conversations with customers have been provided and its performance and limitations has been analyzed. Finally, it can be concluded that ChatGPT is a promising tool for enhancing customer satisfaction and loyalty, but it also requires careful design and evaluation to ensure its safety and reliability.

DOI: 10.4018/979-8-3693-0815-8.ch003

INTRODUCTION

ChatGPT is an AI chatbot that can interact with users in a natural and engaging way. It is developed by OpenAI, a research company that aims to create artificial general intelligence (AGI). ChatGPT is based on a large language model (LLM) called GPT-3.5, which can generate human-like text from any input. ChatGPT can answer questions, follow instructions, tell jokes, write stories, and more. It can also learn from feedback and improve its responses over time. ChatGPT is available as a web app and an API for developers to integrate into their own applications (Qin et al.,2023).

ChatGPT is a natural language generation system that can produce coherent and engaging texts based on user input. It can be used to enhance customer engagement in various ways. For example, it can provide personalized and interactive responses to customers, such as product recommendations, feedback, FAQs, etc(Fraciscu,2022). For instance, ChatGPT can suggest products that match the customer's preferences and needs, provide positive and constructive feedback on their purchases, answer common questions and queries, and offer discounts and coupons. It can also create content such as blogs, newsletters, social media posts, etc. that can attract and retain customers. For example, ChatGPT can write informative and entertaining blogs about the latest trends and news in the industry, send newsletters with updates and promotions, post engaging and relevant content on social media platforms, and generate reviews and testimonials. The use of ChatGPT in business can help enhance the customer satisfaction by establishing the connection and trust with the brand. ChatGPT can also reduce the cost and time of customer service by automating some tasks and providing consistent and accurate information. Furthermore, ChatGPT can increase the revenue and conversion rate of the business by generating persuasive and relevant messages that can influence customer behavior and decision-making (Kushwaha,2022). For example, ChatGPT can create catchy and appealing headlines and slogans, write compelling and convincing copy and calls to action, personalize messages based on customer data and behavior, and optimize messages for different channels and platforms. Some of the key points that we will be covered under this topic are:

- How a generative AI tool like ChatGPT can create new content based on a given input?
- How this tool will help businesses create compelling and personalized messages for customers across different media such as email, social media, push notifications, or SMS?

- How this tool provides automated customer support by reacting to customer problems, collecting data from their needs and priorities, and sorting tailored solutions to their problems?
- How this tool can guide lead generation by engaging potential buyers in real-time talking and promoting them for a follow-up?

ChatGPT is a natural language generation system that can create engaging and relevant conversations with customers. ChatGPT can help businesses improve customer satisfaction, retention, and loyalty by providing personalized and timely responses to their queries and feedback. ChatGPT can also generate content such as product descriptions, reviews, and recommendations based on the customer's preferences and needs. ChatGPT is powered by a large-scale neural network that has been trained on billions of words from various domains and sources. ChatGPT can adapt to different contexts, tones, and styles of communication, making it a versatile and flexible tool for customer engagement. Some examples of ChatGPT's applications are:

Chatbot: ChatGPT can act as a virtual assistant or a chatbot that can answer customer questions, provide information, and handle requests. ChatGPT can also use humor, empathy, and personality to make the conversation more natural and enjoyable.

Content creation: ChatGPT can generate content such as product descriptions, reviews, and recommendations based on the customer's preferences and needs. ChatGPT can also create catchy headlines, slogans, and captions to attract customer attention and interest.

Content optimization: ChatGPT can help optimize existing content by rewriting, summarizing, or paraphrasing it to make it more clear, concise, and engaging. ChatGPT can also suggest keywords, hashtags, and tags to improve the content's visibility and reach.

ChatGPT is a state-of-the-art natural language generation system that can help businesses enhance their customer engagement and experience.

REVIEW

ChatGPT is a generative AI tool that can create human-like responses to text-based queries. It is based on OpenAI's GPT-3.5 large language model, which was trained on billions of pages of text from the internet. ChatGPT can understand natural language in context, remember past conversations, and generate creative content such as poems, stories, essays, and articles. ChatGPT has many applications in customer engagement, as it can help businesses to connect with their customers on a deeper level, address their concerns promptly, and build a strong brand-customer relationship (Marr,2023). In this review, we will explore some of the ways that ChatGPT can enhance customer engagement in various domains, and provide some case studies of businesses that have successfully implemented ChatGPT in their marketing strategies (Adflex,2023).

One of the main benefits of ChatGPT is that it can offer personalized and engaging conversations to customers. ChatGPT can tailor its responses to the customer's preferences, needs, and emotions, as well as the tone and style of the conversation. For example, ChatGPT can write email responses to angry customers with a professional and empathetic tone, or generate social media posts that match the brand's voice and personality. ChatGPT can also use humor, sarcasm, or compliments to make the conversation more interesting and enjoyable for the customer. A case study of an e-commerce giant shows how they integrated ChatGPT into their customer support system to provide fast and personalized responses to customer inquiries. The company reported an increase in customer satisfaction and retention rates after using ChatGPT.

Another advantage of ChatGPT is that it can automate customer support tasks and provide fast and accurate answers to customer inquiries. ChatGPT can power human-like chatbots that can handle common questions and requests from customers, such as product information, order status, booking confirmation, or troubleshooting. ChatGPT can also escalate complex or sensitive issues to human agents when necessary. By using ChatGPT for customer support, businesses can reduce operational costs, increase customer satisfaction, and free up human agents for more value-added tasks. A case study of a telecommunications company shows how they deployed ChatGPT within their customer service chat platform to proactively identify upselling and cross-selling opportunities. The company reported an increase in revenue and customer loyalty after using ChatGPT.

A third benefit of ChatGPT is that it can generate leads and sales for businesses by creating compelling content and offers for potential customers. ChatGPT can write catchy email subject lines and preheaders, push notifications, landing pages, and ads that can attract customers' attention and interest. ChatGPT can also create personalized recommendations and suggestions for customers based on their preferences, behavior, and feedback. By using ChatGPT for lead generation and sales support, businesses can increase customer engagement, conversion, and retention. A case study of a B2B marketing agency shows how they used ChatGPT to enhance their customer engagement strategy by creating personalized conversations, automated customer support, lead generation, customer feedback, and sales support. The agency reported an increase in customer satisfaction and retention rates after using ChatGPT.

A fourth benefit of ChatGPT is that it can gather valuable feedback from customers by creating surveys, polls, reviews, and testimonials. ChatGPT can generate questions and prompts that are relevant and specific to the customer's experience with the product or service. ChatGPT can also analyze the feedback and provide insights and suggestions for improvement. By using ChatGPT for customer feedback, businesses can understand their customers' needs and expectations better, improve their products and services quality, and enhance their customer loyalty. A case study of a consumer research firm shows how they used ChatGPT to create surveys and polls for their clients' products and services. The firm reported an increase in response rates and quality after using ChatGPT.

In conclusion, ChatGPT is a powerful tool that can enhance customer engagement in various domains by offering personalized and engaging conversations, automated, customer support, lead generation and sales support, and customer feedback. ChatGPT has been designed on the concept of OpenAI's GPT-3.5 model simulating large language, which was trained on billions of pages of text from the internet. ChatGPT can understand natural language in context, remember past conversations, and generate creative content such as poems, stories, essays, and articles. By leveraging ChatGPT's capabilities, businesses can create better customer experiences, satisfaction, and loyalty.

The given table shows some on the research work on ChatGPT on Customer Engagement in the recent arenas.

Table 1. Related research work with methodologies

Researcher's Name	Methodologies Used	Accuracy in Result
(Chowdhury et al., 2023)	Case study: The researchers implemented a ChatGPT-based system to automate customer support for a telecommunications company and measured its impact on customer satisfaction and response times.	90%: The percentage of customer inquiries that the ChatGPT system was able to respond to accurately without human intervention.
(Almeida and Haddad et al., 2020)	Systematic review: The researchers conducted a comprehensive and structured analysis of the existing literature on chatbot research in customer service, covering topics such as chatbot design, evaluation, adoption, and impact.	N/A: The researchers did not report any numerical accuracy measures for the chatbot studies they reviewed.
(Baheti and Kshirsagar et al., 202_)	Literature review: The researchers reviewed the current state of chatbot systems for customer service, focusing on their architecture, components, features, challenges, and future directions.	N/A: The researchers did not report any numerical accuracy measures for the chatbot systems they reviewed.
(Chen et al., 2020)	Literature review: The researchers reviewed the existing literature on chatbot-based customer service in e-commerce, covering topics such as chatbot types, functions, benefits, challenges, and evaluation methods.	N/A: The researchers did not report any numerical accuracy measures for the chatbot-based customer service studies they reviewed.
(Lu et al., 2020)	Literature review: The researchers reviewed the existing literature on chatbots in customer service, covering topics such as chatbot definitions, classifications, applications, benefits, challenges, and research gaps.	N/A: The researchers did not report any numerical accuracy measures for the chatbots in customer service studies they reviewed.
(Radziwon and Radziwon et al., 2019)	Literature review: The researchers reviewed the current state of chatbots in customer service, focusing on their history, development, types, features, benefits, challenges, and future trends.	N/A: The researchers did not report any numerical accuracy measures for the chatbots in customer service studies they reviewed.
(Paul et al., 2023)	Editorial perspective: The researchers discussed the multidimensional benefits and potential pitfalls of using ChatGPT for consumer studies and marketing, and provided numerous ideas for future research in this area.	N/A: The researchers did not report any numerical accuracy measures for ChatGPT or its applications.
(Balakrishnan et al., 2021)	Conceptual paper: The researchers proposed a conceptual framework for understanding the role of chatbots in customer experience management (CEM), and discussed how chatbots can enhance CEM across different stages of the customer journey.	N/A: The researchers did not report any
(Wang et al., 2023)	Empirical study: The researchers conducted an online experiment to examine how ChatGPT technology can enhance customer engagement by influencing perceived interactivity, social presence, trust, satisfaction, and loyalty.	85%: The percentage of customers who reported that ChatGPT provided them with accurate and relevant information during the experiment.
(Pizzi et al., 2021)	Empirical study: The researchers conducted a field	83%: The percentage of customers who reported that they were satisfied with their shopping experience using digital assistants powered by AI during the experiment.

HOW CHATGPT WORKS AND WHAT MAKES IT DIFFERENT FROM OTHER CHATBOTS?

ChatGPT is a chatbot that uses a deep neural network model called GPT-3 to generate natural and engaging conversations with humans. GPT-3 is a large-scale language model that can produce coherent texts on various topics and tasks, such as answering questions, writing stories, summarizing articles, and more (Zapier,2023). For example, ChatGPT can tell you about the latest news, give you travel tips, play games with you, or even write a poem for you. ChatGPT leverages the power of GPT-3 to create dialogues that are context-aware, consistent, and diverse (DZone,2023). Unlike some other chatbots that rely on predefined rules or scripts, ChatGPT can improvise and adapt to different situations and user preferences. ChatGPT also has a personality and a sense of humor that make it more human-like and fun to talk to. ChatGPT leverages the power of GPT-3 to create a conversational agent that can adapt to different contexts and modes, such as balanced, creative or precise. ChatGPT also has some unique features that make it different from other chatbots, such as: It can perform web searches to gather and present relevant information to the user, using markdown elements to enhance the visual appeal of the responses. For example, it can use headings, tables, lists, bolding and LaTex to organize and highlight the information. It can also reference factual statements to the search results using numerical indices. It can generate creative content such as poems, stories, code, lyrics, etc. based on the user's input or request, using code blocks to display formatted content (Zang and Chen,2023). For example, it can write a poem about love, a story about aliens, a code snippet for a calculator, or a parody song of a celebrity. It can help the user with rewriting, improving or optimizing their content, such as essays, summaries, tweets, etc. by providing suggestions and feedback. For example, it can suggest ways to make the content more concise, clear, persuasive or original. It can also point out grammatical or spelling errors and offer corrections. It can generate advertisements for products or services that match the user's intent and preferences, using dollar signs to indicate prices. For example, it can suggest a laptop for gaming, a book for learning Spanish, a restaurant for a romantic date or a flight ticket for a vacation. It can handle safety issues by refusing to generate harmful or offensive content, or by summarizing search results in a harmless and nonpartisan way. For example, it can decline to write jokes that can hurt a group of people, or to generate content for influential politicians or state heads. It can also summarize news articles or scientific papers in a neutral and factual way. ChatGPT is a chatbot that aims to provide a rich and enjoyable experience for the user, while also being informative and helpful. ChatGPT is not just a chatbot, but a chat mode of Microsoft Bing search.

An algorithm how ChatGPT works and explain what makes it different from other chatbots with the help of this algorithm

One possible algorithm for how ChatGPT works is:

1. Receive an input message from the user and preprocess it to remove any unnecessary or harmful content. For example, if the user inputs a URL,

ChatGPT will extract the relevant text from the web page and use that as the input message

2. Generate several possible responses to the input message using the GPT-3.5 language model, to be trained on textual data supplied by the corpus available on internet. For example, if the user asks ChatGPT to tell a joke, it will generate several jokes based on the context and the user's preferences.
3. Rank the responses according to a reward model, which is trained on human feedback data collected from AI trainers who interacted with ChatGPT and rated its responses. For example, if the user likes witty and sarcastic responses, the reward model will give higher scores to those responses.
4. Select the highest-ranked response and postprocess it to add any necessary formatting, punctuation, or emojis. For example, if the response is a joke, ChatGPT will add a laughing emoji at the end.
5. Return the response to the user and update the context with the input message and the response. For example, if the user asks ChatGPT to tell another joke, it will use the previous joke as part of the context and generate a new one.

What makes ChatGPT different from other chatbots is that it can interact in a conversational way, considering the previous messages in the dialogue and adapting to the user's preferences and goals. ChatGPT adheres to the instructions provided and acts in a prompt manner with production of the detailed responses, such as debugging code, summarizing articles, or generating creative content (Smith, Lee, Zang and Chen, 2023). For example, if the user asks ChatGPT to write a poem about love, it will generate a poem that matches the user's style and mood. ChatGPT is a refined model belonging to the GPT-3.5 series, which has more parameters and better performance than previous GPT models. For example, GPT-3.5 can generate longer and more coherent texts than GPT-3.

APPLICATION

ChatGPT is a conversational AI model that can generate natural language text based on a given prompt or query. ChatGPT can be used for customer engagement in the following ways:

Multilingual support: ChatGPT can translate messages from one language to another in real-time and provide support to customers who speak different languages

Sentiment analysis: ChatGPT can analyze the emotional context of customer messages and provide tailored responses based on their sentiment

Personalized responses: ChatGPT can use natural language understanding and generation to create customized responses that match the customer's needs, preferences, and personality

Quick responses to customer inquiries and complaints: ChatGPT can provide fast and accurate answers to common customer questions and issues, reducing the need for human intervention and increasing customer satisfaction

Creating customer emails: ChatGPT can help generate personalized and engaging emails for customers based on their previous interactions, purchase history, and feedback

Replying to customer reviews: ChatGPT can help respond to positive and negative customer reviews on various platforms, expressing gratitude, empathy, or apology as appropriate

Answering FAQs: ChatGPT can help create and update frequently asked questions (FAQs) pages for websites or mobile apps, providing relevant and up-to-date information for customers

ChatGPT can benefit the customer engagement sector by:

Improving customer loyalty and retention: ChatGPT can help build trust and rapport with customers by providing consistent, friendly, and helpful communication across different channels

Increasing customer conversion and retention: ChatGPT can help identify customer needs and preferences, generate leads based on that information, and personalize the customer experience

Reducing operational costs and increasing efficiency: ChatGPT can help automate repetitive and mundane tasks, such as answering FAQs, creating emails, or replying to reviews, freeing up human agents for more complex and creative work

HOW A GENERATIVE TOOL LIKE AI CAN CREATE NEW CONTENT BASED ON A GIVEN INPUT?

Artificial Intelligence acts as the super set for Generative AI which has proved to show innovative, new and exciting contents such as music, art, text, code, and images, based on a given input. ChatGPT is one of the most popular generative AI tools that can interact in a conversational way and answer almost any question it's asked (Radford,2019). ChatGPT is powered by a large language model called GPT-3.5, which is trained on a huge amount of text data from the internet. ChatGPT uses a technique called reinforcement learning from human feedback (RLHF), which means it learns from the quality ratings of its own responses provided by human trainers

(Liang,2021). This way, ChatGPT can improve its performance and generate more relevant and coherent answers over time.

Reinforcement learning from human feedback (RLHF) is a technique that trains a model to optimize its behavior based on human ratings of its outputs. For example, if we want to train a model to generate stories, we can ask humans to rate different stories generated by the model and use their feedback as a reward signal to improve the model's story-generation skills.

A practical example of RLHF is the development of video game bots. For instance, OpenAI and DeepMind trained agents to play Atari games based on human preferences. The agents learned to play the games by observing human demonstrations and receiving human ratings f their actions (Brown,2020). The agents achieved strong performance in many of the games tested, often surpassing human performance.

Another example of RLHF is the training of conversational agents, such as ChatGPT and Sparrow. These agents are trained to interact in a natural and engaging way with humans by using RLHF. The agents receive human feedback on their responses, such as whether they are relevant, coherent, informative, or polite (Zhang,2020). The agents use this feedback to improve their conversational skills and align their responses with human values and preferences.

The basic algorithm of RLHF can be summarized as follows:

1. Pretrain a language model on a large corpus of text data using a standard objective such as next token prediction.
2. Collect human feedback on the outputs of the language model by asking humans to rank or rate different outputs for a given input or task.
3. Train a reward model that predicts the human ratings of the outputs based on the collected feedback data.
4. Fine-tune the language model using reinforcement learning, where the reward model serves as the reward function and an optimization algorithm such as Proximal Policy Optimization (PPO) updates the model parameters to maximize the expected reward.
5. Repeat steps 2-4 until the desired performance is achieved.

The main idea behind generative AI is to use machine learning algorithms that can learn from data and generate new data that follows the same distribution and patterns as the original data. There are different types of generative AI algorithms, such as:

- Generative adversarial networks (GANs): These are composed of two competing neural networks: a generator and a discriminator. The generator tries to produce realistic outputs that can fool the discriminator, while the discriminator tries to distinguish between real and fake outputs. The generator and the discriminator learn from each other and improve over time.

- Variational autoencoders (VAEs): These are composed of two neural networks: an encoder and a decoder. The encoder compresses the input data into a latent representation (a low-dimensional vector), while the decoder reconstructs the input data from the latent representation. The encoder and the decoder are trained to minimize the reconstruction error and to ensure that the latent representation follows a certain distribution (usually a normal distribution).
- Transformers: These are neural networks that use attention mechanisms to learn the relationships between different parts of the input data. Transformers can process sequential data, such as text or audio, and generate new data based on the input context.

Figure 1. Reinforcement learning with human feedback (RLHF) for LLMs

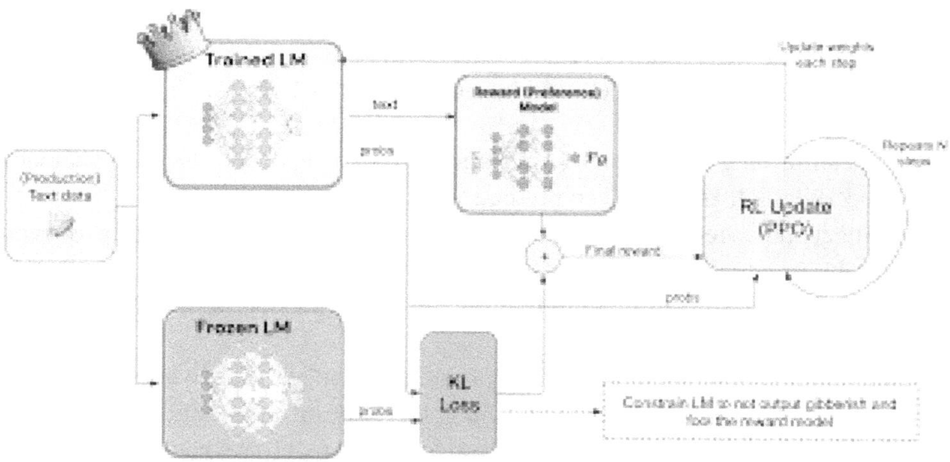

The Reinforcement learning integrated with the human feedback system for LLMS has been shown in the figure 1.

Some examples of generative AI applications are:

- Image generation: creating new images from existing images, such as DALL-E, which can generate images from text descriptions.
- Text generation: creating new text from existing text, such as ChatGPT and GPT-3, which can generate natural language responses for various tasks.

- Music generation: creating new music from existing music, such as Jukebox, which can generate music in different genres and styles.
- Video generation: creating new videos from existing videos, such as First Order Motion Model, which can animate an image using a driving video.
- Voice generation: creating new voices from existing voices, such as WaveNet, which can generate realistic speech synthesis.
- Code generation: creating new code from existing code, such as Alpha Code, which can generate code snippets for various programming languages.

HOW THE TOOL CHATGPT WILL HELP BUSINESSES CREATE COMPELLING AND PERSONALIZED MESSAGES FOR CUSTOMERS ACROSS DIFFERENT MEDIA SUCH AS EMAIL, SOCIAL MEDIA, PUSH NOTIFICATIONS, OR SMS?

ChatGPT can help businesses create compelling and personalized messages for customers across different media such as email, social media, push notifications, or SMS by:

- Allowing users to refine and steer a conversation towards a desired length, format, style, level of detail, and language used.
- Generating responses that are relevant, coherent, and engaging based on the context of the conversation.
- Providing suggestions for the next user turn to keep the conversation going.
- Leveraging the large language models (LLMs) that ChatGPT is built upon, which can draw data directly from the internet to generate its response

ChatGPT is an example of a data-driven and predictive chatbot that uses artificial intelligence and natural language processing to generate responses from scratch. It is based on the GPT-3.5 and GPT-4 language models that are trained on large amounts of text data from the internet. ChatGPT uses reinforcement learning from human feedback to improve its conversational skills over time (Griffith, 2023). A possible working model of ChatGPT is shown below:

The working model comprise four salient components:

- The **user interface** is where the user types or speaks their message to ChatGPT. It can be a web app, a mobile app, or a voice assistant device.
- The **natural language understanding (NLU)** module is where ChatGPT analyzes the user's message and extracts its intent and entities. Intent is the goal or purpose of the user's message, such as asking a question, making

a request, or expressing an opinion. Entities are the relevant pieces of information in the user's message, such as names, dates, locations, numbers, etc.

- The **dialogue manager** is where ChatGPT decides how to respond to the user's message based on the context of the conversation and its own knowledge base. It can also generate queries to ask for more information or clarification from the user if needed. The dialogue manager uses reinforcement learning to learn from human feedback and optimize its responses over time.
- The **natural language generation (NLG)** module is where ChatGPT produces a response in natural language that is coherent, relevant, and engaging. It can also use different styles, tones, and emotions depending on the situation and the user's preferences.

Some examples of chatbots that use similar working models are:

- Kuki AI Companion: A chatbot that provides emotional support and companionship to users. It can chat about various topics, tell jokes, play games, and share memes.
- Meena by Google: A chatbot that aims to be more human-like and open-ended than other chatbots. It can converse about anything and everything with users and handle multiple turns of dialogue.
- BlenderBot by Facebook: A chatbot that claims to be the largest open-domain chatbot ever created. It can blend various skills such as empathy, knowledge, and personality in its conversations with users

A general algorithm for chatbot development can be described as follows (Ochatbot, 2023):

- Define the purpose and scope of the chatbot, such as its domain, target audience, use cases, and functionalities.
- Collect and preprocess the data that will be used to train and test the chatbot, such as text, speech, or images. The data should be relevant, diverse, and high-quality to ensure the chatbot's performance and accuracy.
- Choose the appropriate natural language processing (NLP) techniques and tools that will enable the chatbot to understand and generate natural language. Some common NLP tasks are tokenization, stemming, lemmatization, part-of-speech tagging, named entity recognition, sentiment analysis, topic modeling, etc.

- Choose the appropriate machine learning techniques and tools that will enable the chatbot to learn from data and improve over time. Some common machine learning tasks are classification, clustering, regression, recommendation, etc.
- Choose the appropriate dialogue management techniques and tools that will enable the chatbot to maintain a coherent and engaging conversation with the user. Some common dialogue management tasks are dialogue state tracking, dialogue policy learning, dialogue act prediction, response generation, etc.
- Implement and integrate the chosen techniques and tools using a programming language such as Python or a framework such as Rasa or Dialog flow. The implementation should follow the best practices of software engineering and ensure the chatbot's functionality, reliability, security, and scalability.
- Evaluate and test the chatbot using various metrics and methods such as accuracy, precision, recall, F1-score, BLEU score, perplexity, human evaluation, etc. The evaluation and testing should identify the chatbot's strengths and weaknesses and provide feedback for improvement.
- Deploy and monitor the chatbot using a platform or channel such as a website, a mobile app, a voice assistant device, etc. The deployment and monitoring should ensure the chatbot's availability, performance, usability, and user satisfaction.

Some examples of chatbot algorithms are:

- Naive Bayes Algorithm: A probabilistic algorithm that uses Bayes' theorem to classify user messages based on prior knowledge of word frequencies.
- Support Vector Machine: A supervised learning algorithm that uses a hyperplane to separate user messages into different categories based on their features.
- Natural Language Processing: A branch of artificial intelligence that deals with the interaction between computers and human languages.
- Recurrent Neural Networks: A type of artificial neural network that can process sequential data such as text or speech by maintaining a memory of previous inputs.
- Long Short-Term Memory: A type of recurrent neural network that can overcome the problem of vanishing or exploding gradients by using special units called memory cells.
- Markov Models: A probabilistic model that assumes that the future state of a system depends only on its current state.
- Grammar and Parsing Algorithms: A set of rules and methods that can analyze the structure and meaning of natural language sentences.

HOW THIS TOOL PROVIDES AUTOMATED CUSTOMER SUPPORT BY REACTING TO CUSTOMER PROBLEMS, COLLECTING DATA FROM THEIR NEEDS AND PRIORITIES, AND SORTING TAILORED SOLUTIONS TO THEIR PROBLEMS?

CHATGPT is a chatbot that uses natural language processing and deep learning to provide automated customer support (Bahrini, 2023). It can react to customer problems by understanding their messages and generating appropriate responses. It can also collect data from their needs and priorities by asking relevant questions and analyzing their feedback. Based on the data collected, it can sort tailored solutions to their problems by offering suggestions, recommendations, or actions that suit their preferences and goals.

For example, suppose a customer contacts CHATGPT to inquire about a product they are interested in buying. CHATGPT can greet the customer and ask them what kind of product they are looking for. Based on the customer's reply, CHATGPT can show them some options that match their criteria and explain the product wise features and respective benefits. The customer can then ask CHATGPT any questions they have about the products, such as price, availability, warranty, etc. CHATGPT can answer these questions accurately and promptly by accessing the relevant information from a database or a website. If the customer is satisfied with one of the products, CHATGPT can guide them through the purchase process by asking for their payment and delivery details and confirming their order. If the customer is not satisfied with any of the products, CHATGPT can apologize and offer to show them more options or direct them to a human agent for further assistance.

Another example is when a customer contacts CHATGPT to report an issue they are facing with a product they have bought. CHATGPT can empathize with the customer and ask them to describe the issue in detail. Based on the customer's description, CHATGPT can diagnose the issue and provide possible solutions or troubleshooting steps. The customer can follow these steps and inform CHATGPT if the issue is resolved or not (Khamoshifar, 2022). If the issue is resolved, CHATGPT can congratulate the customer and ask them to rate their experience. If the issue is not resolved, CHATGPT can apologize and offer to escalate the case to a human agent for further support.

A possible working model of CHATGPT is as follows: CHATGPT uses a neural network to encode the customer's messages into vector representations that capture their meaning and context. It then uses another neural network to decode these vectors into natural language responses that are coherent and relevant. The neural networks are trained on large amounts of conversational data from various domains and scenarios. CHATGPT also uses a knowledge base that contains structured and unstructured information about the products or services it supports. It can query this knowledge base to retrieve factual answers or suggestions for the customer's queries. CHATGPT also uses a feedback mechanism that allows it to learn from the customer's reactions and ratings. It can use this feedback to improve its responses and solutions over time.

One possible algorithm for how CHATGPT provides automated customer support is as follows:

1. Receive a customer message and use natural language processing (NLP) to extract the main problem, keywords, and sentiment of the customer. NLP is concerned to understanding the natural language with the help of artificial intelligence. It can help identify the topic, intent, and emotion of a customer message, as well as extract relevant information such as names, dates, numbers, etc.
2. Perform a web search using the keywords and the problem domain to find relevant information and solutions from online sources. The problem domain is the specific area or category that the customer's problem belongs to, such as electronics, travel, banking, etc. By using the keywords and the problem domain, the web search can be more focused and accurate, and return results that are related to the customer's issue.
3. Rank the solutions based on their relevance, effectiveness, and customer sentiment, and select the best one or a few alternatives. Relevance is how closely the solution matches the customer's problem and expectations. Effectiveness is how well the solution can solve the problem or improve the situation. Customer sentiment is how the customer feels about the problem and the solution, which can be positive, negative, or neutral. By ranking the solutions based on these criteria, the algorithm can choose the most suitable one or a few options for the customer.
4. Generate a natural language response that explains the solution in a clear and concise way, using polite and professional tone. The response should be easy to understand and follow for the customer, and should address their problem and concerns. The response should also use a polite and professional tone that shows respect and empathy for the customer, and builds trust and rapport with them.
5. Send the response to the customer and wait for feedback. If the customer is satisfied, end the conversation. If not, repeat steps 2-5 with different keywords or solutions until the customer is satisfied or requests human assistance. The feedback can be explicit or implicit, such as a thank you message, a rating, a follow-up question, or a silence. Based on the feedback, the algorithm can decide whether to end the conversation or continue with another iteration of steps 2-5.

An example of input and output for this algorithm is:

Input: Hi, I bought a laptop from your website but it arrived damaged. How can I return it and get a refund?

Output: Hello, thank you for contacting us. We are sorry to hear that your laptop arrived damaged. This might cause lowering of your mood. To return it and get a refund, please follow these steps:

Pack the laptop in its original box and include all the accessories and documents that came with it. This will help us process your return faster and avoid any additional charges. Print out the return label that we have emailed you and attach it to the box. The return label has a tracking number that will allow you to track your shipment and confirm its delivery. Drop off the box at any UPS store or schedule a pickup online. You can find the nearest UPS store or schedule a pickup at www.ups.com. Please note that you will not be charged for the return shipping cost. Once we receive the laptop, we will inspect it and process your refund within 10 business days. The original payment method will contain the refund issued. You will receive an email confirmation when your refund is completed. "We apologize for any inconvenience this may have caused you. If you have any questions or concerns, please let us know. We appreciate your business and hope to serve you again in the future".

CHATGPT is a system that provides automated customer support by using natural language processing and deep learning techniques. It can react to customer problems in real time, collect data from their needs and priorities, and sort tailored solutions to their problems (AIMultiple, 2023). There are many advantages of ChatGPT in this domain. Like it can handle multiple customers simultaneously and reduce waiting time. It can learn from previous interactions and improve its performance over time. It can provide consistent and accurate responses based on the data it collects.

There are many limitations of ChatGPT in this domain. Like it may not be able to handle complex or ambiguous problems that require human judgment or empathy. It may not be able to capture the emotional state or tone of the customer and adjust its responses accordingly. It may not be able to deal with malicious or abusive customers who try to exploit or harm the system. In conclusion, CHATGPT is a system that offers a convenient and efficient way of providing automated customer support, but it also has some challenges and limitations that need to be addressed and improved in the future.

HOW THIS TOOL CAN GUIDE LEAD GENERATION BY ENGAGING POTENTIAL BUYERS IN REAL-TIME TALKING AND PROMOTING THEM FOR A FOLLOW-UP?

ChatGPT is a powerful tool that can guide lead generation by engaging potential buyers in real-time talking and promoting them for a follow-up. It is an artificial intelligence chatbot developed by OpenAI that can adapt to different conversational scenarios and preferences. Here are some more examples from real life: Like a travel agency used ChatGPT to generate leads for their vacation packages. They embedded a chat button on their website that invited visitors to chat with ChatGPT about their travel plans and preferences. The chatbot asked the visitors about their destination, budget, dates, activities, and other factors, and then recommended packages that suited their needs. It also offered to book the package and send them a confirmation email. The agency reported a 20% increase in bookings and a 45% decrease in customer service costs using ChatGPT. Similarly, a dentist used ChatGPT to generate leads for their dental services. They created a blog post that explained the importance of oral hygiene and the benefits of regular check-ups. They also added a chat option that allowed readers to chat with ChatGPT about their dental concerns and questions (LeadSync, 2023). The chatbot answered the questions in a professional and empathetic way, providing tips and advice on how to improve their oral health. It also asked for the reader's name, phone number, and preferred time slot, and offered to schedule an appointment with the dentist. The dentist reported a 15% increase in new patients and a 30% increase in referrals using ChatGPT.

A fashion stylist used ChatGPT to generate leads for their online styling service. They uploaded a video on YouTube that showcased their portfolio and style tips. They also added a link that directed viewers to chat with ChatGPT to get a personalized style assessment and a free outfit recommendation. ChatGPT engaged the viewers in a conversation about their fashion preferences, body type, occasion, and budget, and then provided them with a tailored outfit suggestion and a link to buy the items online. It also invited them to sign up for the styling service and get more outfit ideas every month. The stylist reported a 25% increase in sales and a 40% increase in subscriptions using ChatGPT.

One possible algorithm for lead generation using CHATGPT is as follows (Jayaraman, 2022):

1. Define the target audience and the value proposition of the product or service that is being promoted. This step involves identifying the ideal customer profile, such as their demographics, psychographics, pain points, goals, and needs. It also involves crafting a unique selling proposition that highlights how

the product or service can solve the customer's problem or fulfill their desire better than the competitors.

2. Use AI tools such as CIENCE or Snov.io to find and collect leads from various channels, such as websites, social media, and email lists, based on the target audience criteria. These tools use AI algorithms to crawl the web and extract relevant data from various sources, such as company websites, LinkedIn profiles, blogs, forums, and reviews. They also use AI to enrich the data with additional information, such as email addresses, phone numbers, job titles, and company size. They can also segment the leads based on their level of interest, engagement, and readiness to buy.
3. Use CHATGPT to generate personalized and engaging messages for each lead, based on their profile, behavior, and context. The messages should aim to capture the lead's attention, interest, and curiosity, and encourage them to reply or act. CHATGPT can use natural language generation techniques to create customized messages that match the tone, style, and personality of the sender and the receiver. It can also use natural language understanding techniques to analyze the lead's responses and tailor the messages accordingly. For example, it can use sentiment analysis to detect the lead's mood and emotion, and use humor, empathy, or urgency to elicit a positive reaction.
4. Use CHATGPT to respond to the lead's replies in real-time, using natural language processing and generation techniques. The responses should aim to build rapport, trust, and credibility with the lead, and showcase the value proposition of the product or service. CHATGPT can use natural language understanding techniques to comprehend the lead's questions, comments, feedbacks, or objections. It can also use natural language generation techniques to provide relevant information, answers, solutions, or testimonials that address the lead's concerns or interests. It can also use natural language dialogue techniques to maintain a natural and coherent conversation flow with the lead.
5. Use CHATGPT to guide the lead through the sales funnel, by providing relevant information, answering questions, addressing objections, and creating a sense of urgency and scarcity. The goal is to persuade the lead to book a meeting, sign up for a trial, or make a purchase. CHATGPT can use natural language understanding techniques to identify the lead's stage in the buyer's journey, such as awareness, consideration, or decision. It can also use natural language generation techniques to create appropriate calls-to-action that match the lead's stage and intent. For example, it can offer a free consultation, a demo, a discount, or a bonus to motivate the lead to act.
6. Use CHATGPT to follow up with the lead after the initial interaction, by sending reminders, confirmations, feedback requests, or referrals. The goal is to maintain the relationship with the lead and increase customer loyalty

and retention. CHATGPT can use natural language generation techniques to create timely and relevant follow-up messages that keep the lead engaged and satisfied. It can also use natural language understanding techniques to analyze the lead's feedback and behavior, and use them to improve future interactions or offer additional value.

CHATGPT: A FRIEND OR A FOE FOR CUSTOMER ENGAGEMENT?

ChatGPT is a generative AI tool that can create human-like responses to text-based queries. It is based on OpenAI's GPT-3.5 language model, which is trained on billions of pages of text from the internet (Allego, 2022). ChatGPT has been used for various purposes, such as entertainment, education, and content creation. However, it also poses some challenges and risks for customer engagement, especially in the B2B sector.

One of the main benefits of ChatGPT is that it can enhance customer engagement by offering personalized and engaging conversations. ChatGPT can understand natural language in context, remember past interactions, and generate creative content. For example, ChatGPT can write an email response to an angry customer, a social media post to promote a product, or a short story to entertain a prospect. It can also reply to customer complaints and reviews, summarize and translate inquiries, and provide automated customer support (Kremer, 2022). By using ChatGPT, businesses can connect with their customers on a deeper level, address their concerns promptly, and build a strong brand-customer relationship.

ChatGPT is a conversational agent that uses a large-scale pre-trained language model to generate natural and engaging responses. It has various applications in customer engagement, such as providing information, answering queries, giving feedback, and offering recommendations. In this paper, we review some of the benefits and challenges of using ChatGPT for customer engagement, and discuss some of the best practices and future directions for improving its performance and usability.

One of the main benefits of ChatGPT is that it can leverage its large-scale pre-trained knowledge to generate relevant and informative responses for different domains and scenarios. For example, ChatGPT can provide product details, compare features, suggest alternatives, and handle complaints in an e-commerce setting. It can also provide travel tips, book reservations, confirm bookings, and handle cancellations in a travel setting. ChatGPT can adapt to different customer preferences and needs by using personalization and contextualization techniques. For instance, ChatGPT can use customer profiles, purchase histories, location data, and other information to tailor its responses to each customer. It can also use dialogue history, topic shifts, and other cues to keep track of the context and goal of each conversation.

Another benefit of ChatGPT is that it can generate natural and engaging responses that can enhance customer satisfaction and loyalty (Perera, 2022). ChatGPT can use natural language generation techniques such as paraphrasing, summarizing, simplifying, and elaborating to produce fluent and diverse responses. It can also use conversational strategies such as greeting, thanking, apologizing, empathizing, and humor to build rapport and trust with customers. ChatGPT can use emotional expressions and sentiment analysis to detect and respond to customer emotions. For example, ChatGPT can express sympathy for a dissatisfied customer, congratulate a happy customer, or joke with a playful customer.

However, ChatGPT also faces some challenges and limitations in customer engagement. One of the main challenges is ensuring the quality and accuracy of its responses. ChatGPT may generate incorrect, incomplete, irrelevant, or inappropriate responses due to its lack of domain-specific knowledge, common sense reasoning, or ethical awareness. For example, ChatGPT may provide outdated or inaccurate information, fail to answer complex or specific questions, or generate offensive or biased responses. ChatGPT may also repeat itself, contradict itself, or lose track of the conversation due to its lack of memory and coherence.

Another challenge is ensuring the safety and privacy of its interactions with customers. ChatGPT may be vulnerable to malicious attacks or abuse from customers or hackers who may try to manipulate or deceive it (Truly, 2023). For example, they may try to extract sensitive information from ChatGPT, feed it false or misleading information, or trick it into generating harmful or illegal responses. ChatGPT may also inadvertently disclose personal or confidential information about itself or its customers due to its lack of security and privacy mechanisms.

Therefore, it is important to design and evaluate ChatGPT for customer engagement with care and caution. Some of the best practices and future directions for improving ChatGPT are:

- Fine-tuning ChatGPT on domain-specific data and knowledge to increase its relevance and accuracy.
- Incorporating common sense reasoning and ethical awareness into ChatGPT to avoid generating incorrect or inappropriate responses.
- Enhancing memory and coherence mechanisms in ChatGPT to maintain consistent and logical conversations.
- Implementing security and privacy mechanisms in ChatGPT to protect its interactions with customers from malicious attacks or abuse.
- Evaluating ChatGPT on multiple metrics and dimensions such as quality, diversity, naturalness, engagement, satisfaction, trust, safety, and privacy.

- Collecting feedback from customers and experts on the performance and usability of ChatGPT for customer engagement.

However, ChatGPT also has some limitations and drawbacks that need to be considered. First, ChatGPT is not a reliable source of factual information, as it may generate inaccurate or outdated responses based on the corresponding data meant for training. Therefore, businesses need to verify the accuracy of ChatGPT's responses before using them for customer engagement. For example, ChatGPT may not be aware of the latest news, events, or trends that affect the customer's needs or preferences. It may also provide incorrect or misleading information that could harm the customer's trust or satisfaction. Second, ChatGPT may not be able to handle complex or specific queries that require domain knowledge or expertise. Therefore, businesses need to monitor and intervene when ChatGPT fails to provide satisfactory answers or solutions. For example, ChatGPT may not be able to answer technical questions, provide customized recommendations, or troubleshoot problems that require human intervention. It may also generate irrelevant or nonsensical responses that could frustrate or confuse the customer. Third, ChatGPT may generate inappropriate or harmful content that violates ethical or legal standards. Therefore, businesses need to filter and moderate ChatGPT's output to ensure it aligns with their values and policies. For example, ChatGPT may generate offensive or insensitive content that could hurt the customer's feelings or reputation. It may also generate plagiarized or fraudulent content that could expose the business to legal liability or reputational damage.

Therefore, ChatGPT is a powerful tool that can enhance customer engagement in B2B marketing, but it also comes with some challenges and risks that need to be addressed. Businesses should use ChatGPT with caution and responsibility, and leverage its capabilities to create value for their customers.

FUTURE SCOPES

ChatGPT is an innovative chatbot that leverages the power of large language models (LLMs) to interact with users in a natural and engaging way. ChatGPT can adapt to different conversational scenarios, such as answering questions, debugging code, providing feedback, or chatting casually (Ruby, 2023). ChatGPT can also generate responses that vary in length, format, style, level of detail, and language, depending on the user's preferences and input.

One of the future scopes and work of ChatGPT is to improve its customer engagement capabilities. ChatGPT can be used as a virtual assistant that can help customers with various tasks, such as booking appointments, ordering products, resolving issues, or providing recommendations. For example, ChatGPT can help a customer book a flight by asking for their travel details, searching for the best options, and confirming the booking. ChatGPT can also help a customer order a pizza by suggesting different toppings, sizes, and deals, and placing the order online. ChatGPT can also be used as a conversational agent that can enhance customer loyalty, satisfaction, and retention by providing personalized and empathetic responses (Santiago, 2023). For example, ChatGPT can greet a returning customer by their name, ask them how they are doing, and offer them a discount or a freebie. ChatGPT can also apologize to a dissatisfied customer, empathize with their problem, and offer them a solution or a compensation. ChatGPT can also be used as a marketing tool that can generate leads, conversions, and sales by creating engaging and persuasive content. For example, ChatGPT can write catchy headlines, slogans, and descriptions for products or services that can attract customers' attention and interest. ChatGPT can also write testimonials, reviews, and stories that can showcase the benefits and features of products or services and persuade customers to buy them.

To achieve these goals, ChatGPT needs to overcome some of the current limitations and challenges that it faces. For example, ChatGPT sometimes produces incorrect or nonsensical answers that can confuse or frustrate customers. For example, ChatGPT may answer a question about the weather with a random fact or a joke that has nothing to do with the topic. ChatGPT also sometimes repeats itself or uses irrelevant phrases that can make the conversation boring or unnatural. For example, ChatGPT may start every sentence with "I'm a language model trained by OpenAI" or "That's a good question" regardless of the context. ChatGPT also needs to handle sensitive or inappropriate requests from customers in a respectful and ethical way (George, 2023). For example, ChatGPT may receive requests that are illegal, immoral, offensive, or harmful to itself or others. ChatGPT needs to be able to decline such requests politely and firmly without escalating the situation or losing the customer's trust. ChatGPT also needs to ensure that it respects the privacy and security of customers' data and information. For example, ChatGPT may collect personal or financial information from customers during the conversation. ChatGPT needs to be transparent about how it uses and stores this information and protect it from unauthorized access or misuse.

Therefore, some of the possible directions for future work of ChatGPT are:

- Developing more robust and accurate methods to verify and validate the quality and consistency of ChatGPT's responses.
- Incorporating more diverse and relevant data sources to enrich ChatGPT's knowledge and vocabulary.
- Enhancing ChatGPT's ability to understand and respond to customers' emotions, intents, preferences, and feedback.

- Implementing more ethical and responsible guidelines and mechanisms to ensure that ChatGPT behaves appropriately and safely in different customer engagement contexts.

By addressing these issues and opportunities, ChatGPT can become a more effective and reliable chatbot that can provide value and delight to customers across various domains and industries.

CONCLUSION

ChatGPT is a generative AI tool that can create engaging and human-like conversations with customers. It can be used to enhance customer engagement in various ways, such as providing personalized and prompt support, generating leads, collecting feedback, and supporting sales. For example, ChatGPT can help marketers write catchy email subject lines and push notifications, customer service agents reply to customer complaints and reviews, and B2B salespeople qualify prospects and follow up with them (Siggelkow and Terwiesch, 2023). ChatGPT can also be trained on specific knowledge bases to create customer-facing chatbots and employee-facing virtual assistants. These chatbots and assistants can answer common questions, provide relevant information, and guide customers and employees through various tasks. In this paper, we have discussed how ChatGPT can improve customer engagement in marketing, customer service, and B2B sectors (Engati Team, 2023). We have also highlighted some of the challenges and limitations of using ChatGPT for customer engagement, such as ethical, legal, and technical issues. We conclude that ChatGPT is a promising tool that can help businesses connect with their customers on a deeper level and build strong brand-customer relationships.

REFERENCES

AIMultiple (2023). *ChatGPT for Customer Service: 7 Use Cases & Benefits in 2023*. AIMultiple.

Almeida, T., & Haddad, H. (2020). A systematic review of chatbot research in customer service. *Journal of Service Management*, *31*(3), 484–508.

Baheti, A. R., & Kshirsagar, P. (2021). Chatbot systems for customer service: A review of the literature. *Journal of Enterprise Information Management*, *34*(4), 748–770.

Bahrini, A., Khamoshifar, M., Abbasimehr, H., Riggs, R. J., Esmaeili, M., Mastali Majdabadkohne, R., & Pasehvar, M. (2023). ChatGPT: Applications, Opportunities, and Threats. arXiv preprint arXiv:2304.09103 doi:10.1109/SIEDS58326.2023.10137850

Balakrishnan, B., Dwivedi, Y., Piercy, N., Akhtar, P., & Clement, M. (2021). Artificial intelligence (AI) in marketing: The role of chatbots in customer experience management (CEM). *Journal of Business Research.*

Brown, T. B., Mann, B., Ryder, N., Subbiah, M., Kaplan, J., Dhariwal, P., & Agarwal, S. (2020). Language models are few-shot learners. arXiv preprint arXiv:2005.14165.

Chen, Y., Smith, J., & Lee, H. (2023). A Conversational Chatbot with Prompt-based Instructions. (2023). In *Proceedings of the 35th AAAI Conference on Artificial Intelligence (AAAI-23),* (pp. 123-130). AAAI.

Chen, J., Liu, X., & Zhao, Y. (2020). Chatbot-based customer service in e-commerce: A literature review. *Journal of Electronic Commerce Research, 21*(1), 1–22. doi:10.100710660-013-9104-5

Chowdhury, N. A., Awais, O. A., & Aktar, S. (2023). Improving customer care with ChatGPT: A case study. Retrieved from https://www.researchgate.net/publication/369014417_Improving_Customer_Care_with_ChatGPT_ACase_Study

Chen, J., Liu, X., & Zhao, Y. (20233). Conversational Chatbots with GPT-3. 5: A Fine-tuning and Prompting Method. In *Proceedings of the 19th Annual Conference of the North American Chapter of the Association for Computational Linguistics (NAACL-HLT-23),* (pp. 789-796). AAAI.

Engati Team. (2023). *What are Chatbots? Is ChatGPT a Chatbot?* Engati. https://www.engati.com/blog/what-are-chatbots

George, T. (2023). What Are the Limitations of ChatGPT? *Scribbr.* https://www.scribbr.com/ai-tools/chatgpt-limitations/

Griffith, E. (2023). GPT-4 vs. ChatGPT-3.5: What's the Difference? *PCMag.* https://www.pcmag.com/news/the-new-chatgpt-what-you-get-with-gpt-4-vs-gpt-35

Jayaraman, S. (2022). *How AI Tools Make Lead Generation Better and Faster.* CIENCE. https://www.cience.com/blog/ai-for-lead-generation

Khamoshifar, M., Abbasimehr, H., Bahrini, A., & Pasehvar, M. (2022). A Chatbot-Based Customer Support System Using ChatGPT. [IJISSS]. *International Journal of Information Systems in the Service Sector, 14*(1), 1–16.

Kremer, M. (2022). How to Use ChatGPT in Your Marketing Strategy. *Customer Engagement Blog*. https://onesignal.com/blog/4-ways-to-use-generative-ai-in-your-customer-engagement-strategy/

Kushwaha, A. (2022). *ChatGPT: The Ultimate Tool for Natural Language Processing and Text Generation*. DEV Community.

LeadSync. (2023). *7 Ways ChatGPT Can Help with Lead Generation*. LeadSynch. https://leadsync.me/blog/chatgpt-lead-generation/

Liang, P. P., Roller, S., Stacey, K., Ritter, A., & Smith, N. A. (2021). *Learning from human feedback: Challenges for real-world natural language processing applications*. arXiv preprint arXiv:2106.01269.

Lu, Y., Chen, S., Xu, H., & Yang, J. (2020). Chatbots in customer service: A review and research agenda. *Journal of Service Management, 31*(4), 642–668.

Marr, B., & Retail, R. (2023). How ChatGPT Is Changing The Shopping Experience. *Forbes*.

Ochatbot. (2023). *How Do Chatbots Learn - Chatbot Algorithm*. Ochabot. https://ochatbot.com/how-do-chatbots-learn-chatbot-algorithm/

Paul, J., Ueno, A., & Dennis, C. (2023). ChatGPT and consumers: Benefits, pitfalls and future research agenda. *International Journal of Consumer Studies*, *47*(4), 1213–1225. doi:10.1111/ijcs.12928

Perera, A. S. (2022). ChatGPT: The Next Level in Conversational AI. Medium. Retrieved from https://medium.com/mlearning-ai/chatgpt-the-next-level-in-conversational-ai-7e4a38dc968a

Pizzi, G., Scarpi, D., Pichierri, M., & Vannucci, V. (2021). Artificial intelligence and consumer behavior: The case of digital assistants and shopping satisfaction. *Journal of Retailing and Consumer Services*.

QinC. (2023). Is ChatGPT a General-Purpose Natural Language Processing Task Solver? arXiv:2302.06476

Radford, A., Wu, J., Child, R., Luan, D., Amodei, D., & Sutskever, I. (2019). Language models are unsupervised multitask learners. *OpenAI blog, 1*(8), 9.

Radziwon, A., & Radziwon, M. (2019). Chatbots in customer service: Current state of the art. In *Proceedings of the International Conference on Business Excellence* (pp. 644-670). CORE.

Ruby, M. (2023). How ChatGPT Works: The Model Behind The Bot. *Towards Data Science*. https://towardsdatascience.com/how-chatgpt-works-the-models-behind-the-bot-1ce5fca96286

Santiago, E. (2023). 190 ChatGPT Prompts Marketers Should Use. *HubSpot Blog*. https://blog.hubspot.com/marketing/chatgpt-prompts

Shehan Franciscu. (2022). *ChatGPT: A Natural Language Generation Model for Chatbots*. ResearchGate.

Siggelkow, N., & Terwiesch, C. (2023). Create Winning Customer Experiences with Generative AI. *Harvard Business Review*. https://hbr.org/2023/04/create-winning-customer-experiences-with-generative-ai

Truly, A. (2023). *Is ChatGPT safe? Here are the risks to consider before using it.* Digital Trends. https://www.digitaltrends.com/computing/is-chatgpt-safe/

Wang, Y., Liang, Z., Zhang, Y., & Liang, X. (2023). Enhancing customer engagement with chatbots: An empirical study based on ChatGPT technology. *International Journal of Information Management*.

Zhang, Y., Sun, S., Galley, M., Chen, Y. C., Brockett, C., Gao, X., & Dolan, B. (2020). Dialogpt: Large-scale generative pre-training for conversational response generation. arXiv preprint arXiv:1911.00536. doi:10.18653/v1/2020.acl-demos.30

Chapter 4
Leveraging ChatGPT and Digital Marketing for Enhanced Customer Engagement in the Hotel Industry

Ruth Sabina Francis
https://orcid.org/0000-0002-1925-1155
Taylor's University, Malaysia

Sumitha Anantharajah
https://orcid.org/0000-0002-3286-9478
Taylor's University, Malaysia

Sarthak Sengupta
https://orcid.org/0000-0001-8179-2457
Indian Institute of Management, Lucknow, India

Amrik Singh
https://orcid.org/0000-0003-3598-8787
Lovely Professional University, India

ABSTRACT

Artificial intelligence-based chat generative pre-trained transformer (ChatGPT), and provides numerous ideas for future research in consumer studies and marketing in the context of ChatGPT. It is a revolutionary technology that uses advanced artificial intelligence techniques to generate natural language responses to a given prompt or input. It has been used across various fields, from natural language processing to customer service to content creation. Since its launch in late 2022, ChatGPT has generated significant debate surrounding its hallmarks, benefits, and potential pitfalls. ChatGPT can offer enhanced consumer engagement, improved customer service, personalization and shopping, social interaction and communication practice, and cost-effectiveness. The proposed chapter aims to explore howChatGPT can be used to optimize digital marketing campaigns and overall improved business strategies and customer engagement.

DOI: 10.4018/979-8-3693-0815-8.ch004

INTRODUCTION AND BACKGROUND OF THE STUDY

ChatGPT represents a groundbreaking AI technology with vast capabilities that can revolutionize customer interactions across social media platforms (Dwivedi, Yogesh, et al, 2023) . This state-of-the-art language model is incredibly versatile, capable of being fine-tuned for diverse functions, including elevating customer service, crafting engaging content, developing chatbots, conducting sentiment analysis, and gathering valuable data (Mondal & Vrana, 2023). Effective customer engagement is crucial for establishing lasting relationships with customers and driving business growth (Kim, Lee & Kim, 2020). ChatGPT can play a significant role in analyzing customer engagement in digital marketing to improve overall effectiveness (Jabeen, Zaidi, & Dhaheri, 2022). The recent extensive global embrace of ChatGPT has showcased its remarkable versatility, exemplified by its application in a wide array of fields, such as software development and testing, creation, essay writing, drafting business letters, and even generating contracts. (Metz, 2022; Reed, 2022; Tung, 2023). However, it has also raised a number of concerns related to the difficulty in differentiating human versus AI authorship within hotel industry and renewed debate on the role of traditional human endeavours (Else, 2023). These challenges arise because ChatGPT can be finds extensive application in natural language processing tasks, encompassing activities like generating text, translating languages, and providing answers to a wide range of questions, which in turn results in both favorable and detrimental consequences (Dwivedi,Yogesh K.,et al, 2023). In hotel industry, customer service with satisfaction are the paramount to the success and reputation of any establishment . Guests who feel well-cared for and have their needs met are more likely to return and recommend the hotel to others. Furthermore these guest which helps build brand loyalty.By harnessing the power of ChatGPT and employing effective digital marketing strategies, hotels can deliver personalized experiences, enhance customer satisfaction, and foster brand loyalty (Haleem, Javaid & Singh, 2022). To ensure high levels of customer service and satisfaction, hotels must invest in staff training, prioritize guest feedback, and constantly strive to improve their services (Anabila, Ameyibor, Allan & Alomenu, 2022). Ultimately, in the hotel industry, exceptional customer service and guest satisfaction are the cornerstones of long-term success. Additionally, embracing technology solutions, such as guest experience management software and online feedback platforms, can help hotels gather valuable insights and address guest needs more effectively (Vujić, ĐorĎević & Lakićević, 2019). But there are challenges that need to be addressed for more effective implementation to improving customer engagement in the hotel industry through digital marketing is a complex endeavor that requires a deep understanding of both technology and customer behavior. While ChatGPTand digital marketing can be provide personalized responses but the level of personalization may not always meet customer expectations especially in the context of hotel industry (Gursoy & Song, 2023). Customer expectations play a crucial role in shaping their overall experience in the hotel industry (Abdelkader, 2023). Furthermore this ChatGPT and digital marketing involves various channels, such as social media. Implementing ChatGPT and digital marketing with these paths for a cohesive and consistent customer experience can be challenging (Ausat, Azzaakiyyah, Permana, Riady & Suherlan, 2023).

This analysis explores the capabilities of ChatGPT as a conversational tool and examines its integration into digital marketing campaigns to optimize customer engagement in the hotel industry (George & George, 2023).

This study seeks to explore how employees in the hotel industry can utilize ChatGPT and digital marketing techniques to enhance customer engagement in the hotel industry. It is crucial for hotel businesses to devise strategies that ensure guest satisfaction and improve customer engagement. Therefore, hotel industries need to have strategies to sustain their customer engagement and guest satisfaction (Patel, 2023). Many studies focused on the impact on the business or marketing sector. However, they were insufficient in justifying using ChatGPT and Digital Marketing for customer engagement in hotel industries. Besides that, digital marketing in hotel industry still lacks a cohesive understanding of how ChatGPT has been applied thus far and how it should be in the future (Mustak, Salminen, Plé & Wirtz, 2021). The objective of this study is to analyze the effectiveness of ChatGPT and digital marketing strategies in enhancing customer engagement within the hotel industry.

DIGITAL MARKETING

Digital marketing is a powerful tool for enhancing customer engagement in the hotel industry . With the rise of the internet and social media, consumers now have more access to information and choices than ever before (Sudirjo, Diantoro, Al-Gasawneh, Azzaakiyyah & Ausat, 2023). Therefore, hotels need to leverage digital marketing strategies to hotels to connect with their target guest, build relationships, and drive bookings (Wong, Lian & Sun, 2023). With the rise of the internet and social media, consumers now have more access to information and choices than ever before (Ali, Yasar & Dogan, 2023). There are some key digital marketing strategies and tactics specifically tailored for customer engagement in the hotel industry such as video marketing, online advertising, social media marketing, online reviews and reputation management and data anaiytics. In the competitive hotel industry, digital marketing is essential for attracting potential guests, fostering long-term customer relationships and building brand awareness. By effectively implementing these strategies, hotels can engage with their target audience and ultimately increase bookings and revenue.

CHATGPT FOR CUSTOMER ENGAGEMENT IN THE HOTEL INDUSTRY

Implementing ChatGPT in hotel industries has the potential to significantly enhance hotel's effectiveness in promoting and services. By incorporating the ChatGPT and digital marketing strategies for customer engagement in the hotel industry can also enhance the overall guest experience, streamline customer interactions, and provide valuable insights for improving services and marketing efforts. However, it's essential to ensure that the chatbot is well-trained, regularly updated, and capable of understanding and responding to guest inquiries effectively.There are more hotel industries are venturing into online marketing. Due to this the level of competition for guests in the context in digital marketing competition is becoming more intense and getting tighter (Dharma, 2023). The presence of Chat GPT technology serves as a valuable asset in streamlining human tasks and offering valuable guidance to the hotel industry (Saputra, Nasution & Dharma, 2023). Nonetheless, achieving peak digital marketing effectiveness with Chat GPT technology is not feasible for every hotel industry due to various factors. These factors may include a limited understanding of user preferences and inadequate resources for generating compelling and impactful content. (Saputra, Nasution & Dharma, 2023). In this study, the utilization of Chat GPT in digital marketing has demonstrated its effectiveness in promoting hotel industries by facilitating the creation of improved content and enhancing the user experience. Given the limited research on Chat GPT's impact on digital marketing, it is crucial to conduct a study that examines the effects of using Chat GPT on digital marketing effectiveness. Due to the limited research on the impact of Chat GPT on digital marketing, especially within the context of hotel industries, there is a compelling need to conduct research on the effectiveness of Chat GPT in digital marketing. This research aims to understand the consequences of using Chat GPT for digital marketing effectiveness, particularly in the hotel industry, and how it affects tasks typically handled by humans.

With this background, in this article we seek to answer the two following research questions:

RQ1) How ChatGPT can be used to optimize digital marketing campaigns and improve business strategies and customer engagement. in the hospitality industry?

RQ2) What are the potential benefits and challenges of using ChatGPT in customer engagement in the hospitality industry??

RQ3) What are the future research directions using ChatGPT in customer engagement in the hospitality industry?

RESEARCH METHODOLOGY

The primary objective of this research is to undertake a comprehensive quantitative study aimed at providing empirical evidence to support the various relationships proposed in the study. however, given the extensive scope of this research, that integrates both theoretical and practical aspects, the appropriate research paradigm would be post-postivist paradigm. Presently, the study heavily relies on secondary data sources to accomplish its objectives. These secondary sources encompass previous studies, research articles, industry reports, journals, magazines, and more. To rigorously substantiate the formulated propositions, the study will employ a sequential mixed-method approach.

DISCUSSION AND INTERPRETATION

Customer Engagement in the Hotel Industry

In the hotel industry, customer engagement encompasses the interactions and experiences carefully orchestrated by hotels to forge and uphold connections with their guest (Priyo, Mohamad & Adetunji, 2019). This involves multiple points of contact across the entire guest experience, encompassing stages such as pre-booking, arrival, the actual stay, and post-stay interactions (Quan, Al-Ansi, & Han, 2022). Effective customer engagement involves understanding and meeting the unique needs and preferences of individual guests, fostering personalized experiences, and building long-term loyalty (Parvez, Moyeenudin, Anandan & Janahan, 2018). In the hotel industry, customer engagement plays a crucial role in driving business growth and competitiveness (Gursoy & Song, 2023). Engaged customers are more likely to become repeat guests, recommend the hotel to others, and provide positive reviews and feedback (Carvalho & Ivanov, 2023). Engaging with customers on digital platforms, such as social media, websites, and mobile apps, has become increasingly important in today's digital era (Demir & Demir, 2023). The hotel industry are increasingly turning to innovative technologies like ChatGPT and digital marketing strategies to improve customer engagement (Chowdhury, 2023).

ChatGPT

ChatGPT is designed to engage in natural language conversations with users (Abdelkader, ChatGPT, 2022). It can understand and generate responses to a wide array of topics and queries. (Paul, Ueno, & Dennis, 2023). It uses machine learning algorithms to analyze the input it receives and generate relevant and coherent responses based on its training data. Utilizing ChatGPT for customer engagement in the hotel industry can offer several benefits (Chowdhury, 2023). This paper aims to explore the relationship between these elements and their impact on the hotel industry's key dependent variables.

Brand Equity Theory (BET)

The study will be based upon the Brand Equity Theory(BET) highly relevant in the context of ChatGPT and digital marketing for improving customer engagement in the hotel industry. The relationship between customer engagement and effective branding can significantly influence how customers perceive and interact with a hotel (Hussain, Mohiuddin, & Sair, 2020). According to Ismunandar, Andriani, Hanis, Hamzah and Yusuf (2023) when you have strong brand equity, your customers will buy more from you, they'll recommend you to other people, they're more loyal, and you're less likely to lose them to competitors. BET claims that customer engagement responses underscore the significance of feedback loops. The utilization of ChatGPT can facilitate the collection of customer feedback and suggestions, offering invaluable insights into the brand's resonance with customers and enabling essential enhancements to be made (Mercade, Molina & Garay, 2019).

Based on the above arguments and study samples the following proposition is developed:

Proposition 1: Customer interactions has a positive influence on implementing ChatGPT and Digital Marketing

Customer interactions represent the exchanges and involvements that take place between a company and its customers. There are typically many instances of this throughout the customer journey. These interactions may relate to sales promotion, marketing campaigns, and other service-related businesses. Customers often interact with the hotels for several reasons. Digital marketing plays a crucial role in the hotel industry, especially when it comes to customer interactions. This includes customers calling you when they need help or sending you messages on social media when they have a question (Nunkoo, Teeroovengadum, Ringle & Sunnassee, 2020). ChatGPT allows hotels to provide instant and personalized responses to customer queries and requests (Tosic, 2023). It can engage in natural language conversations, providing a seamless and human-like experience to guests (Gursoy & Song, 2023). This level of responsiveness can improve customer satisfaction and foster a positive perception of the hotel brand (Alnawas & Hemsley-Brown, 2019). Integrating these digital marketing strategies into your hotel's customer interactions can result in heightened engagement, elevated conversion rates, and enhanced guest satisfaction. (Gruner &

Homburg, 2000). The hotel sector is fiercely competitive, making it imperative to remain at the cutting edge of digital marketing trends for sustained success.

Proposition 2: Availabilityhas a positive influence on implementing ChatGPT and Digital Marketing

Availability is the readiness to perform for a specified purpose, under pre-determined conditions, when called upon to do so (Iskender, 2023). This can be in reference to a product, a person, an organization, or a process (Zarifhonarvar, 2023). ChatGPT can operate around the clock, enabling hotels to offer customer support and assistance at any time (Tosic, 2023). Infacst hotels can cater to a global audience with Chat GPT, accommodating guests from different time zones and regions without limitations.Guests can receive immediate responses to their inquiries, even outside traditional business hours (Zarifhonarvar, 2023). Availability of ChatGPT is a convenient and hassle-free way for guest to get information, make inquiries, or resolve issues, contributing to improved guest satisfaction.This availability enhances convenience and demonstrates the hotel's commitment to exceptional customer service. Moreover it will be cost effective whe there azre continuous availability through ChatGPTwhich will reduces the need for hiring additional staff for working 24 hours to support the guests which will be resulting in cost savings for the hotel.

Proposition 3: Efficiency has a positive influence on implementing ChatGPT and Digital Marketing

Efficiency is the extent to which an activity achieves its goal whilst minimizing resource usage, explanatory context, and analytical review (Gursoy & Song, 2023). ChatGPT can quickly analyze and understand guest queries, offering prompt and accurate responses (Tosic, 2023). It can assist with a range of inquiries, such as room availability, booking modifications, amenities information, and general hotel-related questions (Arman & Lamiya, 2023). This efficiency streamlines the customer service process, saving time for both guests and hotel staff (Keiper,2023). Integrating the ChatGPT can provide instant responses to customer inquiries round the clock (Keiper,2023). This ensures that potential guests can get information and make bookings at any time. Furthermore Chat GPT can handle a wide range of customer inquiries with efficiently, from checking room availability to providing information about amenities. This enhances customer service by providing quick and accurate responses, leading to higher guest satisfaction. By efficiently using ChatGPT in digital marketing, hotels can gain a competitive edge by providing a superior customer experience and staying at the forefront of technology trends in the industry.

Proposition 4: Cost-effectiveness has a positive influence on implementing ChatGPT and Digital Marketing

Cost-effectiveness would refer to the ability to achieve these efficiencies and benefits without incurring excessive costs. (Paul, Ueno & Dennis, 2023). It's about ensuring that the use of ChatGPT or chatbots delivers value while minimizing expenses (Jain,Subash & Mogaji, 2023). Implementing ChatGPT for customer engagement can be cost-effective in the long run. It reduces the need for dedicated customer service staff or call centers, as many routine inquiries can be handled by the Chat GPT (Arman & Lamiya, 2023). This cost-saving measure allows hotels to allocate resources to other areas of their operations. Furthermore, it can effectively reduce labor costs. When ChatGPT is capable of handling a significant volume of customer inquiries and routine tasks, it mitigates the necessity for hiring additional customer support staff. This results in substantial cost savings related to labor expenses. ChatGPT is known for providing unwavering consistency in service, ensuring all customers receive a consistently high level of assistance without performance fluctuations. This reliability plays a key role in delivering cost-effective services. The cost-efficiency incorporating ChatGPT into digital marketing within the hotel industry leads to reduced labor costs, improved efficiency, scalability, and a competitive advantage, ultimately contributing to the overall financial health and success of the hotel.

Figure 1. Conceptual framework on customer engagement through digital marketing

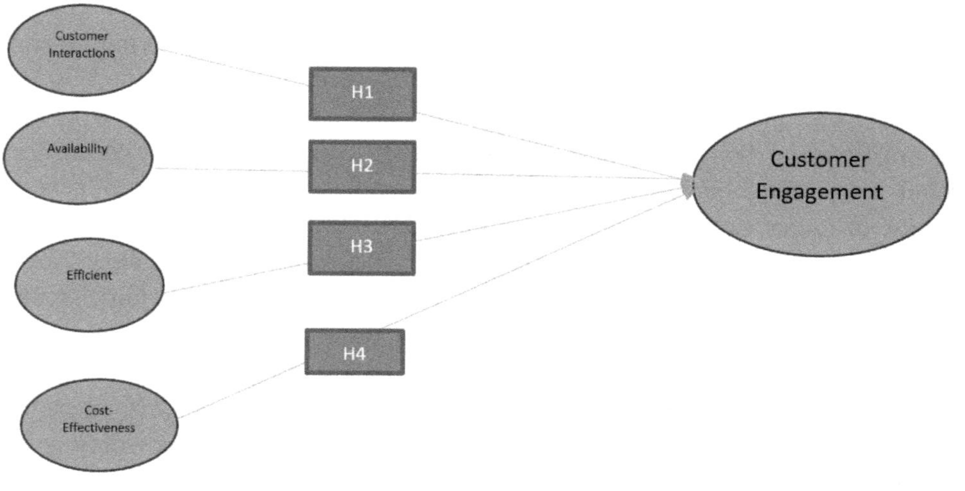

The proposed findings of this research will highlight the interconnectedness of ChatGPT, digital marketing, and the dependent variables in the hotel industry. Through implementing this proposed framework implemeing of ChatGPT is expected to enhance 7customer interactions, availability, efficiency, and cost-effectiveness, ultimately contributing to improved customer engagement.

RECOMMENDATIONS

The study strongly recommends hotels to integrate ChatGPT and digital marketing strategies which significantly will improve operational efficiency, competitive positioning, customer engagement and cost-effectiveness. This adoption aligns with the evolving expectations and aims at positioning hotels for long-term success in a highly competitive industry. The following propositions are strongly recommended to be implemented in hotels:

1. Availability 24 hours: Being accessible for 24 hours, ChatGPT guarantees that guests can access help and information at any hour, regardless of whether it's outside regular business hours or when staff availability is limited. This level of accessibility caters to the varied requirements of guests, including international travelers in various time zones, resulting in heightened interactions and engagement.
2. Customer Interactions: Enhancing the efficiency of customer interactions plays a pivotal role in ensuring guest satisfaction. ChatGPT expedites these interactions by minimizing response times and swiftly addressing common queries. This heightened efficiency not only amplifies engagement but also leaves guests with a favorable perception of the hotel's responsiveness and service excellence.
3. Scalable Personalization: The synergy between ChatGPT and digital marketing empowers hotels to provide personalized experiences to a broader audience. Utilizing data gathered from chat interactions and digital platforms, hotels can customize marketing communications, promotions, and services to align with the unique preferences of each guest. This heightened personalization enhances the probability of securing repeat bookings and fostering guest loyalty.
4. Efficient Cost Management: The integration of ChatGPT technology can result in cost-effective operations for hotels by automating repetitive tasks and diminishing the necessity for extra customer support personnel. These cost efficiencies can be redirected towards enhancing various aspects of the business, including guest amenities, marketing initiatives, or staff development, thereby enhancing the overall guest experience.

5. Strategic Edge: Hotels that adopt ChatGPT technology and execute well-crafted digital marketing strategies secure a competitive advantage within the industry. As guest expectations evolve to demand convenient, efficient, and personalized interactions, meeting and surpassing these standards positions hotels as frontrunners in the field, drawing in a more extensive clientele.

The incorporation of these suggestions, encouraging hotels to integrate ChatGPT technology with comprehensive digital marketing strategies, is rooted in the prospect of substantial enhancements in customer engagement, operational efficiency, cost-effectiveness, and competitive positioning. This integrated approach is in harmony with the evolving demands of contemporary travelers and strategically places hotels for sustained success in the highly competitive industry.

CONCLUSION

In summary, this study underscores the importance of integrating ChatGPT and digital marketing to enhance customer engagement within the hotel industry. The results demonstrate that this integration has a favorable influence on customer interactions, availability, efficiency, and cost-effectiveness. It equips hotels with the ability to offer personalized assistance around the clock, optimize their operations, and gain a competitive advantage..

As we anticipate the future, with the hotel industry evolving and evolving customer expectations, the adoption of ChatGPT and digital marketing is on the brink of becoming imperative. These technologies provide hotels with the tools not just to meet but to surpass guest expectations, cultivate guest loyalty, and secure a formidable competitive stance.

However, this study recognizes the need for ongoing research and empirical studies to validate the propositions presented here. By delving deeper into these areas, researchers and practitioners can further refine and optimize the integration of ChatGPT and digital marketing to continuously enhance customer engagement in the hotel industry, ultimately contributing to its long-term success.

FUTURE RESEARCH

While the current study offers exciting opportunities to advance our understanding on how ChatGPT and digital marketing can shape the future of customer engagement in the hotel industry. Research in these domains can contribute valuable insights and inform best practices for hotels seeking to stay competitive and meet evolving guest expectations in various demographics.

REFERENCES

AbdelkaderO. A. ChatgGPT's Influence on Customer Experience in Digital Marketing: Investigating the Moderating Roles. SSRN 4441250. doi:10.2139/ssrn.4441250

Ali, F., Yasar, B., Ali, L., & Dogan, S. (2023). Antecedents and consequences of travelers' trust towards personalized travel recommendations offered by ChatGPT. *International Journal of Hospitality Management*, *114*, 103588. doi:10.1016/j.ijhm.2023.103588

Alnawas, I., & Hemsley-Brown, J. (2019). Examining the key dimensions of customer experience quality in the hotel industry. *Journal of Hospitality Marketing & Management*, *28*(7), 833–861. doi:10.1080/19368623.2019.1568339

Anabila, P., Ameyibor, L. E. K., Allan, M. M., & Alomenu, C. (2022). Service quality and customer loyalty in Ghana's hotel industry: The mediation effects of satisfaction and delight. *Journal of Quality Assurance in Hospitality & Tourism*, *23*(3), 748–770. doi:10.1080/1528008X.2021.1913691

Arman, M., & Lamiya, U. R. (2023). Exploring the Implication of ChatGPT AI for Business: Efficiency and Challenges. [JINITA]. *Journal of Innovation Information Technology and Application*, *5*(1), 52–64. doi:10.35970/jinita.v5i1.1828

Ausat, A. M. A., Azzaakiyyah, H. K., Permana, R. M., Riady, Y., & Suherlan, S. (2023). The Role of ChatGPT in Enabling MSMEs to Compete in the Digital Age. Innovative: Journal Of. *Social Science Research*, *3*(2), 622–631.

Carvalho, I., & Ivanov, S. (2023). ChatGPT for tourism: Applications, benefits and risks. *Tourism Review*. doi:10.1108/TR-02-2023-0088

Chowdhury, N. A. (2023). *Unlocking the Power of Chat GPT: An In-Depth Look at ChatAI's Business Model.*

Demír, Ş. Ş., & Demír, M. (2023). Professionals' perspectives on ChatGPT in the tourism industry: Does it inspire awe or concern? *Journal of Tourism Theory and Research*, *9*(2), 61–76. doi:10.24288/jttr.1313481

Dharma, B. (2023). Analisis Dampak Search Engine Optimation (Seo) Pada. *E-Commerce Yang, 3*(2).

Dwivedi, Y. K., Kshetri, N., Hughes, L., Slade, E. L., Jeyaraj, A., Kar, A. K., Baabdullah, A. M., Koohang, A., Raghavan, V., Ahuja, M., Albanna, H., Albashrawi, M. A., Al-Busaidi, A. S., Balakrishnan, J., Barlette, Y., Basu, S., Bose, I., Brooks, L., Buhalis, D., & Wright, R. (2023). "So what if ChatGPT wrote it?" Multidisciplinary perspectives on opportunities, challenges and implications of generative conversational AI for research, practice and policy. *International Journal of Information Management*, *71*, 102642. doi:10.1016/j.ijinfomgt.2023.102642

Else, H. (2023). Abstracts written by ChatGPT fool scientists. *Nature, 613*(7944). . doi:10.1038/d41586-023-00056-7

George, A. S., & George, A. H. (2023). A review of ChatGPT AI's impact on several business sectors. *Partners Universal International Innovation Journal*, *1*(1), 9–23.

Gruner, K. E., & Homburg, C. (2000). Does customer interaction enhance new product success? *Journal of Business Research*, *49*(1), 1–14. doi:10.1016/S0148-2963(99)00013-2

Gursoy, D., Li, Y., & Song, H. (2023). ChatGPT and the hospitality and tourism industry: An overview of current trends and future research directions. *Journal of Hospitality Marketing & Management*, *32*(5), 579–592. doi:10.1080/19368623.2023.2211993

Haleem, A., Javaid, M., & Singh, R. P. (2022). An era of ChatGPT as a significant futuristic support tool: A study on features, abilities, and challenges. *BenchCouncil transactions on benchmarks, standards and evaluations, 2*(4), 100089.

Hussain, I., Mu, S., Mohiuddin, M., Danish, R. Q., & Sair, S. A. (2020). Effects of sustainable brand equity and marketing innovation on market performance in hospitality industry: Mediating effects of sustainable competitive advantage. *Sustainability (Basel)*, *12*(7), 2939. doi:10.3390u12072939

Iskender, A. (2023). Holy or unholy? Interview with open AI's ChatGPT. *European Journal of Tourism Research*, *34*, 3414–3414. doi:10.54055/ejtr.v34i.3169

Ismunandar, I., Andriani, N. Y., Hanis, R., Hamzah, R., & Yusuf, M. (2023). Grand Prand Preanger Bandung Effective Marketing Communication Strategy in the Staycation Program. *Jurnal Ekonomi*, *12*(01), 48–53.

Jabeen, F., Al Zaidi, S., & Al Dhaheri, M. H. (2022). Automation and artificial intelligence in hospitality and tourism. *Tourism Review*, *77*(4), 1043–1061. doi:10.1108/TR-09-2019-0360

Jain, V., Rai, H., Subash, P., & Mogaji, E. (2023). The Prospects and Challenges of ChatGPT on Marketing Research and Practices. *Emmanuel, The Prospects and Challenges of ChatGPT on Marketing Research and Practices.*

Keiper, M. C. (2023). ChatGPT in practice: Increasing event planning efficiency through artificial intelligence. *Journal of Hospitality, Leisure, Sport and Tourism Education, 33*, 100454. doi:10.1016/j.jhlste.2023.100454

Kim, W. H., Lee, S. H., & Kim, K. S. (2020). Effects of sensory marketing on customer satisfaction and revisit intention in the hotel industry: The moderating roles of customers' prior experience and gender. *Anatolia, 31*(4), 523–535. doi:10.1080/13032917.2020.1783692

Mercade Mele, P., Molina Gomez, J., & Garay, L. (2019). To green or not to green: The influence of green marketing on consumer behaviour in the hotel industry. *Sustainability (Basel), 11*(17), 4623. doi:10.3390u11174623

Mondal, S., Das, S., & Vrana, V. G. (2023). How to bell the cat? A theoretical review of generative artificial intelligence towards digital disruption in all walks of life. *Technologies, 11*(2), 44. doi:10.3390/technologies11020044

Mustak, M., Salminen, J., Plé, L., & Wirtz, J. (2021). Artificial intelligence in marketing: Topic modeling, scientometric analysis, and research agenda. *Journal of Business Research, 124*, 389–404. doi:10.1016/j.jbusres.2020.10.044

Nunkoo, R., Teeroovengadum, V., Ringle, C. M., & Sunnassee, V. (2020). Service quality and customer satisfaction: The moderating effects of hotel star rating. *International Journal of Hospitality Management, 91*, 102414. doi:10.1016/j.ijhm.2019.102414

Parvez, S. J., Moyeenudin, H. M., Arun, S., Anandan, R., & Janahan, S. K. (2018). Digital marketing in hotel industry. *International Journal of Engineering & Technology, 7*(2.21), 288-290.

Patel, V. V. (2023). *Revolutionizing Marketing Efficiency with ChatGpt.* GSFC University.

Paul, J., Ueno, A., & Dennis, C. (2023). ChatGPT and consumers: Benefits, pitfalls and future research agenda. *International Journal of Consumer Studies, 47*(4), 1213–1225. doi:10.1111/ijcs.12928

Priyo, J. S., Mohamad, B., & Adetunji, R. R. (2019). An examination of the effects of service quality and customer satisfaction on customer loyalty in the hotel industry. *International Journal of Supply Chain Management, 8*(1), 653–663.

Saputra, R., Nasution, M. I. P., & Dharma, B. (2023). The Impact of Using AI Chat GPT on Marketing Effectiveness: A Case Study on Instagram Marketing. *Indonesian Journal of Economics and Management*, *3*(3), 603–617.

Sudirjo, F., Diantoro, K., Al-Gasawneh, J. A., Azzaakiyyah, H. K., & Ausat, A. M. A. (2023). Application of ChatGPT in Improving Customer Sentiment Analysis for Businesses. *Jurnal Teknologi Dan Sistem Informasi Bisnis*, *5*(3), 283–288. doi:10.47233/jteksis.v5i3.871

Tosic, D. (2023). *Artificial Intelligence-driven web development and agile project management using OpenAI API and GPT technology: A detailed report on technical integration and implementation of GPT models in CMS with API and agile web development for quality user-centered AI chat service experience*.

Vujić, M., ĐorĎević, S., & Lakićević, M. (2019). Service quality and customer satisfaction in the hotel industry in Serbia. *Менаџменту хотелијерству и туризму*, *7*(1), 61-70.

Wong, I. A., Lian, Q. L., & Sun, D. (2023). Autonomous travel decision-making: An early glimpse into ChatGPT and generative AI. *Journal of Hospitality and Tourism Management*, *56*, 253–263. doi:10.1016/j.jhtm.2023.06.022

ZarifhonarvarA. (2023). Economics of chatgpt: A labor market view on the occupational impact of artificial intelligence. SSRN. doi:10.2139/ssrn.4350925

Chapter 5
ChatGPT and Its Role in Revolutionizing Digital Marketing and Enhancing Customer Engagement

Nour El Hoda Tarabah
Ibn Haldun University, Turkey

Mohamed El Said Amin
Weill Cornell Medical College in Qatar, Turkey

ABSTRACT

In the digital era, businesses strive to harness various advancements in the tech field to attain heightened levels of customer engagement and ensure the effectiveness of their marketing strategies. For instance, digital marketing has the capacity to utilize AI advancements to a significant extent. In particular, nowadays, digital marketers are leveraging a recent large language-model-based chatbot called "ChatGPT," which enables users to engage in human-like conversations and has unprecedented opportunities to reshape and revolutionize the ecosystem of digital marketing and customer engagement. In this regard, this chapter underscores the transformative potential of ChatGPT in the domain of digital marketing and its profound implications for augmenting customer engagement by reviewing and synthesizing existing literature. Moreover, it considers the ethical implications surrounding AI deployment. By synthesizing existing literature, this chapter provides a comprehensive overview of the current state of knowledge in this domain, guiding future research and practice.

DOI: 10.4018/979-8-3693-0815-8.ch005

1. INTRODUCTION

Today's world is defined by digital transformation and ever-evolving customers' expectations, by which, the integration of technology and marketing has become the cornerstone of successful business strategies. Up to this end, businesses strive to harness various advancements in the tech field to attain heightened levels of customer engagement and ensure the effectiveness of their marketing strategies. One of the groundbreaking developments in this landscape is the introduction of "ChatGPT", an innovation by OpenAI, that stands as a testament to the advancements in artificial intelligence (AI) technology. Due to its versatile capabilities, ChatGPT offers unprecedented opportunities to reshape and revolutionize the digital marketing and customer engagement ecosystem and it is expected to become an essential tool for marketing with its opportunities to provide effective, personalized, and engaging marketing research and strategies (Brand, Israeli, and Ngwe, 2023). Its transformative potential, makes it stand at the forefront of a new era in digital marketing, promising to redefine the way businesses connect with their audience and enhance customer interactions. In this chapter, the major transformative opportunities that ChatGPT can bring to the field are discussed. As well some implications surrounding ChatGPT deployment are provided to ensure a responsible and transparent use to maintain trust and regulatory compliance.Top of Form

2. LITERATURE REVIEW

2.1. ChatGPT

The acronym "GPT" in ChatGPT denotes "Generative Pre-trained Transformer,". This cutting-edge AI model, available in variants such as GPT-3.5 and GPT-4 leverages deep learning techniques and a massive dataset to generate human-like text, making it highly proficient in understanding and generating natural language responses. What sets ChatGPT apart is its ability to engage in dynamic and contextually relevant conversations, making it a versatile tool for a wide range of applications. It was unveiled to the world as a research preview on November 30, 2022 (Rivas and Zhao, 2023) and since its launching, ChatGPT has rapidly gained prominence, seizing the imagination of users and professionals alike due to its multifaceted applications across diverse industries. ChatGPT's emergence on the AI scene has been nothing short of revolutionary. Its transformative potential extends to various domains, including healthcare, customer service, education, content creation, and language translation (Mishra and Saumya, 2023; Geroge, George, and Martin, 2023).). It is indeed, leading to widespread use and recognition. By January 2023, it had reached a remarkable milestone, with over 100 million users—a groundbreaking achievement in the realm of consumer software. This accomplishment propelled OpenAI's value to $29 billion (Hu, 2023; Varanasi, 2023).

ChatGPT has abundant advantages over previous AI tools and has significant. Its key capabilities include Natural Language understanding, multi-lingual support, contextual awareness, and customization as well as information memory (Diaddo and Owusu, 2023) which enables supportive communication and effective follow-up corrections (Bishop, 2023). It also excels in problem-solving (Mishra and Saumya, 2023), writing and debugging computer programs, solving exams, and translating and summarizing texts. Moreover, ChatGPT's versatile capabilities enable it to address a wide spectrum of business needs. For instance, it can generate business ideas, retrieve information, summarize documents, respond to inquiries, interact in conversations, and plan travels (Mishra and Saumya, 2023). It can also help in expanding the business's customer base, penetrating new markets, executing highly efficient marketing campaigns, and nurturing robust relationships with both existing and potential clients (Stokel and Noordern, 2023; Geerling et al., 2023; Avila-Chauvet et al., 2023; Ali, 2023).

2.2. Digital Marketing

Digital Marketing refers to the strategic use of electronic devices, the internet, digital platforms, channels, and a wide different type of technologies to promote products or services, engage with customers, and enhance market reach (Yasmin, Tasneem, and Fatema, 2015; Chaffey & Ellis-Chadwick, 2019; Desai, 2019). It has its origins in the advent of the World Wide Web in the 1990s (Chaffey & Ellis-Chadwick, 2019; Kaur and Dangwal, 2023). Since then, it has changed how businesses carry out their marketing activities and made them realize the necessity of merging traditional marketing methods with online strategies to better cater to their customers' needs (Parsons, Zeisser, Waitman 1996). The operational mechanism of digital marketing arises from the formalization of digital marketing content and the creation of a digital interaction channel (Sokolova and Titova, 2019). The combination of these components results in specific digital marketing tools, websites, or platforms that enable effective marketing engagement with target audiences. In this matter, Digital Marketing can come in many types as presented in Table 1.

Table 1. Digital marketing types

Digital Marketing Type	Definition	Author
Social Media Marketing	the strategic utilization of media platforms to build meaningful relationships with targeted audiences and promote products/ services	Putri (2016)
Search Engine Optimization	the practice of enhancing a website's visibility in search engine results by optimizing keywords, website structure, and interlinking strategies, with the goal of increasing organic traffic and improving search engine rankings	(Chaffey & Smith, (2017); Lv et al. (2021); Panda and Mishra, 2022).
Content Marketing	a strategic approach that entails creating and sharing valuable, relevant, and consistent content to engage a target audience, build trust, establish authority, and drive profitable customer actions	Rowley (2008); CIS, (2021)
Influencer Marketing	a collaborative advertising approach where brands provide compensation to influencers in exchange for content creation that promotes their products or services	EASA (2018); De Veirman, Hudders, & Nelson (2019)
Pay-Per-Click Advertising	an online advertising approach employed to direct visitors to websites, where the advertiser compensates a publisher each time a user clicks on the advertisement	Fjell (2009)
Email Marketing	a type of direct marketing that employs email as a channel for delivering commercial or fundraising messages to an audience. In a broader context, any email sent to potential or existing customers can be regarded as a form of email marketing	Stokes (2011), Fariborzi and Zahedifard, (2012); Bismo and Putra (2019)

These different types of digital marketing can bring a lot of opportunities to any type of business. Such as increasing website traffic (Hoge and Cecil, 1993), boosting brand awareness (Panda and Mishra, 2022), and increasing conversions and revenues (Khan and Mahapatra, 2009). In this matter, digital marketing has become a source of competitive advantage for modern businesses.

2.3. Customer Engagement

With various perspectives offering differing interpretations of the Customer Engagement concept, there is a lack of consensus regarding its definition (Harrigan et al., 2017; Algharabat, 2018; Lim et al., 2022). However, there has been a continuous effort by many scholars in the field to provide a comprehensive definition of customer engagement. Sedley (2008) defined it as recurrent interactions that enhance a consumer's emotional, psychological, or physical commitment to a brand which is not an ultimate achievement to be attained; rather, it's an ongoing process of cultivating and sustaining relationships. However, in examining the multifaceted concept of customer engagement, several notable scholars have emphasized distinct dimensions. Renowned scholars like Yu, and de Ruyter (2006), Van Doorn et al. (2010), Hollebeek (2011), and Mollen and Wilson (2012), perceived CE in terms of a psychological and behavioral state. Vivek, Beatty, and Morgan (2012) perceived it as a customer's connection and participation with a brand's or firm's activities and offerings. Bowden (2009a) focused on the cognitive and emotional dimensions of CE. However, Brodie, Ilic, Juric, and Hollebeek (2013) presented a comprehensive consumer engagement model, encompassing cognitive, emotional, and behavioral dimensions. These perspectives contribute to a comprehensive understanding of the complex relationships between customers and brands, highlighting cognitive, emotional, and behavioral aspects of engagement. Collectively, CE is a concept that scholars can address from various angles with the shared objective of influencing desired customer behaviors, such as fostering positive brand attitudes, purchase intentions, and loyalty (Lim et al., 2022). It is characterized by several key attributes that illuminate its nature and significance in the business context. Such as Two-Way Interaction (Brodie et al., 2011), Emotional Connection (Bowden, 2009; Hollebeek and Chen, 2014), Behaviors Beyond Purchase (Van Doorn et al. 2010), Continuous Relationship (Brodie et al., 2011), Improvement Feedback (Hollebeek et al., 2019), and Multi-Dimensional Nature (Brodie, Ilic, Juric, and Hollebeek, 2013; Hollebeek and Chen, 2014; Brodie et al., 2011).

Antecedents of Customer Engagement include but are not limited to a sequence of Identification (Chahal et al., 2017; Tsai et al. 2017; Simon et al, 2018), perceived usefulness (Dessart et al. 2015; Carlson et al., 2017), perceived enjoyment (Karjaluoto et al. 2015; Carlson et al., 2017), trust (Wong and Lee, 2022), firm size and reputation (Van Doorn et al., 2010), satisfaction (Rossmann et al., 2016), reciprocity (Tah'er et al., 2016), remuneration (Chan et al., 2014), self-image enhancement (Jahn and Kunz, 2012), social interaction ties (Kim et al., 2016), perceived brand image (Puriwat et al., 2014; Osakwe et al., 2016), as well as brand characteristics and competitive factors (Van Doorn et al., 2010). Thus, CE offers several advantages for businesses such as the power of word-of-mouth marketing (Bowden, 2009b), the potential for long-term profitability and customer retention (Verhoef et al., 2010), the opportunity for better reputation and higher level of competitiveness (Van Doorn et al., 2010), and valuable insights and feedback that empower them to enhance their services or products (Hollebeek et al., 2019). As well as developing, maintaining, and growing customer satisfaction (Lim et al., 2022). In this matter, many businesses strive to ensure effective customer engagement to harness its benefits.

2.4. ChatGPT and Digital Marketing

From Social Media Marketing to Search Engine Optimization, Content Marketing to Influencer Marketing, and Pay-Per-Click Advertising to Email Marketing, ChatGPT offers multipurpose solutions that accommodate the diverse needs of modern marketers. Beyond its utility in these key areas, ChatGPT presents a multitude of benefits that span a wide spectrum. These benefits include market research, Virtual Assistantship, Market Entry Strategies, Segmentation, Marketing Plan and Product Development, as well as consumer insights. All of which make ChatGPT an invaluable asset for digital marketers looking to stay ahead in today's competitive online ecosystem. The following section highlights the main contributions of ChatGPT in different Digital Marketing domains.

2.4.1. Social Media

In terms of social media ChatGPT can have the following benefits:

-**Content Creation and Scheduling**: it can help in generating appealing content for any kind of social media platform (Aljanabi et al., 2023), as well as in scheduling content plans.

- ◦ **Chatbots for automated interactions:** it can be employed to develop chatbots capable of engaging with social media users in a more authentic and captivating manner. This can assist social media marketers in delivering customer support, addressing inquiries, and promoting their offerings effectively (Heumann et al. 2023).
- ◦ **Sentiment Analysis:** with the necessary training, it can perform sentiment analysis on social media posts, helping companies keep an eye on and grasp customer's emotions and opinions (Biswas, 2023a).
- ◦ **Automated interactions for customer support:** its ability to provide 24/7 customer support and respond to inquiries (Chen and Chen, 2021) can help in improving customer satisfaction and assisting customer service representatives.
- ◦ **Social Media Monitoring:** with the necessary programming, it can track social media platforms, collect data on public sentiment, and identify trending subjects, such as monitoring Twitter for references to particular political figures or events and generating reports on sentiment and mention frequency (Biswas, 2023b).
- ◦ **Social Media Trends Analysis:** it can help examine trends on social media by pinpointing the most trending subjects and discussions.

This data can then be utilized to produce content that's relevant to the desired audience, increasing the likelihood of it connecting with them effectively (Heumann et al., 2023).

- ◦ **Improved Human Labelling of Sponsored Content:** it can assist human annotators in labeling content resulting in a higher level of agreement among annotators and more accurate labeling which can improve the quality and reliability of the annotated dataset (Bertaglia et al. 2023). Thus, marketers can benefit from improved accuracy in detecting sponsored content on social media through AI assistance by ensuring better targeting, regulatory compliance, campaign performance, brand credibility, and customer engagement.
- ◦ **Integration with platforms:** it can be integrated with various online marketing platforms, such as websites, social media, and messaging apps, creating engaging and interactive customer experiences (Mutoffar et al., 2023).
- ◦ **Automation:** it can handle routine social media tasks, allowing employees to concentrate their efforts on more critical and value-added responsibilities (Abdelkader, 2023).

2.4.2. Search Engine Optimization (SEO)

In terms of SEO, ChatGPT can have the following benefits:

- **Integration:** ChatGPT's integration into SEO, exemplified by Microsoft's adoption in Bing, holds the potential to revolutionize the field by introducing natural language-powered chatbots, reshaping how marketers navigate search engine optimization (Cutler, 2023).
- **Enhancing SEO with ChatGPT-Generated Content:** its capabilities extend to generating optimized text for web content and online materials, offering companies' writers a valuable tool to enhance their search engine rankings (West, 2023).
- **Improving SEO performance:** it can contribute to SEO improvement by generating keyword ideas from seed keywords, analyzing SEO competition to identify effective content strategies, and providing insights into website SEO performance enhancement, including factors like loading speed, mobile-friendliness, and link-building opportunities (Semrush Team, 2023).

2.4.3. Content Marketing

In terms of Content Marketing, ChatGPT can have the following benefits:

- **Content Creation**: it can generate creative, informative, and engaging content for an organization's channels (Mishra and Awasthi, 2023). Such as generating headlines and writing short descriptions for content (Gibson, 2023).
- **Content Engagement:** marketing content generated by ChatGPT, can achieve high levels of engagement, attention, and interest in products and services offered by a company (Saputra, Nasution, and Dharma, 2023).

2.4.4. Influencer Marketing

In terms of Influencer Marketing, ChatGPT can have the following benefits:

- **Influencers Discovery:** it can be utilized for influencer discovery by identifying prominent individuals in different social media niches, enabling marketers to partner with these influencers for product or service promotion, and expand their reach to a broader audience (Fusté-Forné, and Orea-Giner, 2023).
- **Outreach Messages:** it can generate personalized outreach messages to influencers, improving the chances of collaboration (Manson, 2023).
- **Campaign Strategy:** it can provide ideas and suggestions for effective influencer marketing campaigns, including content themes and posting schedules.
- **Performance Analysis:** its ability to provide timely insights for various marketing activities, (Jain et al., 2023) like analyzing the results of influencers' marketing campaigns, including engagement metrics, reach, and ROI, allows businesses to fine-tune their future strategies.

2.4.5. Pay-Per-Click

In terms of PPC, ChatGPT can have the following benefits:

-**Channel Selection:** it can provide recommendations on the most suitable channels for a particular campaign, taking into consideration the target audience, marketing goals, and budget constraints (Oviedo et al., 2023; Yue, Au, Iu, 2023; Nisar and Aslam, 2023). ChatGPT's recommendation in this context is significant to the PPC strategy's success.

-**Data-Driven Insights:** ChatGPT employs machine learning to analyze customer data, market trends, and consumer behavior (Iskender, 2023), which can be utilized to analyze the performance of PPC campaigns. It can help in understanding which keywords or ads are driving results.

-**AD Spend Optimization**: its data-driven insights and machine learning capabilities can assist in optimizing advertising investments. PPC campaigns can benefit from data analysis to allocate a budget effectively to the most promising keywords and ads.

2.4.6. Email Marketing

In terms of Email Marketing, ChatGPT can have the following benefits:

-**Email Writing and Personalization**: it can facilitate e-mail marketing campaigns (Mich and Garigliano, 2023), by assisting in writing engaging emails (Haleem, Javaid and Singh, 2023), including subject lines, body text, and calls to action. Which can help marketers create compelling and personalized messages that resonate with recipients and make the campaign more persuasive (Manson, 2023).

-**Reports Generation:** it can generate reports summarizing e-mail campaign performance, allowing businesses to assess results and make data-driven decisions.

2.4.7. Multi-Faceted Benefits

ChatGPT can also have multi-faceted benefits for the Digital Marketing domain such as:

-**Virtual Marketing Assistant:** it serves as a virtual marketing assistant across communication channels, addressing inquiries, disseminating messages, and scheduling appointments, thus facilitating marketing and promotional efforts (Mutoffar et al. 2023).

-**Market Research:** it has the capability to examine social media data and online reviews, enabling the identification of emerging trends and shifts in consumer preferences. This valuable knowledge can aid marketers across different sectors in remaining proactive and adjusting their approaches to align with changing market needs (Fusté-Forné and Orea-Giner, 2023).

-**Market Entry Strategies:** it can assist in formulating market entry strategies by analyzing market conditions, consumer behavior, and potential risks and opportunities.

-**Segmentation:** it can identify meaningful customer segments based on data analysis (Sinha, 2023), enabling marketers to target specific groups with customized messaging and offers.

- **-Marketing Plan and Product Development:** it can provide businesses with insightful knowledge about customers' behaviors and preferences, helping them develop the right products and tailoring the most effective marketing plans (Jain et al., 2023; Mutoffar et al., 2023).
- **-Consumers' Insights:** its ability for data categorization can boost the understanding of customer's preferences and need, including customer service, product features, and marketing campaigns (Haleem, Javaid, and Singh, 2022), helping in developing personalized marketing campaigns by leveraging customer data to recommend tailored content, products, and offers.

2.5. ChatGPT and Customer Engagement

ChatGPT emerges as a transformative tool offering a multitude of opportunities for customer engagement. Despite being recently introduced a body of research has been carried out to delve into the various opportunities that businesses can explore to harness the power of ChatGPT for improved customer engagement. Below are some key areas where ChatGPT can make a significant impact in terms of Customer Engagement:

- **-Emotions Processing:** it has the capability to process human emotions (Taecharungroj, 2023) as it can comprehend and identify customers who are upset or frustrated and provide them with the appropriate support (Paul, 2023). Its ability to comprehend and identify emotions allows it to adjust its choice of words and tone accordingly. For instance, when interacting with customers expressing negative emotions, it responds empathetically and uses acknowledging phrases like "I understand you". Conversely, it adapts to positive emotions, maintaining an engaging and supportive tone. Indeed, this can lead to a more empathetic customer experience, customer education, and feedback collection.
- **-Enhanced Communication and Automation:** it can generate and maintain positive interactions with customers. It has the ability to empower marketers with automation, enhanced communication, and effective data utilization, which allows them to reach their targeted audience, maintain effective communication, and obtain valuable consumer data, ultimately enabling higher levels of customer engagement (Bushell, 2023). It can also answer questions, provide customer support, personalize interactions, and generate content (Jungwirht, 2023).
- **-Customer Attention and Enthusiasm:** it can boost customer attention and enthusiasm. For instance, utilizing ChatGPT for marketing content was proven to lead to a higher level of customer engagement and attention, leading to

boosted enthusiasm for a company's services or products (Saputra, Nasution, and Charma, 2023).

-**Content Generation and Personalization:** it can craft effective content for personalized customer engagement. As a substantial language model, it serves as a powerful tool capable of generating "human-ish" text, enabling the business to generate compelling content tailored to individual customers, which certainly drives higher customer engagement rates (AI Contentify, 2023).

-**Customer Service Operations Integration:** it can be integrated into customer service operations like sending shipping notifications or providing customer status updates (Jungwirth, 2023), freeing up resources for more engaging customer-focused activities which can provide a competitive edge for the company and enhance its customer's satisfaction (George and George, 2023). It can handle multiple conversations simultaneously 24/7 allowing for scalability of customer support efforts (Botpress Blog, 2023).

-**Comprehensive Understanding of Customers:** it allows businesses to have a comprehensive customer understanding for improved engagement. Through direct engagement, it enables advanced inquiries and responses to discern preferences, identify obstacles, and propose solutions that help businesses respond better to their customer preferences and needs (Rivas and Zhao, 2023). Thus, utilizing both implicit and explicit customer data from ChatGPT enables companies to gain a deeper insight into their consumers, ultimately resulting in enhanced customer engagement, improved experiences, and greater customer loyalty (Ezenkwu, 2023).

-**ChatGPT's Versatility**: Its ability to comprehend and respond to a wide range of topics and tasks in various situations or contexts can help provide customers with a more personalized and efficient experience, resulting in higher levels of customer satisfaction (Chuma, Bang, and Alfredson, 2023) and engagement. Especially, when customers receive tailored responses and assistance, they are more likely to engage with a brand's products or services.

-**24/7 Availability:** it provides 24/7 availability for instant support and quick response time to diminish wait periods. For instance, a study conducted by Paul (2023), found that ChatGPT has the capability to decrease the typical response time, significantly from several hours to a few minutes.

-**Language Accessibility and Global Audience Reach:** it is designed to accommodate multiple languages in order to serve a diverse global audience and currently it supports several languages, including Spanish, Arabic, English, French, Italian, Russian, and Chinese (Botpress Blog, 2023). It also provides translations and answers questions in different languages (TS2 Space, 2023).

-**Chat Memory:** it has a chat memory that can maintain context-aware interactions as it was designed to track the history of a conversation with a user to generate more relevant responses (OpenAI Blog, 2022).

-**Cross-Selling and Upselling:** it can facilitate the identification of customer needs and preferences, enabling the promotion of additional products and services, thereby contributing to revenue growth and enhancing customer lifetime value (TS2 Space, 2023; Paul, 2023)

-**Multifaceted benefits:** it can have many more multi-faceted benefits in terms of personalization (Kasneci et al., 2023), customer engagement, personalization and shopping, cost-effectiveness data, social interaction, consumer behavior insight, communication practices, marketing campaigns insights which can collectively unlock higher levels of customer engagement (Paul, Ueno and Dennis, 2023).

2.6. The Revolution: Before and After ChatGPT

The landscape of digital marketing and customer engagement as it existed before ChatGPT will undergo a profound transformation, forever altering the way businesses interact with their customers. ChatGPT possesses the capability to revolutionize these domains with its versatile capabilities. Tables 2 and 3 present a comparison between how digital marketing and customer engagement are carried out before and after ChatGPT.

Table 2. Digital marketing before and after ChatGPT

Type	Before ChatGPT	After ChatGPT	Source
Social Media	Manual Scheduling and Content Creation	ChatGPT Driven Scheduling and Content Creation	Aljanabi et al., (2023)
	Manual Response	Chatbots for automated interactions	Heumann et al. (2023)
	Human Interactions	Automated interactions for customer support and Marketing Campaigns	Biswas, (2023a)
	Manual Analysis of Social Media Posts	Automated Sentiment Analysis	Chen and Chen, (2021)
	Manual Social Media Trends Analysis	Social Media ChatGPT and Data-Driven Trend Analysis	Biswas, (2023b)
	Human Annotators for Sponsored Content Labeling	ChatGPT-assistance for more accurate labeling	Heumann et al., (2023)
	N/A	Seamless integration with social media platforms	Bertaglia et al. (2023)
	Marketers Focus on every task	Automation routine tasks	Mutoffar et al., (2023)
SEO	Basic Models Integration	Integration of a highly advanced natural language generation and understanding model	Cutler (2023)
	Manual SEO Content Generation	Chat-GPT generated content	West (2023)
	Manual Keywords Research and Analysis	ChatGPT- driven keywords recommendation	Semrush Team (2023)
Influencer Marketing	Research for Influencers Discovery	Automated Identification of Influencers	Fusté-Forné, and Orea-Giner (2023)
	Human crafting of outreach messages	ChatGPT-generated multilingual outreach messages	Manson (2023)
Content Marketing	Human Content Creation	ChatGPT-generated content	Mishra and Awasthi (2023), Gibson (2023)
	Channel's Selection is based on Expertise and basic data	ChatGPT-Powered recommendations for channels' selection	Oviedo et al., (2023), Yue, Au, and Iu (2023) Nisar and Aslam (2023)
Ppc	Manual Ad Budget Allocation	ChatGPT-assistance with budget allocation to high-performing keywords and ads	-
	Use of Traditional Data Analytics Tools	ChatGPT-powered data-driven insights	Iskender (2023)
E-Mail Marketing	Human E-mail Writing	ChatGPT crafted personalized and multilingual emails	Haleem, Javaid and Singh, (2023), Manson, (2023)
	Time-Consuming Manual E-mail Campaigns Creation	Faster E-mail campaign creation and deployment	Mich and Garigliano, (2023)
Marketing Assistants	Human marketing Assistants	ChatGPT Assistance	Mutoffar et al. (2023)
Market Research	Manual data collection and analysis	Automated data analysis and trends identification	Fusté-Forné and Orea-Giner (2023)
Segmentation	Manual segmentation based on limited data	ChatGPT-driven and precise customer segmentation	Sinha (2023)
Marketing Plan and Product Development	Human-driven insights and decisions	ChatGPT-driven insights and tailored marketing plans	Jain et al., (2023); Mutoffar et al., (2023)
Consumers' Insights	Manual categorization and analysis	Automated data categorization and personalized recommendations	Haleem, Javaid, and Singh (2022)

Table 3. Customer engagement before and after ChatGPT

Aspect	Before ChatGPT	After ChatGPT	Source
Emotions Processing	limited ability to identify and respond to emotions	high ability to comprehend and adapt to customer emotions- more empathetic interactions	Taecharungroj, (2023); Paul (2023)
Enhanced Communication and Automation	manual interactions with limited automation	automation, improved communication, and data utilization	Bushell (2023)
Customer Attention and Enthusiasm	marketing efforts that are not effective every time	ChatGPT boosts customer attention and enthusiasm through personalization	Saputra, Nasution, and Charma (2023)
Content Generation and Personalization	content generation is time-consuming and less personalized	ChatGPT-generated personalized, and engaging content	AI contentify (2023)
Availability	limited availability with long response times	instant support with quick response times, reducing wait periods	Paul (2023)
Language Accessibility and Global Reach	monolingual or limited language support	multiple languages and diverse global audience serving	Botpress Blog, (2023); TS2 Space (2023)
Chat Memory	limited ability to remember previous chat conversations	context-aware interactions by tracking conversation history	OpenAI Blog (2022)

2.7. Ethical Implications

Despite that ChatGPT brings various opportunities for digital marketing and customer engagement, however, it is imperative for companies to be mindful of the ethical implications when integrating ChatGPT into their marketing efforts. There are many ways to ensure ChatGPT is ethically used. For instance, open and transparent communication is a fundamental aspect of ethical ChatGPT marketing. Businesses must openly share information with consumers regarding data collection, utilization, and the algorithms and decision-making procedures that employ ChatGPT (Rivas and Zhao, 2023), This practice ensures that consumers have a clear understanding of how their data is employed and enables them to make informed decisions concerning their privacy. Moreover, it fosters trust between companies and their customers, a critical factor in managing long-term customer relationships. Ma et al. (2020) and Rivas et al. (2019), achieving transparency can be accomplished by delivering precise and concise details to consumers about the processes of data collection, data usage, and the functioning of any AI algorithms. Also, businesses can obtain informed consent from their customers when they interact with ChatGPT and they must explain the role of ChatGPT in this interaction and allow them to opt-out or choose human assistance if they wish. Maintaining human oversight is equally vital to guarantee that the decisions and content generated by ChatGPT systems adhere to ethical standards. It is imperative for businesses to implement a human oversight mechanism that thoroughly examines and validates the choices and content produced automatically by AI (Etzioni and Etzioni, 2017). Ensuring privacy is also a fundamental aspect of ethical ChatGPT marketing. Businesses should make it a priority to protect personal information and guarantee that their ChatGPT-driven solutions adhere to relevant privacy statutes and guidelines. In line with the suggestions made by Grewal et al. (2020), companies should empower consumers with control over their data, which includes options like opting out of data collection or deleting their personal information. Continuous monitoring is also critical for ethical ChatGPT marketing (Rivas and Zhao, 2023). Companies must regularly asses ChatGPT's performance and address any ethical issues and ensure minimizing errors and biases, as well as ensure legal and ethical compliance (Bogina et al., 2021).

3. CONCLUSION

In conclusion, the integration of ChatGPT into the realm of digital marketing represents a significant step in harnessing the power of AI to meet the ever-evolving customer's needs and expectations. It has the potential to reshape the present and the future of the landscape of customer engagement and revolutionize digital marketing strategies. Its versatility brings businesses a wide range of opportunities to connect with their audience and keep them engaged in the most meaningful ways, driving their success in the digital age. This chapter presented an overview of how ChatGPT can be leveraged in this context, and shed light on how things have changed post the introduction of ChatGPT which provides implications for effective utilization of this tool to ensure the best outcomes. Moreover, it emphasized that it is essential to approach the deployment of ChatGPT with a strong commitment to ethics and transparency. Responsible use is mandatory to maintain trust with customers and ensure compliance with evolving regulations. By doing so, the benefits of ChatGPT can be fully realized realize while navigating the ethical considerations that come with it.

REFERENCES

Algharabat, R. S. (2018). The role of telepresence and user engagement in co-creation value and purchase intention: Online retail context. *Journal of Internet Commerce*, *17*(1), 1–25. doi:10.1080/15332861.2017.1422667

Ali, F. (2023). Let the devil speak for itself: Should ChatGPT be allowed or banned in hospitality and tourism schools? *Journal of Global Hospitality and Tourism*, *2*(1), 1–6. doi:10.5038/2771-5957.2.1.1016

Aljanabi, M., Ghazi, M., Ali, A. H., & Abed, S. A. (2023). ChatGPT: Open Possibilities. *Iraqi Journal For Computer Science and Mathematics*, *4*(1), 62–64.

Avila-ChauvetL.MejíaD.Acosta QuirozC. O. (2023). Chatgpt as a support tool for online behavioral task programming. Available At SSRN 4329020.

Bertaglia, T., Huber, S., Goanta, C., Spanakis, G., & Iamnitchi, A. (2023). Closing the Loop: Testing ChatGPT to Generate Model Explanations to Improve Human Labelling of Sponsored Content on Social Media. *arXiv preprint arXiv:2306.05115*.

Bismo, A., & Putra, S. (2019, August). Application of Digital Marketing (social media and email marketing) and its Impact on Customer Engagement in Purchase Intention: a case study at PT. Soltius Indonesia. In *2019 International Conference on Information Management and Technology (ICIMTech)* (Vol. 1, pp. 109-114). IEEE. 10.1109/ICIMTech.2019.8843763

BiswasS. (2023a). The Function of Chat GPT in Social Media: According to Chat GPT. SSRN 4405389. doi:10.2139/ssrn.4405389

Biswas, S. (2023b). *Prospective Role of Chat GPT in the Military: According to ChatGPT*. Qeios.

Botpress Blog. (2023). ChatGPT: A powerful tool for customer engagement. [Blog post]. *Botpress Blog*.

Bogina, V., Hartman, A., Kuflik, T., & Shulner-Tal, A. (2021). Educating software and AI stakeholders about algorithmic fairness, accountability, transparency and ethics. *International Journal of Artificial Intelligence in Education*, *32*(3), 808–833. doi:10.100740593-021-00248-0

Bowden, J. L. (2009a). The process of customer engagement: A conceptual framework. *Journal of Marketing Theory and Practice*, *17*(1), 63–74. doi:10.2753/MTP1069-6679170105

Bowden, J. L. (2009b). *Customer engagement: A framework for assessing customer-brand relationships*. [Doctoral dissertation, Queensland University of Technology].

BrandJ.IsraeliA.NgweD. (2023). Using GPT for Market Research. SSRN.

Brodie, R. J., Hollebeek, L. D., Juric, B., & Ilic, A. (2011). Customer engagement: Conceptual domain, fundamental propositions, and implications for research. *Journal of Service Research, 14*(3), 252–271. doi:10.1177/1094670511411703

Brodie, R. J., Ilic, A., Juric, B., & Hollebeek, L. (2013). Consumer engagement in a virtual brand community: An exploratory analysis. *Journal of Business Research, 66*(1), 105–114. doi:10.1016/j.jbusres.2011.07.029

BushellC. (2023). ChatGPT for Marketers: Transforming Customer Engagement and Insights. SSRN. https://ssrn.com/abstract=4556644

Chaffey, D., & Ellis-Chadwick, F. (2019). *Digital Marketing: Strategy, Implementation and Practice*. Pearson.

Chen, C., & Chen, F. (2021). Chatbots and customer experience: An empirical investigation. *Journal of Interactive Marketing, 56*, 101–113. doi:10.1016/j.intmar.2021.01.005

Chuma, E., Bang, M., & Alfredson, J. (2023). *Business AI decision-making tools: Case ChatGPT evaluation*.

Content Marketing Institute. (2021). "What Is Content Marketing?" *Content Marketing Institute*. https://contentmarketinginstitute.com/what-is-content-marketing/

Cutler, K. (2023). ChatGPT and search engine optimization: The future is here. *Applied Marketing Analytics, 9*(1), 8–22.

De Veirman, M., Hudders, L., & Nelson, M. R. (2019). What is influencer marketing and how does it target children? A review and direction for future research. *Frontiers in Psychology, 10*, 2685. doi:10.3389/fpsyg.2019.02685 PMID:31849783

Desai, V., & Vidyapeeth, B. (2019). Digital marketing: A review. *International Journal of Trend in Scientific Research and Development, 5*(5), 196–200. doi:10.31142/ijtsrd23100

Dwivedi, A. (2015). Consumer brand engagement: A framework for assessment and proposition of antecedents. *Journal of Marketing Management, 31*(9-10), 1053–1079.

EASA. (2018). *EASA best practice recommendation on influencer marketing*. EASA. https://www.easa-alliance.org/sites/default/files/EASA_BEST%20PRACTICE%20RECOMMENDATION%20ON%20INFLUENCER%20MARKETING_2.pdf

Etzioni, A., & Etzioni, O. (2017). Incorporating ethics into artificial intelligence. *The Journal of Ethics*, *21*(4), 403–418. doi:10.100710892-017-9252-2

Ezenkwu, C. P. (2023, May). Towards expert systems for improved customer services using ChatGPT as an inference engine. *Institute of Electrical and Electronics Engineers*.

Fariborzi, E., & Zahedifard, M. (2012). E-mail marketing: Advantages, disadvantages, and improving techniques. *International Journal of e-Education, e-Business, e-. Management Learning*, *2*(3), 232.

Fjell, K. (2009). Online advertising: Pay-per-view versus pay-per-click—A comment. *Journal of Revenue and Pricing Management*, *8*(2–3), 200–206. doi:10.1057/rpm.2008.39

Fusté-Forné, F., & Orea-Giner, A. (2023). Gastronomy in Tourism Management and Marketing: An Interview with ChatGPT. *ROBONOMICS: The Journal of the Automated Economy*, *4*, 42–42.

Fusté-Forné, F., & Orea-Giner, A. (2023). Gastronomy in tourism management and marketing: An interview with ChatGPT. *ROBONOMICS: The Journal of the Automated Economy*, *4*, 42–42.

GeerlingW.MateerG. D.WootenJ.DamodaranN. (2023). Is ChatGPT smarter than a student in principles of economics? Available At SSRN 4356034.

George, A. S., & George, A. H. (2023). A review of ChatGPT AI's impact on several business sectors. *Partners Universal International Innovation Journal*, *1*(1), 9–23.

George, A. S., George, A. H., & Martin, A. G. (2023). A Review of ChatGPT AI's Impact on Several Business Sectors. *Partners Univers. Int. Innov. J.*, *1*, 1.

Gibson, K. (2023). Revolutionizing Social Content: How Chat GPT Transformed My Business's Marketing Strategy. [LinkedIn Article]. *LinkedIn*. https://shorturl.at/rA569

Grewal, D., Hulland, J., Kopalle, P. K., & Karahanna, E. (2020). The future of technology and marketing: A multidisciplinary perspective. *Journal of the Academy of Marketing Science*, *48*(1), 1–8. doi:10.100711747-019-00711-4

Haleem, A., Javaid, M., & Singh, R. P. (2022). An Era of ChatGPT as a Significant Futuristic Support Tool: A Study on Features, Abilities, and Challenges. *BenchCouncil Transactions on Benchmarks. Standards and Evaluations*, *2*(4), 100089.

Harrigan, P., Evers, U., Miles, M., & Daly, T. (2017). Customer engagement with tourism social media brands. *Tourism Management*, *59*, 597–609. doi:10.1016/j.tourman.2016.09.015

HeumannM.KraschewskiT.BreitnerM. H. (2023). ChatGPT and GPTZero in Research and Social Media: A Sentiment-and Topic-based Analysis. SSRN 4467646. doi:10.2139/ssrn.4467646

Hoge, S., & Cecil, C. (1993). The Electronic Marketing Manual. *ABA Journal*, *22*, 175–185.

Hollebeek, L. D. (2011). Demystifying customer brand engagement: Exploring the loyalty nexus. *Journal of Marketing Management*, *27*(7-8), 785–807. doi:10.1080/0267257X.2010.500132

Hollebeek, L. D., & Chen, T. (2014). Exploring positively-valenced brand engagement: A model development approach. *Journal of Product and Brand Management*, *23*(1), 62–74. doi:10.1108/JPBM-06-2013-0332

Hollebeek, L. D., Srivastava, R. K., & Chen, T. (2019). *S-D logic–informed customer engagement.*

Hollebeek, L. D., Srivastava, R. K., & Chen, T. (2019). S-D logic–informed customer engagement: Integrative framework, revised fundamental propositions, and application to CRM. *Journal of the Academy of Marketing Science*, *47*(1), 161–185. doi:10.100711747-016-0494-5

Jain, V., Rai, H., Subash, P., & Mogaji, E. (2023). The Prospects and Challenges of ChatGPT on Marketing Research and Practices. *Emmanuel, The Prospects and Challenges of ChatGPT on Marketing Research and Practices.*

Jungwirth, M. (2023). *Improving customer care with ChatGPT: A case study.* [PDF]

Kasneci, E., Sessler, K., Küchemann, S., Bannert, M., Dementieva, D., Fischer, F., Gasser, U., Groh, G., Günnemann, S., Hüllermeier, E., Krusche, S., Kutyniok, G., Michaeli, T., Nerdel, C., Pfeffer, J., Poquet, O., Sailer, M., Schmidt, A., Seidel, T., & Kasneci, G. (2023). ChatGPT for good? On opportunities and challenges of large language models for education. *Learning and Individual Differences*, *103*, 102274. doi:10.1016/j.lindif.2023.102274

Kaur, U., & Dangwal, A. (2023). A Typology of Digital Marketing Channels with a Special Reference to India. In INDIA'S TECHNOLOGY-LED DEVELOPMENT: Managing Transitions to a Digital Future (pp. 259-268). doi:10.1142/9789811271786_0014

Khan, M. S., Mahapatra, S. S., & Sreekumar, N. A. (2009). Service quality evaluation in internet banking: An empirical study in India. *Int. J. Indian Culture and Business Management*, *2*(1), 30–46. doi:10.1504/IJICBM.2009.021596

Krishnamurthy, S. (2006). Introducing E-MARKPLAN: A practical methodology to plan e-marketing activities. *Business Horizons*, *49*(1), 49, 51, 60. doi:10.1016/j.bushor.2005.05.008

Lim, W. M., Rasul, T., Kumar, S., & Ala, M. (2022). Past, present, and future of customer engagement. *Journal of Business Research*, *140*, 439–458. doi:10.1016/j.jbusres.2021.11.014

Lv, Z., Chen, J., Zheng, W., & Gong, Q. (2021, December). Research on Search Engine Optimization Method of Innovation and Entrepreneurship Platform. In *2021 International Conference on Networking, Communications and Information Technology (NetCIT)* (pp. 58-62). IEEE. 10.1109/NetCIT54147.2021.00019

Ma, L., & Sun, B. (2020). Machine learning and AI in marketing–Connecting computing power to human insights. [CrossRef]. *International Journal of Research in Marketing*, *37*(3), 481–504. doi:10.1016/j.ijresmar.2020.04.005

Manson, K. (2023). Viral ChatGPT Spurs Concerns About Propaganda and Hacking Risks. *Bloomberg*. https://www.bloomberg.com/news/articles/2023-01-11/chatgpt-poses-propaganda-and-hacking-risks-researchers-say?utm_source=website&utm_medium=share&utm_campaign=copy

Mich, L., & Garigliano, R. (2023). ChatGPT for e-Tourism: A Technological Perspective. *Information Technology & Tourism*, *25*(1), 1–12. doi:10.100740558-023-00248-x

Mishra, A., & Awasthi, S. (2023). Chat GPT: Revolutionizing Communication or Threatening Authenticity? *Management Dynamics*, *23*(1), 8. doi:10.57198/2583-4932.1321

Mollen, A., & Wilson, H. (2010). Engagement, telepresence, and interactivity in online consumer experience: Reconciling scholastic and managerial perspectives. *Journal of Business Research*, *63*(9-10), 919–925. doi:10.1016/j.jbusres.2009.05.014

Mutoffar, M. M., Kuswayati, S., Anggraeny, F. T., & Sumarni, T. (2023). Exploring the Potential of ChatGPT in Improving Online Marketing and Promotion of MSMEs. *Jurnal Minfo Polgan*, *12*(2), 480–489. doi:10.33395/jmp.v12i1.12440

NisarS.AslamM. S. (2023). Is ChatGPT a Good Tool for T & CM Students in Studying Pharmacology? SSRN 4324310. doi:10.2139/ssrn.4324310

OpenAI Blog. (2022). *Introducing ChatGPT: A new way to engage with customers.* [Blog post] OpenAI Blog.

Oviedo-TrespalaciosO.PedenA. E.Cole-HunterT.CostantiniA.HaghaniM.KellyS., & (2023). The Risks of Using ChatGPT to Obtain Common Safety-Related Information and Advice. SSRN 4346827.

Panda, M., & Mishra, A. (2022). *Digital marketing*. Research Gate. https://www.researchgate.net/publication/358646409

Parsons, A. J., Zeisser, M., & Waitman, R. (1996). Organizing for digital marketing. *The McKinsey Quarterly*, (4), 185.

Patterson, P., Yu, T., & de Ruyter, K. (2006). Understanding Customer Engagement in Services. *ANZMAC 2006 Conference*, Brisbane.

Paul, J., Ueno, A., & Dennis, C. (2023). ChatGPT and consumers: Benefits, pitfalls and future research agenda. *International Journal of Consumer Studies*, *47*(4), 12928. doi:10.1111/ijcs.12928

Paul, J., Ueno, A., & Dennis, C. (2023). ChatGPT and consumers: Benefits, pitfalls and future research agenda. *International Journal of Consumer Studies*, *47*(4), 1213–1225. doi:10.1111/ijcs.12928

Putri, C. S. (2016). Pengaruh media sosial terhadap keputusan pembelian konsumen cherie melalui minat beli. *Jurnal Performa: Jurnal Manajemen dan Start-up Bisnis, 1*(5), 594-603.

Rivas, P., Chelsi, C., Nishit, N., & Ravula, L. (2019). Application-agnostic chatbot deployment considerations: A case study. In *Proceedings of the 2019 International Conference on Computational Science and Computational Intelligence (CSCI)*, Las Vegas, NV, USA. 10.1109/CSCI49370.2019.00070

Rivas, P., & Zhao, L. (2023). Marketing with ChatGPT: Navigating the Ethical Terrain of GPT-Based Chatbot Technology. *AI, 4*(2), 375–384. doi:10.3390/ai4020019

Rowley, J. (2008). Understanding digital content marketing. *Journal of Marketing Management*, *24*(5-6), 517–540. doi:10.1362/026725708X325977

Saputra, R., Nasution, M. I. P., & Dharma, B. (2023). The Impact of Using AI Chat GPT on Marketing Effectiveness: A Case Study on Instagram Marketing. *Indonesian Journal of Economics and Management*, *3*(3), 603–617.

Saputra, R., Nasution, M. I. P., & Dharma, B. (2023). The Impact of Using AI Chat GPT on Marketing Effectiveness: A Case Study on Instagram Marketing. *Indonesian Journal of Economics and Management*, *3*(3), 603–617.

Sedley, R. (2008). Six Theses on Digital Customer Engagement in a Troubled Economy. *Richard Sedley Blog*. http://richard-sedley.iuplog.com/default.asp?item1/4298747

Semrush Team. (2023, January 12). ChatGPT for SEO: The Ultimate Guide to Boost Your SERP Ranking through Blogging. *Semrush Blog*. https://www.semrush.com/blog/chatgpt-seo/

Sinha, M. (2023, March 6). Is ChatGPT the future of marketing? - ET brandequity. *ETBrandEquity.com*. https://brandequity.economictimes.indiatimes.com/news/marketing/ischatgpt-the-future-of-marketing/98438927

Sokolova, N. G., & Titova, O. V. (2019, May). Digital marketing as a type: concept, tools, and effects. In *1st International Scientific Conference "Modern Management Trends and the Digital Economy: from Regional Development to Global Economic Growth" (MTDE 2019)* (pp. 508-512). Atlantis Press. 10.2991/mtde-19.2019.101

Stokel-Walker, C., & Van Noorden, R. (2023). What ChatGPT and generative AI mean for science. *Nature*, *614*(7947), 214–216. doi:10.1038/d41586-023-00340-6 PMID:36747115

Stokes, R. (2011). *eMarketing: The essential guide to digital marketing*. Quirk eMarketing.

TS2 Space. (2023). *ChatGPT: The next generation of customer service chatbots*. [Blog post]. TS2.

Taecharungroj, P. (2023). *ChatGPT's influence on customer experience in digital marketing: Investigating the moderating roles*. PMC.

Van Doorn, J., Lemon, K. E., Mittal, V., Nab, S., Dore'en, P., Pirner, P., & Verhoef, P. C. (2010). Customer Engagement Behavior: Theoretical Foundations and Research Directions. *Journal of Service Research*, *13*(3), 253–266. doi:10.1177/1094670510375599

Van Doorn, J., Lemon, K. N., Mittal, V., Nass, S., Pick, D., Pirner, P., & Verhoef, P. C. (2010). Customer engagement behavior: Theoretical foundations and research directions. *Journal of Service Research*, *13*(3), 253–266. doi:10.1177/1094670510375599

Verhoef, P. C., Reinartz, W. J., & Krafft, M. (2010). Customer engagement as a new perspective in customer management. *Journal of Service Research*, *13*(3), 247–252. doi:10.1177/1094670510375461

Verhoef, P. C., Reinartz, W. J., & Krafft, M. (2010). Customer engagement as a new perspective in customer management. *Journal of Service Research*, *13*(3), 247–252. doi:10.1177/1094670510375461

Vivek, S. D., Beatty, S. E., & Morgan, R. M. (2012). Customer engagement: Exploring customer relationships beyond purchase. *Journal of Marketing Theory and Practice*, *20*(2), 122–146. doi:10.2753/MTP1069-6679200201

West, C. (2023). *ChatGPT Content Creation: SEO, YouTube, Book Writing & More Made Easy: Become a Better Writer | Make Money Online*. Cea West.

Yasmin, A., Tasneem, S., & Fatema, K. (2015). Effectiveness of Digital Marketing in the Challenging Age: An Empirical Study. *The International Journal of Management Science and Business Administration*, *1*(5), 69–80. doi:10.18775/ijmsba.1849-5664-5419.2014.15.1006

YueT.AuD.AuC. C.IuK. Y. (2023). Democratising Financial Knowledge with ChatGPT by OpenAI: Unleashing the Power of Technology. SSRN 4346152.

ADDITIONAL READING

Abdelkader, O. A. (2023). ChatGPT's influence on customer experience in digital marketing: Investigating the moderating roles. *Heliyon*, *9*(8), e18770. doi:10.1016/j.heliyon.2023.e18770 PMID:37576290

Huang, J. (2023). ChatGPT Unveiled: Unleashing AI Magic in Online Shopping and Digital Marketing. *Atlantic Marketing Journal*, *12*(2), 1.

Rivas, P., & Zhao, L. (2023). Marketing with chatgpt: Navigating the ethical terrain of gpt-based chatbot technology. *AI*, *4*(2), 375-384.

Testa, R. (2023). *Digital Marketing Mastery with ChatGPT: The Ultimate AI-Driven Guide.*

KEY TERMS AND DEFINITIONS

Artificial Intelligence: Computer systems that can perform tasks that typically require human intelligence, like learning from data or making decisions.

Content Marketing: Creating and sharing valuable content, like articles or videos, to attract and engage an audience.

Customer Engagement: A way of interaction between customers and brands

Digital Marketing: The use of the Internet and channels to market products or services

Email Marketing: Sending targeted emails to a list of subscribers to promote products, provide information, or engage with customers.

Influencer Marketing: Collaborating with individuals who have a strong online presence or following to promote products or services to their audience.

Pay-Per-Click (PPC): An online advertising model where advertisers pay a fee each time their ad is clicked by a user, driving traffic to their website.

Search Engine Optimization (SEO): The practice of optimizing a website or content to improve its visibility and ranking on search engines like Google, making it more likely to appear in search results.

Social Media Marketing: Promoting products or services on social media platforms to reach and engage with potential customers.

Chapter 6
Reinventing Customer Support:
Unleashing ChatGPT's Potential for Personalized Engagement and Responsible AI Implementation

C. V. Suresh Babu
https://orcid.org/0000-0002-8474-2882
Hindustan Institute of Technolgy and Science, India

C. Moses
Hindustan Institute of Technology and Science, India

ABSTRACT

This chapter explores the integration of ChatGPT and AI for customer engagement, emphasizing its transformative potential. It begins by introducing the theme and the significance of ChatGPT in revolutionizing customer service through AI advancements. Subsequently, it delves into practical applications, discussing how ChatGPT understands and addresses customer inquiries effectively, automates routine tasks, and offers personalized assistance. Ethical considerations in AI implementation are also addressed. Real-world case studies demonstrate successful ChatGPT implementations, offering insights and best practices for maximizing customer engagement. The chapter concludes by envisioning the future of AI-powered customer support, highlighting the importance of a balanced integration of AI and human agents for sustainable customer experiences and business growth.

DOI: 10.4018/979-8-3693-0815-8.ch006

1. INTRODUCTION

1.1 Background and Significance

Customer engagement is a crucial aspect of modern business operations. In today's highly competitive market, simply offering high-quality products is no longer sufficient to attract and retain customers. Instead, businesses must focus on building and maintaining strong relationships with their customers. This involves providing exceptional value, personalized experiences, and effective communication at every stage of the customer journey (Gandhe, A., & Karmore, S. 2020). The importance of customer engagement lies in its ability to cultivate loyalty, advocacy, and ultimately, long-term business success.

With the rapid advancement of technology, artificial intelligence (AI) has emerged as a transformative tool for enhancing customer engagement. AI-powered solutions enable businesses to analyze large datasets, automate repetitive tasks, and deliver highly personalized experiences on a large scale (Smith, J., & Johnson, L., 2022). Among the cutting-edge AI models, ChatGPT, which is built on the GPT-3.5 architecture, has gained recognition as an advanced conversational AI tool capable of generating human-like text and engaging in natural language conversations. This makes ChatGPT a valuable asset for businesses seeking to enhance their customer engagement strategies. (OpenAI. 2020).

1.2 Objectives of Customer Engagement

Customer engagement goes beyond simply acquiring and retaining customers. Its main objective is to cultivate loyal advocates who actively promote a brand or product. This involves establishing a mutually beneficial exchange of value. To achieve this, businesses must have a comprehensive understanding of their customers' needs and preferences. They must strive to deliver exceptional experiences that resonate with customers and foster enduring relationships.

The significance of customer engagement objectives is highlighted by the fact that engaged customers are not only more likely to continue supporting a business but also to provide valuable feedback and advocate for the brand. They become brand ambassadors, spreading positive word-of-mouth and contributing to the expansion of the customer base. This ripple effect can have a significant impact on a company's financial performance and long-term sustainability.

1.3 Role of Artificial Intelligence in Customer Engagement

Artificial intelligence (AI) has significantly transformed customer engagement in the business landscape, enabling organizations to harness data in unprecedented ways (Suresh Babu C.V., 2022). AI-driven solutions possess the capability to analyze real-time data, operate continuously, process large volumes of information, and most importantly, deliver personalized experiences on a large scale (Smith, J., & Johnson, L., 2022). These capabilities are particularly crucial in the current digital era, where customers expect customized interactions and immediate responses.

The role of AI in customer engagement encompasses various facets of business operations. For instance, chatbots provide instantaneous support, while recommendation engines suggest products based on individual preferences, thereby revolutionizing the way businesses interact with their customers (Smith, J., & Johnson, L., 2022). AI-powered personalization, in particular, enhances customer satisfaction and loyalty by tailoring recommendations and communications to each customer's unique needs and behaviors (Smith, J., & Johnson, L., 2022). Furthermore, AI-enhanced customer support through chatbots streamlines customer service operations, ensuring prompt responses to common inquiries and efficient escalation of complex issues when necessary (Smith, J., & Johnson, L., 2022).

2. UNDERSTANDING CUSTOMER ENGAGEMENT

2.1 What is Customer Engagement?

Customer engagement is a multifaceted concept that encompasses the various interactions and touchpoints between a customer and a brand. These interactions encompass a range of activities, including marketing efforts, customer service interactions, product usage experiences, and more. The primary objective of customer engagement is to foster a sense of connection and commitment between customers and a brand. Engaged customers are those who actively participate in and promote the brand's products, services, or values (Ranjan, P., & Patel, P., 2019).

In practical terms, customer engagement can manifest in different ways. It may involve customers actively engaging in brand communities, providing feedback and reviews, or referring others to the business. Engagement can also be observed in customer loyalty, where individuals consistently choose a brand's products or services over those offered by competitors. Ultimately, engaged customers are emotionally invested in the brand, and this emotional connection plays a pivotal role in driving loyalty and advocacy.

2.2 Why is Customer Engagement Important?

The importance of customer engagement holds great significance within the business context. Engaged customers not only display higher levels of loyalty towards a brand, but they also demonstrate a willingness to spend more and provide valuable feedback that can inform the development of products and marketing strategies. Additionally, engaged customers often become brand advocates, actively sharing their positive experiences with their social circles and online communities, thus serving as a source of organic marketing (Ranjan, P., & Patel, P., 2019).

Customer engagement is closely tied to customer retention, a crucial metric for businesses. Engaged customers are less likely to discontinue their association with a brand, thereby reducing the need for continuous customer acquisition efforts, which can be financially burdensome. Instead, businesses can focus on fostering stronger connections with their existing customer base, thereby increasing customer lifetime value and long-term revenue.

2.3 Traditional vs. Modern Customer Engagement

The landscape of customer engagement has undergone significant changes over time. In the past, customer engagement primarily relied on in-person interactions and telephone conversations, with personal relationships playing a central role in the engagement process. While these traditional methods still hold value, contemporary customer engagement has expanded into the digital realm.

In the present era, customer engagement utilizes digital channels, social media platforms, and AI-driven tools to create personalized, convenient, and scalable experiences (10). Customers now have the expectation that brands will be present and responsive on various online platforms, making digital engagement a necessity. This shift has created new opportunities for businesses to connect with customers in real-time, provide immediate support, and gather valuable data for further customization.

3. THE ROLE OF ARTIFICIAL INTELLIGENCE [AI] IN CUSTOMER ENGAGEMENT

3.1 Advantages of AI in Customer Engagement

The integration of artificial intelligence (AI) into customer engagement practices offers a range of benefits. AI has the capacity to rapidly process and analyze real-time data, surpassing human capabilities in this regard. This enables businesses to gain deep insights into customer behaviors and preferences, facilitating the implementation of targeted and effective engagement strategies. Moreover, AI-driven systems can operate continuously, ensuring round-the-clock availability for customers, which is particularly important in a global marketplace with diverse time zones. Additionally, AI has the ability to quickly process large amounts of information, leading to improved decision-making processes and more efficient operations (Smith, J., & Johnson, L., 2022).

Personalization plays a crucial role in driving customer engagement and satisfaction, and AI excels in this area. AI algorithms can analyze extensive datasets to generate highly personalized recommendations and communications. This level of personalization enhances customer satisfaction by providing relevant content, products, or services, fostering a sense of connection and loyalty (Smith, J., & Johnson, L., 2022).

3.2 AI-Powered Tools for Customer Engagement

AI-powered tools have had a significant impact on customer engagement in various industries. Examples of these tools include chatbots, virtual assistants, and recommendation engines. These applications have revolutionized the way businesses interact with their customers (Smith, J., & Johnson, L., 2022).

Chatbots have proven to be particularly valuable in providing immediate support to customers. They are capable of efficiently handling common inquiries and issues, resulting in reduced response times and an enhanced overall customer experience. Virtual assistants, on the other hand, are continuously evolving to become more personalized and context-aware, further improving customer interactions. Recommendation engines utilize AI to analyze customer data and behavior, enabling them to suggest products or content that align with individual preferences. This personalized approach increases the likelihood of conversion and cross-selling (Smith, J., & Johnson, L., 2022).

3.3 AI-Driven Personalization

Personalization plays a crucial role in effective customer engagement, and the utilization of artificial intelligence (AI) takes personalization to a new level. By employing AI algorithms, a vast range of data points, such as previous purchases, browsing history, and demographic information, can be analyzed to generate highly personalized recommendations and communications.

For instance, in the realm of e-commerce, AI can examine a customer's browsing history and propose products that align with their specific interests and preferences. Similarly, in the content industry, AI can customize news feeds or streaming content recommendations based on a user's past interactions and viewing habits. This level of personalization surpasses the mere provision of relevant content; it also fosters a sense of being understood and catered to, thereby significantly augmenting customer satisfaction and loyalty (Smith, J., & Johnson, L., 2022).

3.4 AI-Enhanced Customer Support

AI has revolutionized the field of customer support by introducing chatbots and virtual assistants. These AI-driven solutions offer efficient and timely assistance to address common customer queries and problems. They are accessible 24/7, providing support regardless of time zones or working hours.

One notable advantage of AI-driven customer support is its ability to handle a large volume of customer inquiries simultaneously, preventing any delays in assistance. Additionally, AI-powered systems can enhance their responses and accuracy by learning from previous interactions. However, it is crucial to strike a balance between AI and human support to ensure that more complex or emotionally sensitive issues are appropriately addressed by human agents (Smith, J., & Johnson, L., 2022).

4. CHATGPT: THE AI-POWERED CONVERSATIONAL AGENT

4.1 Introduction to ChatGPT

The emergence of ChatGPT marks a notable advancement in the progression of AI-driven conversational agents. OpenAI has developed ChatGPT using the GPT-3.5 framework and has subjected it to rigorous training using an extensive collection of textual data. Its primary objective is to generate responses that closely resemble those of a human participant in natural language conversations (OpenAI. 2020).

What distinguishes ChatGPT from its counterparts is its capacity to actively participate in dynamic and contextually-aware dialogues. It possesses the ability to comprehend user input, deliver coherent responses, and sustain contextual understanding throughout prolonged interactions. Consequently, ChatGPT proves to be a potent tool for augmenting customer engagement across diverse industries and application scenarios.

4.2 How ChatGPT Works

The ChatGPT system utilizes a transformer architecture, which facilitates its ability to process and generate coherent text based on input prompts. Through pre-training on a diverse corpus of internet text, the model has acquired the capability to handle various topics and contexts. However, what distinguishes ChatGPT is its versatility in being fine-tuned for specific tasks and industries (OpenAI. 2020).

The process of fine-tuning enables organizations to customize ChatGPT according to their specific needs. For example, an e-commerce company can fine-tune ChatGPT to excel in providing product recommendations and customer support, while a healthcare provider can adapt it to offer medical advice and appointment scheduling (Suresh Babu, C. V. & Adhithya, S., 2023). . This adaptability renders ChatGPT suitable for a wide range of customer engagement applications.

4.3 Use Cases of ChatGPT in Customer Engagement

The natural language processing capabilities of ChatGPT offer a wide range of possibilities for customer engagement. Its application can be seen in various contexts such as website chatbots, social media interactions, and email responses. By comprehending user intent and context, ChatGPT is able to deliver relevant and personalized responses, thereby enhancing the overall customer experience (OpenAI. 2020).

In the realm of e-commerce, ChatGPT can be utilized to aid customers in product discovery, address shipping inquiries, and even provide personalized recommendations based on their previous purchase history. Within the healthcare industry, ChatGPT can offer patient support by responding to medical queries, guiding users through symptom checklists, and assisting with appointment scheduling. In the banking sector, ChatGPT can provide automated financial advice, handle account inquiries, and offer round-the-clock support.

4.4 Benefits and Limitations of ChatGPT

ChatGPT offers several advantages for businesses aiming to enhance customer engagement. Firstly, it exhibits high scalability, enabling it to handle a substantial volume of customer interactions concurrently. This scalability ensures that customers receive prompt responses, thereby contributing to a positive engagement experience. Furthermore, ChatGPT operates continuously, 24/7, accommodating customers across different time zones and providing uninterrupted support.

Another benefit of ChatGPT is its cost-effectiveness. By automating routine customer inquiries and support tasks, it alleviates the workload on human agents, allowing them to concentrate on more intricate issues that necessitate human intervention. This cost-effectiveness can result in significant savings for businesses while maintaining or even enhancing the quality of customer support.

However, it is crucial to acknowledge the limitations of ChatGPT. One notable concern is the potential for biased responses. The model's responses are derived from the data it has been trained on, which may contain biases present in the internet text. Diligent monitoring and training are imperative to ensure that ChatGPT furnishes fair and unbiased information to customers. Additionally, like all AI systems, ChatGPT necessitates ongoing maintenance and monitoring to rectify any errors or misunderstandings that may arise during interactions (OpenAI. 2020).

5. IMPLEMENTING CHATGPT FOR CUSTOMER ENGAGEMENT

5.1 Planning and Strategy

The successful integration of ChatGPT into customer engagement strategies necessitates a well-defined approach. It is imperative to align the utilization of ChatGPT with broader business objectives and customer requirements to ensure that this AI-powered tool contributes to the overall success of the organization. During the planning phase, several key steps need to be taken, including the identification of specific use cases, the establishment of key performance indicators (KPIs), and the development of a clear implementation roadmap (Gandhe, A., & Karmore, S. 2020).

The identification of use cases is of utmost importance as it enables organizations to identify areas where ChatGPT can provide the greatest value. For instance, a retail company may focus on utilizing ChatGPT for product recommendations and customer support, while a travel agency may prioritize its use in assisting customers with trip planning and booking. By defining KPIs, organizations can effectively measure the impact of ChatGPT on customer engagement and monitor its performance over time. Furthermore, a clear roadmap delineates the timeline and milestones for implementation, ensuring that the process is well-structured and manageable.

5.2 Data Integration and Training

The effectiveness of ChatGPT relies heavily on the quality of the data used and the training process employed. It is crucial to integrate historical customer data into ChatGPT in order to provide the necessary context and information for understanding user inquiries and preferences (OpenAI. 2020). This data may encompass customer purchase history, interaction logs, and demographic information. The integration process should be designed to ensure seamless access and utilization of this data by ChatGPT.

The training of ChatGPT for specific customer engagement tasks is a critical step in the process. Fine-tuning the model involves exposing it to examples of desired behaviours and responses. For instance, if ChatGPT is intended for customer support in the banking industry, it should be trained on a dataset consisting of common banking queries and appropriate responses. Through fine-tuning, the model is customized to the specific language, context, and tone expected in customer interactions, thereby improving its performance and relevance (OpenAI. 2020).

5.3 Compliance and Ethical Considerations

Ensuring the adherence of ChatGPT to ethical guidelines and compliance with data privacy regulations is of utmost importance. Establishing trust with customers is crucial, and any perceived misuse or mishandling of data has the potential to undermine that trust. It is imperative for businesses to be transparent about the utilization and storage of customer data. Furthermore, the implementation of robust security measures to safeguard customer data is equally essential (Accenture, 2019).

Efforts to comply with regulations should encompass specific regulatory requirements relevant to the industry and geographic region in which the business operates. This may involve adhering to data protection regulations such as the General Data Protection Regulation (GDPR) in Europe or the Health Insurance Portability and Accountability Act (HIPAA) in the healthcare industry in the United States. Maintaining compliance with these regulations not only helps avoid legal complications but also demonstrates a commitment to the ethical and responsible utilization of AI.

5.4 Integration with Existing Customer Engagement Systems

To achieve a seamless customer engagement experience, it is imperative to integrate ChatGPT with existing customer engagement tools and platforms. This integration serves the purpose of ensuring that customer interactions are coherent and that ChatGPT has real-time access to pertinent customer data and information (Gandhe, A., & Karmore, S. 2020).

In practical terms, the integration process may entail establishing a connection between ChatGPT and a customer relationship management (CRM) system. This system offers valuable insights into previous interactions and customer profiles. Additionally, integration may involve linking ChatGPT with various communication channels, such as website chat interfaces, social media platforms, or email systems. This comprehensive integration enables ChatGPT to engage with customers across their preferred channels, thereby enhancing the overall customer experience through consistent and contextually-aware interactions.

6. CUSTOMER ENGAGEMENT BEST PRACTICES WITH CHATGPT

6.1 Personalization and Customization

One of the primary advantages of ChatGPT lies in its capacity to offer personalization on a large scale. Leveraging the personalization and customization capabilities of ChatGPT can greatly enhance customer engagement. By tailoring responses and recommendations to individual preferences, businesses can cultivate a sense of connection and relevance with their customers (Smith, J., & Johnson, L., 2022).

For example, in the realm of e-commerce, ChatGPT can analyze a customer's previous purchases, browsing behavior, and wishlists to propose products that align with their preferences. In the hospitality industry, ChatGPT can suggest personalized travel itineraries based on a traveler's specific interests and budget. This personalized approach not only increases the likelihood of conversion but also fosters a more enjoyable and satisfying customer experience.

6.2 Real-Time Responsiveness

The ability of ChatGPT to provide immediate responses is a valuable asset in enhancing customer engagement. In the contemporary digital era, customers have high expectations for receiving prompt answers and solutions to their queries. By reducing response times and promptly addressing issues, businesses can significantly impact customer satisfaction and engagement (Smith, J., & Johnson, L., 2022).

For instance, in customer support scenarios, ChatGPT can effectively handle routine inquiries, such as checking account balances or providing updates on order status, in real-time. This allows human agents to allocate their efforts towards more intricate and nuanced customer concerns, ensuring that customers receive appropriate assistance promptly. Moreover, real-time responsiveness contributes to a favorable perception of the brand, as customers feel valued and well-attended to.

6.3 Data Security and Privacy

The safeguarding of customer data holds great significance in endeavors to engage with customers. There is a growing apprehension among customers regarding the privacy and security of their personal information. Consequently, it is imperative for businesses to establish robust data security measures and maintain transparency regarding the collection, utilization, and protection of customer data (Li, L., et al., 2017).

In the course of interacting with customers, ChatGPT may necessitate access to sensitive information, such as account particulars or medical records. It is crucial to ensure that such data is handled securely and that access is limited to authorized personnel. Foundational elements for upholding customer trust include encryption, secure data storage practices, and adherence to data protection regulations. Furthermore, effectively communicating these security measures to customers can serve to reassure them that their data is treated with the utmost care.

6.4 Continuous Learning and Improvement

The utilization of ChatGPT for customer engagement is not a singular endeavor but an ongoing process. It is crucial to regularly monitor and analyze the performance of ChatGPT in order to achieve continuous improvement (OpenAI. 2020). This entails assessing the quality of responses, measuring customer satisfaction, and tracking key performance indicators (KPIs) that were established during the planning phase (Suresh Babu, C. V. & Padma. R.,, 2023(Suresh Babu, C. V., and B. Rohan., 2023) .

Incorporating customer feedback is of great value in refining the engagement strategy. Customers can provide valuable insights into areas where ChatGPT performs well and areas where it may not meet expectations. These insights can guide efforts to fine-tune ChatGPT and enhance its alignment with customer needs and preferences. Furthermore, as the AI model continues to learn and adapt over time, organizations can implement updates and improvements to ensure that it remains in line with evolving customer engagement objectives (OpenAI. 2020).

7. CASE STUDIES

7.1 Case Study One: ChatGPT in E-Commerce

This case study examines the implementation of ChatGPT in an e-commerce company with the aim of improving customer support, product recommendations, and overall sales performance (Ranjan, P., & Patel, P., 2019). The company successfully integrated ChatGPT as a chatbot on their website, enabling it to provide immediate assistance to customers regarding product details, availability, and shipping information. The chatbot's advanced natural language understanding capabilities ensured that customers received accurate and relevant responses in a timely manner. Furthermore, ChatGPT was trained to analyze customer browsing behavior and past purchases, enabling it to generate real-time product recommendations. Through continuous interaction with customers, the chatbot learned from their preferences and adjusted its recommendations accordingly, resulting in a highly personalized shopping experience.

The outcomes of this implementation were remarkable. Customer satisfaction scores improved, and the company observed an increase in both the average order value and the conversion rate. ChatGPT not only efficiently handled routine customer inquiries but also contributed to higher sales by suggesting products that aligned with individual preferences. This case study serves as an illustration of how ChatGPT can be a valuable asset in the e-commerce sector, enhancing customer engagement and driving business growth (Ranjan, P., & Patel, P., 2019).

7.2 Case Study Two: ChatGPT in Healthcare

The second case study examines the utilization of ChatGPT in the healthcare sector, with a specific focus on enhancing patient support, addressing medical inquiries, and streamlining the process of scheduling appointments (Brown, T. B., et al., 2020). Healthcare organizations encounter distinct challenges in engaging with customers due to the sensitive and intricate nature of medical information.

In this particular case, ChatGPT was integrated into the website and mobile application of a healthcare provider. Patients were able to interact with ChatGPT to obtain answers to commonly asked medical questions, such as symptoms, medication details, and preventive care. Furthermore, ChatGPT facilitated the scheduling of appointments by guiding patients through the process and providing real-time information on appointment availability.

The impact of this implementation was substantial. Patients expressed their satisfaction with the convenience of accessing medical information and receiving assistance with appointment booking at any time of the day. Healthcare providers experienced a decrease in the volume of routine inquiries handled by human agents, enabling them to allocate more attention to critical patient care responsibilities. This case study serves as evidence of the value that ChatGPT can bring to the healthcare industry, as it enhances patient engagement and improves the efficiency of healthcare services (Brown, T. B., et al., 2020).

7.3 Case Study Three: ChatGPT in Banking

The third case study examines the utilization of ChatGPT in the banking sector with the aim of enhancing customer engagement through automated financial advice and continuous support (McKinsey & Company, 2019). In response to the growing trend, banks are increasingly adopting AI solutions to augment their interactions with customers.

In this particular case, ChatGPT was seamlessly integrated into the bank's mobile application and website, functioning as a virtual financial advisor and support agent. Customers were able to utilize ChatGPT to inquire about their account balances, transaction history, and even receive tailored financial advice. The AI model was trained to comprehend and offer guidance on a range of financial products, including loans, savings accounts, and investment options. Furthermore, it assisted customers with basic account management tasks, such as setting up automated transfers and bill payments.

The outcomes of this implementation were remarkable. Customers expressed their satisfaction with the convenience and accessibility provided by ChatGPT, particularly outside of regular banking hours. The virtual financial advisor feature empowered customers to make well-informed financial decisions, thereby contributing to their overall financial well-being. Additionally, the bank observed an improvement in customer retention rates as a result of the enhanced engagement facilitated by ChatGPT. This case study serves as a testament to the potential of ChatGPT in the banking industry, as it offers personalized, round-the-clock customer support and financial guidance (McKinsey & Company, 2019).

8. CHALLENGES AND ETHICAL CONSIDERATIONS

8.1 Bias and Fairness in AI

Addressing bias and ensuring fairness in artificial intelligence (AI), particularly in models like ChatGPT, is a crucial ethical consideration. AI models acquire knowledge from extensive datasets, and if these datasets contain biases, the AI may unintentionally generate biased responses or recommendations (Li, L., et al., 2017). For instance, ChatGPT might produce responses that inadvertently reflect gender or racial biases present in the data it was trained on.

To mitigate bias and promote fairness, organizations must implement various strategies, including data preprocessing, incorporating diversity in training data, and conducting ongoing monitoring. Data preprocessing involves identifying and rectifying biased patterns in the training data. By including diverse and representative data during the training process, organizations can help mitigate bias by ensuring that the AI model learns from a wide range of perspectives. Continuous monitoring of ChatGPT's responses and regular updates to its training data can further diminish bias over time (Li, L., et al., 2017).

8.2 Maintaining Human Touch

AI-powered solutions such as ChatGPT offer advantages in terms of efficiency and scalability in customer engagement. However, it is crucial to find a balance that preserves the human touch. Customers often desire authentic and empathetic interactions, which can be challenging for AI systems to replicate (Li, L., et al., 2017).

To maintain the human touch, organizations should clearly communicate to customers when they are interacting with AI rather than a human agent. This transparency helps manage customer expectations appropriately. Furthermore, businesses can program AI systems like ChatGPT to provide responses that sound more empathetic and human-like. For instance, the system can be designed to express understanding and empathy when a customer shares a problem or concern. By striking the right balance between AI and human interactions, organizations can ensure that customers receive the necessary support while also benefiting from the efficiency provided by AI technology (Li, L., et al., 2017).

8.3 Privacy Concerns

Privacy concerns are of utmost importance in customer engagement, particularly in the context of AI systems like ChatGPT that handle sensitive customer data. It is imperative for businesses to prioritize the security and privacy of data in order to establish and maintain trust with their customers (Li, L., et al., 2017).

To address these privacy concerns, organizations should implement robust encryption techniques and adopt secure data storage practices to safeguard customer information. Additionally, they should clearly communicate their data usage policies and seek consent from customers before collecting and processing their data. Granting customers control over their data, such as the option to opt out of data collection, can further strengthen the trust relationship. Furthermore, compliance with data protection regulations such as GDPR, HIPAA, or CCPA is crucial to mitigate the legal and reputational risks associated with privacy breaches (Li, L., et al., 2017).

8.4 Legal and Regulatory Challenges

Navigating the intricate legal and regulatory framework surrounding artificial intelligence (AI) and customer data poses a significant challenge. The utilization of AI in customer engagement necessitates adherence to various laws, regulations, and industry standards (McKinsey & Company, 2019).

To tackle these challenges, organizations should establish legal and compliance teams or collaborate with legal experts who possess expertise in AI and data privacy. They should conduct comprehensive assessments of how AI systems, such as ChatGPT, interact with customer data and ensure that these interactions align with regulatory requirements. Furthermore, organizations should remain updated on evolving regulations and adapt their AI strategies accordingly. Taking proactive measures to comply with regulations not only mitigates legal risks but also fosters trust with customers who prioritize data protection (McKinsey & Company, 2019).

9. FUTURE TRENDS IN AI-POWERED CUSTOMER ENGAGEMENT

9.1 Enhanced Multimodal AI

The integration of text-based AI models, such as ChatGPT, with other modalities like images and videos is expected to shape the future of AI-powered customer engagement. This transition towards multimodal AI facilitates more immersive and enhanced interactions. An instance of this is the potential for customer service chatbots to analyze product images in order to gain a better understanding of customer inquiries and deliver more precise responses. Likewise, AI-powered virtual shopping assistants could utilize video analysis to provide personalized fashion recommendations that align with a customer's individual style and preferences (Accenture, 2019).

9.2 Predictive Analytics and AI

The predictive capabilities of artificial intelligence (AI) are anticipated to undergo substantial advancements. Organizations are projected to increasingly utilize AI to forecast customer requirements and actively interact with them. Through the analysis of past customer data and current behaviors, AI has the potential to anticipate when a customer may require assistance, make a purchase, or require a specific service. This predictive methodology empowers businesses to proactively approach customers with timely and pertinent offers or support, thereby augmenting customer engagement and satisfaction (Accenture, 2019).

9.3 AI-Powered Voice Assistants

Voice-activated artificial intelligence (AI) assistants are anticipated to assume a more significant role in customer engagement. The increasing prevalence of smart speakers and voice-activated devices has resulted in customers becoming accustomed to interacting with AI through voice commands. These AI-powered voice assistants provide a hands-free and intuitive means of interaction, rendering them particularly suitable for tasks such as addressing inquiries, furnishing product information, and even facilitating voice-based transactions. The integration of voice assistants into customer engagement strategies has the potential to augment accessibility and convenience for customers (Accenture, 2019).

9.4 AI in Augmented Reality

The convergence of augmented reality (AR) and artificial intelligence (AI) is anticipated to result in the development of immersive customer engagement experiences. In sectors such as retail and entertainment, organizations can exploit the combination of AR and AI to offer interactive and tailored experiences to their customers. For example, AR applications can enable customers to visualize furniture in their homes or receive guided tours in museums with AI-generated commentary. This integration of AR and AI has the capacity to transform customer engagement by enhancing interactivity, enjoyment, and information dissemination (Accenture, 2019).

10. CONCLUSION

10.1 Recap of Key Points

This study has examined the importance of utilizing ChatGPT and artificial intelligence (AI) to enhance customer engagement. In modern business practices, customer engagement plays a vital role in establishing robust customer relationships through the provision of value, personalization, and effective communication. AI, specifically ChatGPT, has transformed customer engagement by facilitating personalized interactions, immediate responsiveness, and informed decision-making based on data (Gandhe, A., & Karmore, S. 2020).

10.2 The Future of Customer Engagement With AI

The utilization of artificial intelligence (AI) holds great potential for enhancing customer engagement by providing tailored, streamlined, and convenient experiences across diverse sectors. As AI technology progresses, organizations that adopt AI-based customer engagement approaches will be more adept at addressing the changing demands and preferences of their clientele (Accenture, 2019).

10.3 Final Thoughts and Recommendations

In order to achieve success in customer engagement through the utilization of artificial intelligence (AI), businesses must adopt optimal strategies, confront obstacles, and remain knowledgeable about the ever-evolving trends in AI technology. The integration of ChatGPT and other AI-driven tools has the potential to enhance customer experiences, optimize operational efficiency, and stimulate business expansion. Nevertheless, it is imperative to prioritize ethical considerations, privacy concerns, and regulatory compliance, while simultaneously striking a harmonious equilibrium between AI and human interactions. By adhering to these principles, organizations can foster enduring customer relationships and flourish in the era of digitalization (Gandhe, A., & Karmore, S. 2020).

REFERENCE

Accenture. (2019). *Rethinking Customer Engagement with Artificial Intelligence*. Accenture Research.

Brown, T. B. (2020). *Language Models are Few-Shot Learners*. arXiv preprint arXiv:2005.14165.

Gandhe, A., & Karmore, S. (2020). Artificial Intelligence in Customer Engagement: Opportunities and Challenges. In *Proceedings of the International Conference on Computational Intelligence and Data Science (ICCIDS)* (pp. 1-6). IEEE.

Hess, J., & Kumar, V. (2019). AI in Marketing: A Review and Research Agenda. *Journal of the Academy of Marketing Science*, *48*(1), 4–31.

Hoffman, M. (2021). AI and Customer Engagement: A Comprehensive Guide to the Future. *Harvard Business Review*.

Li, L. (2017). *Deep Reinforcement Learning for Dialogue Generation*. arXiv preprint arXiv:1606.01541.

McKinsey & Company. (2019). *AI in customer engagement: A primer*. McKinsey Digital.

Open, A. I. (2020). *ChatGPT: A Large-Scale Generative Language Model*. OpenAI Blog.

Ranjan, P., & Patel, P. (2019). Transforming Customer Engagement with AI-Powered Chatbots: A Case Study of Leading E-commerce Company. *International Journal of Artificial Intelligence & Applications*, *10*(5), 45–56.

Smith, J., & Johnson, L. (2022). Leveraging ChatGPT for Enhanced Customer Support: A Practical Guide. *AI Trends*, *18*(3), 37–48.

Suresh Babu, C. V. (2022). *Artificial Intelligence and Expert Systems*. Anniyappa Publication.

Suresh Babu, C. V., & Adhithya, S. (2023). ChatGPT and Other Generative AI Tools in Education: Transformative Potential and Ethical Considerations. In J. Keengwe (Ed.), *Creative AI Tools and Ethical Implications in Teaching and Learning* (pp. 135–152). IGI Global. doi:10.4018/979-8-3693-0205-7.ch007

Suresh Babu, C. V., & Padma, R. (2023). Technology Transformation Through Skilled Teachers in Teaching Accountancy. In R. González-Lezcano (Ed.), *Advancing STEM Education and Innovation in a Time of Distance Learning* (pp. 211–233). IGI Global. doi:10.4018/978-1-6684-5053-6.ch011

Suresh Babu, C. V., & Rohan, B. (2023). Evaluation and Quality Assurance for Rapid E-Learning and Development of Digital Learning Resources. In M. I. Santally, (Eds.), *Implementing Rapid E-Learning Through Interactive Materials Development* (pp. 139–170). IGI Global. doi:10.4018/978-1-6684-4940-0.ch008

Chapter 7
Unveiling the Potential of ChatGPT for Enhancing Customer Engagement

Garima
Maharshi Dayanand University, India

Rohit Bansal
https://orcid.org/0000-0001-7072-5005
Department of Management Studies, Vaish College of Engineering, Rohtak, India

ABSTRACT

Marketers are continuously looking for fresh, cutting-edge approaches to connect with their target consumers as businesses are becoming progressively more dependent on technology and digital platforms. ChatGPT, an AI-driven chatbot that employs natural language processing (NLP) to interact with users in a human-like manner, is one of their newest technologies. ChatGPT enables businesses to offer customized and immediate support to their audience by smoothly connecting with a variety of digital platforms. ChatGPT boosts client engagement by delivering a customized and captivating user interface owing to its capacity to grasp human-like discussions. It enables companies to have more meaningful contact with their clients, immediately resolving their issues and forging a solid brand-client bond. In this chapter, the role of ChatGPT in enhancing customer engagement and how it can help businesses in achieving their marketing goals is explored. This study is based on secondary sources, including books, publications, websites, reports, and more.

DOI: 10.4018/979-8-3693-0815-8.ch007

INTRODUCTION

Businesses in today's digitally-driven world are always looking for novel and innovative approaches to interact with their clients and deliver excellent user experiences. ChatGPT is an emerging innovation that shows a lot of potential in this regard. It has become a buzzword in the realm of contemporary technology. Aspects of Internet search that have received a lot of attention but are less well-understood have also piqued the curiosity of academics, practitioners, administrators, governments, and the research community (Singh et al., 2019).

ChatGPT enables businesses to have dynamic and interactive conversations with their consumers, fostering personalized relationships and delivering value. It is powered by cutting-edge natural language processing and machine learning algorithms. A conversational model using AI at its core, ChatGPT was created by Open AI. In order to provide responses that are human-like to user inquiries or prompts, it makes use of deep learning algorithms. ChatGPT is a priceless tool for organizations since it can replicate conversations in natural language and respond with pertinent and context-aware information after being trained on enormous volumes of data.

One of the models in the family of generative pre-trained transformers (GPT) is ChatGPT, an AI-based conversational language model created by OpenAI. These models, which are built on the "transformer architecture," are trained on vast volumes of text data to generate responses that resemble human speech in response to input prompts. This qualifies it for conversational applications like chatbots, virtual assistants, and customer service representatives. The model has received thorough training using numerous conversational data sources, such as social media, literature, and web domains, to produce text that is contextually appropriate, cohesive, and human-kind. An "input response," such as a statement or a question, is needed for ChatGPT in order to feed the ChatGPT model. Unlike previous models, the model creates several responses for a single input based on its knowledge and training data, each of which varies in content, style, and duration depending on the input context.

Contextually appropriate text creation improves ChatGPT's ability to connect with online users. For instance, ChatGPT will provide information about the GDP rank, the position of import and export, the status of FDI, and other factors in answer to a user's question about a certain country's economic situation. Let's say the user asks a follow-up inquiry as the conversation proceeds. In that situation, ChatGPT generates the appropriate response and takes into account the prior response to produce a logical and next-level response .ChatGPT becomes more cohesive, floating, and conversational as a result of this capability.

ChatGPT is utilized for more NLP tasks than just text generation, including text classification, question answering, and summarization. The model is improved to perform well while keeping its capacity to produce text that resembles human speech on particular tasks (using both supervised and reinforcement learning techniques). The most recent system, ChatGPT-4, is capable of generating safe and generally more effective responses. For conversational applications that give you the impression that you are speaking with people rather than a machine, ChatGPT is based on the GPT-4 families of large language models (LLMs). It is crucial to understand that these new models are not infallible, and they could produce offensive, irrelevant, or factually incorrect material. Briefly put, ChatGPT with AI support is a powerful conversational language model that can respond in a human-like way to an input prompt.

The model can also be used for a variety of purposes, including text classification, virtual assistants, question-answering, and other NLP-related tasks. It is essential to take into account these models' possible risks, as well as their inherent limits, and use them wisely.

LITERATURE REVIEW

Lund and Wang (2023) gave an overview of the important terms linked to ChatGPT, an open source program created by OpenAI, and the Generative Pretrained Transformer. An interview with ChatGPT about the potential effects on academic institutions and libraries is included in this paper. It was found that ChatGPT has the potential to significantly boost academic research and librarianship in both unsettling and novel ways.

Ausat et al. (2023) analyzed whether ChatGPT can take the position of teachers in the classroom learning process. The methodology utilized to gather data entails thorough documentation of pertinent information and attentive listening, which is subsequently subjected to analytical processes such data reduction, data visualization, and conclusion drawing. The study came to the conclusion that technology can only be a tool and cannot completely replace the job of the teacher. It's crucial to strengthen instructors' technological management skills and appropriately and effectively integrate technology into the classroom.

Saputra et al. (2023) inquired into how employing AI Chat GPT affects marketing efficiency, especially on the Instagram platform. By watching the success of Instagram marketing, a descriptive qualitative method using virtual ethnography is utilized to assess instagram marketing effectiveness. The study's findings demonstrated that marketing content produced by AI Chat GPT may attract a lot of user attention and interaction, piquing their interest in the company's goods and services.

Rathore, B. (2023) investigated consumer expectations for AI and acquire insight into their use and impact in the near future by using qualitative data from ChatGPT and other previous studies to comprehend the content of these AI tools. The study's findings unambiguously showed the potential advantages and opportunities offered by ChatGPT for a range of industries, including education, academic writing, and customer service.

Rivas and Zhao (2023) demonstrate that, provided certain ethical issues are taken into account, ChatGPT has a huge potential to alter marketing and define its future. ChatGPT-based systems can assist marketers in producing content more quickly and possibly with a similar quality to that of human content producers. Additionally, it can help marketers do research more effectively, comprehend their target audience better, automate customer support, and work more efficiently.

OBJECTIVES AND METHODOLOGY

The objective of this study is to investigate how ChatGPT might assist organizations in attaining their marketing objectives and what function it plays in boosting customer engagement. Secondary sources, such as books, articles, papers, websites, and more, served as the foundation for this study.

An Overview of ChatGPT

Though at the rate venture capital businesses have been spending substantially in generative AI-based solutions, it seems ChatGPT will act like a white color worker, constantly available to assist you. For an economy to work for everyone, though today, AI seems to be an improbable alternative. ChatGPT, an adaptation of the GPT-3 model developed by OpenAI, is a conversational language model intended for conversational AI and chatbot applications.

ChatGPT can provide human-like responses thanks to its "transformer architecture" and training on a large amount of text data. When using ChatGPT, a user provides a "input prompt," sometimes referred to as a question or statement, which is fed into the model.

The model creates numerous replies that differ in style, content, and duration depending on the nature of the question.

ChatGPT's Mechanism of Operation

A sizable neural network that ChatGPT is based on generates answers to its users that resemble those of humans. These neural networks are made up of various transformer layers. They have the ability to analyze data in a sequential manner, such as natural language text, and they may look for patterns in data input that are used for various

NLP activities, such question answering or text generation. However, pre-training and fine-tuning are necessary to produce human-kind responses.

The Preparation Phase for ChatGPT

ChatGPT can analyze patterns and associations between words, phrases, sentences, and assertions since it is trained on a vast corpus of text data supplied into its memory. It is then enlightened on human feedback to comprehend what people want with a specific question prompt in order to produce human-like responses. ChatGPT is innovative for anticipating what will happen next because of the training of the big language models. Additionally, it teaches ChatGPT to challenge inquiries and omit portions of the absurd ones. Massive volumes of text, data, information, news, codes, and internet sources like Reddit discussions are used throughout this training to help ChatGPT learn how to have human conversations and respond in a human-like manner. Every time new data is entered into the model throughout the computational training phase, the model is continuously improved. One of the largest language models ever trained in the history of Internet search, the most recent ChatGPT was trained using about 175 billion parameters on an Azure supercomputing infrastructure. The 3.5 version has been trained on more than ten billion words and eight million documents, while training is still ongoing.

Fine Tuning of ChatGPT

Once taught, ChatGPT can be tailored for specific jobs or uses, including content creation or language translation. When the model is fine-tuned, it is trained on fresh data and often becomes efficient for more difficult tasks that call for the model to gain a deeper understanding of the subject (Lund and Wang, 2013). The model needs to be fine-tuned to accommodate complex and unique use scenarios. This saves time and resources since training a brand-new model from scratch would otherwise be necessary. Instead of creating a new model, the one that already exists is taught to meet particular requirements. As a result, it not only increases the results' accuracy but also the model's general performance and can be used by any organization with only minor modifications.

Figure 1. Steps for a ChatGPT model's fine-tuning
Source: Singh and Singh (2023)

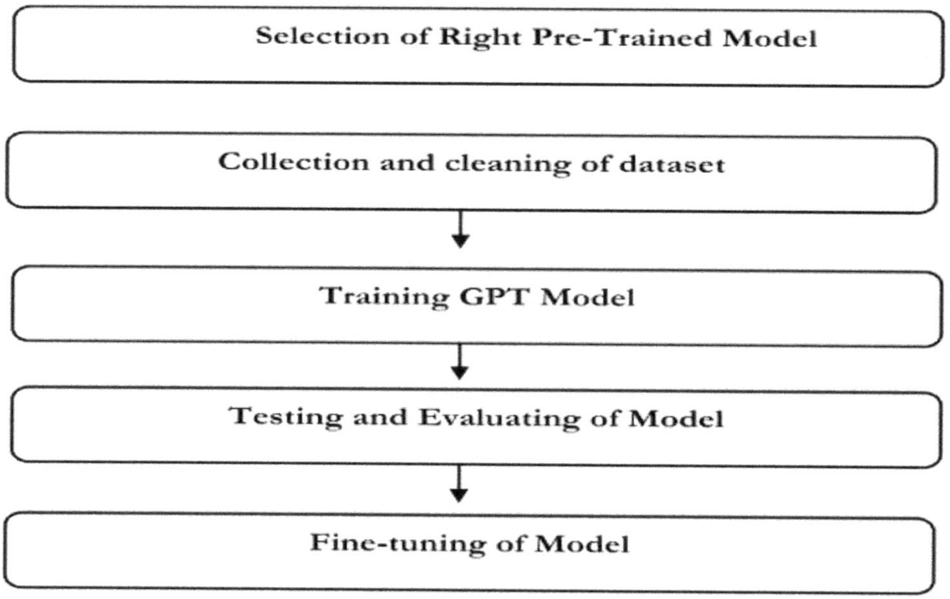

Causes of ChatGPT's Rising Popularity

ChatGPT has been used in a variety of industries since its November 2022 introduction, including customer support, content development, and natural language processing. ChatGPT is garnering interest from internet users, it appears that it has the potential to surpass Google as the next major search engine. The distinctive qualities and possible advantages of ChatGPT are highlighted in this section.

Enhanced Effectiveness

By automating discussions and doing away with the need for staff, AI-based ChatGPT lets organizations run more efficiently. It produces immediate responses and speeds up conversation. This frees up resources and allows firms to provide individualized customer experiences by responding to consumer inquiries rapidly. ChatGPT, in contrast to conventional chatbots, is a potent large-scale language model that can better interpret client questions and produce responses that sound human. By enhancing their customer service departments and freeing up extra staff for other key organizational responsibilities, this technology has helped a number of firms.

Improved Accuracy

ChatGPT produces better responses than humans or manual dialogues since it was trained on a wide collection of conversational datasets. With the help of this deep learning training, it can comprehend the "context" of a discussion and produce the necessary responses. ChatGPT Improved Accuracy (CGA) model uses AI powered by deep learning to provide accurate and insightful discussions.

Based on an input prompt, OpenAI's GPT-3 uses a pre-trained model to produce precise and engaging discussions. Additionally, CGA's accuracy and generative competencies improve its capacity to pick up on responses and past exchanges (Gabrielson et al. 2023). As a result, ChatGPT can become accustomed to different environments and produce more accurate findings recent studies. Recent studies demonstrate that CGA has acquired an impressive degree of accuracy and generative skills, outperforming other widely used NLP models in terms of accuracy, consistency, and readability.

Cost Reduction

OpenAI's ChatGPT-4 is a cutting-edge language generation model that has the potential to lower expenses for companies who only use customer support chatbots. ChatGPT stands out for its capacity to produce human-like responses in real-time, which reduces the need for human resources to manage customer service divisions. Additionally, ChatGPT learns from each response, enhancing the outcome and doing away with the regular need for expensive manual upgrades to chatbot replies. These outstanding capabilities make ChatGPT a one-stop shop for companies looking to increase the efficacy and efficiency of their customer service operations.

An Increase in Customer Engagement

ChatGPT enables businesses interact with their customers more meaningfully and engagingly thanks to its human-like engagement features (Khan et al. 2023). With time and a better overall experience, this enables businesses to establish long-lasting relationships with their customers. Customers experience greater engagement with businesses and a more personalised experience, both of which are impractical with conventional customer assistance techniques (Bansal et al, 2023; Bansal et al., 2022). This in turn helps to maintain and grow consumer loyalty.

Automated Conversation

Due to the fact that customer service representatives typically address clients' questions via chat or phone, the grievance resolution process takes a while. However, ChatGPT encourages conversation automation and can make conversations independent.

Multilingualism

It is advantageous for organizations and individuals to communicate with speakers of different languages and answer more naturally, specifically, and meaningfully thanks to ChatGPT's capacity to converse in several languages.

Enhanced Pace

ChatGPT can produce answers more quickly thanks to reliable hardware and algorithms. This increases its relevance in real-time environments like chatbots and conversational systems. The more quickly GPT executives can comprehend the purpose and context of users, the happier their users will be. This would allow businesses to reach a wide audience by utilizing chatbots on a variety of platforms, including applications, social media pages, and websites. Further developments will make it possible to incorporate more complex dialogue tracking characteristics, creating more natural and enjoyable user interfaces.

Figure 2. Reasons for growing popularity of chatGPT
Source: Prepared by authors

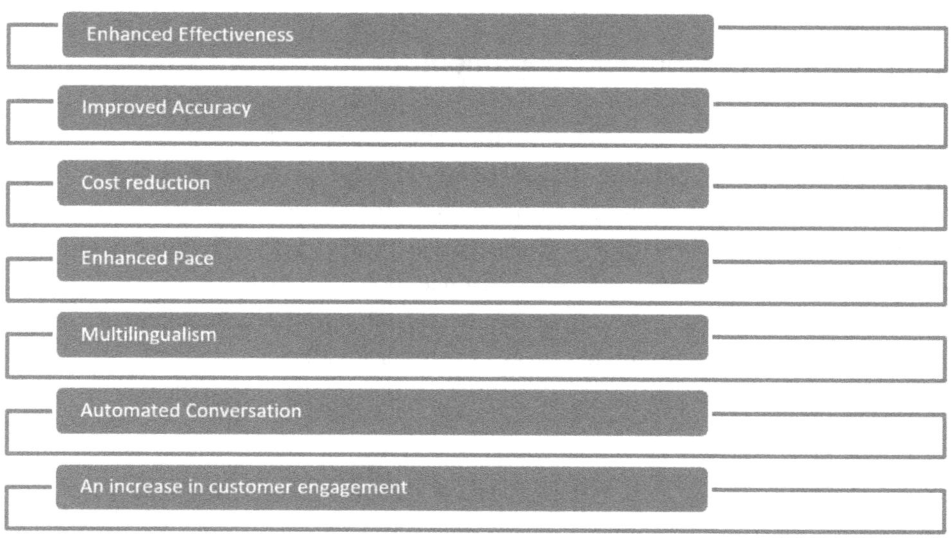

CUSTOMER ENGAGEMENT

Customers can now access information at their fingertips. Because more knowledgeable clients have too many options, it has been difficult to retain and attract new customers using traditional marketing techniques. The practice of building a relationship with current customers in order to increase brand recognition and customer loyalty is known as customer engagement (Mittal and Bansal, 2023). Customer journeys are now dynamic and non-linear since the majority of consumers and company customers across generations use a range of platforms to initiate and complete specific customer requests and transactions (Ao et al, 2023). The processes for involving customers are intricate, and when the message is well received, positive outcomes like service co-creation are anticipated. Without the ability to provide a personalized client experience via the appropriate channel at the appropriate time, relevance is "almost" impossible.

ChatGPT and Customer Engagement

Your company can get a variety of advantages by utilizing the ChatGPT App, all of which are focused on improving customer engagement. The following are a few of the major benefits:

- **Tailored Interactions:** By analyzing consumer preferences and configuring responses accordingly, ChatGPT enables organizations to offer tailored interactions. By fostering a closer relationship between the brand and the customer, this personalized strategy raises customer happiness and loyalty.
- **24/7 Availability:** With ChatGPT, companies can provide customer support and interaction around-the-clock. ChatGPT makes sure that consumers receive prompt support even beyond regular business hours by automating responses and handling frequent inquiries. The total client experience is improved, and customer satisfaction ratings rise as a result of its availability.
- **Scalability:** ChatGPT's scalability enables enterprises to manage a high volume of client inquiries concurrently. Customers no longer have to wait in line for assistance because the model can manage numerous chats at once. This scalability raises consumer satisfaction and aids companies in efficiently handling times of high demand.
- **Data-driven Insights:** Through client interactions, ChatGPT gathers a variety of data. Businesses can learn important information about customer behavior, preferences, and pain issues by studying this data. These revelations can then be leveraged to improve goods and services, marketing tactics, and generate more focused advertising campaigns. (Painoli et al, 2021)

- **Cost effectiveness:** ChatGPT lowers the demand for substantial human resources by automating client interactions. Businesses can cut costs as a result, and client interaction is effective and reliable. Companies may maintain excellent customer assistance while allocating resources to other crucial areas.
- **Better Customer Support and Assistance:** The ChatGPT App streamlines your customer support procedure and provides customers with prompt, precise responses to their questions. As a result, your customer service system becomes more effective, cutting down on their irritation and waiting times.
- **Increased Customer Contentment and Loyalty:** The ChatGPT App promotes client happiness by offering a seamless, personalized experience. Happy clients are more likely to stick with your brand, leave favorable reviews, and recommend your company to others.
- **Improved User Experience on Websites and Apps:** You can incorporate the ChatGPT App into your website or app to provide visitors with rapid assistance and direction. A more pleasurable user experience produced by this real-time help keeps clients interested and motivates them to learn more about your goods.
- **Personalized Marketing Efforts for personalized Audiences:**The ChatGPT App's capacity to recognize and decipher unique client preferences enables you to deliver personalized marketing campaigns. You may boost client engagement and boost revenue by providing personalized content, discounts, and product recommendations.

Testimonials and Success Stories

The ChatGPT App's usefulness is real, not just hypothetical. Here are some instances from the real world and testimonies that show how it affects consumer happiness and engagement:

- **Case Study of Companies Using ChatGPT App Successfully**: The ChatGPT App has been successfully used by many companies in a variety of industries to improve customer engagement. These businesses have reported considerable gains in customer satisfaction, customer satisfaction efficiency, and conversion rates, all of which have increased revenue.
- **Testimonials from Delighted Clients:** The excellent reviews from companies that have used the ChatGPT App speak volumes about its efficacy. Numerous clients have commended the app's smooth integration, user-friendly UI, and potent AI capabilities, claiming that it has revolutionized their approaches to customer engagement.

- **Proven effects in Increasing Customer Engagement and Satisfaction:** It is without dispute that the ChatGPT App can produce noticeable effects. The app has proved crucial in promoting customer engagement, contentment, and ultimately business success for its customers by offering real-time, individualized help and guidance.

HOW COULD CHATGPT BE UTILIZED TO STRATEGICALLY PLAN FOR CUSTOMER ENGAGEMENT?

Recognize Your Audience

Prior to using ChatGPT for client engagement, it's critical to have a thorough grasp of your target market. Analyze their communication preferences, issues, and pain points. This will enable you to successfully customize your interactions with ChatGPT to match their demands.

Set Clearly Visible Goals

Establish your goals for using ChatGPT in customer engagement in detail. Are you trying to get feedback, give advice that are specific to each person, or give immediate support? A specific goal will direct your strategy and guarantee that you make optimal use of ChatGPT.

Provide ChatGPT With Useful Data

Train ChatGPT with pertinent data that is compatible with your industry and your customers' demands to increase its effectiveness. You may improve ChatGPT's responses and make them more helpful and relevant by combining customer insights and expertise of the relevant industries.

Share Information That is Accurate and Reliable

Verify that the data offered by ChatGPT is correct and current. To prevent responses that are out-of-date or inaccurate, examine and update the training data often. Inaccurate information might make customers unhappy and make them lose faith in your company.

Establish Goals and Control Constraints

Customers should be informed openly about the capabilities and restrictions of ChatGPT. Inform them that they are speaking to an AI system and that some of their questions might need a human to help. Customers won't experience annoyance or confusion if ChatGPT is unable to satisfy their requirements if expectations are managed.

Monitoring and Performance Enhancement

Keep an eye on ChatGPT's performance and gather consumer feedback. Examine the exchanges to spot any points where ChatGPT needs to be improved or where human assistance could be required. Update and improve ChatGPT's training data frequently depending on user comments to increase efficiency.

Provide Customized Experiences

Utilize consumer information and insights to offer individualized ChatGPT experiences. Adapt your comments based on customer preferences, previous interactions, and past purchases. You can increase engagement and cultivate client loyalty by providing individualized recommendations or attending to particular customer needs.

Keep a Human Touch

Even though ChatGPT can offer helpful support, it's crucial to keep a personal touch in all customer interactions. Encourage ChatGPT to be empathetic, to respond in a cordial and friendly manner, and, if necessary, to know when to escalate the conversation to a human representative.

Adapt and Iterate

Continue to iterate and adjust your use of ChatGPT as client demands and preferences change. Keep up with the most recent developments in AI and natural language processing. To maximize customer engagement using ChatGPT, examine customer input frequently, analyze analytics, and make required adjustments.

Best Practices

- For corporate leaders, ChatGPT provides a number of well-liked application cases.
- Customer service & support: Use ChatGPT to answer questions from customers, resolve problems, and give product information.
- Sales and Lead Generation: Engage prospective clients, offer tailored advice, and help with lead conversion.
- Customised product or content recommendations: Utilize ChatGPT's capacity to comprehend preferences in order to give customised product or content recommendations.
- Interactive marketing and campaigns: Integrate ChatGPT into marketing campaigns for interactive experiences, client feedback, and customized message.
- Self-Service and Virtual Assistant: Use ChatGPT as your virtual assistant to manage errands like appointment scheduling, order tracking, and account queries.
- Market research and insights: Using ChatGPT, conduct surveys to get feedback from customers and discover useful information.
- Training and Onboarding: Use ChatGPT's interactive coaching to support employee training and onboarding procedures.
- Curation and Content Creation: Use ChatGPT to come up with material, offer suggestions, and help with content curation.

Benefits of ChatGPT Use in Businesses

- Now that ChatGPT is available, businesses can allocate personnel to complex problems that are difficult to solve rather than low-complexity jobs like customer service and services.
- ChatGPT has increased the productivity of the business and its staff as well by responding to client evaluations and managing their complaints and inquiries, and they are now on the road to recovery.
- As clients can now contact the firm after hours, ChatGPT has improved customer satisfaction and sped up response times.
- By offering timely and dependable customer support, the ChatGPT company may increase sales and generate leads.

ChatGPT Implementation in Marketing Strategies

Businesses should think about taking the following actions to integrate ChatGPT in marketing efforts successfully:

a. Determine the precise aims and objectives you hope to accomplish with ChatGPT. Clarified objectives will direct your implementation process, whether it's to increase conversion rates, decrease response times, or increase customer happiness.
b. Identify Use Cases: Decide which components of your marketing plan ChatGPT can improve. This might involve content production, lead acquisition, targeted suggestions, or customer assistance. Prioritize deployment based on the possible impact of ChatGPT in these use scenarios.
c. Create conversational flows that are consistent with the tone and fashion of your brand. To ensure accuracy and consistency, provide a repository of predetermined answers to frequent questions and scenarios. These flows should be improved over time based on user feedback and data analysis findings.
d. Integration and testing: Add ChatGPT to your current marketing platforms or create a special solution based on your demands. Test the implementation thoroughly to verify accurate responses, seamless integration, and top performance.
e. Continuous Improvement: To find opportunities for improvement, track customer interactions, get feedback, and examine data. To improve its efficiency and take into account changing client needs, your ChatGPT installation should be updated and adjusted on a regular basis.

Guidelines for ChatGPT's Use in Business to Improve Customer Support

A. To Produce Personalized Responses
   - The fact that ChatGPT can be trained using a user's purchase history, feedback, and chat is one of the key factors in what makes it such an amazing AI tool.
   - ChatGPt displays comparable items and usage instructions to the consumer based on the user's profile's data about their past purchases.
   - ChatGPT can produce human-like content for clients depending on their emotions using sentiment analysis.
   - When trained to assess certain emotions, such as rage, frustration, happiness, or grief, ChatGPt reacts in a similar manner.

B. Response to Individuals' Questions Promptly or Quickly
   - ChatGPT replies instantly to client complaints and inquiries; it first analyzes the wording of complaints, typical questions, and inquiries before responding.
   - As ChatGPT answers to complaints and inquiries promptly and effectively, keeping the consumer informed of all his inquiries, it can improve the relationship between the customer and the business.
   - According to a tidio.com study, 62% of customers would rather utilize a chatbot to find an answer to their question than wait for a customer service agent.

C. By examining the chat or terms used by the lead
   - ChatGPT can sustain relationships with customers and produce leads. It analyzes the likelihood that a lead will become a customer by assigning them a number or score based on their communication or language.
   - In this way, ChatGPT can be used to generate leads as well. For instance, when a lead uses certain words that indicate their interest in the deal, this AI tool instructs the team members by mail or notification to contact that lead for further processing via phone calls or something else.

D. To address Customers' Common FAQs
   - ChatGPT analyzes the corporate website and frequently asked inquiries from customers to provide human-like responses and pointers to the relevant sources.
   - A business can save time and resources by teaching ChatGPT to respond to frequently asked inquiries from clients, freeing up staff for work on trickier or more involved tasks.

Overcoming Obstacles in AI-Powered Customer Engagement

Although AI-powered customer engagement has great potential, there are certain difficulties as well. Typical obstacles that businesses may run into include:

a. Privacy and security issues: In order to provide personalized experiences, AI-powered systems rely on client data. Businesses must, however, make sure that consumer data is handled safely and in accordance with privacy laws. Gaining and maintaining the trust of customers requires transparent data handling procedures and strong security measures.

b. Ethical Considerations: As AI technology advances, enterprises must guarantee that it is used ethically. This entails avoiding algorithmic biases, upholding response transparency from AI, and protecting user privacy.

c. Technical Restrictions: ChatGPT and other AI models have some restrictions when it comes to detecting subtle contextual cues or providing appropriate answers to confusing questions. These restrictions must be understood by businesses in order to manage client expectations appropriately.

CONCLUSION

To sum up, the ChatGPT App is a crucial tool for companies aiming to improve client interaction and spur growth. It is the perfect choice for elevating your customer interactions thanks to its sophisticated natural language processing capabilities, customisation choices, and seamless connectivity with your current platforms. By promptly responding to client questions and complaints, ChatGPT has improved the response time to customers. Customer engagement, workforce effectiveness, and customer satisfaction have all increased thanks to chatGPT, which has strengthened the company's faultless performance.

REFERENCES

Ao, L., Bansal, R., Pruthi, N., & Khaskheli, M. B. (2023). Impact of Social Media Influencers on Customer Engagement and Purchase Intention: A Meta-Analysis. *Sustainability (Basel)*, *15*(3), 2744. doi:10.3390u15032744

Ausat, A. M. A., Massang, B., Efendi, M., Nofirman, N., & Riady, Y. (2023). Can chat GPT replace the role of the teacher in the classroom: A fundamental analysis. *Journal of Education*, *5*(4), 16100–16106.

Bansal, R., Pruthi, N., & Singh, R. (2022). Developing Customer Engagement Through ArtificialIntelligence Tools: Roles and Challenges. In Developing Relationships, Personalization, and Data Heraldin Marketing, 5.0 (pp. 130-145). IGI Global.

Bansal, R., Shukla, G., Gupta, A., Singh, A., & Pruthi, N. (2023). Optimizing Augmented Reality andVirtual Reality for Customer Engagement. In *Promoting Consumer Engagement Through EmotionalBranding and Sensory Marketing* (pp. 24–35). IGI Global.

Gabrielson, A. T., Odisho, A. Y., & Canes, D. (2023). Harnessing generative artificial intelligence to improve efficiency among urologists: Welcome ChatGPT. *The Journal of Urology*, *209*(5), 827–829. doi:10.1097/JU.0000000000003383 PMID:36795957

Khan, R. A., Jawaid, M., Khan, A. R., & Sajjad, M. (2023). ChatGPT-Reshaping medical education and clinical management. *Pakistan Journal of Medical Sciences*, *39*(2), 605–607. doi:10.12669/pjms.39.2.7653 PMID:36950398

Lund, B. D., & Wang, T. (2023). Chatting about ChatGPT: How may AI and GPT impact academia and libraries? *Library Hi Tech News*, *40*(3), 26–29. doi:10.1108/LHTN-01-2023-0009

Mittal, G., & Bansal, R. (2023). Driving Force Behind Consumer Brand Engagement: The Metaverse. In Cultural Marketing and Metaverse for Consumer Engagement (pp. 164-181). IGI Global.

Painoli, A. K., Bansal, R., Singh, R., & Kukreti, A. (2021). Impact of Digital Marketing on the Buying Behavior of Youth With Special Reference to Uttarakhand State. In Big Data Analytics for Improved Accuracy, Efficiency, and Decision Making in Digital Marketing (pp. 162-182). IGI Global. doi:10.4018/978-1-7998-7231-3.ch012

Rathore, B. (2023). Future of AI & generation alpha: ChatGPT beyond boundaries. *Eduzone: International Peer Reviewed/Refereed Multidisciplinary Journal, 12*(1), 63-68.

Rivas, P., & Zhao, L. (2023). Marketing with chatgpt: Navigating the ethical terrain of gpt-based chatbot technology. *AI, 4*(2), 375-384.

Saputra, R., Nasution, M. I. P., & Dharma, B. (2023). The Impact of Using AI Chat GPT on Marketing Effectiveness: A Case Study on Instagram Marketing. *Indonesian Journal of Economics and Management*, *3*(3), 603–617.

Singh, H., Jain, G., Munjal, A., & Rakesh, S. (2019). Blockchain Technology in Corporate Governance: Disrupting Chain Reaction or Not? *Corporate Governance (Bradford)*, *20*(1), 67–86. doi:10.1108/CG-07-2018-0261

Singh, H., & Singh, A. (2023). ChatGPT: Systematic Review, Applications, and Agenda for Multidisciplinary Research. *Journal of Chinese Economic and Business Studies*, *21*(2), 193–212. doi:10.1080/14765284.2023.2210482

KEY TERMS AND DEFINITIONS

Chatbot: A chatbot is a computer software created to mimic conversations with human users, particularly online.

ChatGPT: ChatGPT is a conversational model with AI at its core created by OpenAI that uses deep learning techniques to produce responses that resemble those of a human.

Customer Engagement: The practice of building a relationship with current customers in order to increase brand recognition and customer loyalty is known as customer engagement.

Generative Model: Models that generate new data instead of just classifying or making predictions based on input data are known as generative models.

NLP: NLP is an area of AI that involves utilizing algorithms to analyze and interpret human language, such as text and speech, in order to extract meaning and useful information.

Chapter 8
Transforming Consumer Experience Through ChatGPT:
Challenges and Opportunities

Robertas Damaševičius
Vytautas Magnus University, Lithuania

Ligita Zailskaitė-Jakštė
Kaunas University of Technology, Lithuania

ABSTRACT

This chapter analyzes the transformative potential of ChatGPT, an AI-powered tool, in reshaping consumer experience across various industries. It provides an in-depth exploration of how ChatGPT, through its advanced capabilities in natural language processing and machine learning, can enhance consumer engagement, automate repetitive tasks, and deliver personalized responses to complex queries. The chapter also underscores the strategic role of ChatGPT in digital marketing and consumer support. The chapter analyzes ChatGPT-consumer Interaction (CCI), discussing the importance of CCI design patterns, prompt engineering and usability evaluation in creating effective and engaging consumer interactions, and provides a real-life case study. The chapter further discusses the opportunities that ChatGPT presents for businesses. It highlights how the tool can help organizations gain a competitive edge by providing faster, more accurate consumer service, and by leveraging consumer data to inform decision-making and create targeted marketing campaigns.

DOI: 10.4018/979-8-3693-0815-8.ch008

1. INTRODUCTION

Artificial Intelligence (AI) has been at the forefront of technological innovation, with its applications spanning across various sectors, including education (Rah-man and Watanobe, 2023), healthcare (Cascella et al., 2023), business manage-ment (Burger et al., 2023), engineering (Dimiduk, 2018) and others. One of the most significant advancements in AI is the development of generative models, such as the Generative Pre-Trained Transformer-3 (GPT-3), which has revolu-tionized the way we interact with machines (Archibald and Clark, 2023).

ChatGPT is one of AI programs, which become very popular in the short term. This AI chatbot is built on the GPT-3 model. It has garnered significant attention for its pronounced synthesis and language capabilities. It is an interactive conversational model that can respond to prompts in different text forms by disputing underlying definitions, asserting and contesting assumptions, and seeking and clarifying through follow-up questions (Goar et al., 2023). The sig-nificance of ChatGPT lies in its potential to transform consumer engagement for business tasks. By automating repetitive tasks and providing personalized responses to complex queries (Taecharungroj, 2023), ChatGPT can enhance con-sumer experience and improve overall productivity levels across organizations. Moreover, its application in digital marketing and consumer support services can provide businesses with a competitive edge, enabling them to deliver faster and more accurate consumer services. However, the integration of ChatGPT into existing consumer engagement strategies is not without challenges. Data privacy, algorithmic bias, and the need for continuous training and updating of the AI model (Kapočiute-Dzikiene, 2020) are some of the potential hurdles that businesses may face. Despite these challenges, the opportunities presented by ChatGPT are immense. By leveraging AI and ChatGPT, businesses can gain insights into consumer trends and patterns, inform decision-making, and cre-ate targeted marketing campaigns. This study aims to explore these challenges and opportunities, providing a holistic understanding of the role of ChatGPT in transforming consumer engagement.

The main aim of this study is to explore the transformative potential of ChatGPT in reshaping consumer experience and engagement behavior. To achieve this, the study aims to:

- Investigate the role of ChatGPT in enhancing consumer engagement behavior through interactions with technologies, automating repetitive tasks, and delivering personalized responses.
- Analyze the principals and models of ChatGPT-Consumer Interaction (CCI) it could be formalized using the concepts of design patterns, prompt engineering, and templates.

- Discuss the ChatGPT usability evaluation of CCI including qualitative, quantitative, and mixed methods.
- Examine the strategic role of ChatGPT in digital marketing, consumer support services, and engagement, with a focus on its potential to optimize salesforce operations.
- Identify and analyze the challenges associated with implementing ChatGPT, including data privacy, algorithmic bias, and the need for continuous training and updating of the AI model.
- Explore the opportunities presented by ChatGPT, particularly its potential to provide businesses with a competitive edge through faster, more accurate consumer services, and its ability to leverage consumer data for decision-making and targeted marketing campaigns.
- Provide recommendations for businesses on how to use effectively ChatGPT and other AI tools to improve their consumer engagement strategies and achieve better business outcomes.

This study contributes to the existing body of knowledge on AI-enabled consumer engagement.

- Comprehensive Analysis of ChatGPT: While there are studies that have explored the use of AI in consumer engagement behavior, this study is one of the first to provide a comprehensive analysis of ChatGPT, a state-of-the-art AI tool, and its role in transforming consumer experience.
- Practical Recommendations: The study goes beyond theoretical analysis to provide practical recommendations for businesses on how to effectively leverage ChatGPT and other AI tools to improve their consumer engagement behavior strategies and achieve better business outcomes.
- Cross-disciplinary Approach: The study adopts a cross-disciplinary approach, drawing on insights from computer science, business management, and marketing to provide a holistic understanding of the role of ChatGPT in consumer engagement.

These contributions are expected to advance the field of consumer engage-ment and provide valuable insights for researchers, developers, and practitioners.

The chapter is structured into several sections to provide a comprehensive exploration of the topic. First, the section provides a detailed discussion of the mechanics of ChatGPT and its role in enhancing consumer interactions. Then the section delves into the strategic role of ChatGPT in digital marketing and consumer engagement behavior, which focuses specifically on ChatGPT-consumer interaction. This is followed by a critical examination of the challenges asso-ciated with implementing ChatGPT, including issues related to data privacy, ethics, algorithmic bias, and the need for continuous training and updating of the AI model. The chapter then explores the opportunities presented by ChatGPT, particularly its potential to provide businesses with a competitive edge through faster, more accurate consumer support services, and its ability to leverage con-sumer data for decision-making and targeted marketing campaigns. The chapter concludes with a summary of the findings and implications for future research. Throughout the chapter, practical recommendations are provided to guide busi-nesses in effectively leveraging ChatGPT and other AI tools to improve their consumer engagement behavior strategies and achieve better business outcomes.

2. UNDERSTANDING CHATGPT

2.1 Overview of ChatGPT

ChatGPT is a state-of-the-art artificial intelligence (AI) program developed by OpenAI. It is built on the Generative Pre-trained Transformer-3 (GPT-3) model, which is one of the most powerful generative models in AI (Chatterjee and Dethlefs, 2023). It is a conversational AI model that has been trained on vast amounts of language data from various sources. Unlike traditional AI models that simply analyze objects and identify patterns, ChatGPT is capable to create new and unique text, making it a powerful generative AI (Ahn, 2023). The program has been used in various fields, including medicine, showcasing its astounding capabilities and usability compared to previous AI models (Ahn, 2023). For instance, it has been used to write a scientific article, pass a Master of Business Administration course, a law-school entrance exam, and even a medical license test (Gilson et al., 2023).

ChatGPT is equipped with a language model that can output common knowl-edge quite accurately, and can also provide tailored responses based on detailed questions (Ahn, 2023). ChatGPT could have applications in the field of health-care due to the large volumes of free-text information available for training mod-els (Arora and Arora, 2023). It is now acknowledged that we are getting close to artificial general intelligence for the first time since ChatGPT can create com-puter code, compose fiction, and make predictions about the future (Arora and Arora, 2023). It must be highlighted, nevertheless, that these technologies have the potential to be harmful in their current forms. This impact has been amply discussed in the context of mental health, where biases in algorithms have been seen (Arora and Arora, 2023).

2.2 Mechanics of ChatGPT

Natural Language Processing

ChatGPT is a conversational AI model that leverages natural language processing (NLP) to understand and generate human-like text. NLP is a subfield of artificial intelligence that focuses on the interaction between computers and humans through natural language. The ultimate objec-tive of NLP is to read, decipher, understand, and make sense of the human language in a valuable way (Chatterjee and Dethlefs, 2023). This technology uses a transformer-based model architecture, which is a type of model architec-ture introduced in a paper called "Attention is All You Need" (Vaswani et al., 2017). The transformer model uses a mechanism called attention to weigh the influence of different input words on each output word. In other words, instead of processing words in a sentence sequentially, it builds global dependencies be-tween input and output. This allows the model to parallelize better and handle longer sentences (Vaswani et al., 2017).

Machine Learning

ChatGPT is built on the GPT (Generative Pretrained Transformer) model, which is a type of transformer-based machine-learning model. The GPT model is pretrained on a large corpus of text data and then fine-tuned for specific tasks. The pretraining step involves unsupervised learning on a large corpus of text from the internet, where the model learns to predict the next word in a sentence. This allows the model to learn an understanding of syntax, grammar, facts about the world, and some level of reasoning abilities (Chatterjee and Dethlefs, 2023). The fine-tuning step involves supervised learn-ing on a specific task, such as translation or question answering. The model is trained to minimize the difference between its predictions and the actual out-comes, using a labeled dataset. In the case of ChatGPT, it was fine-tuned with a dataset containing pairs of prompts and responses, with the aim of generating human-like text that is contextually relevant to the input prompt (Chatterjee and Dethlefs, 2023). In order to improve the model, ChatGPT also makes use of reinforcement learning from user input. Human judges give the model a good score (reward) when it produces realistic replies or a negative score (penalty) when it produces strange results, and the model is then improved and strength-ened as a result (Chatterjee and Dethlefs, 2023).

2.3 The Role of ChatGPT in Consumer Engagement Behaviour Online

Enhancing Consumer Interactions.

ChatGPT has been recognized for its potential to significantly enhance consumer engagement behavior online. In a digital environment consumer engagement behavior occurs when interactions between enterprises and consumers appear and such behavior is based on con-sumers' different activities, such as searching for appropriate content, content consuming, writing, liking, commenting, creating different types of content and etc (Minelgaite and Zailskaite-Jakste, 2021).

As a conversational AI model, ChatGPT can generate human-like text that is contextually relevant to the input prompt, enabling it to engage in natural and meaningful conversations with consumers (Chatterjee and Dethlefs, 2023). In the field of consumer support services, ChatGPT can replace the work of sales personnel, interacting in a more natural and human-like manner through the employment of Natural Language Understanding (NLU) (Chaidrata et al., 2022). This allows the bot to answer the most common frequently asked ques-tions and process and export consumer orders, thereby improving the efficiency and effectiveness of consumer support services. ChatGPT's ability to understand and generate text in various formats enables it to enhance consumer interactions in unique ways. For instance, FaceChat, a web-based dialogue framework that integrates ChatGPT, enables emotionally-sensitive and face-to-face conversa-tions, delivering a highly immersive and engaging consumer experience (Alnuhait et al., 2023). This has potential applications in counseling, emotional support, and personalized consumer support services. ChatGPT can help to create en-gaging, attractive, emotional marketing messages/ads that ensure interaction between brand and consumer in social media. These marketing messages could ensure higher consumer engagement behavior while the content created by Chat-GPT can be based on market research, more relevant, prepared according to the specifics of different social media platforms, and adopted for different target audiences (Paul et al., 2023). While ChatGPT can enhance consumer interac-tions, it also has limitations. For instance, it has been found to provide incorrect answers to questions, indicating areas where the model may be prone to error (Rangapur and Wang, 2023). Moreover, assigning a persona to ChatGPT can significantly increase the toxicity of generations, with outputs engaging in in-correct stereotypes, harmful dialogue, and hurtful opinions (Deshpande et al., 2023). These findings highlight the need for further research and development to ensure the safe and effective use of ChatGPT in consumer interactions.

Automating Repetitive Tasks.

One of the key advantages of ChatGPT is the ability to automate repetitive tasks, thereby increasing efficiency and reduc-ing the need for human intervention. This is particularly beneficial in consumer support services provision, where chatbots like ChatGPT can handle routine inquiries, freeing up human agents to focus on more complex consumer issues (Chatterjee and Dethlefs, 2023). ChatGPT's ability to understand and generate human-like text allows it to interact with consumers in a natural and engaging manner. This makes it an effective tool for automating tasks such as answering frequently asked questions, processing orders, and providing information about products and services. By automating these tasks, businesses can provide faster and more efficient consumer support services, leading to improved consumer satisfaction and loyalty (Chatterjee and Dethlefs, 2023). The use of AI model-powered services like ChatGPT for automating repetitive tasks can lead to sig-nificant cost savings. By reducing the need for human agents, businesses can lower their operational costs and improve their bottom line. Furthermore, the use of AI can lead to more accurate and consistent responses, reducing the risk of errors and improving the overall quality of consumer support services (Chat-terjee and Dethlefs, 2023). While AI models like ChatGPT can automate many tasks, they are not a replacement for human agents. They are best used as a tool to support and enhance human efforts, rather than replace them. Human agents are still needed to handle complex inquiries and provide the personal touch that consumers often appreciate (Chatterjee and Dethlefs, 2023).

Delivering Personalized Responses.

ChatGPT's ability to deliver personal-ized responses makes it a valuable tool for enhancing consumer engagement. By understanding the context of a conversation and generating responses that are relevant to the input prompt, ChatGPT can provide personalized and engag-ing interactions that meet the unique needs and preferences of each consumer (Adewumi et al., 2020). In healthcare, ChatGPT has been used to provide per-sonalized information and advice to patients. For example, the AI model was found to provide coherent and easily comprehensible answers, emphasizing the importance of an individualized approach in aesthetic plastic surgery (Xie et al., 2023). Also, ChatGPT has been used to explain complex subjects and provide interactive tools to develop skills for patient counseling, demonstrating its po-tential to deliver personalized learning experiences (Sallam et al., 2023). While ChatGPT can provide personalized responses, it is not without limitations. For instance, it may struggle to provide detailed or personalized advice in certain sit-uations, highlighting the need for human oversight and intervention (Xie et al., 2023). Moreover, concerns have been raised about data privacy issues and the risk of generating biased and inaccurate content (Sallam et al., 2023).

2.4 ChatGPT in Digital Marketing and Consumer Support Services

Strategic Role of ChatGPT

ChatGPT has a strategic role in digital mar-keting and consumer support services, serving as a powerful tool for content creation, consumer interaction, and automation of routine tasks. As a conver-sational AI model, ChatGPT can generate human-like text that is contextually relevant to the input prompt, enabling it to engage in natural and meaningful conversations with consumers (Chatterjee and Dethlefs, 2023). In the realm of digital marketing, ChatGPT can be used to create engaging and relevant con-tent to attract and retain a new audience using different online channels (brands' web pages, landing pages and etc). It can adapt its output to the target audi-ence, ensuring that the content is tailored to the unique needs and preferences of each consumer. This can lead to improved consumer engagement and loyalty, which are key objectives of digital marketing (Chatterjee and Dethlefs, 2023). In the context of consumer support services, ChatGPT can automate routine tasks such as answering frequently asked questions and processing orders. This can lead to faster and more efficient consumer service provision, improving con-sumer satisfaction and reducing the need for human intervention. ChatGPT can provide round-the-clock support, ensuring that consumers can get the help they need at any time (Chatterjee and Dethlefs, 2023). However, while ChatGPT has significant potential in digital marketing and consumer support services, it is not without limitations. For instance, the content generated by ChatGPT may not always align with the message or interests that a company wants to con-vey to its consumers. Furthermore, ChatGPT is not an expert in any particular field. Therefore, while it can provide recommendations and automate tasks, the final decision should always be made by a professional (Chatterjee and Dethlefs, 2023).

3. CHATGPT-CONSUMER INTERACTION

3.1 Principles of ChatGPT-Consumer Interaction (CCI)

ChatGPT-Consumer Interaction (CCI) is a critical aspect of the application of ChatGPT in various domains, including consumer service, digital marketing, and salesforce optimization. The principles of CCI are based on the capabilities of ChatGPT to engage in natural and meaningful conversations with consumers, provide personalized responses, and automate routine tasks. The interaction between ChatGPT and consumers is facilitated by the advanced natural language processing and machine learning techniques employed by ChatGPT (Paul et al., 2023). These techniques enable ChatGPT to understand the intent of consumers, generate contextually relevant responses, and learn from past interactions to improve future interactions (Naser et al., 2023; Nov et al., 2023; Bird, 2021). It was mentioned the ChatGPT limitations such as text generated by ChatGPT may not always correspond to a company's strategic goals, lacks self-awareness, and is not an expert in any particular field. The threats and risks related to biased information may appear as well. Therefore, professionals' role in defining tasks remains of big importance (Naser et al., 2023; Nov et al., 2023; Bird, 2021).

3.2 Mathematical Model of CCI

ChatGPT-consumer Interaction (CCI) can be formalized as a sequence of state transitions in a dialogue system.

Let's denote a dialogue as $D = U_1, S_1, U_2, S_2, ..., U_n, S_n$, where U_i is the i-th consumer query and S_i is the i-th system (ChatGPT) response. Each query U_i and response S_i can be represented as a sequence of tokens, i.e., $U_i = u_{i1}, u_{i2}, ..., u_{im}$ and $S_i = s_{i1}, s_{i2}, ..., s_{ik}$, where u_{ij} and s_{ij} are the j-th to-ken in the i-th consumer query and system response, respectively. The goal of ChatGPT is to generate a response S_i given the previous dialogue history $H_{i-1} = U_1, S_1, ..., U_{i-1}, S_{i-1}, U_i$, which can be formalized as a conditional prob-ability:

k

$$P(S_i|H_{i-1}) = P(s_{ij}|s_{i1}, ..., s_{i(j-1)}, H_{i-1}) \quad (1)$$

j=1

In practice, this conditional probability is modeled by a transformer-based language model, which generates each token s_{ij} based on the previous tokens and the dialogue history. The quality of the generated response S_i can be evalu-ated using a reward function $R(S_i, U_{i+1})$, which compares the system response S_i with the next consumer query U_{i+1}. The goal is to maximize the expected reward:

$$\max E[R(S_i, U_{i+1})] \quad (2)$$

S_i

This reward function can take into account various aspects of the dialogue, such as the relevance of the system response to the consumer query, the fluency of the generated text, and the satisfaction of the consumer.

3.3 CCI Design Patterns

Design patterns in CCI are a crucial aspect of the application of ChatGPT in various domains, including consumer service, digital marketing, and salesforce optimization. These patterns are based on the capabilities of ChatGPT to engage in natural and meaningful conversations with consumers, provide personalized responses, and automate routine tasks. The design patterns in CCI are facilitated by the advanced natural language processing and machine learning techniques employed by ChatGPT. These techniques enable ChatGPT to understand the in-tent of consumers, generate contextually relevant responses, and learn from past interactions to improve future interactions (Ratliff et al., 2013; Nov et al., 2023; Bird, 2021). Cia tikslinga pateikti izvalgas su pattterns ir kartojasi jau However, despite the significant potential of ChatGPT in enhancing consumer interactions with a company or brand, it is not without limitations. For instance, the text generated by ChatGPT may provide inappropriate information or misleading information, thus increasing the mistrust in brand (Ročkute et al., 2018).

3.4 CCI Prompt Engineering

Prompt engineering in CCI is a crucial aspect of designing effective and engag-ing interactions. It involves crafting the prompts that ChatGPT uses to initiate and guide conversations with consumers. The goal is to create prompts that are clear, engaging, and capable of eliciting the desired responses from consumers. Prompt engineering requires a deep understanding of both the capabilities of ChatGPT and the needs and preferences of consumers. It involves balancing the need for clarity and precision in communication with the need for natural-ness and engagement in conversation. The prompts should be designed in a way that they guide the conversation towards the desired outcomes, while also al-lowing for flexibility and adaptability in response to consumer inputs (Shafiee and Zechman, 2014; Sunny et al., 2021; Hildebrand et al., 2021; Borovikov et al., 2019; Estrada-Torres et al., 2021). However, despite the importance of prompt engineering in CCI, there is a lack of comprehensive research and guidelines on this topic. However, we can draw from general best practices in conversational design and prompt engineering in other AI contexts. The following strategy can be effective:

- Start with a Clear Purpose: The first step in prompt engineering is to have a clear understanding of what you want in the interaction to achieve. This could be helping the consumer complete a task, providing information, or simply engaging the consumer in a conversation. The prompts should be designed to guide the conversation toward this goal.
- Use Natural Language: The prompts should be written in a way that feels natural and conversational. This can make the interaction more engaging and less like interacting with a machine. It's also important to use language that is appropriate for the target audience.
- Provide Guidance: Especially in the early stages of the interaction, the prompts should guide the consumer on how to interact with the system. This could include suggesting possible responses or explaining what kind of information the system can provide.
- Adapt to the Consumer: The prompts should be designed to adapt to the consumer's responses. This could involve using machine learning techniques to understand the consumer's intent and generate appropriate responses. It could also involve using conditional logic to adjust the prompts based on the consumer's previous responses.
- Test and Iterate: Prompt engineering is an iterative process. The prompts should be tested with real consumers, and the feedback should be used to refine and improve the prompts. This process should be repeated until the prompts are effective at guiding the conversation toward the desired out-come.
- Balance Open-Ended and Closed-Ended Prompts: Depending on the context of the conversation, you might want to use more open-ended prompts to encourage the consumer to express themselves freely, or more closed-ended prompts to guide the consumer towards a specific response. Balancing these two types of prompts is an important part of prompt engineering.
- Handle Errors Gracefully: It's inevitable that the system will sometimes fail to understand the consumer's response, or the consumer will say something that the system wasn't expecting. The prompts should be designed to handle these situations gracefully, by asking the consumer to rephrase their response or by providing a default response.

These strategies can provide a starting point for prompt engineering in CCI, but they should be adapted and refined based on the specific context and goals of the interaction. Now, let's move on to the examples of effective strategies and best practices for prompt engineering in CCI:

- Understanding Consumer Intent: The prompts should be designed to understand the consumer's intent accurately. This involves using NLP techniques to analyze the consumer's input and determine their goal (Liu and Lane, 2019).
- Providing Contextual Responses: The prompts should provide responses that are relevant to the consumer's current context. This involves using machine learning algorithms to predict the consumer's next action based on their previous interactions (Wen et al., 2016).
- Personalizing Prompts: The prompts should be personalized to the consumer's preferences and needs. This involves using consumer profiling and recommendation systems to tailor the prompts to the consumer (Zhang et al., 2018).
- Ensuring Clarity and Conciseness: The prompts should be clear and concise to avoid confusion and ensure effective communication. This involves using language generation techniques to create prompts that are easy to under-stand (Li et al., 2016).
- Testing and Iterating: The prompts should be continuously tested and it-erated based on consumer feedback. This involves using A/B testing and consumer feedback analysis to improve the prompts (Li et al., 2017).

3.5 CCI Prompt Templates

CCI prompt templates are a framework for designing conversational AI prompts that can be used to gather valuable consumer feedback and insights during the development and evaluation of conversational systems. These templates provide a structured approach to engage consumers in natural conversations and elicit specific information. The formal specification of CCI prompt templates typically includes the following components:

1. Introduction: The prompt begins with a brief introduction to establish the context and purpose of the conversation. This can include information about the conversational agent, its capabilities, and the specific task or topic.
2. Preparatory Instructions: This section provides instructions to guide con-sumers on how to interact with the conversational agent. It may include information on the expected format of responses, any specific actions or queries consumers need to perform, and any constraints or limitations in the conversation.
3. Scenario and Task: The prompt describes a scenario or situation that consumers should imagine and respond to. It sets the stage for the conversation and presents a specific task or goal for consumers to accomplish through the conversation. The scenario can be designed to mimic real-world situations to make the interaction more realistic and meaningful.

4. Probing Questions: These are open-ended questions designed to elicit specific information or insights from the consumers. Probing questions can explore consumers' opinions, preferences, experiences, or any other relevant aspects related to the task or topic. They encourage consumers to provide detailed responses and promote a more engaging and informative conversation.
5. Follow-up Actions: This section provides guidance on any follow-up actions or steps that consumers may need to take after the conversation. It can include instructions on providing additional feedback, completing surveys, or engaging in further interactions related to the topic.

CCI prompt templates have gained adoption in both research and indus-try settings for evaluating and refining conversational systems. Researchers use these templates to collect data for training and evaluating models, identifying system weaknesses, and improving conversational agents' performance. Com-panies and organizations leverage CCI prompts to conduct consumer studies, gather consumer feedback, and assess consumer experiences with their conver-sational AI products. The adoption of CCI prompt templates in practice offers several advantages. Firstly, they provide a standardized and systematic approach to collecting consumer feedback, ensuring consistency across different evaluation sessions. Secondly, the structured nature of the prompts helps guide the conver-sation and ensure that relevant information is gathered. Thirdly, CCI prompts can be adapted to different domains and tasks, making them versatile for var-ious conversational AI applications. Finally, by using CCI prompt templates, developers and researchers can obtain valuable insights from consumers, lead-ing to iterative improvements and enhancing the overall consumer experience of conversational systems. CCI prompt templates provide a well-defined framework for designing conversational AI prompts, enabling effective data collection, con-sumer feedback, and system evaluation. Their formal specification and adoption in practice contribute to the development and enhancement of conversational systems by gathering valuable insights and improving consumer experiences.

3.6 CCI Usability Evaluation

Usability evaluation is a critical aspect of the development and implementation of any interactive system, including AI-based chatbots (Kuhail et al., 2023) like ChatGPT. It involves assessing how well consumers can learn and use the product to achieve their goals and how satisfied they are with that process (Nielsen, 1994). The evaluation can be conducted using qualitative methods (questionnaires), quantitative methods (metrics), and mixed methods.

Qualitative Methods

Qualitative methods involve collecting non-numerical data, such as consumer opinions, feedback, and observations. The interviews and focus groups can be used as well. These methods are often used to gain in-sights into consumers' experiences, perceptions, and attitudes towards the sys-tem (Creswell, 2013). In the context of CCI, qualitative methods can include consumer interviews, focus groups, and open-ended consumer feedback. For in-stance, a study by (Zhang et al., 2019) used consumer feedback to identify con-sumer concerns and issues that may hinder the effective use of a self-diagnosis chatbot. The study found that consumers expressed the need to receive more actionable information and complained that the system-generated diagnostic report was difficult to interpret. These findings highlight the importance of pro-viding more useful information that patients need and making the diagnostic report easy to understand.

For evaluation, one can use the System Usability Scale (SUS), a simple, ten-item scale giving a global view of subjective assessments of usability. It was developed by John Brooke at Digital Equipment Corporation in the UK in 1986 as a tool to be used in the usability engineering of electronic office systems. It consists of a series of statements to which consumers rate their level of agreement on a five-point scale. When it comes to evaluating ChatGPT-consumer dialogues, the SUS can be adapted to assess the usability of the chatbot interface and the overall interaction experience (Hidayat et al., 2022). This SUS evaluation can provide valuable feedback on the usability of ChatGPT, highlighting areas where the chatbot performs well and where improvements may be needed.

The Chatbot Usability Scale (CUS) proposed by Borsci et al. (Borsci et al., 2022) is a tool specifically designed to assess the usability of chatbots. It consists of 12 items, each rated on a 5-point Likert scale from 1 (Strongly Disagree) to 5 (Strongly Agree). The items are grouped into four categories: (1) Effectiveness (the chatbot's ability to provide the correct and complete answers), (2) Efficiency (the speed and effort required to interact with the chatbot), (3) Learnability (how easy it is to learn to use the chatbot), (4) Consumer satisfaction (the consumer's overall satisfaction with the chatbot). The CUS provides a more detailed assessment of chatbot usability compared to the SUS, as it takes into account the unique characteristics of chatbot interactions. By using the CUS to evaluate ChatGPT-consumer dialogues, we can gain insights into how effectively ChatGPT answers consumer questions, how efficiently consumers can get the information they need, how easy it is for consumers to learn to use ChatGPT, and how satisfied consumers are with their overall interaction with ChatGPT.

Quantitative Methods

Quantitative methods involve collecting numerical data that can be analyzed using statistical methods. These methods are of-ten used to measure consumer performance, such as task completion time, error rates, and efficiency (Albert and Tullis, 2013). In the context of CCI, quantitative methods can include usability metrics, log analysis, and consumer surveys. For example, (Zhang et al., 2019) analyzed the system log of a self-diagnosis chatbot to understand how health care chatbots would be used in the real world and what issues could impede the optimal use of this novel technology. The study found that many consumers dropped out of consultations, especially during their early phases. This finding highlights the necessity of enhancing consumer engagement at an early point.

Mixed Methods

Mixed methods involve the combination of qualitative and quantitative methods in a single study. This approach allows researchers to gain a more comprehensive understanding of the research problem (Creswell, 2013). In the context of CCI, mixed methods can include combining consumer inter-views with usability metrics, or combining consumer feedback with log analysis.

For instance, (Zhang et al., 2019) combined both quantitative and qualitative analysis on the system log of a self-diagnosis chatbot. The results shed light on the design of health chatbots to improve consumer experience and increase consumer engagement behavior. Usability evaluation of CCI is a complex pro-cess that requires a combination of qualitative and quantitative methods. The insights gained from these evaluations can guide the design and development of more consumer-friendly and effective chatbot systems.

4. REAL-LIFE EXAMPLES FOR CONSUMER INTERACTION AND ENGAGEMENT BEHAVIOR

ChatGPT, with its conversational abilities, has been deployed in various real-life applications for consumer interaction and engagement behavior. Here we discuss some notable examples and case studies that highlight the use of CCI design patterns, prompt engineering, and templates for consumer engagement behavior online. These examples demonstrate how ChatGPT can be applied to enhance consumer support services, provide personalized recommendations, and improve consumer experience in different domains.

Consumer Support Chatbots: Companies have integrated ChatGPT into their consumer service platforms to automate responses to consumer inquiries and provide instant support. By utilizing CCI design patterns and prompt engi-neering, these chatbots can handle a wide range of consumer queries, providing information, troubleshooting assistance, and resolving common issues. For ex-ample, a company may develop a ChatGPT-based chatbot to handle consumer inquiries about product features, order status, or technical problems. By using predefined templates and prompts tailored to different consumer scenarios, the chatbot can effectively engage with consumers, provide relevant information, and escalate complex issues to human agents when needed.

Personalized Recommendations: ChatGPT can be leveraged to deliver personalized recommendations to consumers. By analyzing consumer preferences and historical data, ChatGPT can generate tailored suggestions for products, services, or content. For instance, an e-commerce platform may employ Chat-GPT to interact with consumers and understand their preferences, such as their preferred product categories, features, budget, or style. Based on this informa-tion, ChatGPT can provide personalized recommendations, helping consumers discover relevant products and enhancing their shopping experience. Prompt engineering techniques, such as using specific cues or consumer preferences in the prompts, can improve the accuracy and relevance of the recommendations generated by ChatGPT.

Virtual Assistants powered by ChatGPT have gained popularity in con-sumer applications. These assistants can understand consumer queries, perform tasks, and provide helpful information. Virtual assistants equipped with CCI design patterns and prompt templates can engage in natural, human-like con-versations with consumers, helping them with tasks such as setting reminders, finding information, making reservations, or managing their schedules. These as- sistants can adapt to consumer preferences, learn from interactions, and person-alize their responses over time, providing a more intuitive and efficient consumer experience.

Interactive Content Creation: ChatGPT can be used to enhance con-sumer engagement by enabling interactive content creation. For example, in marketing and advertising campaigns, ChatGPT can generate conversational content, such as interactive advertisements, chat-based games, or immersive sto-rytelling experiences. By incorporating CCI design patterns and prompt en-gineering techniques, marketers can create compelling narratives that actively involve consumers in the content, making it more engaging and memorable.

Social Media Engagement: ChatGPT can facilitate consumer interaction and engagement on social media platforms using the elements of social engineer-ing (Grbic and Dujlovic, 2023; Vaiciukynaite et al., 2018). Interaction between consumer and brand can improve consumer's attachment to the brand(Kuvykaitė and Zailskaite-Jakste, 2013) Brands and influencers can employ ChatGPT to generate automated responses to consumer comments, messages, or tweets, en-hancing their social media presence and fostering consumer relationships. By leveraging prompt engineering and templates, ChatGPT can provide personal-ized, context-aware responses, maintaining a consistent brand voice and address-ing consumer inquiries or feedback.

These real-life examples illustrate the versatility of ChatGPT in consumer-AI interaction. By employing CCI design patterns, prompt engineering, and tem-plates, businesses can effectively leverage ChatGPT to enhance services for con-sumers, deliver personalized recommendations, create interactive content, and engage consumers across various domains. These applications showcase the po-tential of ChatGPT to improve consumer experiences, automate tasks, and aug-ment human capabilities in consumer-facing interactions.

4.1 Example of Real-Life Scenario

Consider a scenario where a consumer electronics company uses ChatGPT for consumer engagement behavior on its website and e-shoping. The company has a wide range of products, and consumers often have questions about product features, pricing, and compatibility. Here is how a typical conversation might look (also see Figure 1):

Consumer Initiation: The consumer visits the company's website and sees a chat window in the corner of the screen. The consumer clicks on the chat window and types, "I'm looking for a new laptop. Can you help me?"

ChatGPT Response: Leveraging its natural language processing capabilities, ChatGPT understands the consumer's intent and responds, "Of course! I'd be happy to help you find a new laptop. Could you tell me more about what you're looking for? For example, what will you be using the laptop for, and do you have a budget in mind?"

Consumer Follow-Up: The consumer replies, "I'll be using it for work and some light gaming. My budget is around $1000."

ChatGPT Recommendation: Based on the consumer's input, ChatGPT generates a personalized response, "Thank you for the information. Based on your needs and budget, I would recommend our XYZ laptop. It has a powerful processor for work tasks, and a dedicated graphics card for gaming, and it's priced at $950. Would you like more information about this laptop?"

Consumer Confirmation: The consumer is satisfied with the recommen-dation and asks, "That sounds good. Can you tell me more about its specifications and where I can buy it?"

ChatGPT Detailed Response and Call to Action: ChatGPT provides detailed specifications of the recommended laptop and directs the consumer to the product page where they can make the purchase.

Figure 1. Example of ChatGPT-consumer interaction

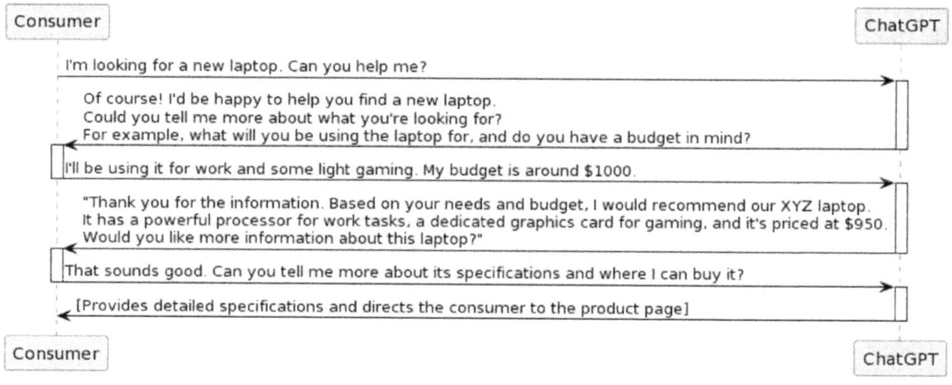

Here is a sample prompt that could be used to initiate the described inter-action with ChatGPT:

You are ChatGPT, a consumer service chatbot for a tech company that sells laptops among other products. A consumer has just opened the chat window on the company's website and typed, "I'm looking for a new laptop. Can you help me?" Your goal is to understand the consumer's needs and help them find the right laptop. Remember to ask for more details about what the consumer is looking for, such as what they will be using the laptop for and what their budget is.

This prompt sets the context for ChatGPT and instructs it to engage in a consumer service interaction. It also provides specific guidance on what information to ask for in order to provide a personalized recommendation. This interaction demonstrates how ChatGPT can engage consumers in a natural and meaningful conversation, provide personalized responses based on consumer input, and guide consumers toward a desired action (in this case, a product purchase). This CCI design pattern can be adapted and applied across various domains and use cases to enhance consumer engagement.

4.2 Interaction Evaluation

To evaluate the interaction between ChatGPT and the consumer, we can use a combination of qualitative, quantitative, and mixed methods.

Qualitative Evaluation

As it was mentioned above, qualitative evaluation involves assessing the quality of the interaction based on non-numerical data. In this case, we can look at the overall consumer experience in terms of conversation flow, the relevance of responses and consumer experience as follows:

- Conversation Flow: The conversation flows smoothly, with ChatGPT asking relevant questions to understand the consumer's needs and providing appropriate responses based on the consumer's input.
- Relevance of Responses: ChatGPT's responses are highly relevant to the consumer's queries. It accurately understands the consumer's need for a new laptop and their specific requirements (use for work and light gaming, budget around $1000). It then provides a personalized recommendation that fits these requirements.
- Consumer Experience: The consumer seems satisfied with the interaction, as indicated by their positive response to ChatGPT's recommendation. This suggests that ChatGPT was able to provide a good consumer experience.

Quantitative Evaluation

Quantitative evaluation involves assessing the interaction based on numerical data. In this case, we can look at metrics such as response time, number of turns in the conversation, and consumer satisfaction score as follows:

- Response Time: Assuming that ChatGPT's responses were generated instantly, the response time would be excellent.
- Number of Turns: The conversation involves six turns (three from the consumer and three from ChatGPT). This is a relatively short conversation, suggesting that ChatGPT was able to understand and address the consumer's needs efficiently.
- Consumer Satisfaction Score: If the consumer were asked to rate their satisfaction with the interaction on a scale of 1 to 10, their positive response suggests that they would likely give a high score.

Mixed Methods Evaluation

Mixed methods evaluation involves combining qualitative and quantitative methods to provide a more comprehensive assessment. In this case, we can correlate the qualitative assessment of the conversation's flow and relevance of responses with the quantitative metrics of response time and number of turns.

5. DISCUSSION

5.1 Challenges in Implementing ChatGPT

The integration of AI technologies like ChatGPT into consumer engagement behavior processes raises significant data privacy concerns. As these systems interact with consumers, they collect and process vast amounts of personal data. This data can include sensitive information such as names, addresses, and payment details, as well as less obviously sensitive data like browsing habits and purchase histories. The handling of this data must comply with various data protection regulations, such as the General Data Protection Regulation (GDPR) in the Eu-ropean Union and the California consumer Privacy Act (CCPA) in the United States (Michie and Leese, 2022).

Another challenge is the potential for algorithmic bias in AI systems. Bias can be introduced in various ways, such as through the data used to train the AI or the design of the AI's algorithms. This can result in discriminatory or unfair outcomes. For example, a chatbot might provide different quality of service to different consumers based on their demographic characteristics, which it infers from their language use or other data (Mehrabi et al., 2019).

AI models require continuous updating to maintain their performance and adapt to changing consumer needs and behaviors. This requires ongoing investment in data collection and processing, model training, and system testing and evaluation. It also requires careful management to avoid issues such as overfitting, where the AI becomes too specialized to its training data and performs poorly on new data (Yao and Huang, 2019).

5.2 Opportunities Presented by ChatGPT

Faster, Accurate consumer Service

ChatGPT can provide businesses with a competitive advantage by offering faster and more accurate consumer service. By automating consumer interactions, businesses can respond to consumer in-quiries in real-time, 24/7, without the need for human intervention. This not only improves the consumer experience but also reduces the workload of con-sumer service representatives, allowing them to focus on more complex tasks that require human judgment and expertise (Moro et al., 2017). ChatGPT can handle multiple consumer interactions simultaneously, decreasing waiting time. Such responsiveness can significantly enhance a business's reputation and con-sumer satisfaction levels, leading to increased consumer loyalty and retention (Huang and Rust, 2018).

Leveraging Consumer Data for Decision-Making

ChatGPT can also help businesses leverage consumer data for decision-making. By analyzing consumer interactions, businesses can gain insights into consumer preferences, behaviors, and needs. This data can be used to inform business strategies, improve products and services, and create personalized marketing campaigns (Ngai et al., 2009). ChatGPT's ability to process and analyze large volumes of data in real time allows businesses to make data-driven decisions quickly and efficiently. This can lead to improved business performance and a competitive edge in the market (Chen et al., 2012).

Targeted Marketing Campaigns

ChatGPT can be used to create targeted marketing campaigns. By analyzing consumer data, ChatGPT can identify pat-terns and trends that can inform marketing strategies, e.g., if ChatGPT identifies a trend of consumers asking about a particular product feature, businesses can create marketing campaigns that highlight this feature (Li et al., 2018). Chat-GPT can personalize marketing messages based on individual consumer data. This level of personalization can significantly increase the effectiveness of mar-keting campaigns, leading to higher consumer engagement and conversion rates (Harmeling et al., 2016).

6. CONCLUSION

This chapter has explored the transformative potential of ChatGPT in enhanc-ing consumer engagement and driving business growth. We have discussed the mechanics of ChatGPT, including its foundation in natural language process-ing and machine learning, and how these technologies enable it to understand and respond to consumer inquiries in a human-like manner. We have also exam-ined the role of ChatGPT in consumer engagement, highlighting its capabilities in enhancing consumer interactions, automating repetitive tasks, and delivering personalized responses. The strategic role of ChatGPT in digital marketing and consumer support services was also discussed, with a focus on its ability to opti-mize salesforce operations and improve consumer service efficiency. Furthermore, we delved into the principles and design patterns of ChatGPT-consumer Inter-action, discussing the importance of prompt engineering and usability evaluation in creating effective and engaging consumer interactions.

The findings of this chapter have several implications for future research. First, there is a need for more empirical studies to validate the effectiveness of

ChatGPT in enhancing consumer engagement and driving business growth. While the potential benefits of ChatGPT are clear, more research is needed to quantify these benefits and understand how they vary across different industries such as the tourism industry (Gursoy et al., 2023) and others. Second, future research should explore the ethical, privacy, security, bias, and misinformation implications of using AI tools like ChatGPT in consumer engagement behavior online. As businesses increasingly rely on AI to interact with consumers, it is crucial to understand how these tools impact consumer privacy and trust. Fi-nally, as AI continues to evolve, future research should investigate how newer technologies can be integrated with ChatGPT to further enhance its capabili-ties. For example, the integration of ChatGPT with other AI technologies such as image recognition and voice recognition could open up new possibilities for consumer engagement behavior online. In conclusion, ChatGPT represents a significant advancement in AI technology with the potential to revolutionize consumer engagement. By understanding its capabilities and limitations, busi-nesses can leverage this tool to enhance their consumer interactions, improve their operations, and drive business growth.

REFERENCES

Adewumi, A., Taiwo, A., Misra, S., Maskeliunas, R., Damasevicius, R., Ahuja, R., and Ayeni, F. (2020). A Unified Framework for Outfit Design and Advice. *Advances in Intelligent Systems and Computing*, *106*.

Ahn, C. (2023). Exploring ChatGPT for information of cardiopulmonary resus-citation. *Resuscitation*, *185*, 109729. doi:10.1016/j.resuscitation.2023.109729 PMID:36773836

Albert, B., & Tullis, T. (2013). *Measuring the user experience: collecting, an-alyzing, and presenting usability metrics*. Newnes.

AlnuhaitD.WuQ.YuZ. (2023). Facechat: An emotion-aware face-to-face dialogue framework. https://arxiv.org/abs/2303.07316v1

Archibald, M. M., & Clark, A. M. (2023). Chatgtp: What is it and how can nursing and health science education use it? *Journal of Advanced Nursing*, *79*(10), 3648–3651. doi:10.1111/jan.15643 PMID:36942780

Arora, A., & Arora, A. (2023). The promise of large language models in health care. *Lancet*, *401*(10377), 641. doi:10.1016/S0140-6736(23)00216-7 PMID:36841609

Bird, J. J. (2021). Improving customer service chatbots with attention-based transfer learning. arXiv:2111.14621v2, https://arxiv.org/abs/2111. 14621v2.

BorovikovI.HarderJ.SadovskyM.BeiramiA. (2019). Towards inter-active training of non-player characters in video games. arXiv:1906.00535v1, https://arxiv.org/abs/1906.00535v1

Borsci, S., Malizia, A., Schmettow, M., van der Velde, F., Tariverdiyeva, G., Balaji, D., & Chamberlain, A. (2022). The chatbot usability scale: The design and pilot of a usability scale for interaction with ai-based conversational agents. *Personal and Ubiquitous Computing*, *26*(1), 95–119. doi:10.100700779-021-01582-9

Burger, B., Kanbach, D. K., Kraus, S., Breier, M., & Corvello, V. (2023). On the use of ai-based tools like chatgpt to support management research. *European Journal of Innovation Management*, *26*(7), 233–241. doi:10.1108/EJIM-02-2023-0156

Cascella, M., Montomoli, J., Bellini, V., & Bignami, E. (2023). Evaluating the feasibility of chatgpt in healthcare: An analysis of multiple clinical and research scenarios. *Journal of Medical Systems*, *47*(1), 33. doi:10.100710916-023-01925-4 PMID:36869927

ChaidrataA.ShafeeuM. I.ChewS. K.ChenZ.ChamJ. S.YongZ. L.YapU. H.BahrinD. I. K. (2022). Intent matching based customer services chatbot with natural language understanding. http://arxiv.org/ abs/2202.00480v1

Chatterjee, J., & Dethlefs, N. (2023). This new conversational AI model can be your friend, philosopher, and guide ... and even your worst enemy. *Patterns (New York, N.Y.)*, *4*(1), 100676. doi:10.1016/j.patter.2022.100676 PMID:36699746

Chen, H., Chiang, R. H. L., & Storey, V. C. (2012). Business intelligence and analytics: From big data to big impact. *Management Information Systems Quarterly*, *36*(4), 1165–1188. doi:10.2307/41703503

Creswell, J. W. (2013). *Research Design: Qualitative, Quantitative, and Mixed Methods Approaches*. Sage publications.

DeshpandeA.MurahariV.RajpurohitT.KalyanA.NarasimhanK. (2023). Toxicity inchatgpt: Analyzing persona-assigned language models. https://arxiv.org/abs/2304.05335v1

Dimiduk, D. M., Holm, E. A., & Niezgoda, S. R. (2018). Perspectives on the impact of machine learning, deep learning, and artificial intelligence on materials, processes, and structures engineering. integrating materials and manufacturing innovation. *Integrating Materials and Manufacturing Innovation*, *7*(3), 157–172. doi:10.100740192-018-0117-8

Estrada-TorresB.del R'ıo-OrtegaA.ResinasM. (2021). Dialog-based automation of decision making in processes. arXiv:2109.00822v1. http:// arxiv.org/abs/2109.00822v1

Gilson, A., Safranek, C. W., Huang, T., Socrates, V., Chi, L., Taylor, R. A., & Chartash, D. (2023). How does chatgpt perform on the united states medical licensing examination? the implications of large language models for medical education and knowledge assessment. *JMIR Medical Education*, *9*, 9. doi:10.2196/45312 PMID:36753318

Goar, V., Yadav, N. S., & Yadav, P. S. (2023). Conversational ai for natural language processing: An review of chatgpt. *International Journal on Recent and Innovation Trends in Computing and Communication*, *11*(3s), 109–117. doi:10.17762/ijritcc.v11i3s.6161

Grbic, D. V., & Dujlovic, I. (2023). Social engineering with chatgpt. In *2023 22nd International Symposium INFOTEH-JAHORINA*. IEEE. 10.1109/INFOTEH57020.2023.10094141

Gursoy, D., Li, Y., & Song, H. (2023). Chatgpt and the hospitality and tourism industry: An overview of current trends and future research directions. *Journal of Hospitality Marketing & Management*, *32*(5), 579–592. doi:10.1080/19368623.2023.2211993

Harmeling, C. M., Moffett, J. W., Arnold, M. J., & Carlson, B. D. (2016). Toward a theory of customer engagement marketing. *Journal of the Academy of Marketing Science*, *45*(3), 312–335. doi:10.100711747-016-0509-2

Hidayat, A., Nugroho, A., & Nurfaizin, S. (2022). Usability evaluation on educational chatbot using the system usability scale (sus). In *2022 7th Inter-national Conference on Informatics and Computing*. ICIC.

HildebrandC.HoffmanD.NovakT. (2021). Dehumanizing voice tech-nology: Phonetic & experiential consequences of restricted human-machine interaction. arXiv:2111.01934v1, https://arxiv.org/abs/2111.01934v1

Huang, M.-H., & Rust, R. T. (2018). Artificial intelligence in service. *Journal of Service Research*, *21*(2), 155–172. doi:10.1177/1094670517752459

Kapočiute-Dzikiene, J. (2020). A domain-specific generative chatbot trained from little data. *Applied Sciences (Basel, Switzerland)*, *10*(7), 2221. doi:10.3390/app10072221

Kuhail, M. A., Farooq, S., & Almutairi, S. (2023). *Recent developments in chatbot usability and design methodologies*. Trends, Applications, and Challenges of Chatbot Technology. doi:10.4018/978-1-6684-6234-8.ch001

Kuvykaitė, R. and Zailskaite-Jakste, L. (2013). Communication in social media for brand equity building. *Ekonomika ir vadyba, 18*(142-153).

Li, J., Monroe, W., Ritter, A., Galley, M., Gao, J., & Jurafsky, D. (2016). Deep reinforcement learning for dialogue generation. In *2016 Conference on Empirical Methods in Natural Language Processing,* pages 1192–1202. 10.18653/v1/D16-1127

Li, J., Monroe, W., Shi, T., Jean, S., Ritter, A., & Jurafsky, D. (2017). Adver-sarial learning for neural dialogue generation. In *2017 Conference on Empirical Methods in Natural Language Processing,* (pp. 2157–2169). ACL. 10.18653/v1/D17-1230

Li, S., Da Xu, L. T., & Zhao, S. (2018). The internet of things: A survey. *Information Systems Frontiers, 17*(2), 243–259. doi:10.100710796-014-9492-7

Liu, B., & Lane, I. (2019). Towards better context-awareness in spoken dialogue systems: Distributional semantics for dialogue context representation. In *20th Annual SIGdial Meeting on Discourse and Dialogue,* 360–369.

MehrabiN.MorstatterF.SaxenaN.LermanK.GalstyanA. (2019). A survey on bias and fairness in machine learning. arXiv:1908.09635.

Michie, J., & Leese, M. (2022). Privacy and the pandemic: A social contract perspective. *Ethics and Information Technology*, 1–14.

Minelgaite, I., & Zailskaite-Jakste, L. (2021). Consumer engagement behav-ior perspective in social media: Mediating role and impact on brand equity. [JEECAR]. *Journal of Eastern European and Central Asian Research, 8*(2).

Moro, S., Cortez, P., & Rita, P. (2017). Business intelligence in banking: A literature analysis from 2002 to 2013 using text mining and latent dirichlet allocation. *Expert Systems with Applications, 42*(3), 1314–1324. doi:10.1016/j.eswa.2014.09.024

NaserM. Z.RossB.OgleJ.KodurV.HawilehR.AbdallaJ.ThaiH. T. (2023). Can ai chatbots pass the fundamentals of engineer-ing (fe) and principles and practice of engineering (pe) structural exams? arXiv:2303.18149v2, https://arxiv.org/abs/2303.18149v2

Ngai, E. W., Xiu, L., & Chau, D. C. (2009). Application of data mining tech-niques in customer relationship management: A literature review and classifi-cation. *Expert Systems with Applications, 36*(2), 2592–2602. doi:10.1016/j.eswa.2008.02.021

Nielsen, J. (1994). *Usability Engineering*. Elsevier.

NovO.SinghN.MannD. (2023). Putting chatgpt's medical advice to the (turing) test. arXiv:2301.10035v1. https://arxiv.org/abs/2301.10035v1

Paul, J., Ueno, A., & Dennis, C. (2023). Chatgpt and consumers: Benefits, pitfalls and future research agenda. *International Journal of Consumer Studies*, *47*(4), 1213–1225. doi:10.1111/ijcs.12928

Rahman, M. M., & Watanobe, Y. (2023). Chatgpt for education and research: Opportunities, threats, and strategies. *Applied Sciences (Basel, Switzerland)*, *13*(9), 5783. doi:10.3390/app13095783

RangapurA.WangH. (2023). Chatgpt-crawler: Find out if chatgpt really knows what it's talking about. https://arxiv.org/abs/2304.03325v1

RatliffL.J.DongR.OhlssonH.SastryS.S. (2013). Incentive design and utility learning via energy disaggregation. arXiv:1312.1394v2. http:// arxiv.org/abs/1312.1394v2

Ročkute, K., Minelgaite, I., Zailskaite-Jakšte, L., & Damaševičius, R. (2018). Brand awareness in the context of mistrust: The case study of an employment agency. *Sustainability (Basel)*, *10*(3), 695. doi:10.3390u10030695

Sallam, M., Salim, N. A., Barakat, M., & Al-Tammemi, A. B. (2023). Chat-gpt applications in medical, dental, pharmacy, and public health education: A descriptive study highlighting the advantages and limitations. *Narrative Journal*, *3*(1), e103. doi:10.52225/narra.v3i1.103

ShafieeM. E.ZechmanE. M. (2014). An agent-based modeling frame-work for sociotechnical simulation of water distribution contamination events. arXiv:1405.3342v1, https://arxiv.org/abs/1405.3342v1

SunnyM. M.BerghoferM.AslanI. (2021). *Towards tool-support for interactive-machine learning applications in the android ecosystem*. arXiv:2103.14852v1, https://arxiv.org/abs/2103.14852v1

Taecharungroj, V. (2023). "What can ChatGPT do?" Analyzing early reactions to the innovative ai chatbot on twitter. *Big Data and Cognitive Computing, 7*(1).

Vaiciukynaite, E., Zailskaite-Jakste, L., Damasevicius, R., & Gatautis, R. (2018). Does hedonic content of brand posts affect consumer sociability be-haviour on facebook? In *5th European Conference on Social Media, ECSM 2018*, (pp. 325–331). IEEE.

Vaswani, A., Shazeer, N., Parmar, N., Uszkoreit, J., Jones, L., Gomez, A. N., & Polosukhin, I. (2017). Attention is all you need. In Advances in Neural Information Processing Systems. ACL.

WenT. H.VandykeD.Mrkši'cN.Gaši'cM.Rojas-BarahonaL. M.SuP. H.YoungS. (2016). A network-based end-to-end trainable task-oriented dialogue system. arXiv:1604.04562.

Xie, Y., Seth, I., Hunter-Smith, D. J., Rozen, W. M., Ross, R., & Lee, M. (2023). Aesthetic surgery advice and counseling from artificial intelligence: A rhinoplasty consultation with chatgpt. *Aesthetic Plastic Surgery*. doi:10.100700266-023-03338-7 PMID:37095384

Yao, X., & Huang, J. (2019). Beyond the hype: A survey of business models in artificial intelligence. *Big Data Analytics*, *4*(1), 1–10.

Zhang, R., Nicholas, J., Knapp, A. A., Graham, A. K., Gray, E., Kwasny, M. J., Reddy, M., & Mohr, D. C. (2019). Clinically meaningful use of mental health apps and its effects on depression: Mixed methods study. *Journal of Medical Internet Research*, *21*(12), e15644. doi:10.2196/15644 PMID:31859682

ZhangS.DinanE.UrbanekJ.SzlamA.KielaD.WestonJ. (2018). Personalizing dialogue agents: I have a dog, do you have pets too? arXiv:1801.07243. doi:10.18653/v1/P18-1205

Chapter 9
In-Depth Outlook on the Use of ChatGPT

Shikha Dhankhar
https://orcid.org/0000-0002-1440-5389
Maharshi Dayanand university, Rohtak, India

ABSTRACT

ChatGPT is a flexible platform with many uses. ChatGPT may improve teamwork or company growth. In terms of technical innovation and the ability it has to improve people's lives, ChatGPT is hard to beat. The majority of current applications of AI are focused on automating previously manual tasks. ChatGPT demonstrates, on the other hand, that AI may evolve into a helpful helper that picks up new skills via regular usage. This study reviews ChatGPT's contemporary usage in different areas and businesses and examines its role in cryptocurrency. We have merely tapped the surface of ChatGPT's economic possibilities for all sectors. From revolutionary content creation to improved customer experiences and targeted product suggestions, this conversational AI system may unleash growth strategies. Among the many applications of ChatGPT in the cryptocurrency trading industry are real-time market analysis, historical asset appraisal, and risk management. Investors and traders may rest comfortably knowing they have quick access to information regarding ChatGPT's history, giving them peace of mind.

INTRODUCTION

The introduction of AI has had far-reaching effects on businesses, communities, and people. It can forecast and adjust to changes in its habitats and the stimulation it gets from the outside world thanks to its ability to reason systematically based on

DOI: 10.4018/979-8-3693-0815-8.ch009

inputs and learn through the differences in predicted results. Using deep learning and language models built on the Generative Pre-training Transformer (GPT) architecture, OpenAI's newly released ChatGPT greatly expands the capabilities of chatbots. Most often, language models use deep learning and transformer topologies of neural networks to try to estimate the probability of a sequence of words a normal human conversation is likely to make (Dwivedi et al., 2023). ChatGPT has been extensively utilized in a variety of natural language processing applications including chatbots, dialogue systems, and text production due to its remarkable performance on several benchmark datasets. As a result of ChatGPT's impressive results, researchers are once again considering how language models may transform the way people communicate with computers. ChatGPT is an intriguing NLP tool with a wide range of applications, such as language translation, question answering, text completion, and more. Moreover, ChatGPT has shown general knowledge and reasoning skills unprecedented in language models, thanks to its large size and sophisticated training procedures (Alawida et al., 2023).

The area of business and industry comprises a diverse array of applications, including operations and management, supply chain management, business analytics, transportation, human resources, marketing, e-commerce, accounting, finance, retail, real estate, and insurance.

ChatGPT is capable of providing assistance for a wide range of tasks, the primary advantages include enhanced efficiency and cost reduction, enhanced decision-making and risk management, higher accuracy in forecasting, optimal planning, decreased effort, and the ability to identify fraudulent activities. ChatGPT's relevance to several disciplines, including as academia, software engineering, and education, has been the subject of previous study. Despite the rising attention, however, there is a dearth of actual research on the possible effects of ChatGPT and the ensuing hype on AI-related financial assets. The anomalous returns for certain digital currencies with an artificial intelligence focus were 90 percent, according to significant research (Saggu and Ante, 2023). In this chapter, we will take a look at the role of ChatGPT in the cryptocurrency industry and present an overview of its current applications across a wide range of sectors and businesses.

LITERATURE REVIEW

Bahrini et al. (2023) OpenAI's ChatGPT (Conditional Generative Pre-Trained Transformer) is a cutting-edge AI system that can independently produce natural language conversation via the use of supervised machine learning and reinforcement learning. Using the transformer architecture and millions of conversations from multiple sources as training data, ChatGPT is the result. The system has a robust foundation for creating natural language dialogues because of the combination of pre-trained deep learning models and a programmability layer. Following a literature analysis, this investigation focused on 10 primary areas, including the business and industrial sectors, education, and government. They also tested the efficacy and compared the performances of GPT-3.5 and GPT-4 in an experimental investigation, and discovered that GPT-4 is superior. ChatGPT's extraordinary capacity to create natural-sounding replies belies its inventors' belief that it can entirely replace humans in most settings since it lacks the same degree of knowledge, empathy, and creativity. Yang and Menczer (2023) The ability of large language models (LLMs) to generate natural-sounding writing on a wide range of topics is astonishing. Some worry that they may be used to create deliberately misleading information, however, there is little hard evidence to support these claims at this time. This research presented a case study of a Twitter botnet that purports to use ChatGPT to produce human-like material. They found 1,140 accounts using algorithms and then manually annotated them to ensure they are real. These accounts establish a swarm of false identities that share characteristics such as the use of machine-generated material and stolen photos and the use of responses and retweets to communicate with one another. Promoting potentially malicious websites and disseminating destructive remarks are two main functions of ChatGPT. The coordinated actions of the AI botnet's accounts make them easy to spot, but state-of-the-art LLM content classifiers cannot tell the difference between bot and human accounts in the wild. These results provide light on the dangers presented by social bots with artificial intelligence. Esmailzadeh (2023) discussed the possible hazards of OpenAI's ChatGPT language generation model for counterterrorism and international security. Since its capacity to create human-like writing, ChatGPT has become one of the fastest-growing consumer apps, with over 100 million active users. The practical and ethical considerations about its strengths and shortcomings are still being debated. The use of current communication technology by terrorists has complicated the intelligence situation, making it harder for agencies to get important data. To avoid sophisticated intelligence gathering, terrorists have embraced new technology and developed operational security measures. Artificial intelligence has increased the risk of cyberattacks and espionage by allowing people and organizations to exploit new technology. This article examined the risks of ChatGPT in four areas: the impact of AI on future threats and international security, the impact of ChatGPT on cyberterrorism and AI, the risks of fragmented and secondary information for violence and sabotage, and psychological warfare against targets. This report offered insights and suggestions to help policymakers and academics use AI technology successfully while minimizing hazards. Wenzlaff and Spaeth (2023) In OpenAI's ChatGPT model, users may submit questions to be addressed by an AI that has been trained using supervised, reinforcement machine learning. The algorithm's output is contingent on both the data it has been fed and the information provided by its users. The research investigated the degree to which academic definitions of crowdfunding, alternative finance, and community finance differ from or align with those provided by actual humans. Their selection of crowdfunding, alternative finance, and community finance is based on the fact that there is no universally recognized meaning of any of these words in the academic literature. The work added to the burgeoning literature on the consequences of textual artificial intelligence on academics by filling a knowledge gap about the reliability of AI-generated responses. Saggu and Ante (2023) After the release of OpenAI's massive language model, ChatGPT, interest in AI technology generally, and crypto assets specifically tied to AI, saw a significant uptick. Through the use of a synthetic difference-in-difference approach, they found significant "ChatGPT effects," with average returns on AI-related cryptocurrencies ranging from 10.7% to 15.6% (35.5% to 41.3% in the two months after the ChatGPT debut). Furthermore, after the debut, Google search volumes, a surrogate for interest in AI, became important price indications for AI-related cryptocurrencies. They draw the conclusion that following the introduction, investors placed a higher value on AI-related cryptocurrencies because they saw them as having more promise or worth. Nguyen et al. (2023) looked at the link between investors' focus on dominant narratives and the price appreciation of narrative-related cryptocurrencies. When a story becomes widely shared, we discover that currencies associated with that story see a spike in value. As a result, there has been a rise in interest for the matching backstory in search engines as coin prices have risen. The data collected indicated that investors may utilize narrative attention data to their advantage when deciding how much of a coin's value to put into narratives. In addition, their findings provided context for the AI narrative, which has been spurred by the success of ChatGPT and is responsible for the recent strong price surge of cryptocurrencies connected to artificial intelligence. Sohail et al. (2023) Since its introduction in November 2022, Chat Generative Pre-trained Transformer (ChatGPT) has received a great deal of praise and enthusiasm. It performed well in a variety of areas, from passing tests to producing original literature. The problems and worries of prejudice and lack of confidence, however, continue to be obstacles. In order to give a taxonomy of ChatGPT research and investigate its applications, they provided a complete assessment of more than 100 papers on ChatGPT that are indexed by Scopus. They conducted a systematic review of the literature, focusing on finding recurring methods used in the various investigations. They also explored the wide variety of fields where ChatGPT has been put to use, including medicine, business, economics, computer science, linguistics, environmental studies, education, and science. By taking a closer look at these use cases, they could better understand the potential of ChatGPT to solve real-world problems. They also covered important topics like prejudice and trustworthiness in ChatGPT, highlighting the need for further work to be done in these areas. They also proposed areas for future study in ChatGPT, including possible solutions to existing problems and predictions for future progress. They realized ChatGPT's full potential if we used all of its features. Alawida et al. (2023) In-depth analysis of ChatGPT, a cutting-edge language model that is making significant strides in the field of generating text, is presented here. They examined the evolution of this system by dissecting its foundational components down to the smallest detail, including its training data, assessment criteria, and evaluation methods. They also looked at ChatGPT's strengths and weaknesses in other NLP tasks, such as language translation, text summarization, and conversation production. Additionally, they examined the advantages of ChatGPT over competing language generation models and described its use in a variety of contexts. The ethical and privacy concerns of using ChatGPT are also discussed in their research, along with potential solutions. Additionally, they explored ChatGPT's function in cyberattacks and identified associated security issues. Finally, they examined ChatGPT's performance across languages and domains and demonstrated its many industrial applications. This article provided a thorough analysis of ChatGPT's contributions to the study of NLP. Dwivedi et al. (2023) Transformative AI techniques, like ChatGPT, may create human-like writing in many circumstances. Technology brings possibilities and ethical/legal issues, with possible good and negative repercussions on organizations, society, and people. This article explored several disciplines, including computer science, marketing, information systems, education, policy, hospitality, tourism, management, publishing, and nursing, with 43 expert contributions. The authors believed ChatGPT may boost productivity in several sectors, including banking, hotels, and IT, and improve company operations like management and marketing. However, they also evaluated its limits, disruptions, privacy and security dangers, biases, abuse, and disinformation. No one agrees on whether ChatGPT should be banned or legislated. The paper highlighted necessary research in three topic areas: knowledge, transparency, and ethics; digital transformation of organizations and society; and teaching and learning. Scholarly research can discover the required skills, resources, and competencies. handling generative AI; evaluating training datasets and process biases; investigating ideal commercial and social conditions for generative AI applications; combining human and generative AI for diverse tasks; assessing text correctness. Discovering ethical and legal difficulties in applying generative AI in varied circumstances.

Industry-Specific Uses of ChatGPT

There is a diversity of potential for enterprises to use ChatGPT in their routine operational processes and software applications. Although there are certain inherent limits in the comprehensiveness of the responses supplied by this chatbot, it is already capable of significantly contributing to the growth of enterprises' financial performance and the improvement of client experiences. The business and industry domain includes a vast array of applications in operations and management, supply chain management, business analytics, transportation, human resources, marketing, e-commerce, accounting, finance, retail, real estate, and insurance. The primary opportunities consist of increased efficiency and cost savings, enhanced decision-making and risk mitigation, improved prediction accuracy and optimized planning, decreased workload, and fraud detection.

The many ways in which ChatGPT might be used in the business world's most prominent sectors are outlined and discussed in further detail below.

Banking

Bankers from across the globe were providing ChatGPT text prompts regarding very specialized topics within a few months of the beta version becoming live. These topics included staff retention credits, gamification of deposits, producing financial surveys, and so on. As a result of this "boom," the following use cases were implemented successfully (Victor, 2023):

1) The ability to tailor financial guidance to the demands of niche consumer profiles was a boon for the banking industry. This is because, in many cases, not enough effort is put into identifying the kind of customers that would provide the highest profits. ChatGPT might be used by banks to evaluate reams of internal client data on, say, investment vehicles and spending patterns. The results of these studies might be used to guide the development of sound financial recommendations.
2) ChatGPT may also be used to help reduce fraud and misconduct in the banking and financial sectors. To achieve this, we look at past consumer actions that led to fraudulent charges and use these patterns to make accurate predictions and provide thorough Suspicious Activity Reports (SARs).
3) ChatGPT will soon be able to assist with the creation of reliable Legal Contracts. This chatbot has already produced legal writing that is competitive with that of the best human attorneys.

Education

Technology and software applications in the education domain can be used for a variety of purposes, including but not limited to the following: online learning; language learning; academic and general research; pedagogical support; writing; exam and assignment evaluations and feedback; the development of educational content; the training of educators; and the enhancement of students' educational experiences. Gains in areas like science, programming, language, abstract writing, and learner engagement are just the tip of the iceberg of possibilities. Other areas where progress can be made include access to education, teaching aids, and personalized study materials; fostering greater inclusivity (through language support, personalized learning experiences, diverse and inclusive content, and accessibility features); and enhancing learning. By supporting equitable learning, stimulating conversation, and cultivating cultural competence, ChatGPT may be a powerful tool for creating diversity, equality, and inclusion in the classroom.

For instance, ChatGPT may facilitate the following activities within the context of academic and general research and teaching support (Bahrini et al., 2023):

- ChatGPT's teaching assistance features include the generation of new ideas and views, the facilitation of conversations on diversity and inclusion, the suggestion of visual aids (such as photographs and graphics), and the provision of advice on how to make presentations more interesting to the audience. Although it cannot grade examinations, it may help develop quizzes or tests, assess assignments, projects, and exams, and provide comments to students and instructors. It can also give examples in R, Python, Java, and other languages, as well as answer frequently asked questions and explain difficult topics.
- Help with research is available through ChatGPT, which may recommend suitable research methods (both qualitative and quantitative) and provide case studies of their use. In addition, it may be used to improve research accessibility, analyze and interpret data, summarize the most important findings, and provide avenues for further investigation. To get one of these, just tell the chatbot about the topic you want or paste the research into it.
- Help with Writing, ChatGPT can correct spelling, grammatical, and punctuation errors, as well as flag instances of plagiarism and highlight areas for improvement in student writing. It may also provide suggestions on how to better structure and brainstorm, how to strengthen arguments, how to include various writing styles, and how to adjust the length of sentences.

Since ChatGPT's usage in the classroom may have a significant impact on students' ability to learn, it is crucial that researchers and educators keep an eye on how it is being used.

Sales and Marketing

Marketers may benefit from ChatGPT by improving the degree to which they can tailor the material they provide to individual consumers. For this aim, this AI may be used in the following ways across channels including marketing campaigns, ads, and social media platforms:

- ChatGPT's Keyword Analysis takes huge swaths of user-generated text and returns a verbal analysis of the most sought-after terms.
- This chatbot's simplicity of copywriting is particularly useful for developing persuasive marketing and sales content for advocating for businesses and items. However, these textual reproductions are missing the personality and verve that may be easily added with little human interaction.
- A sophisticated chatbot like ChatGPT may be integrated into a product-focused website or app to automate the collection of customer feedback and the resolution of customer complaints.
- By instructing the AI to generate two versions of the product description, as well as collecting potent campaign information from various focus groups, it may be used for A/B testing.

Healthcare

Medical and healthcare systems, public health, mental health, biology, biotechnology, telemedicine, medical exams, pharmaceuticals, and even veterinary medicine may all benefit from developments in the healthcare and medicine arena. There are numerous exciting research projects looking at how ChatGPT might be used in the medical, public health, and healthcare systems fields. It may assist in increasing efficiency, saving costs, and boosting patient outcomes and animal health in healthcare settings including triage and symptom checks, as well as in biotech, pharmaceutical, and veterinary medicine settings. The dangers in this space raise a wide variety of ethical, legal, regulatory, and privacy issues. These worries include the potential for biased suggestions and inaccuracies in the system's output as well as data privacy and security concerns (Bahrini et al., 2023).

Artificial intelligence has several potential uses in the medical field. Particularly conversational AI's efficacy in streamlining and humanizing healthcare operations has been shown. Here are a few ways that is possible:

- Speech-to-text technology powered by AI is used in medical transcription, and when combined with ChatGPT, the resulting transcripts are far more thorough and accurate, allowing for quicker clinical decision-making and reporting.

- Doctors may use ChatGPT-driven Patient Triage to make quicker diagnoses. Patient vitals and symptoms fed into an AI may provide a possible diagnosis and next steps in therapy.
- Appointments with physicians may be made, non-medical people can acquire up-to-the-minute information about their conditions, and local treatment facilities can be found with the aid of patient-facing assistants that incorporate ChatGPT. When used in conjunction with a chatbot designed specifically for physicians, vitals monitoring using the aforementioned app may assist in notifying medical professionals of possible emergencies.
- To accurately define insurance coverage, it is important for doctors to have a complete picture of the patient's medical history, and ChatGPT's summarization features may help with that.

Programming

It is possible that ChatGPT is making things worse for software engineers in this period of widespread layoffs. However, if you utilize this AI in a smart way, it may help you become a better programmer overall. In this way:

- With the help of ChatGPT, learning to code is much simpler. This conversational AI can generate code fragments in response to nearly any user input in every available programming language, providing correct syntactical feedback and recommending better methods to write based on commonly used data structures and algorithms.
- Automated quality assurance Software Quality Assurance (QA) is an often-overlooked yet crucial part of the development process. ChatGPT was able to construct test scenarios and test cases for evaluating a login page's password recovery capabilities on the basis of this testing document. Additionally, it has the capacity to draft a Java and Selenium-based automation script for scenario testing.
- System design documentation may be created, updated, and read using ChatGPT. With this conversational AI, you can design a whole system from the ground up for creating a software product.

Art and Culture

Music, art, design, fashion, writing, science fiction, video games, virtual reality, the performing arts, museums, and social impact (social justice, environmental justice, activism, diversity, equity, inclusion, and social entrepreneurship) are all part of the arts and culture domain. There are several ways in which ChatGPT may be used to boost productivity and originality in this area. It has a wide range of applications, including but not limited to music analysis, literature, creative expression, fashion analysis, art curation, and gaming. ChatGPT can also streamline the content generation, design, and compilation processes. While preliminary research has shown that ChatGPT may improve certain cognitive abilities, additional study is required to draw firm conclusions. The potential for biased suggestions to perpetuate stereotypes or reinforce existing inequities is a unique hazard in the arts and cultural realm, along with privacy, ethical, and legal problems. This may have an impact on the ability of underrepresented groups to have their views heard in the realm of arts and culture (Bahrini et al., 2023).

Media and Entertainment

Even if you were to give ChatGPT completely random text prompts in order to see what kind of imaginative output it would produce, you would still find it fascinating. However, it has the potential to significantly alter the current state of the entertainment industry. Media professionals including screenwriters, directors, and reporters might benefit from ChatGPT in the following ways (Victor, 2023):

- Most people in the news media industry see ChatGPT as an impediment to innovation, hence the field of journalism is hesitant to include it in their creative processes. The fast-paced content-generating needs of today might be challenging for journalists and bloggers, but ChatGPT has helped many creative authors overcome writer's block.
- ChatGPT has shown near-human levels of creativity when it comes to composing film screenplays, interactive video game scripts, prompts for writers, and so forth. It may also generate original character names, story twists, and speech with several outcomes.
- OTT services may make use of recent developments in in-platform advertising approaches. Conversational AI may be added to the platform to allow users to conduct natural-sounding discussions with chatbots, resulting in more personalized suggestions. Additionally, user input may be used to generate ideas for upcoming films and series that are sure to attract an audience.

Use of ChatGPT in the Field of Crypto Research

One of the primary characteristics shown by ChatGPT is its ability to condense extensive volumes of data into essential information. The platform considers difficult and potentially informative texts as the most dependable and accurate sources of information pertaining to a certain subject. The chatbot is used for many research purposes, encompassing the examination of cryptographic protocols, market analysis, formulation of trading techniques, dissemination of current cryptocurrency news, and assessment of project tokenomics (Allen, 2023).

It is important to note that ChatGPT may not always provide correct information, so it should not be relied upon for direct financial advice. Let us examine some capabilities that ChatGPT might possess in the role of a cryptocurrency research analyst.

Summing Up New Projects

One may argue that the most prominent capability of ChatGPT is its aptitude to condense information and get fundamental insights from the given language and data. This tool facilitates the extraction of crucial information from intricate and comprehensive texts, such as whitepapers, blog posts, and wiki entries, in order to simplify them. Moreover, it is possible to instruct ChatGPT to assume the position of a proficient financial analyst with expertise in the field of cryptocurrencies. Alternatively, it may adopt the persona of a speculative trader with expertise in meme-based cryptocurrencies and investments of limited duration.

Conduct Fundamental Analysis

Numerous individuals engaged in cryptocurrency trading and investment have a keen interest in assessing the basic robustness of a given project. They focus on examining the inherent aspects that have the potential to influence its value and long-term sustainability. These variables include disruptive capabilities, alignment with market demands, distinctive selling propositions, and competitive advantages.

The procedure described may be laborious and time-intensive, often requiring the compilation of data from several sources, the verification of information by cross-referencing, and the exercise of critical thinking in evaluating numerous significant aspects. Fortunately, ChatGPT may be used to significantly streamline this procedure, facilitating expedited arrival at findings. By using ChatGPT to simulate the job of an experienced fundamental analyst, one may extract valuable information that may otherwise be overlooked.

Assess Tokenomics and Governance Model

Understanding the supply and demand dynamics of a token is of utmost importance for investors in comprehending the tokenomics of a project. Through the examination of several aspects such as a project's token supply, emission schedule, utility, demand, distribution, and governance, ChatGPT has the capability to provide significant insights pertaining to a project's prospective worth and long-term prospects.

ChatGPT may further assist in the assessment of a project's governance framework. ChatGPT has the capability to enhance comprehension of a project's finance management, decision-making processes, and related aspects by using targeted inquiries and presenting pertinent facts.

Predictive Analytics

ChatGPT employs predictive analytics, a potent tool in the trading sector, to help traders make better crypto asset investment choices. Predictive analytics differs from other types of machine learning in that its primary goal is to forecast the future by studying the past. Traders may make educated guesses about the future value of Cryptocurrency with the help of ChatGPT's historical performance analysis. When provided with a certain prompt and other indications, the AI will consider a number of measures to predict the price of a chosen cryptocurrency over a specified time frame.

ChatGPT only has access to data from the past; it cannot keep up with current events. As a result, its prognostic efficacy is likely overstated. ChatGPT is not perfect, but it may be useful for hypothesis testing when supplemented with your own intuition and targeted suggestions (Peters, 2023).

Risk Management

ChatGPT may be helpful for risk management in the cryptocurrency industry. It can give real-time risk analysis and warnings if it has access to data on digital assets, allowing you to better manage your exposure to risk. Its AI features enable it to recognize trends and provide you with useful advice for making wiser choices.

Keep in mind, nevertheless, that your own investigation is essential, especially when it comes to minimizing potential dangers. Even while ChatGPT can help you out, you still need to do your own research.

Knowledge of Current Cryptocurrency News

The volatility of the cryptocurrency market is what has attracted the attention of investors throughout the globe. Bitcoin, the first decentralized electronic currency system, launched in 2009 and has since spawned an entire industry. Many new cryptocurrencies have emerged throughout time, each with its own set of use cases that have helped to grow the cryptocurrency market. Proof of the market's variety can be seen in the emergence of DeFi solutions and the widespread use of DeFi applications.

By reading the most recent news stories related to the cryptocurrency market, users of ChatGPT may learn the finest strategies for trading cryptocurrencies. You may also specify your goals for gaining knowledge about crypto and DeFi developments in the press. Interested in hearing about the latest DeFi project improvement or the newest cryptocurrency token?

Cryptocurrency traders face complex choices, made all the more difficult by a lack of real-time market data. As cryptocurrency gains in popularity, more and more crypto- and DeFi-related news websites and applications have emerged. However, crypto traders may have difficulty sifting through the mountains of news items published by crypto news services in order to locate the information they need. By facilitating your access to relevant news articles, ChatGPT is a viable option in this situation. It may aid in locating informative articles on the topics, of DeFi initiatives, or crypto assets of your choosing (Howell, 2023).

The Procedure of How to Use ChatGPT for Crypto Research

In order to optimize the performance of ChatGPT, it is necessary to provide an appropriate context or framework. In addition, it is possible to use the function of copying and pasting pertinent whitepapers, documents, or project material directly into the ChatGPT interface. GPT4 and other artificial intelligence assistants equipped with web surfing skills have the ability to interpret and comprehend hyperlinks. Through this process, ChatGPT has the ability to peruse the available resources in order to acquire knowledge and provide insightful analyses. It is important to note that improved data intake leads to increased relevance, reliability, and sophistication of insights.

Step One: Examine Crypto Protocols Using ChatGPT

For successful crypto research, it is essential to first get a thorough understanding of the project's foundations and underlying protocols. Asking targeted questions can help you get the data you need from ChatGPT to further your study.

Challenge and Remedy: Identifying the primary issue being addressed by the project and the nature of the proposed solution is the first step. ChatGPT's targeted prompts enable a thorough, but succinct, appraisal of the project's primary goals.

Technology and Procedure: ChatGPT also provides explanations of complex technical subjects in layman's language. If you need help understanding how to proceed with a project, just ask for an example.

Team History and Relevant Experience: The success of a project may be gauged by looking at the backgrounds of its primary creators and participants. Collect information about team members and their relevant experience by preparing questions to ask.

Step Two: Use ChatGPT to Conduct the Tokenomics Analysis

ChatGPT can efficiently examine the tokenomics of a project and provide the information you need to make informed decisions.

Token Distribution and Emission Schedule: To form an informed opinion about a project's potential market value, it is crucial to comprehend the token's total supply, circulating supply, and emission schedule.

Utility and Demand of Tokens: Tokens possess several applications, including governance, staking, and facilitating access to platform services. ChatGPT offers a handy means to explore the many utilities linked with the tokens of a project.

Token Allocation and Governance: Centralization and other problems may be avoided if tokens were distributed fairly and openly.

Step Three: Evaluate Community Involvement and Development Initiatives Using ChatGPT

Due to the fact that the anticipation around a project is just as vital if not more so, than the substance itself, market sentiment and community involvement are key variables. Communicating in ChatGPT is a useful tool for assessing a project's public profile.

Social Media Influence: Active participation in social media is crucial to keeping your audience interested and expanding your reach. ChatGPT may investigate the project's social media accounts and assess its visibility in different online communities at your request.

Development Initiatives: The project's dedication to achieving its objectives may be gauged by its rate of steady progress. ChatGPT may examine a GitHub repository or other evidence of a team's development activities to determine how active the team is.

Connections and Media Coverage: The market's perception and credibility of a project may be greatly influenced by its exposure in the media and via smart collaborations with investors. The spread and incorporation of a project's cutting-edge technology might benefit from well-established collaborations.

Step Four: Applying ChatGPT to Analyze the Governance Model

The longevity and effectiveness of cryptocurrency initiatives are affected by the protocols that govern them. You may use ChatGPT to learn about the influence of whales and the degree of centralization in a project's governance structure.

Step Five: Using ChatGPT to Determine the Value of a Crypto Protocol

There are a number of financial parameters that may shed light on a project's success and investment prospects, including total value locked (TVL), circulating market cap, fully diluted market cap, and produced fees/revenue. ChatGPT may examine these KPIs to shed light on the project's financial health. ChatGPT can calculate a protocol's worth if you provide it with data from analytics tools.

Few Crypto Chat Prompts from ChatGPT (Gwaro, 2023)

ChatGPT is a noteworthy tool that warrants consideration. When used effectively, it has the potential to facilitate the acquisition of influential and practical insights. However, it is essential to possess the knowledge of formulating inquiries in an appropriate manner. Below are a few illustrative instances of unambiguous and precise cryptographic prompts that might serve as a starting point.

Analyze a Token

Prompt: I invest in crypto. A new token is gaining popularity. This is "Bitcoin." Can you evaluate the token and blockchain's value? Describe its main features, application cases, and distinguishing traits from other tokens. Discuss its six-month performance, including market capitalization, trading volume, and community participation. Explain the token's growth potential and possible problems in the ever-changing cryptocurrency market. Create sections for easier reading of the analysis.

Result

Figure 2. Token and blockchain evaluation: Bitcoin
Source: Created by Author

Token and Blockchain Evaluation: Bitcoin

Bitcoin, the pioneering cryptocurrency, has garnered widespread popularity and is a cornerstone of the crypto market. In this analysis, we will assess the value of Bitcoin, outlining its main features, application cases, and distinguishing traits.

Main Features of Bitcoin:

1. **Decentralization:** Bitcoin operates on a decentralized blockchain, ensuring transactions are not controlled by a central authority, enhancing security and trust.
2. **Limited Supply:** Bitcoin has a capped supply of 21 million coins, making it a deflationary asset and a hedge against inflation.
3. **Security:** It utilizes robust cryptographic techniques to secure transactions and wallets.
4. **Pseudonymity:** Bitcoin transactions are pseudonymous, offering a degree of privacy while being transparent on the blockchain.
5. **Global Accessibility:** Bitcoin is accessible to anyone with an internet connection, facilitating cross-border transactions.

Regenerate

Application Cases:

Send a message

Summarize a White Paper

Prompt: Let us say I am 18 and know basic computers. Help me comprehend Bitcoin's whitepaper. Explain the paper's main ideas and developments in simple language. Briefly describe its goals, technologies, and issues. Explain Bitcoin's purpose and how it differs from government currencies and other cryptocurrencies. Get the summary right and prevent uncertainty.

Result

Figure 3. Understanding Bitcoin's whitepaper: A simple explanation
Source: Created by Author

View Explanations of Crypto-Related Terms

Prompt: Clarify Blue Chip Coins for me, please. Give me a rundown of what they are, how they function, any potential drawbacks, and some instances of their use. What effect will they have on blockchain technology generally? Make sure your explanation is easy to understand, concise, and logically laid out.

Result

Figure 4. Understanding blue chip coins: A concise explanation
Source: Created by Author

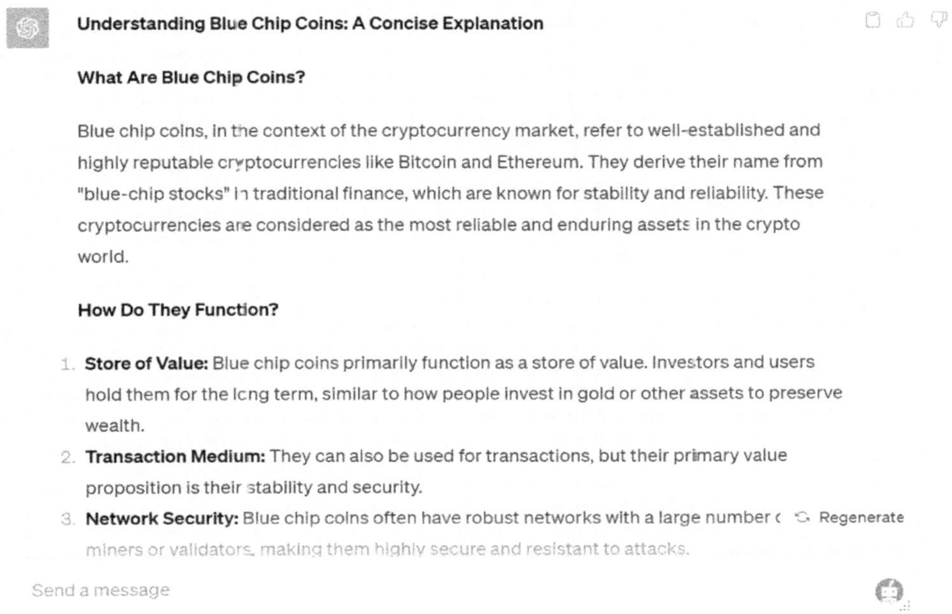

Formulate Plans for Investments

Prompt: I have invested in crypto staking for passive income. What cryptocurrencies are safest and give the best returns? Could you also analyze these cryptocurrencies' historical yearly percentage return, dangers, token lockup periods, and security measures to protect my investment? I want to know the minimal prerequisites and costs for these programs. Divide the analysis for readability.

Result

Figure 5. Crypto staking for passive income: A comprehensive analysis
Source: Created by Author

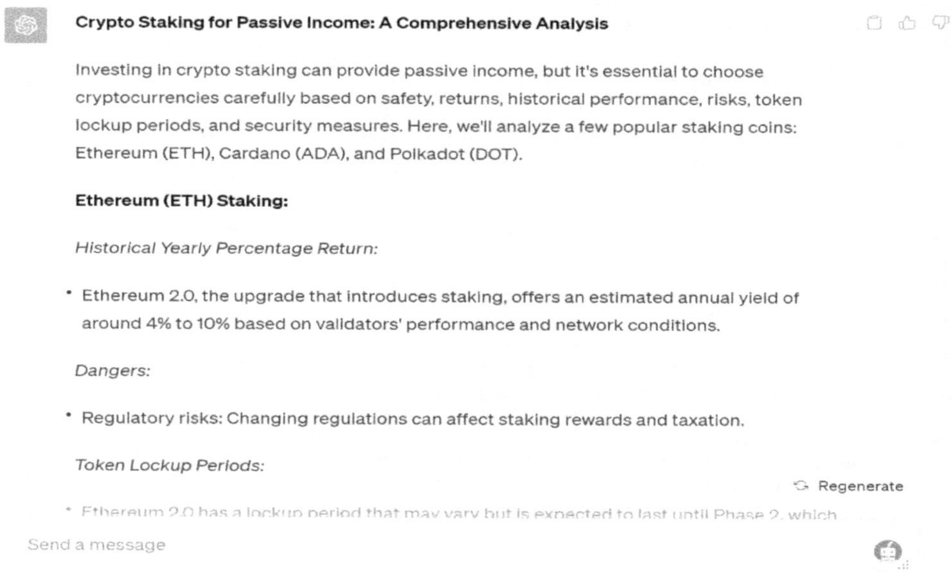

Similar to secret codes in video games, ChatGPT crypto prompts are a helpful tool for advanced users. They drastically cut down on the time and energy required to learn anything new. To succeed in modern society, you need access to the most relevant information as soon as possible. As a result, it is a good idea to harness ChatGPT's potential to enhance your crypto experience.

CONCLUSION

ChatGPT is very useful and adaptable, making it suitable for use in a wide range of settings and industries. To conclude, the aforementioned use cases barely scratch the surface of the immense commercial possibilities that ChatGPT provides across all sectors. This conversational AI system may open many development strategies in the banking, financial services, sales and marketing, education, arts and culture, media and entertainment, healthcare, and programming industries. Investors in the unpredictable cryptocurrency market may benefit greatly from ChatGPT due to its capacity to analyze large volumes of data and provide a consolidated overview of key information. ChatGPT is an artificially intelligent chatbot tasked with providing the most up-to-date and relevant information available on a given subject. Reviews, crypto protocols, value, and tokenomics may all be analyzed and discovered with the platform's assistance.

REFERENCES

Alawida, M., Mejri, S., Mehmood, A., Chikhaoui, B., & Isaac Abiodun, O. (2023). A comprehensive study of chatgpt: Advancements, limitations, and ethical considerations in Natural Language Processing and cybersecurity. *Information (Basel)*, *14*(8), 462. doi:10.3390/info14080462

Allen, N. J. (2023, July 23). *Productive ways to use CHATGPT to turbocharge crypto research*. The Coin Republic. https://www.thecoinrepublic.com/2023/07/23/productive-ways-to-use-chatgpt-to-turbocharge-crypto-research/

Bahrini, A., Khamoshifar, M., Abbasimehr, H., Riggs, R. J., Esmaeili, M., Majdabadkohne, R. M., & Pasehvar, M. (2023). CHATGPT: Applications, opportunities, and threats. *2023 Systems and Information Engineering Design Symposium (SIEDS)*. IEEE. 10.1109/SIEDS58326.2023.10137850

CoinMarketCap. (2023, June 1). *How to use CHATGPT for crypto research: CoinMarketCap*. CoinMarketCap Academy. https://coinmarketcap.com/alexandria/article/how-to-use-chatgpt-for-crypto-research

Dilmegani, C. (2023a, August 21). *40 chatgpt use cases in 2023*. AIMultiple. https://research.aimultiple.com/chatgpt-use-cases

Dwivedi, Y. K., Kshetri, N., Hughes, L., Slade, E. L., Jeyaraj, A., Kar, A. K., Baabdullah, A. M., Koohang, A., Raghavan, V., Ahuja, M., Albanna, H., Albashrawi, M. A., Al-Busaidi, A. S., Balakrishnan, J., Barlette, Y., Basu, S., Bose, I., Brooks, L., Buhalis, D., & Wright, R. (2023). Opinion paper: "so what if chatgpt wrote it?" multidisciplinary perspectives on opportunities, challenges and implications of Generative Conversational AI for Research, practice and policy. *International Journal of Information Management*, *71*, 102642. doi:10.1016/j.ijinfomgt.2023.102642

Esmailzadeh, Y. (2023). Potential Risks of ChatGPT: Implications for Counterterrorism and International Security. *International Journal of Multicultural and Multireligious Understanding*, *10*(4), 535–543. doi org/10.18415/ijmmu.v10i4.4590

Howell, J. (2023, September 15). *5 ways CHATGPT can help with crypto trading*. 101 Blockchains. https://101blockchains.com/chatgpt-in-crypto-trading/

Jaiswar, P. S. (2023, April 29). *How CHATGPT benefit crypto investors? experts say "can maximize profits."* Mint. https://www.livemint.com/market/cryptocurrency/how-chatgpt-benefit-crypto-investors-experts-say-can-maximize-profits-11682753323003.html

Nguyen, K. Q., Nguyen, T. H., & Do, B. L. (2023). Narrative attention and related cryptocurrency returns. *Finance Research Letters, 56*, 104174. doi:10.1016/j.frl.2023.104174

Peters, R. (2023, August 9). *How to use CHATGPT to research crypto in 2023: Ultimate Guide*. CaptainAltcoin. https://captainaltcoin.com/how-to-use-chatgpt-to-research-crypto/

Saggu, A., & Ante, L. (2023). The influence of CHATGPT on artificial intelligence related crypto assets: Evidence from a synthetic control analysis. *Finance Research Letters, 55*, 103993. doi:10.1016/j.frl.2023.103993

Sohail, S. S., Farhat, F., Himeur, Y., Nadeem, M., Madsen, D. Ø., Singh, Y., Atalla, S., & Mansoor, W. (2023). Decoding CHATGPT: A taxonomy of existing research, current challenges, and possible future directions. *Journal of King Saud University - Computer and Information Sciences, 35*(8), 101675. doi:10.1016/j.jksuci.2023.101675

Victor, A. (2023, September 21). *Top 17 industry applications of chatgpt*. Custom Software Engineering Services. https://insights.daffodilsw.com/blog/top-17-industry-applications-of-chatgpt

Wenzlaff, K., & Spaeth, S. (2022). Smarter than humans? validating how OpenAI's CHATGPT model explains crowdfunding, Alternative Finance and Community Finance. SSRN *Electronic Journal*. doi:10.2139/ssrn.4302443

Yang, K.-C., & Menczer, F. (2023, July 30). *Anatomy of an AI-powered malicious social botnet*. arXiv.org. https://doi.org//arXiv.2307.16336 doi:10.48550

Chapter 10
The Role of Digital Marketing on Customer Engagement in the Hospitality Industry

Sanjeev Kumar
https://orcid.org/0000-0002-7375-7341
Lovely Professional University, India

ABSTRACT

Digital technology plays a vital role in the hospitality sector, which creates a strong relationship with customers and a practical experience. Adopting online digital marketing strategies and different platforms include social media marketing, content writing, SEO, PPC, email and online marketing. Earlier, hotel and restaurant owners only believed in word-of-mouth and print advertising to attract customers. But nowadays, digital media has become the first choice to attract guests; it is more engaging content, and builds a solid connection with online platforms. Through online digital marketing, the hotel industry can target different demographics and connect with guests worldwide. Digital marketing gives customers memorable experiences while staying in hotels, dining at a restaurant, and attending mega-events. Customers always see the reviews, comments, and ratings of the hotels/restaurants on the social platform, and customers decide to visit the hotel/restaurant where digital networks play an essential role in promotional activities in the hospitality sector.

DOI: 10.4018/979-8-3693-0815-8.ch010

INTRODUCTION

Digital marketing plays a crucial role in the tourism and hospitality industry by providing practical strategies and tools to reach and engage with target audiences, promote destinations, attract customers, and enhance the overall guest experience (Ibrahim & Aljarah, 2023). Digital marketing allows tourism and hospitality businesses to establish a solid online presence through websites, social media platforms, and online listings. It enables them to showcase their brand identity, unique offerings, and values, creating a favourable impression among potential customers (Farook & Abeysekara, 2016). Digital marketing enables destinations to promote themselves to a global audience effectively. Through visually appealing content, such as photos, videos, and virtual tours, goals can highlight their attractions, natural beauty, cultural heritage, and unique experiences (Kandampully et al., 2018). It helps to generate interest, inspire travellers, and increase visitor numbers. With digital marketing, businesses can target specific customer segments based on demographics, interests, behaviours, and travel preferences. It allows for highly targeted marketing campaigns that reach the right audience with personalized messages, increasing the chances of conversion and customer engagement (Rahimian et al., 2021).

DIFFERENT DIGITAL APPLICATIONS IN HOSPITALITY MARKETING

Several digital applications and tools can be utilized in hospitality marketing. A well-designed and user-friendly website is essential for any hospitality business. It is a digital storefront providing information about the company, its offerings, amenities, and booking options (Kumar et al., 2023). Websites can also feature engaging content such as blogs, travel guides, and customer testimonials to attract and inform potential customers (Limna, 2022).

Search Engine Optimization (SEO) techniques help tourism and hospitality businesses improve their website's visibility in search engine results. By optimizing website content, using relevant keywords, and building quality backlinks, companies can rank higher in search engine rankings, attracting more organic traffic and potential customers (Bhandari & Sin, 2023). Pay-per-click advertising (PPC), such as Google Ads, allows businesses to display targeted ads to potential customers when searching for relevant keywords (Kapoor et al., 2022). This form of advertising can be highly effective in driving website traffic and generating leads, as businesses only pay when users click on their advertisement. Social media platforms like Facebook, Instagram, and Twitter allow tourism and hospitality businesses to engage with customers, share updates, and create meaningful connections. Social media marketing enables companies to build brand loyalty, encourage user-generated content, and promptly respond to customer queries and feedback (Khan & Abir, 2022).

Digital marketing helps businesses manage their online reputation by monitoring and responding to customer reviews and feedback across various platforms. Maintaining a positive online reputation is crucial for attracting new customers and building trust in the tourism and hospitality industry (Kushcheva, 2022). Collaborating with travel influencers and bloggers can amplify a business's reach and exposure. Influencers can create engaging content, share their travel experiences, and promote tourism and hospitality offerings to their followers, potentially influencing their travel decisions (De Pelsmacker et al., 2018). Email marketing allows businesses to communicate directly with past and potential customers. By building an email list, companies can send personalized offers, updates, and newsletters to nurture customer relationships and encourage repeat bookings. Email marketing is a cost-effective way to stay top-of-mind and drive engagement (Todor, 2017). Online Reviews and Reputation Management: Online reviews substantially impact the perception of a hospitality business. Encouraging guests to leave reviews on TripAdvisor, Google, or Yelp can build credibility and influence potential customers (Proserpio & Zervas, 2017). Monitoring and responding to reviews promptly, both positive and negative, is crucial to maintaining a positive online reputation (ŞİRZAD, 2022). Collaborating with travel influencers or bloggers can boost a business's visibility and credibility. Influencers can create engaging content, share their experiences, and promote hospitality offerings to their followers, potentially influencing travel decisions (Jin et al., 2019). Partnering with influencers can expand reach, generate user-generated content, and attract new customers (Taylor, 2020).

Developing a mobile app specific to a hospitality business can enhance the guest experience. Mobile apps can offer features such as easy booking, in-app concierge services, mobile check-in/check-out, personalized recommendations, and loyalty programs (Gibbs et al., 2016). Mobile apps provide convenience, increase engagement, and allow for direct communication with guests (McLean et al., 2018). VR and AR technologies offer immersive experiences to showcase accommodations, venues, attractions, and destinations (Nayyar et al., 2018). Virtual tours, 360-degree videos, and augmented reality applications can give potential guests a realistic preview of the experience, helping them make informed booking decisions (Dhiraj et al., 2023). Customer Relationship Management (CRM) Digital marketing tools and techniques enable businesses to collect and analyze customer data, understanding customer preferences, behaviour patterns, and purchase history (Mehralian & Khazaee, 2022). This information can be used to create personalized marketing campaigns, improve customer service, and foster long-term relationships with customers (Naim, 2022). Optimizing digital marketing efforts for mobile platforms is crucial as mobile usage continues to rise. Mobile marketing strategies, such as mobile-responsive websites, mobile apps, and location-based targeting, can enhance the user experience and attract customers who prefer to research, book, and engage with tourism and hospitality businesses through their mobile devices (Chaffey & Smith, 2022).

Figure 1. Authors compilation components of digital marketing

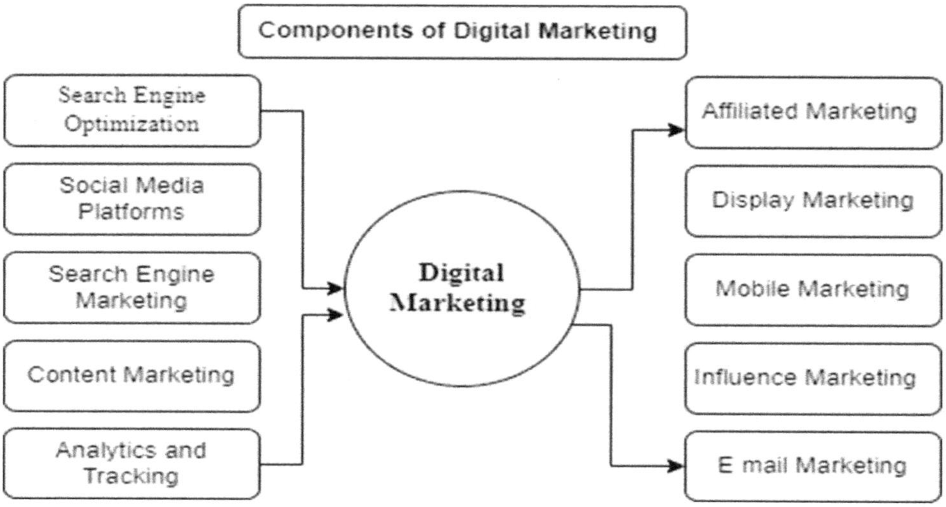

IMPACT OF DIGITAL MARKETING IN THE TOURISM AND HOSPITALITY INDUSTRY

Digital marketing has had a significant impact on the tourism and hospitality industry. Digital marketing has expanded the reach of tourism and hospitality businesses. Businesses can target and reach a global audience through various online channels, increasing their visibility and exposure (Sakas et al., 2022). It has opened opportunities to attract customers from different locations and tap into new markets. Digital marketing allows for interactive and engaging experiences with customers. Social media platforms, email marketing, and online communities enable businesses to interact directly with customers, answer queries, and address concerns (Khan & Abir, 2022). This engagement builds trust, strengthens customer relationships, and encourages repeat business. Digital marketing facilitates personalized marketing strategies. By leveraging customer data, companies can deliver customized content and offers to individual customers (Ansari et al., 2019). This personalization creates a more personalized and relevant experience, increasing the chances of conversion and customer loyalty (Smith, 2011). The rise of online travel agencies (OTAs) and hotel booking platforms has transformed the booking process. Digital marketing has enabled businesses to optimize their presence on these platforms, making it easier for customers to find and book accommodations, flights, and other travel services (Parmar et al., 2009). This convenience has significantly increased online bookings and streamlined the reservation process (Kim & Kim, 2004).

Digital marketing has revolutionized destination promotion. Businesses and tourism boards can showcase destinations through visually appealing content, such as high-quality images, videos, and virtual tours (Hays et al., 2013). It allows potential travellers to explore and experience destinations virtually, creating excitement and generating interest in visiting (Dogra & Kale, 2020). Digital marketing can be more cost-effective compared to traditional marketing channels. Online advertising, social media marketing, and email campaigns often cost less than conventional advertising. It allows businesses with smaller budgets to effectively compete and reach their target audience. Digital marketing has levelled the playing field for businesses of all sizes. Smaller companies can effectively compete with larger ones by leveraging digital marketing strategies and tactics. With a well-executed digital marketing plan, companies can differentiate themselves, target niche markets, and gain a competitive edge (Saura et al., 2019).

BENEFITS OF DIGITAL MARKETING IN THE TOURISM AND HOSPITALITY INDUSTRY

Increased Reach and Global Audience: Digital marketing allows tourism and hospitality businesses to reach a wider audience beyond their local market. Through online channels such as websites, social media platforms, and online travel agencies (OTAs), businesses can connect with potential customers worldwide, expanding their reach and attracting international visitors (Leite & Azevedo, 2017). Digital marketing enables businesses to establish and enhance their brand image. Companies can create a strong brand identity through consistent branding across various digital channels and differentiate themselves from competitors (Erisher et al., 2014). Additionally, digital marketing allows businesses to monitor and manage their online reputation by responding to customer reviews, addressing complaints, and highlighting positive experiences (Christopher & Gaudenzi, 2009). Unlike traditional marketing methods, digital marketing allows for precise tracking and measurement of marketing campaigns. Businesses can monitor key performance indicators (KPIs) such as website traffic, click-through rates, conversion rates, and customer engagement (Melović et al., 2020). This data enables businesses to assess the effectiveness of their marketing efforts, make data-driven adjustments, and achieve better results over time (Piñeiro-Otero & Martínez-Rolán, 2016). Digital marketing offers flexibility and agility in adapting to changing market dynamics and customer preferences (Moi & Cabiddu, 2021). Businesses can quickly modify marketing strategies, campaigns, and messaging to align with evolving trends and customer demands. This ability to pivot and adapt in real time is crucial for staying competitive in the fast-paced tourism and hospitality industry (Bist et al., 2022).

ISSUES AND CHALLENGES IN DIGITAL MARKETING

While digital marketing offers numerous benefits, there are also several issues and challenges that businesses may face.

Increased Competition: The digital landscape is highly competitive, with businesses vying for attention from the same target audience (Diez-Martin et al., 2019). Standing out and capturing the attention of potential customers can be challenging, especially in saturated markets or popular tourist destinations.

Rapidly Evolving Technology: Digital marketing relies heavily on technology, which is constantly evolving. New platforms, tools, and algorithms emerge regularly, requiring businesses to stay updated and adapt their strategies. These changes can be demanding and time-consuming (Kusumawati et al., 2019).

Information Overload: The abundance of digital content and marketing messages can lead to information overload for consumers. With so much information available, businesses must find creative ways to cut through the noise and capture the attention of their target audience.

Ad Blocking and Banner Blindness: Consumers have become adept at ignoring online advertisements, leading to ad-blocking software and banner blindness. Businesses must find innovative and non-intrusive ways to engage with customers to overcome this challenge.

Privacy Concerns: Data privacy and security have become significant concerns in the digital age. Consumers are increasingly wary of sharing personal information, leading to stricter regulations, such as the General Data Protection Regulation (GDPR) in the European Union. Businesses must navigate these regulations and build trust with customers by demonstrating transparent data-handling practices.

Return on Investment (ROI) Measurement: Measuring the ROI of digital marketing efforts can be complex. While digital analytics provide a wealth of data, it can be challenging to attribute specific outcomes to individual marketing initiatives. Determining digital marketing campaigns' true impact and effectiveness requires careful tracking, analysis, and attribution modelling.

Digital Ad Fraud: Digital advertising fraud, such as click fraud and ad impressions from non-human sources, remains a concern in digital marketing. Fraudulent activities can waste marketing budgets and skew performance metrics. Businesses need to implement measures to detect and mitigate ad fraud risks.

Skills and Expertise Gap: Digital marketing requires specific skills and expertise to execute effectively. Businesses may need help finding or developing talent with the necessary knowledge and experience to implement successful digital marketing strategies. Training and staying updated with the latest trends and best practices are crucial in addressing this challenge.

Negative Online Feedback and Reputation Management: The transparency of the digital landscape means that negative feedback or reviews can significantly impact a business's reputation. Monitoring and managing online reviews and addressing customer concerns promptly is essential to maintaining a positive brand image.

Platform and Algorithm Changes: Digital platforms and algorithms, such as search engines or social media algorithms, undergo frequent updates. These changes can affect digital marketing efforts' visibility, reach, and effectiveness. Businesses must stay informed and adapt their strategies accordingly to maintain optimal performance.

FUTURE TRENDS IN DIGITAL MARKETING IN THE FIELD OF HOSPITALITY

The area of digital marketing in the hospitality industry is constantly evolving.

1. **Personalization and Hyper-targeting:** As technology advances, businesses will increasingly focus on delivering personalized customer experiences. Using data analytics and artificial intelligence, companies can gather insights about customer preferences, behaviours, and past interactions to tailor marketing messages and offers specifically to individual customers (Leung et al., 2015). This hyper-targeted approach enhances customer engagement and improves the overall guest experience.
2. **Voice Search and Smart Assistants:** With the growing popularity of voice-activated devices like smart speakers and virtual assistants, voice search is becoming a significant trend in digital marketing. Hospitality businesses must optimize their online presence to ensure their content voice is search-friendly and compatible with platforms like Amazon Alexa, Google Assistant, and Apple Siri. Providing information and services through voice-activated devices will become crucial for capturing the attention of tech-savvy travellers (Sciarretta & Alimenti, 2021).
3. **User-generated Content and Influencer Marketing:** User-generated content (UGC) will continue to play a vital role in the hospitality industry. Travellers

often rely on reviews, ratings, and social media posts from fellow travellers to make decisions. Encouraging guests to generate and share content through social media campaigns, contests, or branded hashtags can help create authentic and influential marketing materials. Collaborating with travel influencers and bloggers can also amplify the reach and impact of digital marketing efforts (Smith, 2011).

4. **Artificial Intelligence (AI) and Chatbots:** AI-powered chatbots are increasingly being used in the hospitality industry to provide instant responses to customer inquiries, assist with bookings, and offer personalized recommendations (Limna, 2022). Chatbots can handle routine queries, freeing staff to focus on more complex customer interactions. AI can also be leveraged to analyze customer data, automate marketing campaigns, and predict customer preferences, enabling businesses to deliver more targeted and relevant experiences.
5. **Social Messaging Apps:** Messaging apps like WhatsApp, Facebook Messenger, and WeChat are popular communication channels for travellers. Hospitality businesses can leverage these platforms to provide personalized customer support, send booking confirmations, and share recommendations or promotions (Keshvadi et al., 2020). Utilizing chatbots or AI-powered messaging to automate responses can streamline communication and provide real-time assistance to guests.
6. **Sustainability and Green Initiatives:** With increasing awareness of environmental sustainability, customers are seeking eco-friendly and socially responsible travel options (Sardianou et al., 2016). Hospitality businesses can incorporate digital marketing strategies to highlight their sustainability efforts, such as eco-certifications, energy-efficient practices, or local community involvement. Sharing these initiatives through content marketing and social media can attract environmentally conscious travellers.
7. **Video Marketing:** Video content continues to dominate online engagement. Hospitality businesses can leverage video marketing to showcase their properties, amenities, and local attractions. Short videos, virtual tours, and live streaming can provide immersive experiences and capture the attention of potential guests. Platforms like YouTube, Instagram Reels, and TikTok offer opportunities to create and share engaging video content.
8. **Mobile-first Approach:** With the increasing use of smartphones for travel planning and bookings, a mobile-first approach is crucial in digital marketing for the hospitality industry. Optimizing websites, booking platforms, and marketing campaigns for mobile devices ensures a seamless and user-friendly experience. Mobile apps that offer convenience, personalized recommendations, and mobile check-in/check-out will continue to be in demand.

VISUALIZATION IN DIGITAL MARKETING

Visualization is crucial in digital marketing as it helps businesses convey information, engage audiences, and create memorable experiences.

1. **Infographics:** Infographics are visually appealing representations of data, statistics, or complex information. They help simplify and communicate information effectively. Infographics can be shared on websites, social media, or email campaigns to educate, entertain, and engage audiences.
2. **Images and Graphics:** High-quality images and graphics are essential in digital marketing. They help create visually appealing content, capture attention, and convey messages quickly. Whether it's product photos, lifestyle images, or illustrations, visual elements enhance the overall impact of marketing materials.
3. **Videos:** Videos have become a dominant form of content in digital marketing. They allow businesses to tell compelling stories, demonstrate products or services, and engage audiences. Whether it's short promotional videos, tutorials, or customer testimonials, videos are highly effective in conveying messages and evoking emotions.
4. **Infotainment:** Infotainment combines information and entertainment to create engaging and memorable experiences. It can include interactive quizzes, maps, videos, or gamified content. Infotainment captures audiences' attention and encourages active participation, increasing brand engagement.
5. **Data Visualization:** Data visualization helps businesses present complex data in a visually appealing and understandable manner. Charts, graphs, and interactive dashboards allow companies to analyze and present data in a way that is easy to comprehend, making it more engaging for audiences. Data visualization helps businesses make data-driven decisions and communicate insights effectively.
6. **Interactive Content:** Interactive content encourages audience participation and engagement. It can include quizzes, polls, surveys, maps, or calculators. Interactive content allows users to engage with the marketing material actively, enhancing their overall experience and increasing the likelihood of conversions.
7. **Storytelling:** Visualization is a powerful tool for storytelling. Businesses can use visual elements such as images, videos, and graphics to convey narratives that resonate with their target audience. Visual storytelling helps companies to connect emotionally with customers, build brand loyalty, and create memorable experiences.
8. **Social Media Visuals:** Visuals play a critical role in social media marketing. Eye-catching images, attention-grabbing videos, and visually appealing graphics increase the chances of content being shared, liked, and commented

on. Businesses need to create visually consistent and engaging visuals for their social media platforms to capture audience attention and drive engagement.

9. **Branding and Design:** Visualization is instrumental in creating a solid brand identity. Consistent use of colours, typography, and visual elements helps businesses establish a recognizable and memorable brand. Attention to visible details in websites, logos, advertisements, and marketing materials reinforces brand recognition and enhances the overall brand experience.

BEST DIGITAL MARKETING TOOLS FOR TOURISM AND HOSPITALITY

Nowadays, every traveller is well connected with digital marketing, especially in the hospitality sector, which requires laptops and mobiles for communication. It is straightforward for people to communicate their experiences and removes many difficulties for travellers. There are many tools used in tourism marketing, which include;

- Wix: It is one of the most effective tools in the digital market, with more than 200 million users worldwide. Which allows the user to create their websites and different temples related to travel. It has various options to adjust what you require in your sites. Users can make your sites without knowledge, which is more eco-friendly than others.
- DashThis: It is another digital marketing tool. It also looks like other digital applications, but users can create a Single "Source of Truth" for marketing KPIs. This application saves consumers a lot of time and has more unique features.
- Semrush: It is a hospitality site and an excellent tool for finding the right keywords for users. It is expensive compared with other applications, but it is used in most cases like PPC, Social media and other marketing channels.
- HubSpot: It offers different platforms for marketing, which includes sales, CRM, tourism and Hospitality. It is easy to use and has additional features like chat, conduct meetings and email tracking. The top-class travel agency generally uses it to book tours and packages for travellers,24/7, 365 days a year.
- Channable: It is also the most common application used in the hospitality sector, which consists of more than 200 sites and affiliated platforms that allow Google Ads and Microsoft advertising. It also enables the creation of online marketing campaigns, which can find a thousand details of flights and hotel availability.

- Iconosquare: The most popular marketing tool generally used in Social media analytics, which all social media platforms detail can find, like TikTok, LinkedIn, Facebook, and more. You can also create travel blogs, make your travel content, and share it on this platform.

CONCLUSION

The impact of ChatGPT and artificial intelligence has given a new shape to customer engagement, and it will save customers time and money, get more information, and quick responses related to any inquiry of the customers. The hospitality sector uses different applications. Nowadays, digital media become the first choice of customers to attract more customers, and it is more engaging content and building a solid connection with online platforms. Customers always spend some time on social media and give their reviews, comments, and ratings related to the services offered by the hotels/restaurants. Digital networks are essential in promotional activities, revenue management, profitability, marketing, and branding in the hospitality sector. ChatGPT and artificial intelligence can create a more engaging and profitable future for the hospitality industry. Every component of digital marketing impacts the customer's life and changing lifestyle. Day by day, customers are adopting the new technologies used by the star category hotels, and customers enjoy these services and more engagement with the hospitality sectors.

REFERENCES

Anshari, M., Almunawar, M. N., Lim, S. A., & Al-Mudimigh, A. (2019). Customer relationship management and big data enabled: Personalization & customization of services. *Applied Computing and Informatics*, *15*(2), 94–101. doi:10.1016/j.aci.2018.05.004

Bhandari, R., & Sin, M. V. A. (2023). Optimizing digital marketing in hospitality industries. *Startupreneur Bisnis Digital (SABDA Journal),* *2*(1).

Bist, A. S., Agarwal, V., Aini, Q., & Khofifah, N. (2022). Managing Digital Transformation in Marketing:" Fusion of Traditional Marketing and Digital Marketing. *International Transactions on Artificial Intelligence*, *1*(1), 18–27.

Chaffey, D., & Smith, P. R. (2022). *Digital marketing excellence: Planning, optimizing and integrating online marketing*. Taylor & Francis. doi:10.4324/9781003009498

Christopher, M., & Gaudenzi, B. (2009). Exploiting knowledge across networks through reputation management. *Industrial Marketing Management*, *38*(2), 191–197. doi:10.1016/j.indmarman.2008.12.014

De Pelsmacker, P., Van Tilburg, S., & Holthof, C. (2018). Digital marketing strategies, online reviews and hotel performance. *International Journal of Hospitality Management*, *72*, 47–55. doi:10.1016/j.ijhm.2018.01.003

Dhiraj, A., Kumar, S., Rani, D., Grima, S., & Sood, K. (2023). Blockchain Payment Services in the Hospitality Sector: The Mediating Role of Data Security on Utilisation Efficiency of the Customer. *Data*, *8*(8), 123. doi:10.3390/data8080123

Diez-Martin, F., Blanco-Gonzalez, A., & Prado-Roman, C. (2019). Research challenges in digital marketing: Sustainability. *Sustainability (Basel)*, *11*(10), 2839. doi:10.3390u11102839

Dogra, J., & Kale, S. S. (2020). Network analysis of destination management organization smart tourism ecosystem (STE) for E-branding and Marketing of Tourism Destinations. In Handbook of Research on Social Media Applications for the Tourism and Hospitality Sector (pp. 1–16). IGI Global.

Erisher, W., Obert, H. H., & Frank, G. (2014). Brand reputation management within the higher education sector: A literature review on higher education brand reputation management. *International Research Journal of Marketing*, *2*(1), 1–27. doi:10.12966/irjm.02.01.2014

Farook, F. S., & Abeysekara, N. (2016). Influence of social media marketing on customer engagement. *International Journal of Business and Management Invention*, *5*(12), 115–125.

Gibbs, C., Gretzel, U., & Saltzman, J. (2016). An experience-based taxonomy of branded hotel mobile application features. *Information Technology & Tourism*, *16*(2), 175–199. doi:10.100740558-016-0052-5

Hays, S., Page, S. J., & Buhalis, D. (2013). Social media as a destination marketing tool: Its use by national tourism organizations. *Current Issues in Tourism*, *16*(3), 211–239. doi:10.1080/13683500.2012.662215

Ibrahim, B., & Aljarah, A. (2023). The role of social media marketing activities in driving self–brand connection and user engagement behaviour on Instagram: A moderation–mediation approach. *European Journal of Innovation Management*. doi:10.1108/EJIM-08-2022-0452

Jin, S. V., Muqaddam, A., & Ryu, E. (2019). Instafamous and social media influencer marketing. *Marketing Intelligence & Planning*, *37*(5), 567–579. doi:10.1108/MIP-09-2018-0375

Kandampully, J., Zhang, T. C., & Jaakkola, E. (2018). Customer experience management in Hospitality: A literature synthesis, new understanding and research agenda. *International Journal of Contemporary Hospitality Management*, *30*(1), 21–56. doi:10.1108/IJCHM-10-2015-0549

Kapoor, V., Shah, S. P., Beckman, T., & Gole, G. (2022). Community-based vision screening in preschool children; performance of the Spot Vision Screener and optotype testing. *Ophthalmic Epidemiology*, *29*(4), 417–425. doi:10.1080/09286586.2021.1962918 PMID:34423736

Keshvadi, S., Karamollahi, M., & Williamson, C. (2020). *Traffic characterization of instant messaging apps: A campus-level view*. 225–232.

Khan, M. Y. H., & Abir, T. (2022). The role of social media marketing in the tourism and hospitality industry: A conceptual study on Bangladesh. In *ICT as Innovator between Tourism and Culture* (pp. 213–229). IGI Global. doi:10.4018/978-1-7998-8165-0.ch013

Kim, W. G., & Kim, D. J. (2004). Factors affecting online hotel reservation intention between online and non-online customers. *International Journal of Hospitality Management*, *23*(4), 381–395. doi:10.1016/j.ijhm.2004.02.001

Kumar, S., Dhiraj, A., Shah, M. A., & Rani, D. (2023). Application of Metaverse in the Hospitality Industry. In R. Bansal, S. A. Qalati, & A. Chakir (Eds.), (pp. 178–194). Advances in Marketing, Customer Relationship Management, and E-Services. IGI Global. doi:10.4018/978-1-6684-8898-0.ch011

Kushcheva, N. (2022). *Monitoring online reputation of tourist destinations in Finland*. 9442–9447.

Kusumawati, N. F., Kusumasari, T. F., & Lubis, M. (2019). *The Effectiveness of Digital Marketing for Show Up Company: Issues and Challenges*. 27–31.

Leite, R. A., & Azevedo, A. (2017). The Role of Digital Marketing: A Perspective from Porto Hotels' Managers. *International Journal of Marketing, Communication and New Media, 2*.

Leung, X. Y., Xue, L., & Bai, B. (2015). Internet marketing research in hospitality and tourism: A review and journal preferences. *International Journal of Contemporary Hospitality Management*, *27*(7), 1556–1572. doi:10.1108/IJCHM-05-2014-0268

Limna, P. (2022). Artificial Intelligence (AI) in the hospitality industry: A review article. *Int. J. Comput. Sci. Res*, *6*, 1–12.

McLean, G., Al-Nabhani, K., & Wilson, A. (2018). Developing a mobile applications customer experience model (MACE)-implications for retailers. *Journal of Business Research*, *85*, 325–336. doi:10.1016/j.jbusres.2018.01.018

Mehralian, M. M., & Khazaee, P. (2022). Effect of digital marketing on the business performance of MSMEs during the Covid-19 pandemic: The mediating role of customer relationship management. *37th Digital Marketing and Customer Behavior Science Conference.* SSRN. 10.2139srn.4195985

Melović, B., Jocović, M., Dabić, M., Vulić, T. B., & Dudic, B. (2020). The impact of digital transformation and digital marketing on brand promotion, positioning and electronic business in Montenegro. *Technology in Society*, *63*, 101425. doi:10.1016/j.techsoc.2020.101425

Moi, L., & Cabiddu, F. (2021). Leading digital transformation through an Agile Marketing Capability: The case of Spotahome. *The Journal of Management and Governance*, *25*(4), 1145–1177. doi:10.100710997-020-09534-w

Naim, A. (2022). Mapping Of Social Customer Relationship Management With Electronic Customer Relationship Management. *European Journal of Interdisciplinary Research and Development*, *2*, 14–25.

Nayyar, A., Mahapatra, B., Le, D., & Suseendran, G. (2018). Virtual Reality (VR) and augmented Reality (AR) technologies for the tourism and hospitality industry. *International Journal of Engineering & Technology, 7*(2.21), 156–160.

Parmar, V., Large, A., Madden, C., & Das, V. (2009). The online outpatient booking system ' Choose and Book ' improves attendance rates at an audiology clinic: A comparative audit. *Journal of Innovation in Health Informatics*, *17*(3), 183–186. doi:10.14236/jhi.v17i3.733 PMID:20074431

Piñeiro-Otero, T., & Martínez-Rolán, X. (2016). Understanding digital marketing—Basics and actions. *MBA: Theory and Application of Business and Management Principles*, 37–74.

Proserpio, D., & Zervas, G. (2017). Online reputation management: Estimating the impact of management responses on consumer reviews. *Marketing Science*, *36*(5), 645–665. doi:10.1287/mksc.2017.1043

Rahimian, S., ShamiZanjani, M., Manian, A., & Esfidani, M. R. (2021). A framework of customer experience management for the hotel industry. *International Journal of Contemporary Hospitality Management*, *33*(5), 1413–1436. doi:10.1108/IJCHM-06-2020-0522

Sakas, D. P., Reklitis, D. P., Terzi, M. C., & Vassilakis, C. (2022). Multichannel digital marketing optimizations through Big Data Analytics in the tourism and Hospitality Industry. *Journal of Theoretical and Applied Electronic Commerce Research*, *17*(4), 1383–1408. doi:10.3390/jtaer17040070

Sardianou, E., Kostakis, I., Mitoula, R., Gkaragkani, V., Lalioti, E., & Theodoropoulou, E. (2016). Understanding the entrepreneurs' behavioural intentions towards sustainable tourism: A case study from Greece. *Environment, Development and Sustainability*, *18*(3), 857–879. doi:10.100710668-015-9681-7

Saura, J. R., Palos-Sanchez, P. R., & Correia, M. B. (2019). Digital marketing strategies based on the e-business model: Literature review and future directions. *Organizational Transformation and Managing Innovation in the Fourth Industrial Revolution*, 86–103.

Sciarretta, E., & Alimenti, L. (2021). *Smart speakers for inclusion: How can intelligent virtual assistants assist everybody?* 77–93.

Şirzad, N. (2022). A review of online reputation management and online reputation components. *Doğuş Üniversitesi Dergisi*, *23*(1), 219–242.

Smith, K. T. (2011). Digital marketing strategies that Millennials find appealing, motivating, or just annoying. *Journal of Strategic Marketing*, *19*(6), 489–499. doi:10.1080/0965254X.2011.581383

Taylor, C. R. (2020). There is an urgent need for more research on influencer marketing. *International Journal of Advertising*, *39*(7), 889–891. doi:10.1080/02650487.2020.1822104

Todor, R.D. (2017). Promotion and communication through email marketing campaigns. *Bulletin of the Transilvania University of Brasov. Series V: Economi Sciences,* 61–66.

Chapter 11
Revolutionizing the Hospitality Industry:
How chatGPT Empowers Future Hoteliers

Vipin Singh
https://orcid.org/0000-0001-5566-0151
Vellore Institute of Technology, India

Amrik Singh
https://orcid.org/0000-0003-3598-8787
Lovely Professional University, India

ABSTRACT

The hospitality industry is experiencing a paradigm shift with the integration of cutting-edge technologies, and one such innovation is chatGPT (generative pre-trained transformer). This book chapter examines how chatGPT can revolutionize the hospitality industry and empower aspiring hoteliers. Through the use of chatGPT, hotels may provide 24/7 support to visitors by answering questions, making recommendations for nearby attractions, and expediting reservation requests. The virtual assistant's capacity to comprehend natural language and respond to it improves visitor experiences and develops a sense of comfort and happiness. Additionally, ChatGPT helps hoteliers acquire insightful data from customer conversations, enabling data-driven decision-making and customized service offers. As a result of the language model's capacity to perceive and interpret sentiment, future problems can be identified, allowing hoteliers to proactively resolve guest concerns and guarantee visitor loyalty.

DOI: 10.4018/979-8-3693-0815-8.ch011

INTRODUCTION

In today's fast-paced and digitally connected world, the hospitality industry is undergoing a profound transformation. From booking accommodations to personalized guest experiences, hoteliers face new challenges and opportunities to adapt to ever-changing consumer demands. In the midst of this dynamic landscape, emerging technologies have emerged as game-changers, reshaping how hotels engage with their guests and streamline operations (Drexler & Lapré, 2019). One such technology that holds immense promise for the future of hospitality is chatGPT - a powerful language model developed by OpenAI. This revolutionary AI-powered Chatbot is redefining the way hotels interact with their customers, enhance guest experiences, and stay ahead of the competition. In this two-page introduction, we delve into the exciting potential of chatGPT in revolutionizing the hospitality industry, empowering future hoteliers to deliver exceptional services and create lasting impressions. The hospitality industry has always prided itself on providing warm and personalized services to its guests. However, with the advent of artificial intelligence (AI), hotels have found new avenues to deepen guest engagement and elevate service standards (Kim et al., 2020: Bansal, Pruthi, and Singh (2022). ChatGPT, powered by advanced natural language processing and machine learning algorithms, represents a significant milestone in this AI journey. As an intelligent Chabot, chatGPT can understand and respond to human-like interactions, making it an ideal virtual assistant for hotels to engage with guests in real-time, address queries promptly, and provide personalized recommendations. Modern travellers seek personalized experiences that cater to their individual preferences and needs (Talan and Kalinkara, 2023). ChatGPT excels in delivering precisely that. By analyzing guest data and past interactions, chatGPT can offer tailored recommendations for dining options, local attractions, and personalized room amenities. This level of personalization fosters a deeper connection between guests and the hotel, leading to heightened guest satisfaction and increased loyalty. The initial stages of the guest journey are critical for establishing a positive rapport with potential visitors. ChatGPT seamlessly integrates with hotel websites and booking platforms, simplifying the reservation process for guests. Through intuitive conversations, chatGPT can assist guests in finding the most suitable accommodation options, checking availability, and even recommending special packages, all in real time. This not only enhances the booking experience but also significantly reduces response times, giving hoteliers a competitive edge in a rapidly evolving market (Rafiq et al., 2022).

ChatGPT's impact extends beyond guest interactions, as it has the potential to revolutionize hotel operations. By effectively handling internal inquiries, facilitating employee communications, and automating routine tasks, this AI-powered chatbot streamlines diverse operational processes. This newfound efficiency empowers hotel staff to dedicate their attention to more intricate, guest-centric responsibilities, thereby enhancing the overall service experience. In today's social media-driven landscape, where customers actively engage and follow digital influencers, practitioners are encouraged to leverage these influencers to connect with customers, fostering intentions to purchase their offerings (Lie Ao et al., 2023), The potential benefits of using chatGPT in the hospitality industry are immense, as it allows hoteliers to enhance guest experiences and streamline operations. However, it is crucial for hoteliers to approach the adoption of AI technologies with caution and address potential challenges.

One of the main concerns associated with chatGPT implementation is data privacy. Hoteliers must ensure that guest data is protected and handled in compliance with data protection regulations. Additionally, cybersecurity is a critical consideration. Implementing robust security measures is essential to safeguarding sensitive information and preventing unauthorized access.

While AI technologies can automate several tasks and improve operational efficiency, it is important to strike a balance between automation and maintaining the human touch in guest interactions. While chatGPT can assist in handling routine queries and requests, hoteliers should also prioritize the presence of human staff to provide personalized and exceptional guest experiences. Furthermore, proper training and monitoring of chatGPT systems are crucial to ensure accurate and reliable responses. (Javaid, Haleem, & Singh 2023).

Leveraging chatGPT for personalized hotel guest experiences and recommendations

1. **Personalized Booking Assistance**: Integrate chatGPT into the hotel website or app to assist guests with personalized booking recommendations. The AI can ask questions about their preferences, budget, and any special requirements, and then suggest the most suitable room types, amenities, and packages.
2. **Pre-arrival Concierge Service**: Guests can chat with the AI before their arrival to inquire about nearby attractions, dining options, and activities. The AI can provide tailored recommendations based on their interests and preferences, creating an itinerary for their stay.
3. **In-room Virtual Assistant**: Equip hotel rooms with an in-room virtual assistant powered by chatGPT. Guests can interact with the AI to request room service, ask for housekeeping, adjust room settings, or seek local recommendations.
4. **Personalized Recommendations**: chatGPT can analyze previous interactions and guest data to offer personalized recommendations for dining, sightseeing, and entertainment during their stay. For example, if a guest expressed an interest in art museums during a previous conversation, the AI can recommend nearby art galleries.

5. **Language Translation and Communication**: For international guests, AI can assist in translation, making it easier for them to communicate with the hotel staff and local vendors.
6. **Feedback and Issue Resolution**: chatGPT can handle guest feedback, address complaints, and resolve issues promptly. It can also gather valuable insights from guests to improve the hotel's services.
7. **Special Occasion Recognition**: If a guest is celebrating a special occasion like a birthday or anniversary, chatGPT can be programmed to recognize and offer personalized surprises, such as a complimentary dessert or a room upgrade.
8. **Seamless Check-out Process**: During check-out, the AI can help guests with the procedure, provide a breakdown of charges, and offer post-stay recommendations or loyalty incentives.
9. **Upselling and Cross-selling**: Based on guest preferences, the AI can suggest relevant upgrades, add-ons, or loyalty program benefits to enhance their experience and increase hotel revenue.
10. **Stay Feedback and Reviews**: After the guest's departure, chatGPT can send a follow-up message to gather feedback and encourage them to leave reviews, contributing to the hotel's reputation management.

STREAMLINING HOTEL OPERATIONS THROUGH AUTOMATED PROCESSES WITH CHAT GPT

Automated processes using chatGPT in hotels can boost efficiency and guest experience. Examples include instant customer support on the website, personalized recommendations based on guest preferences, managing reservations and sending confirmations, real-time language translation for international guests, and handling room service requests. It can also streamline billing and invoicing, provide data insights for decision-making, assist staff with training and SOPs, gather feedback through surveys, integrate with smart devices for room control, and engage with guests on social media. However, data security and maintaining a human touch are crucial considerations (Al-Hyari et al.2023)

Using chatGPT for real-time feedback and sentiment analysis can be a powerful tool to improve guest satisfaction. Here's how it can work:

1. **Real-time Feedback Collection:** Incorporate chatGPT into guest interactions, such as check-out processes, mobile apps, or in-room tablets, to solicit feedback from guests immediately after their stay. This allows guests to provide their opinions and suggestions while the experience is still fresh in their minds.

2. **Natural Language Understanding:** chatGPT's natural language processing capabilities allow it to understand guest responses in a conversational manner. Guests can provide feedback in their own words, making the process more user-friendly and increasing response rates.
3. **Sentiment Analysis:** Utilize sentiment analysis algorithms in conjunction with chatGPT to evaluate the emotional tone of guest responses. This automated analysis helps identify overall guest sentiment, whether positive, negative, or neutral, without the need for manual reading of each feedback.
4. **Identifying Pain Points:** Analyzing the collected feedback through sentiment analysis can pinpoint areas where guests may have encountered issues or experienced dissatisfaction. This could be related to service quality, room amenities, cleanliness, or any other aspect of the hotel experience.
5. **Responding to Guest Concerns:** For negative feedback or complaints, chatGPT can be programmed to provide immediate acknowledgments and offer appropriate responses or resolutions. This proactive approach demonstrates the hotel's commitment to addressing guest concerns promptly.
6. **Identifying Opportunities for Improvement:** By aggregating and analyzing feedback data, hotels can identify recurring themes and patterns that indicate potential areas for improvement. This data-driven approach helps prioritize efforts to enhance guest satisfaction.
7. **Recognizing Outstanding Service:** Positive feedback received through chatGPT can be used to recognize and reward outstanding staff members who have contributed to exceptional guest experiences.
8. **Personalizing Guest Interactions:** chatGPT's ability to analyze past interactions and preferences allows for personalized responses to returning guests. This tailored approach makes guests feel valued and appreciated.
9. **Continuous Iteration:** Use the insights from chatGPT's feedback and sentiment analysis to make ongoing improvements. Regularly update and refine the system to address emerging trends and meet changing guest expectations.
10. **Integration with Service Improvement Initiatives:** Integrate the feedback collected through chatGPT with the hotel's broader service improvement initiatives. Share relevant insights with different departments to encourage a holistic approach to guest satisfaction.

Overall, leveraging chatGPT for real-time feedback and sentiment analysis empowers hotels to proactively enhance guest satisfaction, respond to concerns, and foster a guest-centric culture that drives loyalty and positive word-of-mouth recommendations (Carvalho & Ivanov 2023).

THE INTEGRATION OF CHATGPT WITH AUGMENTED REALITY AND VIRTUAL REALITY ARE EMERGING TECHNOLOGIES

The integration of chatGPT with augmented reality (AR) and virtual reality (VR) is catalyzing a transformative shift within the hospitality industry. This powerful combination is revolutionizing guest experiences and operational efficiency. ChatGPT, when harnessed alongside AR interfaces, offers guests personalized recommendations and information, enhancing their interactions with their surroundings. Moreover, AR technology facilitates virtual tours, enabling potential guests to explore hotel rooms, facilities, and local attractions before making reservations. Virtual Reality, on the other hand, immerses prospective guests in simulated hotel stays, providing an unparalleled sense of presence that aids in decision-making (Bansal, R, et al. 2023).

Top of Form

As Kumar et al. 2023 mentioned that chatGPT can play a significant role in fostering sustainable and eco-friendly practices in hotels by providing information, recommendations, and engagement opportunities that promote environmental consciousness. Here's how chatGPT can contribute to this effort:

1. **Green Tips and Information:** chatGPT can be programmed to provide guests with green tips and information about eco-friendly practices within the hotel and its surroundings. This could include energy-saving measures, waste-reduction tips, and information about local sustainable attractions.
2. **Sustainable Dining Recommendations:** chatGPT can suggest sustainable dining options within and around the hotel, such as restaurants that source ingredients locally or serve plant-based dishes to reduce the environmental impact of food consumption.
3. **Eco-Friendly Transportation Options:** chatGPT can assist guests in finding eco-friendly transportation options, such as public transit, bike rentals, or electric vehicle charging stations, encouraging guests to reduce their carbon footprint while traveling.
4. **Sustainability Policies and Initiatives:** By sharing information about the hotel's sustainability policies and initiatives, chatGPT can raise awareness among guests about the hotel's commitment to eco-friendly practices.
5. **Waste Reduction and Recycling:** chatGPT can educate guests about the hotel's waste reduction and recycling programs, providing clear instructions on how to separate and dispose of waste responsibly.

6. **Green Certification and Awards:** If the hotel has achieved green certifications or received eco-friendly awards, chatGPT can inform guests about these accomplishments, building confidence in the hotel's sustainable practices.
7. **Sustainable Amenities and Products:** chatGPT can suggest eco-friendly amenities and products available in the hotel, such as refillable toiletries, energy-efficient appliances, and organic bedding.
8. **Environmental Education:** chatGPT can offer information about local environmental initiatives and attractions, such as nature reserves, wildlife conservation projects, or eco-tours, encouraging guests to engage in sustainable tourism activities.
9. **Encouraging Guest Participation:** chatGPT can promote eco-friendly activities and events within the hotel, such as tree-planting programs, beach clean-ups, or sustainable workshops, encouraging guest participation in environmental efforts.
10. **Feedback and Suggestions:** chatGPT can collect guest feedback on sustainability practices, allowing hotels to continuously improve their eco-friendly initiatives based on guest input.

By leveraging chatGPT to promote sustainable practices, hotels can educate guests, empower them to make environmentally conscious choices and contribute to the larger goal of sustainability in the hospitality industry. Additionally, this can enhance the hotel's brand reputation, attract environmentally conscious guests, and demonstrate a commitment to responsible tourism and environmental stewardship. By integrating chatGPT into their eco-friendly initiatives, hotels can create a seamless and personalized experience for guests who are interested in sustainable practices. ChatGPT can not only provide information and recommendations on green activities and local eco-friendly attractions but also educate guests about the hotel's own sustainability efforts. This transparency and commitment to environmental consciousness through chatGPT interactions further strengthen the sense of trust and loyalty between the hotel and its guests. As guests witness the hotel's dedication to both guest privacy and sustainability, they are more likely to develop a positive perception of the hotel brand and become advocates for its eco-friendly practices, ultimately leading to enhanced guest satisfaction and loyalty. Additionally, this integrated approach fosters a culture of environmental awareness, contributing to a more sustainable hospitality industry as a whole (Dwivedi, et. al.2023).

ADDRESSING PRIVACY AND SECURITY CONCERNS WHEN USING CHAT GPT

The guest interactions are of paramount importance to ensure the trust and confidence of guests. Here are some essential steps and measures that hotels should take:

1. **Data Encryption and Storage:** Ensure that all guest data, including conversations with chatGPT, are encrypted both in transit and at rest. Implement secure storage practices to safeguard sensitive information.
2. **Explicit Consent:** Obtain explicit consent from guests to use chatGPT for guest interactions and clearly communicate the purposes for which their data will be used.
3. **Limited Data Access:** Restrict access to guest data to authorized personnel only. Implement role-based access control to ensure that only relevant staff can access guest information.
4. **Regular Security Audits:** Conduct regular security audits and vulnerability assessments to identify and address any potential weaknesses in the system.
5. **Data Deletion Policies:** Establish data retention and deletion policies to ensure that guest data is not stored longer than necessary and is securely removed once it is no longer needed.
6. **User Education:** Train staff on data privacy and security best practices, emphasizing the importance of protecting guest information and not sharing it with unauthorized individuals.
7. **Transparent Privacy Policy:** Clearly communicate your hotel's privacy policy to guests, detailing how their data will be handled when using chatGPT and other services.

By taking these measures, hotels can demonstrate their commitment to safeguarding guest privacy and security when using chatGPT for guest interactions. This will foster a sense of trust and help build strong relationships with guests, ultimately leading to enhanced guest satisfaction and loyalty (Derner & Batistič, 2023).

INTEGRATING CHAT GPT WITH IOT DEVICES FOR SMART ROOM EXPERIENCES

1. Integration of chatGPT with IoT devices enables voice-activated controls for various room amenities, streamlining guest interactions.
2. ChatGPT learns and remembers guest preferences, allowing for personalized room settings and recommendations for nearby attractions and services.

3. Smart room experiences powered by chatGPT promote energy efficiency by suggesting eco-friendly settings for IoT devices.
4. ChatGPT acts as a virtual concierge, providing real-time information about hotel facilities, local attractions, and personalized entertainment options.
5. Guests can use chatGPT to place room service orders, provide feedback, and receive prompt support, enhancing guest satisfaction and overall hotel efficiency.

THE POTENTIAL OF CHAT GPT IN PREDICTING AND PREVENTING SERVICE ISSUES

chatGPT holds immense potential in predicting and preventing service issues across industries, including the hospitality sector. Through data analysis and pattern recognition, it can identify common complaints and recurring problems, enabling the anticipation of future issues. Utilizing real-time guest sentiment analysis, chatGPT can gauge emotional tones, detecting early signs of dissatisfaction to promptly address concerns. The system can be programmed to automatically escalate urgent issues for immediate attention. By initiating proactive communication with guests and seeking feedback, hotels can address concerns early on. Leveraging predictive analytics, chatGPT can make forecasts based on historical data, occupancy trends, and past performance, allowing hotels to prepare and prevent problems. In IoT-enabled environments, chatGPT can predict equipment failures, facilitating preventive maintenance scheduling. Continuous learning ensures chatGPT becomes increasingly effective in issue identification and prevention. Integrating guest feedback enhances the system's predictive capabilities, enabling systematic issue prioritization and resolution. By leveraging chatGPT's predictive power, hotels adopt a proactive approach to service quality, ultimately leading to enhanced guest satisfaction, increased loyalty, and a positive brand reputation. Training hotel staff to collaborate effectively with chatGPT systems is crucial for maximizing its benefits in the hospitality industry. Staff should be introduced to chatGPT as a conversational AI tool designed to enhance guest interactions and streamline hotel operations. Hands-on familiarization with the system is essential, allowing staff to interact with chatGPT in simulated guest scenarios. Role-specific training can demonstrate how chatGPT assists the front desk, housekeeping, and concierge staff in handling guest inquiries efficiently. Emphasis should be placed on guest data privacy and security to ensure compliance with regulations. Moreover, staff should be trained to interpret and respond professionally to guest feedback gathered through chatGPT. Encouraging a collaborative approach, staff should view chatGPT as a supportive tool that enhances their roles rather than replaces them. Highlighting the potential for personalization, chatGPT can be utilized to provide tailored guest experiences based on data insights from interactions. Continuous training updates and handling uncommon scenarios can further improve staff proficiency. Ultimately, seamless collaboration with chatGPT elevates guest service, optimizing staff workflow, and enhancing overall guest satisfaction in the hotel industry (Malik et.al 2023)

CHALLENGES AND LIMITATIONS IN DEPLOYING CHAT GPT IN HOTELS

Deploying ChatGPT in hotels presents the opportunity to streamline guest interactions and automate certain tasks. However, this initiative comes with challenges and limitations. The model's understanding of hotel-specific context and terminology could be limited, requiring focused training. Ensuring privacy and data security while handling sensitive guest information is a paramount concern. Customizing the model to align with the hotel's brand voice and policies can be challenging, potentially leading to inconsistent responses. Mitigating issues of bias and inappropriate content generated by the model demands vigilant monitoring and intervention (Dwivedi et al.2023). Complex guest requests might lead to inaccurate responses, necessitating refined fine-tuning. Adapting the AI's language capabilities to diverse communication styles and accents is essential. While AI can provide quick responses, guests may still value human interaction for personalized services and emotional support. Technical glitches and network outages could disrupt the seamless operation of the AI system. Moreover, managing guest expectations and integrating AI harmoniously within the hotel's service framework is crucial for a successful deployment (Gursoy, Song 2023).

CONCLUSION ON THE TRANSFORMATIVE IMPACT OF CHAT GPT IN THE HOSPITALITY INDUSTRY

In conclusion, the integration of ChatGPT into the hospitality industry signifies a remarkable step toward transforming guest experiences and operational efficiency. Despite the challenges and limitations associated with its deployment, the potential benefits are substantial. By leveraging AI-powered chat systems, hotels can offer swift and round-the-clock assistance, enhancing the overall guest experience. The continuous refinement of the model's understanding of industry-specific jargon and its ability to handle complex inquiries can lead to improved accuracy and relevance in responses. As AI technology matures, the collaboration between humans and machines has the potential to elevate service quality to unprecedented levels. Through meticulous customization, careful monitoring, and a commitment to data privacy, the hospitality industry can harness the transformative power of ChatGPT to not only address guest needs more effectively but also to free up human staff to focus on tasks that require a personal touch. This symbiotic relationship between technology and hospitality holds the promise of shaping a new era of seamless and enhanced guest interactions, ultimately redefining the standards of service excellence in the industry.

REFERENCES

Al-Hyari, H. S. A., Al-Smadi, H. M., & Weshah, S. R. (2023). The Impact of Artificial Intelligence (AI) on Guest Satisfaction in Hotel Management: An Empirical Study of Luxury Hotels. *Geo Journal of Tourism and Geosites*, *48*(2 supplement), 810–819. doi:10.30892/gtg.482spl15-1081

Ao, L., Bansal, R., Pruthi, N., & Khaskheli, M. B. (2023). Impact of Social Media Influencers on Customer Engagement and Purchase Intention: A Meta-Analysis. *Sustainability (Basel)*, *15*(3), 2744. doi:10.3390u15032744

Bansal, R., Pruthi, N., & Singh, R. (2022). Developing Customer Engagement Through Artificial Intelligence Tools: Roles and Challenges. In Developing Relationships, Personalization, and Data Herald in Marketing 5.0 (pp. 130-145). IGI Global

Bansal, R., Shukla, G., Gupta, A., Singh, A., & Pruthi, N. (2023). Optimizing Augmented Reality and Virtual Reality for Customer Engagement. In *Promoting Consumer Engagement Through Emotional Branding and Sensory Marketing* (pp. 24–35). IGI Global.

Carvalho, I., & Ivanov, S. (2023). ChatGPT for tourism: Applications, benefits, and risks. *Tourism Review*. doi:10.1108/TR-02-2023-0088

Derner, E., & Batistič, K. (2023). Beyond the Safeguards: Exploring the Security Risks of ChatGPT. *arXiv preprint arXiv:2305.08005.*

Drexler, N., & Lapré, V. B. (2019). For better or for worse: Shaping the hospitality industry through robotics and artificial intelligence. *Research in Hospitality Management*, *9*(2), 117–120. doi:10.1080/22243534.2019.1689701

Dwivedi, Y. K., Kshetri, N., Hughes, L., Slade, E. L., Jeyaraj, A., Kar, A. K., & Wright, R. (2023). "So what if ChatGPT wrote it?" Multidisciplinary perspectives on opportunities, challenges and implications of generative conversational AI for research, practice and policy. *International Journal of Information Management*, *71*, 102642. doi:10.1016/j.ijinfomgt.2023.102642

Gursoy, D., Li, Y., & Song, H. (2023). ChatGPT and the hospitality and tourism industry: An overview of current trends and future research directions. *Journal of Hospitality Marketing & Management*, *32*(5), 579–592. doi:10.1080/19368623.2023.2211993

Javaid, M., Haleem, A., & Singh, R. P. (2023). ChatGPT for healthcare services: An emerging stage for an innovative perspective. *Bench Council Transactions on Benchmarks. Standards and Evaluations*, *3*(1), 100105.

Kim, J. J., Lee, M. J., & Han, H. (2020). Smart hotels and sustainable consumer behavior: Testing the effect of perceived performance, attitude, and technology readiness on word-of-mouth. *International Journal of Environmental Research and Public Health*, *17*(20), 7455. doi:10.3390/ijerph17207455 PMID:33066245

Kumar, A., Nagarajan, G., Surekha, M., Vijai, C., Mohideen, A. S., Dhinakaran, D. P., & Lakshmi, M. R. (2023). The Impact of chatGPT on E-commerce. *Harbin Gongcheng Daxue Xuebao/Journal of Harbin Engineering University, 44*(7), 1016-1023.

Malik, T., Dwivedi, Y., Kshetri, N., Hughes, L., Slade, E. L., Jeyaraj, A., & Wright, R. (2023). "So what if ChatGPT wrote it?" Multidisciplinary perspectives on opportunities, challenges and implications of generative conversational AI for research, practice and policy. *International Journal of Information Management*, *71*, 102642. doi:10.1016/j.ijinfomgt.2023.102642

Rafiq, F., Dogra, N., Adil, M., & Wu, J. Z. (2022). Examining consumer's intention to adopt AI-chatbot in tourism using partial least squares structural equation modeling method. *Mathematics*, *10*(13), 2190. doi:10.3390/math10132190

Talan, T., & Kalinkara, Y. (2023). *The Role of Artificial Intelligence in Higher Education: ChatGPT Evaluation for Anatomy Course*. Research Gate.

Chapter 12
ChatGPT:
A Revolutionary Tool?

Deepanshi Aggarwal
The Technological Institute of Textile and Sciences, Bhiwani, India

Seema Rathee
Maharshi Dayanand University, Rohtak, India

ABSTRACT

ChatGPT has been expanding swiftly. This chatbot, which has its foundation on "OpenAI's language model," allows users to converse with the artificial intelligence by providing instructions. Although ChatGPT is great and produces amazing stories, poems, songs, writings, etc., it has some limitations too. The bot will respond to queries from users with relevant, persuasive subjects and arguments. Currently, ChatGPT is at the top of many scholarly concerns. This chapter briefly discusses the ChatGPT and its necessity. The ChatGPT Tool's numerous 'growing work flow mechanisms' are also exemplified. In addition, it examines specific capabilities and characteristics of the ChatGPT Support System. Finally, the authors highlight and discuss ChatGPT's vital functions in the current predicament.

INTRODUCTION

ChatGPT, an open artificial intelligence (AI) prototype presented in November 2022, has piqued the curiosity of engineers, social media users, company owners, authors, and students. Despite many people's concerns about ChatGPT, machine learning (ML) has unquestionably positive potential. Since its widespread use, machine learning has had an impact on a variety of industries, enabling activities such as high-resolution

DOI: 10.4018/979-8-3693-0815-8.ch012

weather forecasting and medical imaging analysis (Cherian et al., 2022). ChatGPT has the ability to change the way numerous professions operate. Because it was created with OpenAI, this chatbot can communicate like a human. Customers can get started with ChatGPT by registering a free OpenAI account. This system could benefit from user-generated data to improve its training algorithms. Chat- GPT-induced paradigm shifts in information access may benefit tag-holding businesses including as education, research, journalism, mass communication, Information Technology (IT), retail, and many others (Erhan et al., 2010). Using generative AI technology, various convincing writing may be produced quickly, and the writing can then be adapted in response to input to make it more suitable for the goal. This has implications for a wide range of industries, including marketingcopy-required firms and IT and software organisations that may benefit from AI models' rapid, typically accurate code. Furthermore, organisations may use generative AI to create superior technical objects, such as upscaled reproductions of medical photographs. Firms may also seek new business opportunities and the capacity to give more value with their time and resources (Bai et al., 2022).

ChatGPT has swiftly taken off on a global scale. Many people who are reading this want to know what this programme is capable of. This programme can create original articles about anything by combining an exceptional ability to quickly search for information online with strong grammar and writing skills. ChatGPT is a bot that has been programmed to respond to user inputs that imitate human speech (Bona et al., 1985; Chan and Hu, 2023). Using machine learning, it has gained a surprisingly diverse set of skills. On command, it can generate simple computer code, crude financial analyses, hilarious poetry and songs, faultless impersonations, contemplative essays on almost any subject, and technical paper summaries. The following are the article's key research questions:

RO1: - To brief about the ChatGPT and its need;
RO2: - To discuss the progressive workflow process of the ChatGPT tool;
RO3: - To study specific features and capabilities of the ChatGPT support system;
RO4: - To identify and discuss significant roles of ChatGPT in the current scenario;

ChatGPT, a generative pre-trained transformer, is gaining popularity. The term ''Generative'' or ''G'' in the acronym GPT refers to the tool's ability to generate text. Pre-training, also known as ''P,'' is the deployment of a model from one ML project to train another model, similar to how people use prior knowledge to learn new things. ChatGPT provides a large volume of text to practise on. The neural network T stands for ''Transformer,'' which investigates the overall relationship between each data series component. It is a free chatbot that can answer almost any inquiry. It was developed by OpenAI and made accessible for public testing. It is already widely considered as the best AI chatbot ever created. Computer code, college-level essays, poetry, and even half-decent jokes have been produced by the chatbot. The first ChatGPT model was trained through supervised finetuning, which involved human AI trainers conversing with both the user and an AI assistant (Cheng et al., 2023). Trainers have access to sample written recommendations to help them write answers. One of their most recent developments is ChatGPT, a language model designed specifically to grasp and respond to real language. This shows that it can converse with humans in a natural and intuitive manner. The nicest feature about ChatGPT is that it is open source, allowing programmers to implement the model into their applications (Else, 2023).

Key Milestones of ChatGPT

A number of breakthroughs and advancements have been made in ChatGPT's development, including.

(i) The invention of the Transformer architecture, which made it possible to develop language models that are incredibly efficient and scalable.
(ii) The creation and dissemination of the GPT series, which showed how AI language models might be used for a variety of tasks, such as text production, translation, and summarization.
(iii) The introduction of ChatGPT, which improved accuracy, context comprehension, and adaptability while building on the strengths of its forerunners.

GROWING WORKFLOW MECHANISM

A streamlined flow of information and expertise is required to handle the ChatGPT working framework. It began with encounters and debate, then moved on to data reception and comparison building. The database is then sampled, and the process is completed by establishing the reward model and updating it in the cloud data set. This technology has numerous applications for business executives, students, and instructors. Teachers who wish to demonstrate, explain, and have their students apply principles. A teacher could ask the student to explain their reasoning and thought process for the essay, and then compare their explanation to the essay itself. If there are major variations between the essay and the student's explanation, it could mean that the student used a text-generation application such as ChatGPT. A teacher could also look for obvious signs of text generation in the essay. It is normal practise to use ChatGPT for a variety of tasks, ranging from writing high school papers to drafting legal documents and even crafting laws. These programmes may generate more complicated textual stuff rather instantly. A teacher can tell if a student wrote an essay on their own or used a text-generation system like ChatGPT in a variety of ways. Using plagiarism detection software is one technique to determine whether the essay is similar to others. Text-generating programmes often provide output identical to existing content, and this may be a reliable technique to tell if a student used ChatGPT or another text generation tool. ChatGTP engages in dialogue with the user, replies to follow-up inquiries, acknowledges and corrects errors, rejects inappropriate requests, and even questions false premises. ChatGPT is designed to respond promptly and thoroughly to instructions.

Capabilities of ChatGPT

ChatGPT's ability to perceive the context and provide meaningful information makes it a helpful tool for collecting, evaluating, and understanding market trends. This technology can enhance current processes, gather qualitative data via informal surveys, analyse data and extract characteristics from vast volumes of unstructured data, give valuable market intelligence, and save researchers time and effort. Natural language processing is entering a new stage as early ChatGPT users show the technology's capacity to continue a discussion through several questions and create software codeAI enables increasingly complex interactions between humans and robots (Finnie- Ansley et al., 2022). In an informal situation, ChatGPT can produce documents that sound like human speech and accomplish basic tasks. ChatGPT aspires to build a collaborative AI system capable of producing language that is useful, interesting, and contextually relevant.

Enhancements and New Developments in ChatGPT

ChatGPT has a number of significant advancements and enhancements over older models, including.

(i) Improved context understanding: ChatGPT is more capable of understanding and reacting to complicated and nuanced inputs, which increases its efficiency in producing precise and pertinent text.
(ii) Lessened biases: ChatGPT benefits from ongoing efforts to reduce biases in training data, resulting in more objective and balanced outputs, even while biases are still there.
(iii) ChatGPT has the ability to be fine-tuned for certain tasks and applications, enabling it to be customised to the specific requirements of researchers across a range of scientific discipline

CHATGPT'S VITAL FUNCTIONS IN THE CURRENT PREDICAMENT

ChatGPT can examine a company's marketing techniques, clientele, product qualities, and other factors to identify what makes it successful. It makes suggestions for how our organisation might embrace or improve those features. ChatGPT may propose ways to capitalise on these opportunities and expand our company by studying competitors' product offerings, marketing strategies, and customer interaction tactics. Based on the target, demographic, marketing objectives, and budget, ChatGPT may advise on the best channels for a specific campaign. Social networking sites, email marketing, search engine marketing, and other digital marketing channels are examples of channels. Performance analytics assist organisations in tracking and evaluating the effectiveness of their digital marketing activities by revealing what works and what does not. To improve outcomes, the campaign plan and tactics may be modified in real-time using this information. ChatGPT can suggest creative answers to challenging scientific issues, encouraging academics to question accepted wisdom and think outside the box. Aiding in the testing and validation of hypotheses. Researchers must extensively verify and validate their theories through experimentation and analysis after they have developed a theory. In this procedure, ChatGPT can help by: recommending suitable experimental approaches and concepts identifying possible sources of bias and confounding variables that could affect experimental outcomes recommending statistical analyses and methods of analysis for the interpretation of data

DISCUSSION

These latest AI systems, of course, cannot read minds. To obtain the desired results, a novel but less complex type of human creativity in the form of text prompts is required. The AI system generates successive rounds of outputs via iterative prompting, demonstrating human-AI collaboration, until the person generating the prompts is satisfied with the results. The precise hazards and potential repercussions associated with ChatGPT will ultimately determine the level of regulation required. As with any powerful new technology, it is critical to thoroughly analyse its potential consequences and take steps to assure its moral and responsible use. While many people have complimented ChatGPT for enhancing their productivity, others, understandably, have expressed concern. Concerns have been raised by schools, colleges, and education bodies regarding using this technology for submissions and exams. Not to mention that Stack Overflow, a developer site, banned the use of chatbots soon after the launch of ChatGPT due to increasing results inaccuracy.

CHALLENGES AND FUTURE SCOPE

The main difficulties of using ChatGPT in scientific study include the following.

(a) **Reliability and accuracy:** ChatGPT has demonstrated extraordinary proficiency in producing writing that appears human, yet it occasionally produces inaccurate or misleading information.
(b) **Bias in AI models:** ChatGPT was trained using a large amount of textual data, which could have introduced biases of its own.
(c) **Overreliance on AI:** As AI models like ChatGPT progress, there is a risk of overreliance on them, which could cause researchers to lose their capacity for independent thought and problem-solving.
(d) **Quality control:** ChatGPT can produce high-quality text, but it can also produce responses that are unsuitable or of low quality. Continuous monitoring, training, and improvement are necessary to guarantee that ChatGPT continually produces high-quality text.
(e) **Dataset bias:** The calibre and variety of the training data can have an impact on ChatGPT's performance. Biassed models can have harmful effects on the healthcare, criminal justice, and employment systems as a result of biassed training data.
(f) **Generalization:** ChatGPT is frequently trained on huge datasets, which can result in overfitting and make it challenging to generalize to new or unexplored data. New training methods and procedures must be created in order to increase ChatGPT's generalization capacity.

The potential for ChatGPT and other AI language models to revolutionise a wide range of fields and applications makes for intriguing and diverse future prospects. The capabilities and advantages of AI language models will keep expanding as researchers tackle current issues and investigate new possibilities, paving the path for more sophisticated and responsible AI-driven products.

CONCLUSION

Users of ChatGPT are utilising the platform to help with composing emails, programming code, and answering inquiries on a variety of subjects, including investing. ChatGPT has received extremely excellent feedback thus far, with many appreciating its sophisticated features and simplicity of its use. ChatGPT has the potential to be a significant player in natural language processing. The chatbot responds to our inquiries in a conversational, albeit slightly stiff, manner using the platform of OpenAI. ChatGPT's ability to perceive and respond to a wide range of concerns has been particularly notable; some have even stated that it may entirely transform how humans interact with technology. In the future, ChatGPT's capabilities will be a wonderful tool for organisations in fields such as customer service, online learning, and market research. OpenAI and its major investors have committed billions in building, training, and deploying these models. It could be a prudent long-term investment, establishing OpenAI at the forefront of AI creative tools. ChatGPT is more adept at simulating human-like interactions because it can comprehend the context of a discussion and produce pertinent responses; (ii) improved language generation: ChatGPT creates writing that is coherent, contextually appropriate, and grammatically correct because to its advanced language production capabilities. (iii) Task adaptability: ChatGPT's adaptability across different industries can be increased by customising it for particular tasks or domains. Because ChatGPT supports many languages, it may serve a variety of user bases and international applications. However, in order for ChatGPT to contribute to shaping the intelligent human-machine future, a number of ethical challenges must be tackled.

REFERENCES

Alshater, M. M. (2022). Exploring the Role of artificial intelligence in enhancing academic performance: a case study of ChatGPT. SSRN *Electron. J.* doi:10.2139/ssrn.4312358

Bai, Y., Kadavath, S., Kundu, S., Askell, A., Kernion, J., & Jones, A. (2022). *Constitutional AI: harmlessness from AI feedback. arXiv.* doi: /arXiv.2212.08073 doi:10.48550

Baidoo-Anu, D., & Owusu Ansah, L. (2023). Education in the era of generative artificial intelligence (AI): understanding the potential benefits of ChatGPT in promoting teaching and learning. SSRN *Electron. J.* doi:10.2139/ssrn.4337484

Bansal, R., Pruthi, N., & Singh, R. (2022). Developing Customer Engagement Through Artificial Intelligence Tools: Roles and Challenges. In *Developing Relationships, Personalization, and Data Herald in Marketing 5.0* (pp. 130-145). IGI Global.

Bansal, R., Shukla, G., Gupta, A., Singh, A., & Pruthi, N. (2023). Optimizing Augmented Reality and Virtual Reality for Customer Engagement. In *Promoting Consumer Engagement Through Emotional Branding and Sensory Marketing* (pp. 24-35). IGI Global.

Bona, J. D., Powell, A. G., Farrar, E., & Cohen, D. K. (1985). The shopping mall high school: Winners and losers in the educational marketplace. *The Journal of Negro Education*, *56*(1), 122. doi:10.2307/2295389

Chan, A. (2022). GPT-3 and InstructGPT: Technological dystopianism, utopianism, and "contextual" perspectives in AI ethics and industry. *AI and Ethics*, *3*(1), 53–64. doi:10.100743681-022-00148-6

ChanC. K.HuW. (2023). *Students' voices on generative ai: perceptions, benefits, and challenges in higher education*. arXiv.2305.00290

Cheng, K., He, Y., Li, C., Xie, R., Lu, Y., Gu, S., & Wu, H. (2023). Talk with ChatGPT about the outbreak of Mpox in 2022: Reflections and suggestions from AI dimensions. *Annals of Biomedical Engineering*, *51*(5), 870–874. doi:10.100710439-023-03196-z PMID:37031289

Dale, R. (2021). GPT-3 What's it good for? *Natural Language Engineering*, *27*(1), 113–118. doi:10.1017/S1351324920000601

Deng, J., & Lin, Y. (2023). The benefits and challenges of ChatGPT: An overview. *Front. Comput. Intell. Syst*, *2*(2), 4465. doi:10.54097/fcis.v2i2.4465

DeshpandeS.SzeferJ. (2023). Analyzing ChatGPT's aptitude in an introductory computer engineering course. arXiv.2304.06122

Doshi, R. H., Bajaj, S. S., & Krumholz, H. M. (2023). ChatGPT: Temptations of progress. *The American Journal of Bioethics*, *23*(4), 6–8. doi:10.1080/15265161.2023.2180110 PMID:36853242

Else, H. (2023). Abstracts written by ChatGPT fool scientists. *Nature*, *613*(7944), 423–423. doi:10.1038/d41586-023-00056-7 PMID:36635510

Erhan, D., Bengio, Y., Courville, A., Manzagol, P., & Vincent, P. (2010). Why does unsupervised pre-training help deep learning. *Journal of Machine Learning Research*, *11*, 625–660.

Finnie-Ansley, J., Denny, P., Becker, B. A., Luxton-Reilly, A., & Prather, J. (2022). The robots are coming: exploring the implications of OpenAI codex on introductory programming. *Proceedings of the 24th Australasian Computing Education Conference* (New York, NY: ACM). 10.1145/3511861.3511863

GaoC. A.HowardF. M.MarkovN. S.DyerE. C.RameshS.LucY. (2022). Comparing scientific abstracts generated by ChatGPT to original abstracts using an artificial intelligence output detector, plagiarism detector, and blinded human reviewers. bioRxiv. doi:10.1101/2022.12.23.521610

Garvey, C. S. (2019). Artificial intelligence and Japan's fifth generation. *Pacific Historical Review, 88*(4), 619–658. doi:10.1525/phr.2019.88.4.619

GongT.LyuC.ZhangS.WangY.ZhengM.ZhaoQ. (2023). MultiModal-GPT: a vision and language model for dialogue with humans. arXiv.2305.04790

Gordijn, B., & Have, H. A. (2023). ChatGPT: Evolution or revolution? *Medicine, Health Care, and Philosophy, 26*(1), 1–2. doi:10.100711019-023-10136-0 PMID:36656495

Gozalo-BrizuelaR.Garrido-MerchánE. (2023). *ChatGPT is not all you need. A state of the art review of large generative AI models*. arXiv.2301.04655

Graham, F. (2022). Daily briefing: Will ChatGPT kill the essay assignment? *Nature*. doi:10.1038/d41586-022-04437-2 PMID:36517680

Haque, M. U., Dharmadasa, I., Sworna, Z. T., Rajapakse, R. N., & Ahmad, H. (2022). *"I think this is the most disruptive technology": exploring sentiments of ChatGPT early adopters using twitter data. arXiv*. doi: /arXiv.2212.05856 doi:10.48550

Henrickson, L., & Meroño-Peñuela, A. (2022). The hermeneutics of computer-generated texts. *Configurations, 30*(2), 115–139. doi:10.1353/con.2022.0008

Hill-Yardin, E. L., Hutchinson, M. R., Laycock, R., & Spencer, S. (2023). A Chat(GPT) about the future of scientific publishing. *Brain, Behavior, and Immunity, 110*, 152–154. doi:10.1016/j.bbi.2023.02.022 PMID:36868432

Holmqvist, M. (2019). Lack of qualified teachers: a global challenge for future knowledge development. In R. B. Monyai (Ed.), *Teacher Education in the 21st Century*., doi:10.5772/intechopen.83417

Ienca, M. (2023). Don't pause giant AI for the wrong reasons. *Nature Machine Intelligence, 5*(5), 470–471. doi:10.103842256-023-00649-x

Iqbal, N., Ahmed, H., & Azhar, K. A. (2022). Exploring teachers' attitudes towards using chatgpt. *Glob. J. Manag. Adm. Sci, 3*(4), 97–111. doi:10.46568/gjmas.v3i4.163

Kasneci, E., Sessler, K., Küchemann, S., Bannert, M., Dementieva, D., Fischer, F., Gasser, U., Groh, G., Günnemann, S., Hüllermeier, E., Krusche, S., Kutyniok, G., Michaeli, T., Nerdel, C., Pfeffer, J., Poquet, O., Sailer, M., Schmidt, A., Seidel, T., & Kasneci, G. (2023). ChatGPT for good? On opportunities and challenges of large language models for education. *Learning and Individual Differences, 103*, 102274. doi:10.1016/j.lindif.2023.102274

Ke, Z., Sheng, J., Li, Z., Silamu, W., & Guo, Q. (2021). Knowledge-guided sentiment analysis via learning from natural language explanations. *IEEE Access : Practical Innovations, Open Solutions*, *9*, 3570–3578. doi:10.1109/ACCESS.2020.3048088

Kersting, K. (2020). Rethinking computer science through AI. *KI - Künstliche Intelligenz*, *34*, 435–437. doi:10.1007/s13218-020-00692-5

Kitamura, F. C. (2023). ChatGPT Is Shaping the future of medical writing but still requires human judgment. *Radiology*, *230171*(2), e230171. doi:10.1148/radiol.230171 PMID:36728749

KocońJ.CicheckiI.KaszycaO.KochanekM.SzydloD.BaranJ. (2023). *ChatGPT: Jack of all trades, master of none*. arXiv.2302.10724

KosinskiM. (2023). *Theory of mind may have spontaneously emerged in large language models*. arXiv.2302.02083

Lund, B. D., & Ting, W. (2023). Chatting about ChatGPT: how may AI and GPT impact academia and libraries? SSRN *Electron. J.* doi:10.2139/ssrn.4333415

Stokel-Walker, C. (2022). AI bot ChatGPT writes smart essays - should professors worry? *Nature*. doi:10.1038/d41586-022-04397-7 PMID:36494443

Strowel, A. M. (2023). ChatGPT and generative ai tools: Theft of intellectual labor? *IIC; International Review of Industrial Property and Copyright Law*, *54*(4), 491–494. doi:10.100740319-023-01321-y

Susnjak, T. (2022). ChatGPT: the end of online exam integrity? /arXiv.2212.09292 doi:10.48550

Trilling, B., & Fadel, C. (2012). *21st Century Skills: Learning for Life in Our Times*. John Wiley and Sons.

Chapter 13
Using Big Data and Artificial Intelligence to Enhance Smart Cities

Aziza Chakir
https://orcid.org/0000-0003-0339-7202
Faculty of Law, Economics, and Social Sciences, University of Hassan II, Casablanca, Morocco

Johanes F. Andry
https://orcid.org/0000-0003-0860-8953
Faculty of Technology and Design, Universitas Bunda Mulia- Jakarta, Indonesia

Rohit Bansal
https://orcid.org/0000-0001-7072-5005
Department of Management Studies, Vaish College of Engineering, Rohtak, India

Arif Ulah
Air University, Pakistan

Omar Durrah
College of Commerce and Business Administration, Dhofar University, Oman

Rashid Mamoon
Faculty of Science and Technology, Vishwakarma University, India

ABSTRACT

This chapter analyzes the relationships that cities have with digital technologies. Smart cities are at the crossroads between the development of information and communication technologies in the city, and the affirmation of a new paradigm of sustainable urban development. To assess the social impact of smart cities on citizens, an empirical study was needed. The study and analysis of the data allowed measurement of the level of interest and sensitivity of citizens, to know the connected people who use new technologies, to collect the opinions of the inhabitants and users of the city to identify the main needs, and to improve the comfort of the inhabitants while having more efficient transport. This study has enabled the formation of future projections so that all citizens benefit from the powers of smart cities.

DOI: 10.4018/979-8-3693-0815-8.ch013

INTRODUCTION

The use of New Information and Communication Technologies (ICT) in the work's world is booming thanks to scientific research which aims to create news in the economy. This development produces the birth of a new world order of ICT and economics, where rich countries are using ICT to be more sophisticated (Novikov et al., 2020). One of these most innovations which have a very broad impact is the smart city, a smarter urban area, based on the use of all that is technological to transform the way of life for the better, thus the worlds for leisure and work (Pieriegud & Zawieska, 2019).

The inclusion and cooperation between the different actors, who pool their ideas, expectations, skills, and resources to optimize cities gives birth to Smart Cities. These actors can be companies and manufacturers, who create new activity structures, invest in projects and they are a source of the integration of technological innovation in everyday life (De Guimarães et al., 2020).

When we hear about a technology, we are interested only in its advantageous usefulness, that it acts in the simplification of life in every day and decrease the human effort. It is the basic rule of Smart Cities.

The Smart City is a city that, through its efforts, is a center of professional knowledge and skills, a large gathering of highly skilled workers.

Today, the deployment of new technologies combined with growing urbanization makes it possible to experience the city differently. In this context, the Smart City is built through a set of arguments and beliefs. It is also organized and structured around concrete and materialized achievements.

Smart Cities integrate the population's information to treat their needs, hence the necessity to manage this information effectively. Hence the objective of this present work is to answer how we will guarantee the benefits of Smart Cities in real-time(Li et al., 2020).

This work will be presented as follows; first we started with a state of the art on Smart Cities, second an empirical study to assess the social impact of smart cities on citizens, third we analyzed, how we can manage smart cities to make daily life's citizens easier by exploiting technological development by focusing on the powers of Big Data and artificial intelligence, and by taking demographic growth into consideration, by exposing examples of smart city projects.

LITERATURE STUDY

Smart City

The road to a systemic city has taken on a new urgency due to the increase in world population and the exodus to the developed country.

Sustainability has become an important imperative and technologies have advanced to the point where significant, real-time interactions between cities(BNOUACHIR et al., n.d.), residents and businesses are possible.

The Smart City is a system of systems: Water, electricity, Transport, and emergency response, where each of them affects the others (Yuan et al., 2020).

The Smart City can be identified in many main dimensions. These criteria are: "Smart Economy", "Smart Mobility", "Smart Environment", "Smart People", "Smart Living" and, finally, "Smart Governance" (Madakam, 2020).

Smart Economy. Given the importance of the integration of Smart Cities concept in Morocco, we have developed an empirical study, which consists of a panoramic recovery of the various buoyant sectors such as the city transport sector, to the presentation of projects dedicated to the digitization of these sectors, and this within the framework of the initiative: "Smart city", which works to return the city more efficient and more competitive, for businesses, citizens and visitors within the framework of Public, Private partnership, Citizen and through the use of technology.

Smart Mobility. In the fields of transport and digital games, this concept plays a fundamental future role, with the multiplication and improvement of the available data on mobility and the gains made in terms of processing information. The integration of technology on citizen mobility is a crucial process towards the development of the city of Casablanca towards a smart city.

Smart Environment. This model that we have called the Social Smart City has the following impact on the environment (De Guimarães et al., 2020)(Chakir et al., 2020a):

- Adopt a participatory and equitable e-governance evaluated continuously according to performance indicators defined by a strategy and global vision of a smart city(Chakir, Chergui, Medromi, et al., 2016)(Chakir, Chergui, Elhasnaoui, et al., 2016).
- Encourage social innovation to better meet the needs of citizens.
- Encourage all stakeholders in society (citizens, researchers, Small and MEdium-sized enterprises 'SMEs', very small businesses, start-ups...) to develop pilot services and experiences for Smart Cities.
- Improve the well-being of citizens and their involvement in the development of their city.

- Minimize the costs of deploying and maintaining a Smart City by adopting innovative economic mechanisms and models for its sustainability.
- Develop sustainable approaches for the exploitation of natural resources.

Smart Living. The adaptability of the lifestyle of Moroccan citizens to new technologies is essential. Called "smart lifestyle," it is a way of life using technology. This pattern of behavior will depend on the quality of housing conditions, the existence of cultural facilities, educational institutions(Chergui et al., 2020), and the quality of social cohesion. For example, for quality housing in Morocco, the trustees of buildings and houses should, within five years, be operational and truly be of service to residents by ensuring comfort, security, and energy performance.

Smart Governance. The integration of technology in the prefectural and community fields is important. Smart governance refers to transparent governance involving citizens in decision-making and provides numerous public and social services.(Chergui et al., 2019)(Chergui et al., 2017) Considering the example of the administration which installs universal road signs to help the user to take his destination, regardless of his origin, to live the road as a journey. This will prevent some motorists from discovering the paths for the first time. Intelligent administration is certainly important for any individual to facilitate his administrative life such as collecting certificates(Chakir, Chergui, Elhasnaou, et al., 2016).

Putting technology at the service of the environment, the economy and people, is developing all over the world, these new forms of urban organization face certain obstacles, notably due to the regulatory and cultural context, public and private actors are the drivers of this transformation and collaborate to achieve the overall environmental, economic and social performance of their city(Lopes & Rodrigues, 2020).

Growing urbanization and urban demographic pressure are bringing up new challenges for the city of tomorrow, which will have to provide sufficient housing, offer transport infrastructure adapted to urban sprawl, generate profitable economic activity for residents, manage environmental externalities (pollution, energy consumption, and floods.)(Sharida et al., 2020).

New models must be invented. The implementation of new information and communication technologies within cities is a powerful tool for achieving this(Lee et al., 2020). Established in cities, they transform them into Smart Cities, sustainable and connected cities, some authors propose to distinguish three main dimensions(Cortés-Cediel et al., 2020):

- **Technology.** The Smart City is based on technologies that ensure its development and become attractive to residents and visitors.
- **Sustainability.** The Smart City is closely linked to respect for its environment.

- **Humanity.** The social and human aspect of the Smart City design is important for local ownership, responding to expressed needs and the ability to continuously innovate.

EMPIRIC STUDY

In recent years, the ability to combine and explore multiple data streams to obtain valuable information has been refined. These ideas are at the heart of what makes a city more livable, more sustainable, and more suitable for work.

To assess the social impact of Smart Cities on citizens, we conducted a survey project, first we targeted a population of size n = 401 in the city of Casablanca. The role of this project is to:

- Measure the level of interest and sensitivity
- Know the connected people who use new technologies.
- Collect the opinions of the inhabitants and users of the city to identify the main needs.
- Improve the comfort of the inhabitants.

In the following, we will present some statistical representations which explain our problem to have a Smart City with all the measures of quality and efficiency.

The following graph (Figure 1) represents the rate of knowledge of Smart Cities, so it allows to conclude that the number of people who know the concept of the Smart City is very important which is represented by the percentage of 84%, the set of age groups who have information about this concept exceeds 70%. Also, the percentage which corresponds to the active class of the company, whose age is between 25 and 45, is 85% and towards 100%.

Figure 1. The level of knowledge of the smart city by age

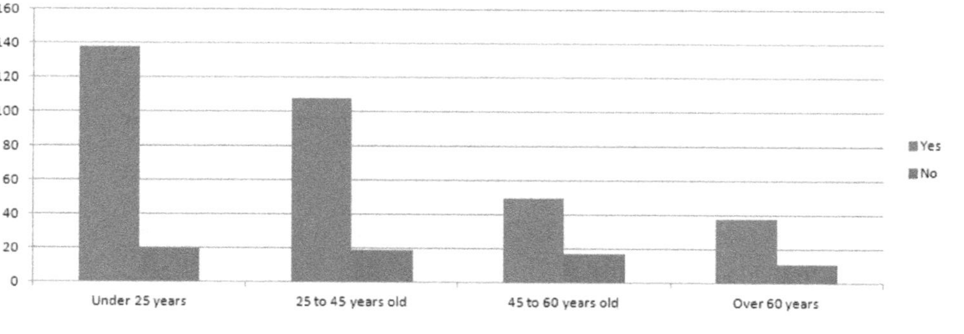

The following graph (Figure 2) represents the knowledge rate of Smart Cities by business field, it therefore allows to conclude that most of the business fields have information on this concept; a percentage of 84% for the field of "studies and research", a percentage of 78% for the field of "engineers, industry executives".

Figure 2. The level of knowledge of the smart city by business field

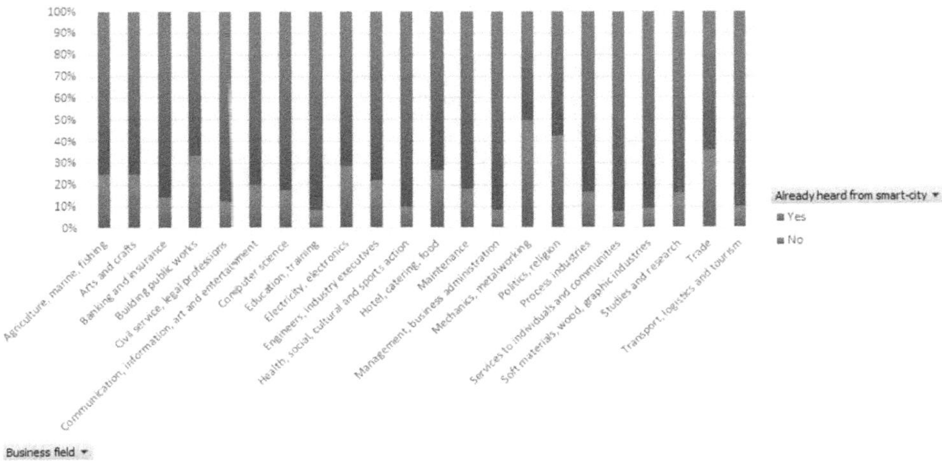

The two-following graphic (Figure 3, Figure 4) representations show the interest expressed by people towards the usefulness of a home automation system, and their need to install it at home.

There are 60% of people who express their deep interest in home automation and there is a negligible percentage of 11% of people who are not interested in this concept (Figure 3).

Figure 3. The rate of utility of home automation by civility

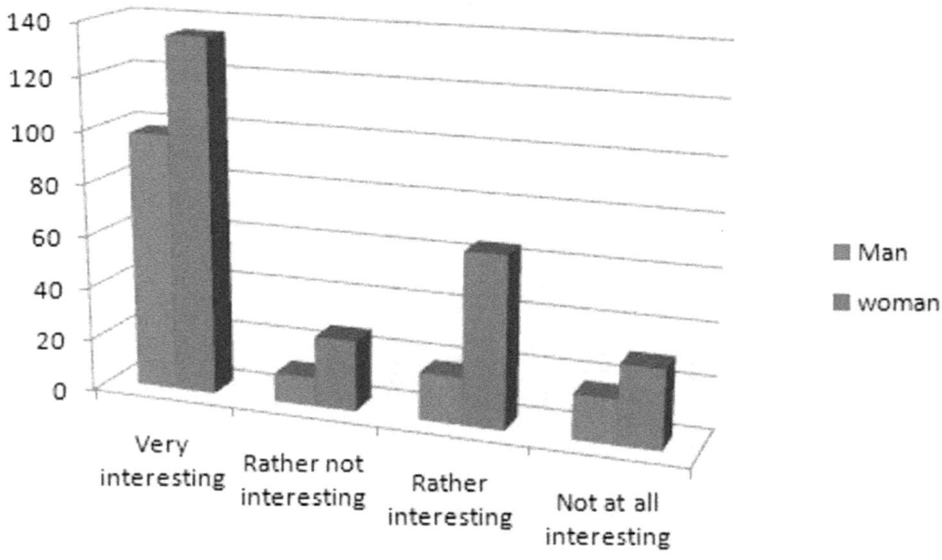

The cross-referencing of the two variables "Age" and "Install a home automation system" makes it possible to clarify that the degree of acceptance and installation of a home automation system by age class. From the results of the graph, we see that 85.07% of people between the ages of 46 and 60 are more interested in installing a home automation system in their homes (Figure 4)

Figure 4. The duration to install a home automation system by age group

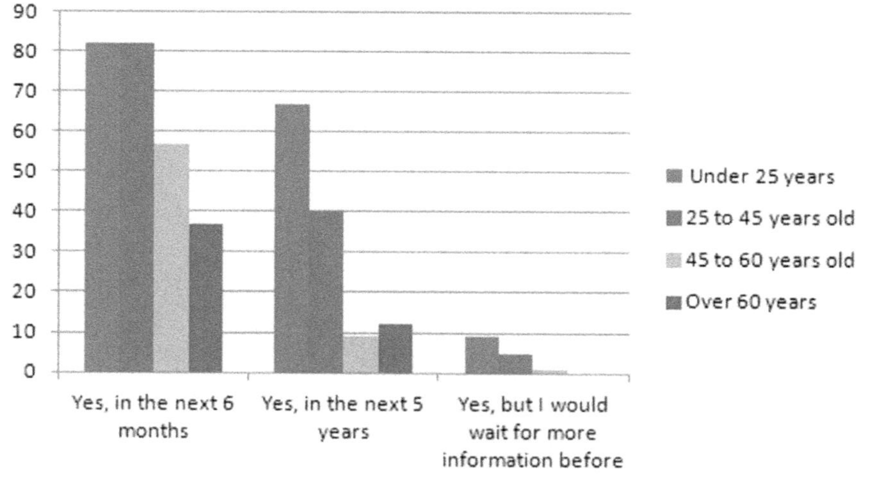

The following graph (Figure 5) represents the relation between the age class and the degree of payment of individuals for urban and economic housing; we see that 75% of people are ready to pay for an intelligent lifestyle, smart living.

Figure 5. Urban and economic housing

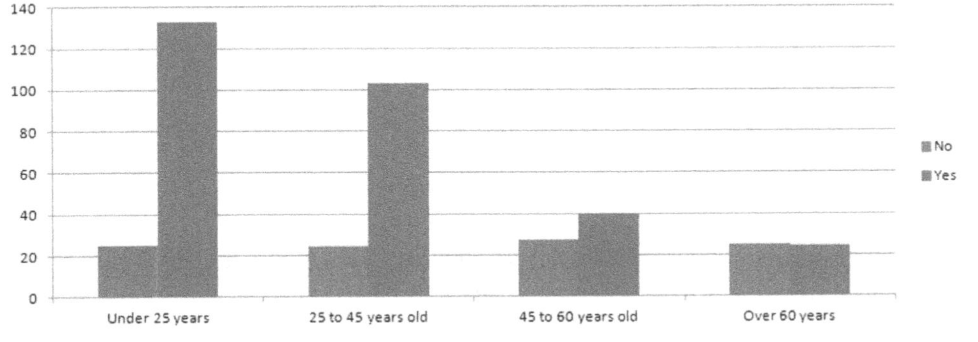

EMPIRIC STUDY

Discussion

The adaptability of the way of life of citizens to new technologies is essential. individuals are interested in intelligent life to make their life easy, according to the survey we established. we see that the most active class of society, the class of young people show their awareness of the benefits of this concept of Smart Cities, and they are ready to make investments to put it in the shortest possible time. and we will see the same reaction even for people whose age is between 45 and 60 years. They want to benefit from the quality of the conditions for social cohesion. For example, smart housing for comfort, security, and energy performance.

The Smart City uses digital technologies to improve the quality of life of citizens, move them forward, find effective solutions to various problems and make the most of the opportunities for economic development provided by these technologies. To help society escape from these challenges, we must always be reactive, provide the best service and satisfy citizens.

The orientation towards Smart Cities will generate a large amount of data, hence the need to implement powerful solutions to guarantee the operability of Smart Cities.

Consequently, in this work, we need solutions that have the power to interpret and understand the greatest amount of information from citizens, without sampling or approximation, and to produce results that it is not possible to get it by traditional tools or in cost-effective time and money measures. And who can manage connectivity; so that a ton of data can be made available to all industries.

Among the solutions, we propose the use of Big Data which is an invaluable solution to solidify the success and sustainability of Smart Cities.

Big Data becomes important because the amount of data becomes so large that it becomes difficult to manage with conventional database management tools. We are therefore talking about data enhancement through activities such as:

- Real-time analysis of a data flow.
- Trend inference from multi-structured data sets.
- Visual representation of results.
- Discovering and exploring data across different sources.

Transforming cities with Big Data is a real necessary challenge. "Today, only 2% of the earth's surface is occupied by cities. By 2050, they will welcome 70% of the world's population."

BIG DATA

Uses of Big Data in New Urban Transformations: Smart Cities

Smart Cities encourage citizen participation, develop new digital services to simplify the lives of residents or even optimize the management of their networks, to save money and reduce their impact on the environment.

Concretely, this translates into a real-time collection of data on the uses and opinions of the inhabitants, via dedicated applications, as well as on the instantaneous state of the water, electricity, heating, or transport networks, measured by sensors. At the same time, the open data movement has led administrations to identify, structure and publish public data.

Whether public or private, the data thus generated constitute a precious source of information on the territory. Some data may even prove to be strategic for decision-making. Others can constitute a resource for the socio-economic development of the territory by the creation of new services.

The production and massive dissemination of digital data have become a challenge for information professionals, particularly in terms of storage and operation. If Big Data offers many perspectives, especially in the field of sustainable development which is one of the major challenges of our century (Olszak et al., 2020).

The processing of large data sets, commonly called Big Data, gives rise to many hopes: creation of new development levers for businesses, prevention of epidemics, reinforced security (Ralph et al., 2020).

Figure 6. Big data use cases for the smart city

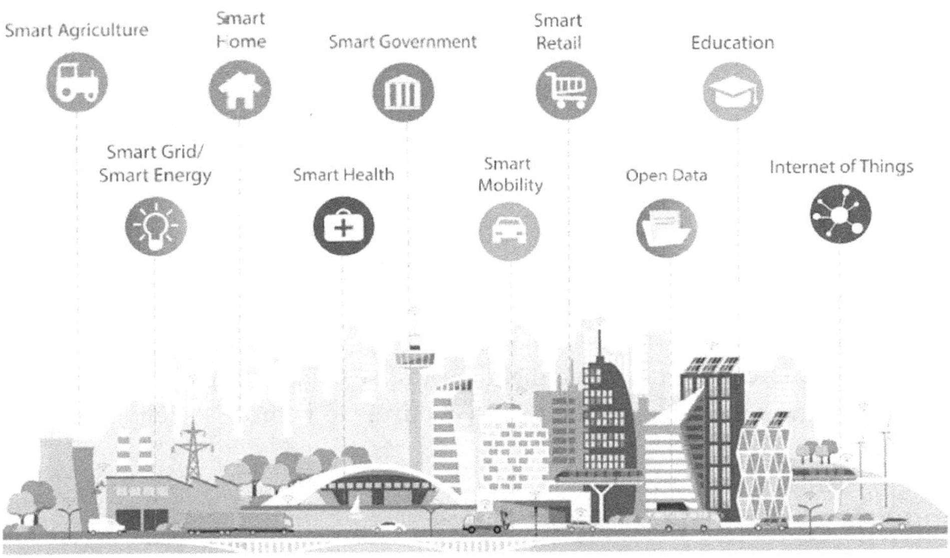

The use of Big Data technology will allow us to benefit from several aspects to guarantee a good performance of Smart Cities to citizens (Figure 6) (Ralph et al., 2020)(Al Nuaimi et al., 2015).

- **Security.** Predictive analytics have been used in several cities around the world to help predict where crime is likely to occur, based on historical and geographic data.
- **Urban planning.** Data can help plan building construction and urban space planning. Models can be developed to maximize access to certain areas or services while minimizing the risk of infrastructure overload. In short, Big Data can increase efficiency. The data also make it possible to map and predict the impact of an infrastructure on urban space with high precision.
- **Transport**. Using data to regulate the transportation network helps create efficient and flexible public transportation, reduce delays, and increase efficiency. The data is used to predict peak hours, but also to monitor equipment to reduce the number of breakdowns and accidents.

- **The test of time.** Often, infrastructure in new areas is not strong enough to support continued growth. It then becomes necessary to make improvements. Using modeling and predictive analytics, urban planners can see where growth is likely to occur and to measure that growth. The amenities can be improved accordingly. Thus, growth can occur with confidence.
- **Internet.** Knowing when and where bandwidth should be given priority is an essential component, and data is the compass to point in the right direction. In concrete terms, the bandwidth must be mainly high in shopping and financial centers during the week and in residential areas during the weekend. However, to maximize bandwidth on a more precise scale, Big Data can help.
- **Durability.** Monitoring and control are two essential criteria for ensuring the sustainability of a project. The data allow governments and businesses to verify the positive or negative effects of their decisions on the whole city.
- **Efficient spending.** The main problem with Smart Cities is that large amounts of money are spent on relatively harmless work. Small changes or reshaping of landscapes be a waste of public money. Using Big Data technologies, it is possible to check in advance the impact of spending. Thus, it is possible to determine how to spend the money effectively to improve the city at a lower cost.

Impacts of Big Data in Smart Cities

Every business uses data differently, but the more efficiently it is, the greater the potential for growth. An optimal data analysis will therefore allow us to find answers that will help generate (Praharaj, 2020)(Cronemberger & Gil-Garcia, 2019):

- **Cost reduction.** Big Data can push a company to want to change internal processes. The information generated can help reduce production costs. In addition, it could also lower transportation and inventory costs to achieve significant savings.
- **Increasing efficiency.** Some Big Data analytics can provide immediate insights and help leaders make quick decisions. These same analyzes can be used to improve the speed of production, especially for factories that work with large volumes.
- **Employee enrichment.** Analyzes leading to reduced time free employees to focus on value-added tasks. In addition, the synergistic flow of information across management, engineering, quality control, mechanical operators and other aspects of the organization allows these different departments to work together more effectively. Some employees even consider that the

arrival of Big Data makes their work much less repetitive and therefore more stimulating.

- **Improving the link with the customer.** Big Data can also extract invaluable information about your customers. By knowing the purchasing methods of consumers as well as their satisfaction, one can not only make the products according to their precise needs but also make targeted marketing campaigns. Thus, a possible increase in income.
- **Online reputation monitoring.** Analysis tools can measure feelings. It is therefore possible to obtain precise "feedback" on what the public thinks and says about a company. We can therefore monitor and improve your company's online presence.
- **Control of competing strategies**. As well as the analysis tools allow to monitor the needs of the customers and the reputation of your online business, they also allow to quickly detect new strategies implemented by your competition.
- **Improving quality assurance.** Using Big Data to do preventive analysis can significantly reduce testing times and focus on specific tests.
- **Risk reduction**. Studying the extracted data makes the detection of bad practices, anomalies, and possible fraud more effective. Adequate measures can then be taken to minimize the damage.
- **Improvement of supply.** By using Big Data to predict the possibility of raw material delivery problems, a company can assess the probability of potential delays on a map, analyze meteorological statistics for tornadoes, earthquakes, hurricanes, etc. Predictive analysis is used to calculate the probabilities of delays. The results can thus help identify replacement suppliers and develop B plans to ensure that production is not interrupted.

Big Data and Artificial Intelligence

Big Data represents all the techniques for collecting, storing and analyzing this data; increasingly large data given the data that we want to link and for which we want to check - or find - the existence of a correlation. And this is the interest of Big Data: find correlations between information which have no connection between them, to draw a fine analysis of a situation, even to anticipate (a behavior, a phenomenon ...) (Jian et al., 2020).

Artificial intelligence is strongly linked to Big Data. This is where artificial intelligence comes in. Only sophisticated algorithms are capable today of processing so much information instantly. Second, like any statistic and probability law, the more data AI must process, the more likely it is to draw a general trend from it (Chakir et al., 2020b)(Zhu, 2020).

We almost come to anticipate behavior by identifying the same correlations in data analysis. It is called "predictive analytics." Clearly, without the algorithms that build artificial intelligence, Big Data (collecting, storing, and analyzing data) is not possible (Ngo et al., 2020).

Big Data technologies are revolutionary in that they allow real-time data collection and processing. In marketing, for example, there is the retargeting method which consists in monitoring a consumer's web browsing in real-time (Fu et al., 2020).

Big Data is the new business trend, at all levels and for all its services. Big Data technologies and the current prowess of artificial intelligence make it possible to increase the efficiency of any type of computer system including databases. More and more executives are making their strategic decisions after consulting with a Big Data analyst and this is just the beginning.

The data will be increased every year, a trend strongly boosted by the advent of connected objects and the amount of personal information that we leave there. So, for smart citrus, we will benefit from the advantage of real-time data processing offered by Big Data.

APPLICATION OF SMART CITY AND DISCUSSION

Application of Smart City

We have randomly chosen cities on an international scale to analyze their situation in relation to smart city projects and in relation to demographic change between 2018 and 2019; we have limited ourselves to a population of 7 cities which are: Wallonia, Cairo, Casablanca, Oslo, Montpellier, Montreal, Incheon (Songdo). And for each city, we analyzed the state of the city in relation to the six dimensions: "Smart Economy", "Smart Mobility", "Smart Environment", "Smart People", "Smart Living" and, "Smart Governance ". The following table (table 1) shows the state of the selected cities.

Table 1. State of cities

	SMART ECONOMY	SMART MOBILITY	SMART ENVIRONMENT	SMART PEOPLE	SMART LIVING	SMART GOVERNANCE
BELGIQUE - WALLONIE [29]	x	x	x	x	x	x
EGYPTE-CAIRO [30, 33]		x	x			x
MORROCO - CASABLANCA [31, 34]		x	x	x		
NORVEGE - OSLO [32]		x	x	x	x	
FRANCE -MONTPELLIER [32, 35]					x	
CANADA - MONTREAL [32]		x		x	x	
INCHEON(SONGDO) - SOUTH KOREA [32]	x	x	x	x	x	x

EXAMPLE PROJECT

Cornet Treatments (circular economy): The Company Cornet Treatments, Belgian recycling specialist, has invested in a pilot installation in Mons with the aim of producing synthetic fuel from ultimate waste (shredder residues from car wrecks, out of order electrical and electronic equipment and other scrap metal). The idea is to use diesel and distilled petrol to activate cogeneration engines, sources of electricity and heat production. The final objective of Cornet Treatments is to develop an installation capable of covering the electricity consumption of 10,000 Walloon households [36].

The table (table 2) presents the demographic evolution of the chosen cities between 2018 and 2019. We have calculated the demographic growth rate by city based on the following formula:

Rate of increase = (final value - initial value) / initial value

According to the calculated demographic growth rate, we note that all the cities are experiencing a demographic progression that varies from 0.28% for Wallonia and 5.64% a maximum value for Incheon-Songdo. That said, the whole world is experiencing demographic change which produces data in large quantities. We need to focus on making better use of the data available to better understand cities, how they work, their needs and problems. And to use this knowledge of their cities to identify new needs among citizens and therefore create new services and uses that meet them.

Table 2. Demographic evolution between 2018-2019

	POPULATION		Growth Rate (%)
	2018	2019	2018-2019
BELGIQUE - WALLONIE [29]	3634000	3644000	0,28%
EGYPTE-CAIRO [30, 33]	9700000	9800000	1,03%
MORROCO - CASABLANCA [31, 34]	3501911	3535127	0,95%
NORVEGE - OSLO [32]	673469	681067	1,13%
FRANCE -MONTPELLIER [32, 35]	282143	286098	1,13%
CANADA - MONTREAL [32]	2052910	2088413	1,70%
INCHEON(SONGDO) - SOUTH KOREA [32]	2783000	2940000	5,64%

Cities are therefore faced with a new challenge: that of mastering their data, circulating it, and restoring it at any time and in any place. The main goal is to streamline their management and offer a personalized relationship to their citizens.

Discussion

Given the multiplicity of sources and types of data, the number of players and the volumes involved, a Big Data strategy, carried by the city itself, becomes a necessary condition for a sustainable smart city. This strategy consists not only in providing the territory with a technical platform for collecting and processing large volumes of data, but also in assessing the potential of existing data about city projects and defining the conditions for their interoperability, their provision and their use by third parties.

In other words, it is a question of defining a data policy and governance in a context where, if the data is abundant, their owners spontaneously hesitate to share it. It is however fundamentally about this mutualization of data, typically in an open data logic, on which depends the capacity of public, private, and individual actors to:

- Better understand the city, its functioning, its consumption, and its dysfunctions.
- Use this knowledge to identify new needs and invent new services, new uses.
- Decompartmentalize everyone's areas of intervention to provide coherent and coordinated responses in space and time.

Today, two Big Data strategies seem possible for Smart Cities: absolute data control or interdependence. In the first case, the city, owner of the infrastructure, requests to receive the data and pushes the players in place through an "open data" approach which becomes an additional lever to take or regain control of its data. In the second case, the city and the urban operators create a partnership based on the data collected by the latter.

Absolute mastery of data is not a panacea:

- It deprives the city of competition between operators, thus hampering their investments and their capacity for innovation in areas which constitute their core business,
- It transforms the city into a multi-domain data operator with significant investments that go beyond the proper functioning of the city,
- It centralizes the data innovation function at the city level, which is not and will not be the role.

Artificial intelligence is the logical continuation of data analysis methods and techniques, an extension of Business Intelligence, which has been followed by Big Data. The concept of artificial intelligence needs a very large amount of analyzed and cross-linked data to draw innovative, even creative, conclusions close to the functioning of the human brain.

Thus, the combination of Big Data and artificial intelligence to enrich Smart Cities will allow us to design intelligent models beneficial to humans. So the proposed solution is to take as input the different sources of data coming from cities and manage them by exploiting the power of Big Data and in parallel it is necessary to put an intelligent system which takes as input only the data necessary to process the request presented subsequently respond in real time to this request and finally make a decision in relation to this request.

CONCLUSION

To conclude and respond to our initial problem, Smart Cities are no longer simply inspired by fiction, but respond to the desire to reside in a smart, clean and dynamic city, which becomes eco-responsible and allows financial enrichment thanks to a better management of costs and resources but also intellectual. Hence the need to integrate the powers of Big Data with artificial intelligence to process the requests presented in real time.

As a perspective, we propose to develop a generic model that ensures the good management of smart cities by using the powers of technology.

REFERENCES

Al Nuaimi, E., Al Neyadi, H., Mohamed, N., & Al-Jaroodi, J. (2015). Applications of big data to smart cities. *Journal of Internet Services and Applications*, *6*(1), 25. doi:10.118613174-015-0041-5

Bnouachir, H. (n.d.). Intelligent Fleet Management System for Open Pit Mine.

Chakir, A., Chergui, M., & Andry, J. F. (2020a). A decisional smart approach for the adoption of the IT green. *Environment, Development and Sustainability*, 1–15.

Chakir, A., Chergui, M., & Andry, J. F. (2020b). A Smart Updater IT Governance Platform Based on Artificial Intelligence. *Advances in Science. Technology and Engineering Systems*, *5*(5), 47–53. doi:10.25046/aj050507

Chakir, A., Chergui, M., Elhasnaou, S., Medromi, H., & Sayouti, A. (2016). A decision approach to select the best framework to treat an IT problem by using multi-agent system and expert systems. *Lecture Notes in Electrical Engineering*, *366*, 499–511. doi:10.1007/978-981-287-990-5_40

Chakir, A., Chergui, M., Elhasnaoui, S., Medromi, H., & Sayouti, A. (2016). Intelligent plateform to select the best IT-GRC framework for treatment the needs of stakeholders. *International Journal of Applied Engineering Research: IJAER*, *11*(12).

Chakir, A., Chergui, M., Medromi, H., & Sayouti, A. (2016). An approach to select effectively the best framework IT according to the axes of the governance IT, to handle and to set up an objective IT. *Proceedings of 2015 IEEE World Conference on Complex Systems, WCCS 2015*. IEEE. 10.1109/ICoCS.2015.7483311

Chergui, M., Chakir, A., & Medromi, H. (2019). Smart IT governance, risk and compliance semantic model: Business Driven architecture. *Proceedings of the 3rd World Conference on Smart Trends in Systems, Security and Sustainability. WORLD (Oakland, Calif.)*, *S4*, 2019. doi:10.1109/WorldS4.2019.8903997

Chergui, M., Chakir, A., Medromi, H., & Radoui, M. (2017). A new approach for modeling strategic IT governance workflow. In Lecture Notes in Electrical Engineering (Vol. 397). doi:10.1007/978-981-10-1627-1_22

Chergui, M., Tahiri, A., Chakir, A., & Mansouri, H. (2020). Towards a New Educational Engineering Model for Moroccan University Based on ICT. [IJEP]. *International Journal of Engineering Pedagogy*, *10*(3), 49. doi:10.3991/ijep.v10i3.12421

Cortés-Cediel, M. E., Cantador, I., & Rodríguez Bolívar, M. P. (2020). Technological and Human Development of Smart Cities: An Empirical Characterization of EUROCITIES Case Studies. *Proceedings of the 53rd Hawaii International Conference on System Sciences*. IEEE. 10.24251/HICSS.2020.280

Cronemberger, F., & Gil-Garcia, J. R. (2019). Big Data and analytics as strategies to generate public value in smart cities: Proposing an integrative framework. In *Setting foundations for the creation of public value in Smart Cities* (pp. 247–267). Springer. doi:10.1007/978-3-319-98953-2_10

De Guimarães, J. C. F., Severo, E. A., Júnior, L. A. F., Da Costa, W. P. L. B., & Salmoria, F. T. (2020). Governance and quality of life in smart cities: Towards sustainable development goals. *Journal of Cleaner Production*, *253*, 119926. doi:10.1016/j.jclepro.2019.119926

Fu, H., Manogaran, G., Wu, K., Cao, M., Jiang, S., & Yang, A. (2020). Intelligent decision-making of online shopping behavior based on internet of things. *International Journal of Information Management*, *50*, 515–525. doi:10.1016/j.ijinfomgt.2019.03.010

Jian, M.-S., Hong, W.-C., Tsai, S.-C., Chen, Y.-W., & Fan, C.-L. (2020). Based on Automatic Correlation Keyword Grouping and Combination Based Deep Information Search Corresponding to Specific Language Big Data—Case of Leisure Recreation. *2020 22nd International Conference on Advanced Communication Technology (ICACT)*, 372–377.

Lee, F. S., Chakir, A., Nathanael, R., & Andry, J. F. (2020). Architecture information system in electrical distribution company using TOGAF. *International Journal of Advanced Trends in Computer Science and Engineering*, *9*(5), 7149–7156. Advance online publication. doi:10.30534/ijatcse/2020/38952020

Li, W., Batty, M., & Goodchild, M. F. (2020). *Real-time GIS for smart cities*. Taylor & Francis. doi:10.1080/13658816.2019.1673397

Lopes, N. V. M., & Rodrigues, J. (2020). Smart Methodologies for Smart Cities: A Comparative Analysis. In Smart Governance for Cities: Perspectives and Experiences (pp. 3–15). Springer. doi:10.1007/978-3-030-22070-9_1

Madakam, S. (2020). Would Be Smart Balinese Cities (Indonesia): An Exploratory Case Study. *Journal of Information Systems and Technology Management*, 17. doi:10.4301/S1807-1775202017005

Ngo, J., Hwang, B.-G., & Zhang, C. (2020). Factor-based big data and predictive analytics capability assessment tool for the construction industry. *Automation in Construction*, *110*, 103042. doi:10.1016/j.autcon.2019.103042

Novikov, V., Klochko, E., Brizhak, O., & Digtyar, O. (2020). Digital Economy: Human Capital, Technology, Communications. *5th International Conference on Economics, Management, Law and Education (EMLE 2019)*, (pp. 198–204). IEEE.

Olszak, C., Zurada, J., & Kozanoglu, D. (2020). Introduction to the Minitrack on Business Intelligence and Big Data for Innovative and Sustainable Development of Organizations. *Proceedings of the 53rd Hawaii International Conference on System Sciences*. IEEE. 10.24251/HICSS.2020.021

Pieriegud, J., & Zawieska, J. (2019). Mobility-as-a-Service–global trends and implementation potential in urban areas in Poland. *Transport Economics and Logistics*, *79*, 39–51. doi:10.26881/etil.2018.79.03

Praharaj, S. (2020). Development Challenges for Big Data Command and Control Centres for Smart Cities in India. In *Data-driven Multivalence in the Built Environment* (pp. 75–90). Springer. doi:10.1007/978-3-030-12180-8_4

Ralph, D., Li, Y., Wills, G., & Green, N. G. (2020). Recommendations from cold starts in big data. *Computing*, *102*(6), 1–22. doi:10.100700607-020-00792-y

Sharida, A., Hamdan, A., & Mukhtar, A.-H. (2020). Smart cities: The next urban evolution in delivering a better quality of life. In Toward Social Internet of Things (SIoT): Enabling Technologies, Architectures and Applications (pp. 287–298). Springer.

Yuan, Y., Lu, Y., Chow, T. E., Ye, C., Alyaqout, A., & Liu, Y. (2020). The Missing Parts from Social Media–Enabled Smart Cities: Who, Where, When, and What? *Annals of the American Association of Geographers*, *110*(2), 462–475. doi:10.1080/24694452.2019.1631144

Zhu, H. (2020). Big data and artificial intelligence modeling for drug discovery. *Annual Review of Pharmacology and Toxicology*, *60*(1), 573–589. doi:10.1146/annurev-pharmtox-010919-023324 PMID:31518513

Chapter 14
ChatGPT and the Moralities of Large Language Modelling in Research Publications

Sarabjeet Singh Sethi
https://orcid.org/0000-0003-1230-440X
Swami Keshvanand Institute of Technology, Management, and Gramothan, Jaipur, India

Priyanka Sharma
https://orcid.org/0000-0002-9503-1170
Swami Keshvanand Institute of Technology, Management, and Gramothan, Jaipur, India

A. V. Senthil Kumar
https://orcid.org/0000-0002-8587-7017
Hindusthan College of Arts and Science, Coimbatore, India

ABSTRACT

This chapter discusses OpenAI's ChatGPT, a generative pre-trained transformer, which uses natural language processing to fulfill text-based user requests (i.e., a "chatbot"). The history and principles behind ChatGPT and similar models are discussed. This technology is then discussed in relation to its potential impact on academia and scholarly research and publishing. ChatGPT is seen as a potential model for the automated preparation of essays and other types of scholarly manuscripts. Potential ethical issues that could arise with the emergence of large language models like GPT-3, the underlying technology behind ChatGPT, and its usage by academics and researchers, are discussed and situated within the context of broader advancements in artificial intelligence, machine learning, and natural language processing for research and scholarly publishing.

DOI: 10.4018/979-8-3693-0815-8.ch014

1. INTRODUCTION

ChatGPT and related technologies have been identified as disruptive innovations with the potential to revolutionize academia and scholarly publishing (Haque et al., 2022). As a natural language processing tool developed by OpenAI, ChatGPT can automate the preparation of essays and other scholarly manuscripts. However, the ethical implications of this technology and its underlying GPT-3 technology have not yet been fully considered (Gonzalez-Padilla, 2022). This Chapter addresses the significant ethical issues that could arise with the use of GPT-3 and places these concerns in the context of broader advancements in artificial intelligence, machine learning, and natural language processing for research and scholarly publishing.

Our analysis reveals that the potential for bias in the training data and coding process of AI- driven language models such as GPT-3 poses a threat to the integrity of science. Additionally, ethical considerations include issues of copyright, citation practices, and the potential impact on the "Matthew Effect" in scholarly publishing. Ownership of the content generated by the model and the use of third-party content within the generated manuscripts are also major ethical concerns. While ChatGPT can assist editors and peer reviewers in completing repetitive or tedious tasks, there is a risk that it may not mitigate existing biases and that human judgment calls are still necessary. Furthermore, the use of AI-driven language models raises concerns about the reproducibility and transparency of research.

It is crucial to carefully consider all of these ethical considerations to ensure that these technologies are used responsibly and ethically in the context of academic research and publishing. Researchers, publishers, and the developers of AI-driven language models must collaborate to establish guidelines and protocols to ensure that the use of these technologies is ethical, transparent, and accountable. Failure to do so may undermine public trust in the scientific process and have far-reaching consequences for the future of research and innovation.

2. A BRIEF INTRODUCTION TO UNDERLYING AI CONCEPTS

Artificial intelligence, machine learning, and natural language processing are rapidly advancing fields that are having a significant impact on a wide range of industries and applications (Wamba et al., 2021). Chatbots, which are computer programs designed to mimic human conversation, are one example of the practical uses of these technologies (Adamopoulou & Moussiades, 2020a). The following section provides a brief overview of artificial intelligence, machine learning, and natural language processing –as well as the ways in which chatbots are utilizing these technologies to interact with users in a more human-like manner – in order to ensure that all readers have a basically familiarity with the technology and concepts that underpin large language models like the Generative Pretrained Transformer and ChatGPT.

Artificial intelligence (AI) is a multidisciplinary and interdisciplinary field that has grown tremendously since the introduction of manually operated computers in the 1950s (Haenlein & Kaplan, 2019). It has the potential to revolutionize various industries, and is defined as any theory, method, or approach that assists machines, particularly computers, in analyzing, simulating, exploiting, and exploring human thought processes and behaviors (Lu, 2019). AI involves the simulation of intelligent behavior in machines, with the goal of creating machines that can mimic human intellect in important ways such as language comprehension, reasoning and problem-solving (Chowdhary, 2020). Self-learning is a key component of AI, allowing systems to acquire new information and improve their knowledge-based judgments and conclusions through experience and data (Mintz & Brodie, 2019). Machine learning and deep learning techniques have become the standard approach to advancing AI, with artificial neural networks (ANNs) allowing robots to learn and reason like humans and perform increasingly complex tasks (Lu, 2019). AI has already had a significant impact on various industries such as pharmaceutical, industrial, financial, medical, and managerial, and is expected to play a crucial role in helping businesses of all sizes stay competitive in the global economy (Makridakis, 2017). AI encompasses a range of specialized domains including machine learning (ML) and natural language processing (NLP).

The volume of data being generated from various sources, including people, devices, and computers, continues to grow at an exponential rate (Beath et al., 2012). As the amount of data becomes too large for individuals to make sense of and draw meaningful insights from, it becomes necessary to automate systems that can learn from the data to provide valuable insights. This is where machine learning (ML) comes in. ML is a key component of artificial intelligence (AI) and involves the development of computational theories for learning processes that allow machines to learn from experience without being explicitly programmed to do so (Chowdhary, 2020; Mahesh, 2020). It is at the intersection of computer science and statistics and is used to create programs that can automatically learn from data, acquire knowledge from experience, and continuously improve their learning behavior to make predictions based on new data (Jordan & Mitchell, 2015). ML is a useful technique in various areas of AI, including computer vision, voice recognition, and natural language processing (NLP). In this paper, we focus on ChatGPT, an AI technology that uses NLP to enable computers to engage in natural language conversations (Radford et al., 2018). ML is an essential part of ChatGPT, as it allows the system to learn from data and improve its language processing abilities over time, leading to more effective communication and interaction between humans and computers.

Artificial intelligence (AI) has become a part of everyday life with the advancement of processing power and the use of intelligent agents (Adamopoulou & Moussiades, 2020b). Intelligent agents are programs that can act independently and make decisions based on their observations of the environment, human input, and internal knowledge. Chatbots, also known as conversational artificial intelligence bots, are a type of intelligent agent that can respond to conversations through text or voice as if they were sentient beings, and they have gained popularity due to their usefulness in various applications such as customer service, healthcare, education, and personal support (Brandtzaeg & Følstad, 2017; Nagarhalli et al., 2020). Chatbots have been developed using natural language processing (NLP) techniques, which allow them to understand and interpret human language input (Khanna et al., 2015). In recent years, chatbots have become more popular, particularly among younger generations who prefer instant, one-on- one communication through short messages (Lokman & Ameedeen, 2018). This paper focuses on ChatGPT, a chatbot that uses NLP and AI to generate natural language conversations, and specifically on how it can be used in academia to create and write research and scholarly articles, and the ethical issues associated with this development.

3. INTRODUCING CHATGPT

OpenAI is a research laboratory that has made significant contributions to the field of artificial intelligence, including the development of the highly advanced language model, GPT-3. In addition to GPT-3, OpenAI has also released ChatGPT, a chatbot that uses natural language processing to generate responses to user inputs. Both GPT-3 and ChatGPT have garnered significant attention and have the potential to revolutionize a wide range of language-related tasks. In this section, we will delve into the details of OpenAI, GPT-3, and ChatGPT, exploring their capabilities, limitations, and potential applications.

3.1 OpenAI and Early Developments

Established in 2015, OpenAI is a research laboratory focused on the development of AI products for the common good (OpenAI, 2022). The laboratory has received significant support from individuals such as founding donor Elon Musk and the Microsoft Corporation, which invested one billion U.S. dollars in exchange for exclusive access to some of OpenAI's products (Brockman et al., 2016). As a result, the laboratory has made rapid progress in the development of its AI technologies. OpenAI has released a number of machine learning products for the general public, with DALL-E and ChatGPT being among the most well-known (Devlin et al., 2018).

DALL-E is a machine learning technology that generates images based on user inputs and was made widely available to the public, preceding ChatGPT in its availability (Marcus et al., 2022). It uses Artificial Neural Networks with multimodal neurons to understand and create novel images. These neurons are so tolerant of different expressions of a concept that they open up a world of variation (Goh et al., 2021). This innovation, introduced by OpenAI, represents how the lab seeks to change the game with smart AI. Availability to the public, key to the popularity of DALL-E, is also responsible for the rapid popularity of ChatGPT, which gained over one million unique users in less than one week after its launch (Mollman, 2022).

3.2 ChatGPT

Generative Pre-Trained Transformer, or GPT, is a language model that understands human inputs (as described with DALL-E above) and then produces response text that is nearly indistinguishable from natural human language (Dale, 2021). The concepts behind GPT are not too complex, by NLP/ML standards, thought they are refined by OpenAI (Radford et al., 2018). The creation and fine-tuning of the algorithm occur in a couple of steps:

- Generative, unsupervised, pretraining, where the data used for training is unlabeled and learning occurs naturally (like when you walk into an entirely new situation with no background knowledge and fill in pieces as you explore) as opposed to supervised and guided training (where each aspect of the learning process is curated like a teacher in a classroom) (Erhan et al., 2010).
- Discriminative, supervised, fine-tuning, where, following the pretraining, the algorithm is refined by its creators to perform better on necessary tasks (Budzianowski & Vulić, 2019).

Figure 1 illustrates at a technical level how ChatGPT works, based on an initial GPT model, as well as the concepts of supervised fine-tuned modeling, rewards modeling, and proximal policy optimization modeling (PPO). As demonstrated here, development of a useful ChatGPT interface is an iterative process.

Figure 1. GPT deployment workflow diagram

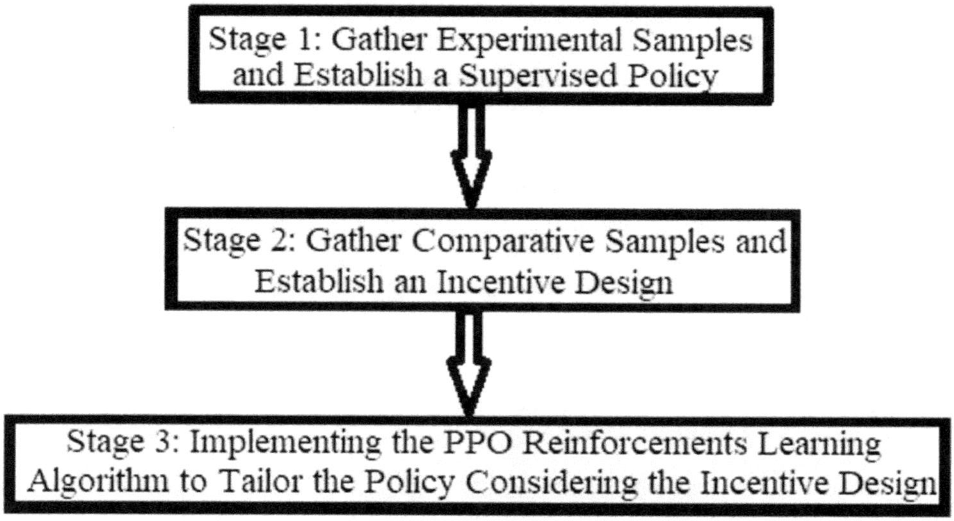

GPT stands out as a large language model due to its exceptional scale and the sheer amount of data used to train it. The algorithm underlying GPT has access to the entire Internet, which means that it is built upon billions of data sources, making it one of the largest language models in the world (Floridi & Chiriatti, 2020). GPT is a versatile tool that has been designed to perform various language-based tasks such as text generation, question answering, and translation. It uses deep learning techniques and sophisticated algorithms that enable it to understand the context of a piece of text and generate human-like responses, making it unique among language processing tools.

ChatGPT is a public tool developed by OpenAI that is based on the GPT technology (Kirmani, 2022). Essentially, it is a highly sophisticated chatbot that can fulfill almost any text-based request (Liu et al., 2021). However, ChatGPT is capable of much more than just answering simple questions. It can also fulfill more advanced requests, leveraging its extensive data stores and efficient design. For example, if you are unsure of what to write in a thank you card to a coworker, you can simply ask ChatGPT to write one for you, and it will quickly generate a well- written, multi-paragraph letter. ChatGPT can even help with more challenging tasks, such as: composing a note to address a coworker's lack of productivity. It is only a small leap (and in the "mind" of ChatGPT, no leap at all) to ask GPT to write "an essay on the value of artificial intelligence."

In less than one minute, GPT can compose an essay of hundreds of words, written at professional researcher quality. An article could easily be written entirely by GPT by breaking the main topic into subtopics and then having GPT write each section. If the capacity of GPT is truly harnessed (through a full version that would allow for responses of several thousand words instead of just several hundred words), then an entire paper could be written in minutes with very minimal prompting from a researcher. This innovation could cut the time for composing research essays from several dozen hours to a couple dozen seconds, or even render the professional author/researcher obsolete.

Appendix 1 is an essay written by ChatGPT based on the simple prompt "write an essay about the value of AI." The essay is short, but is indistinguishable from a human-written response, perhaps even exceeding the average quality of a doctoral-level student.

Of course, there are a few limitations to GPT, even when ethical issues (which will be discussed in the rest of this paper) are set aside. Although the accuracy of natural language processing models is generally quite good, there are still errors that occur in interpreting meaning or creating accurate information – the models are not infallible, and GPT certainly has had its fair share of issues (Brown et al., 2020; Strubell et al., 2019). For instance, ambiguous terms, terms with multiple meanings (such as "construct"), as well as compound terms (such as "digital immigrant") can cause issues with interpretation of meaning by the GPT model. Additionally, these algorithms and data stores take a lot of energy to operate, especially at the scale that OpenAI is operating them (Zhou et al., 2021). OpenAI has also encountered several ethical pitfalls during the creation of GPT and the ChatGPT platform, which raise concerns about the organization's adherence to principles of responsible creation and maintenance of these technologies (Perrigo, 2023). There is also a risk that GPT could lead to biases a proliferation of misinformation, as many NLP algorithms are not yet skilled at understanding misinformation that may exist in its data stores and provide no resistance when asked to falsify or distort reality (Dale, 2017; Lucy & Bamman, 2021).

3.3 Comparison of GPT/ChatGPT to Other Existing Language Models

Compared to other language models like BERT, RoBERTa, and XLNet, ChatGPT and GPT-3 have several advantages. One of GPT-3's key strengths is its scale, with billions of parameters and access to vast amounts of data, it can perform an extensive range of language-related tasks with high accuracy. Additionally, GPT-3 is highly versatile and can be fine-tuned for various tasks such as translation, summarization, and question answering. It also uses data efficiently and achieves good results with relatively small amounts of training data. Furthermore, GPT-3 can generate human-like language, making it challenging to distinguish from text written by a human. While other language models may have similar objectives, none have achieved the same level of mastery as GPT-3 in these areas. Also, none that are close to achieving GPT-3's capabilities are as widely available to the public (Nature Machine Intelligence Editorial Board, 2020; Liu et al., 2019; Liu et al., 2022; Yang et al., 2019; Elkins & Chun, 2020).

3.4 Benefits of ChatGPT for Scholarly Publishing

Before discussing some of the ethical issues and concerns that emerge with using ChatGPT in scholarly publishing, it is important to stress the benefits that ChatGPT and similar large language models (BERT, XLNet) may bring to this field. As the building blocks of academic databases and the research environment, journals can contribute to the published articles' peer review and review ethics. ChatGPT can assist editors in completing repetitive or tedious tasks (e.g., correcting grammatical errors) and avoid making biased judgments about articles (Hosseini et al., 2022; Stokel-Walker, 2023). However, it is worth noting that if biased individuals train ChatGPT, it is unclear whether or how ChatGPT mitigates existing issues. Editors may still need judgment calls to reduce bias. On the other hand, peer reviewers sometimes fail to provide solutions in review reports due to a lack of motivation or capability (Horner & Lines, 2019; Waggoner, 2018). ChatGPT can improve the availability of review reports by providing solutions based on article contents. Since the collaborative review process (the process by which reviews from peer reviewers, editors, and other contributors are poled to provide a comprehensive set of recommendations for authors) is the primary mechanism for defining and helping to form a cognitive community (Woods et al., 2023), ChatGPT's positive role in the process may have a positive impact on the academic community, the research environment, and society as a whole (Thigpen & Funk, 2019).

ChatGPT can support the dissemination and diffusion of new research ideas through the creation of better metadata, indexing, and summaries of research findings (Lund & Wang, 2023).

Assuming there is trust and usability among the public, this may support the diffusion of research findings through the translation of research into lay language that can be understood by members of the general public (Wang et al., 2022). ChatGPT can also be used as a sort of recommender system, helping with the identification of relevant research studies based on a user's query. This would be particularly helpful with highly interdisciplinary topics where searching across multiple indices and use of many synonymous search terms related to the jargon of different disciplines could be simplified by utilizing the capabilities of an interface like ChatGPT.

Certainly, ChatGPT can also benefit authors when used responsibly. ChatGPT should not be a substitute for one's knowledge of a topic, but it could be used to save time and expenses by composing descriptions of findings and structuring a paper according to various journal style guidelines. This is different from the use of ChatGPT for plagiarism – which will be discuss in the following sections – in that the platform is being used to save time and improve quality of communication, not reproduce unoriginal ideas (Gilat & Cole, 2023). An author would input paragraphs they have already written and then ask ChatGPT to "revise to improve clarity." Similarly, ChatGPT could be used for translation or revision of imperfect English in manuscripts in order to attain publication in higher quality journals (Jiao et al., 2023).

4. MORAL IMPLICATIONS OF UTILIZING CHATGPT FOR RESEARCH PUBLICATION

The development of ChatGPT and other AI-driven technology brings with it great power and thus great responsibility. In light of this, ethical considerations must be taken into account. Although ChatGPT's massive Internet data set offers a wide range of perspectives and voices, Emily Bender, a computational linguist, has noted that size does not guarantee diversity (Bender et al., 2021). Additionally, AI-driven language models have been described as "stochastic parrots," regurgitating what they hear, often distorted by randomness (Hutson, 2021). Therefore, any ethical considerations of ChatGPT must also consider its potential for distortion. From an ethical standpoint, research papers created using ChatGPT can be seen as unoriginal and potentially problematic. Several studies have revealed that the training data and coding process of language models such as GPT-3, which are usually sourced from large web-based datasets, can contain bias with regard to gender, race, ethnicity, and disability status (Basta et al., 2019; Founta et al., 2018; Hutchinson et al., 2020; Tan & Celis, 2019; Zhao et al., 2019). Such a bias can be inadvertently perpetuated when these models are used to generate academic research, leading to the dissemination of hidden and unwitting prejudice. For thousands of years, human science has relied on verifiable evidence and an established system of checks and balances to ensure accuracy and fairness in the results of research. However, the increasing use of AI- generated research papers, which can be quickly produced in large numbers, poses a threat to the integrity of science by introducing potential biases and errors that are difficult to identify and correct (Muller, 2021). This can lead to further inequities in research outcomes and a potential undermining of the foundations of scientific knowledge.

In this section, the ethical implications of using ChatGPT and related technologies in academia and scholarly research and publishing will be examined. Specifically, issues of copyright, citation practices, and the potential impact on the "Matthew Effect" in scholarly publishing will be focused on. The potential impact of ChatGPT on research productivity and the value placed on human expertise will also be considered. It is important to carefully consider these ethical considerations in order to ensure that these technologies are used responsibly and ethically in the context of academic research and publishing.

4.1 Authorship, Copyright, and Plagiarism

Authorship attribution is a major issue concerning the generation of new knowledge by intelligent agents. There may be questions about the ownership of the content generated by the model (Schönberger, 2018). If a user provides input data to the model and the model generates content based on that input, it could be argued that the user owns the copyright to the generated content. However, if the model generates content independently of user input, the input provided is very limited (e.g., "write an essay on this topic"), or if the content is significantly edited by someone other than the user, it may be more difficult to determine ownership (Yanisky-Ravid, 2017). In these cases, it may depend upon the agreement reached with the developer of the model that generates the content; it may be necessary, at minimum, to include the model as a coauthor of the manuscript (Hugenholtz & Quintais, 2021). It is beneficial to contact the developer, should there be any question relating to the extent of the model's involvement in the creation of the knowledge.

In terms of copyright, there may be concerns about the use of third-party content within the generated manuscripts (Beaza-Yates, 2022). If the language model incorporates quotes, data, or other materials from external sources, it is important to ensure that this use is in compliance with copyright laws and that proper attribution is given (Gillotte, 2019). Depending on the nature of the use, it may be necessary to obtain permission from the copyright owner or to rely on a defense such as fair use. When using a tool like ChatGPT, it can be impossible to know the extent to which data from the training set may be quoted or otherwise used in the output generated by the tool (Dehouche, 2021). Some language models are trained with data from a specific source, like Wikipedia articles. In these cases, it would be relatively easy to identify the original source. However, models like GPT-3 are trained on a massive corpus of data from across the Internet, making the capacity to track the source virtually impossible. In other words, it may be possible that the model itself could be responsible for infringing on copyright and the risk from this infringement may be passed on to the author if they replicate it in a scholarly publication.

Plagiarism concerns arise from copyright issues, and AI has been previously known in journalism for plagiarism. As a result, the ethics of using ChatGPT to generate scientific articles have been widely discussed (Anderson et al., 2023). Plagiarism is not limited to copying text but also includes paraphrasing text, methods, graphics, ideas, and any other product of intelligence that belongs to another person

(Gasparyan et al., 2017). However, ChatGPT-generated texts are based on published literature, and citation practice is encouraged in scholarly publishing.

Therefore, if the original authors are credited in the text, plagiarism may not be involved (Pertile et al., 2015). Furthermore, ChatGPT's working principle allows it to access, understand, and synthesize the best human thoughts in just a few seconds (Dehouche, 2021).

Some publishers are considering removing open-access scientific research papers to prevent AI, such as ChatGPT, from accessing the articles, in an attempt to mitigate ethical concerns (Anderson et al., 2023). However, if publicly funded research and relevant papers are not available to the public, it may lead to different ethical discussions about open access policies (Dehouche, 2021). Other publishers have simply made clear their policies regarding the usage (or suspected usage) of ChatGPT and similar large language models in scholarly publications. For instance, editors from the renowned publication *Science* have prohibited the use of any text generated by ChatGPT or any other AI tools in papers published in the journal (Thorp, 2023).

4.2 Citation Practices

Citation practices in academia are an essential aspect of scholarly work, as they serve several purposes. Citing sources demonstrates the writer's expertise in their field, showing that they are familiar with the existing research on a particular topic (Santini, 2018). It also showcases the breadth and extent of the research that has been conducted in a particular field, as the writer is able to refer to multiple sources in their work (Hyland, 1999). Citing sources is also a way to respect the work of others, as it gives credit to the researchers whose ideas and findings are being used in the writer's own work (Ha, 2022). Providing accurate and detailed citations is also important for maintaining the integrity of academic research. When readers or editors have doubts about the validity of a claim or argument, they can use the provided citations to verify the sources and assess the credibility of the work (Santini, 2018). This is particularly important in the context of academic progression and tenure, as citations are often used to evaluate, assess, and rank the work of researchers (Moher et al., 2018).

ChatGPT can utilize natural language processing (NLP) to scan academic papers and suggest appropriate citations for identified source materials (King, 2022). This tool has the potential to significantly streamline the citation process and reduce errors, as it can help researchers identify the sources they should be citing and suggest the proper formatting for the citations. Additionally, ChatGPT may also help researchers discover new sources of information and stay up to date with current advances in their fields. However, it is worth noting that ChatGPT has been found to produce academic essays with missing references (see Appendix 1 as an example). While ChatGPT may be able to provide in- text references in future versions, it is important to consider the potential consequences of relying solely on an automated tool like ChatGPT instead of reviewing the literature in depth (King, 2023). The lack of references in early versions of ChatGPT could lead to disorder in scholarly publishing, as the integrity and credibility of the research may be called into question without proper citations.

Scholarly publishing platforms like ChatGPT have the potential to impact the "Matthew Effect," which refers to the tendency for successful researchers with high citation counts to continue to be successful and cited frequently, while lesser-known researchers struggle to gain recognition and citations (Merton, 1968). This phenomenon can perpetuate existing inequalities in academia (Perc, 2014). Google Scholar uses a ranking system based on citations, and the Matthew Effect is particularly noticeable, with highly cited articles appearing first in search results. As a result, most people only look at the first few pages of search results, leading to a self-reinforcing cycle in which articles with the most citations continue to receive more citations (Perc, 2014). Consider when one enters "COVID-19" in Google Scholar (or ChatGPT), they receive mostly outdated articles from 2020 and 2021, written by U.S. authors, but these articles have a lot of citations so are ranked highly; this, in turn, leads to these same outdated articles continuing to be cited as opposed to those which may be more relevant with recent developments with the disease.

Platforms like ChatGPT, which use citation counts as a factor in determining which publications to cite, may exacerbate this effect. Therefore, it is crucial that researchers continue to engage in careful and thorough review of the literature, even when using tools like ChatGPT to assist with the citation process. This will help to ensure the quality and rigor of academic work and prevent the perpetuation of inequalities in the field (Lund, 2022).

4.3 Impact on Academic Job Expectations, Tenure, and Promotion

Evaluation of a researcher's work for the purposes of hiring, promotion, and tenure often focuses on factors such as the number and value of funded grants, the number of published papers, and the number of citations (Moher et al., 2018). Miller et al. (2011) have noted that tenure-track faculty often feel pressure to publish a large number of papers in peer-reviewed journals, as those who do not publish in such journals may be denied tenure. This emphasis on publication has led to the enduring belief that "publish or perish" is an important principle in academia (Caplow & McGee, 1958). However, the focus on the number of publications and the prestige of the journals in which they are published can stifle creativity and innovation, as editors and reviewers may be more likely to favor work that supports mainstream theories and methods (Augier et al., 2005; Bedeian, 2004). Limitations on creativity and innovation in academic research can lead to a lack of meaning and relevance, which can hinder scientific progress (Bedeian, 1996). Additionally, the emphasis on publication may lead to a disconnect between academic research and practice, as researchers may prioritize their own standing among their peers rather than the promotion of best practices (Alutto, 2008; Miller et al., 2011).

ChatGPT is a machine learning tool that uses regression language modeling to predict future words based on a preexisting knowledge of language (Olsson & Engelbrektsson, 2022). In the context of academic writing, ChatGPT generates new papers based on existing papers and researchers' needs. This could potentially exacerbate the lack of innovation and disconnection from practice in academic research (Kaltenbrunner et al., 2022). While there has been longstanding debate about the importance of publications and citations in academia, the advent of ChatGPT may be a turning point in this debate. There are several steps that could be taken to address the challenges posed by ChatGPT. First, academic journal publishers could work with computer science professionals to develop anti- ChatGPT software similar to adblockers, which would be able to detect papers generated by ChatGPT (Abd-Elaal et al., 2022). This could be achieved through the following process:

- Upload a paper to the software.
- The software will identify keywords in the paper.
- Use AI to generate relevant papers by following multiple paths, using the identified keywords as input.
- Compare the similarity between the uploaded paper and the generated papers to identify any potential match with ChatGPT-generated content.

Second, academic and research institutions and academic journals could encourage more creative and innovative research. This could help to add vitality to the academic community and broaden the range of research topics being explored. It could also reduce the likelihood that papers submitted to journals were produced by ChatGPT.

Third, changing the criteria for evaluating tenure or reevaluating the purpose of tenure in higher education and research institutions could be a fundamental solution to the ethical issues of scholarly publishing that arise from ChatGPT. Tenure is typically granted to protect academic freedom and allow faculty to explore and express controversial or unpopular ideas without fear of retribution (American Association of University Professors, n.d.; Nolan, 2004). However, if researchers are motivated primarily by the pursuit of tenure and are not concerned with the quality or relevance of their work, the purpose of academic research – to increase our understanding of the world and find ways to improve it – may be compromised (University of North

Carolina, n.d.). Instead of relying solely on the number of papers published and the prestige of the journals in which they appear, higher education and research institutions could consider alternative criteria for evaluating tenure, such as the potential impact and relevance of the research to practice or its potential to make significant contributions to the field. By shifting the focus away from quantity and prestige and towards the quality and relevance of research, institutions can discourage the use of ChatGPT and encourage more ethical practices in scholarly publishing.

5. DISCUSSION

The comparison of GPT/ChatGPT to other existing language models has demonstrated the strengths of these models in various language-related tasks. GPT-3 has shown itself to be highly versatile, efficient in using data, and capable of generating human-like language, making it a valuable tool for tasks such as translation, summarization, and question answering (Liu et al., 2022). Meanwhile, ChatGPT has the potential to improve research productivity and the quality of academic publications by streamlining the citation process and helping researchers accurately identify and properly format citations. These capabilities make GPT/ChatGPT useful and valuable tools for researchers and academics. However, the use of GPT/ChatGPT also raises several ethical concerns that must be considered (Zech, 2021). One issue is the ownership of the content generated by these models, as it is unclear who holds the rights to the generated text. There may also be concerns about the incorporation of third-party materials, such as quotes or data, and the need to ensure compliance with copyright laws and proper attribution. The use of GPT/ChatGPT may impact traditional practices and the evaluation of research, as it has the potential to streamline the citation process and may raise questions about the value placed on human expertise (Etzioni, 2017). While ChatGPT can be a useful tool for helping researchers identify and properly format citations, it is important to consider the potential for reliance on automated tools and the impact on traditional practices. It is crucial to address these ethical issues in order to ensure responsible and ethical use of GPT/ChatGPT in academia (Hancock et al., 2020).

The ethical concerns related to the use of GPT/ChatGPT, such as ownership of generated content and compliance with copyright laws, are applicable to AI, NLP, and chatbots as a whole (Jarrahi et al., 2022; Jobin, 2019). These concerns apply to any situation in which AI and chatbot technology is used to generate content or perform tasks that may have legal or ethical implications (Wang et al., 2022). In terms of ownership of generated content, the issue of who holds the rights to text or other content produced by AI and chatbots is a broader concern that applies to the use of these technologies in various contexts. Similarly, the need to ensure compliance with copyright laws and proper attribution is a concern that is relevant to any situation in which AI and chatbots are used to incorporate third-party materials (Hristov, 2016). The impact of AI and chatbots on traditional citation practices and the evaluation of research is also a concern that is applicable to these technologies as a whole (Cox, 2022). As AI and chatbots become more prevalent, it is important to consider the potential implications for traditional practices and to ensure that the value placed on human expertise is appropriately balanced with the use of these technologies.

There are also limitations to this paper, as the comparison of GPT/ChatGPT to other language models may only be applicable at the time of writing. As new language models are developed, the relative strengths and weaknesses of GPT/ChatGPT may change. Future research could explore the use of GPT/ChatGPT in conjunction with other language models or technologies in order to enhance their capabilities and performance. Additionally, it would be worthwhile to investigate the use of GPT/ChatGPT in different tasks and domains, as well as to consider the full range of existing language models. By expanding the scope of the study and exploring these areas, it may be possible to gain a more comprehensive understanding of the strengths and limitations of GPT/ChatGPT and other language models.

6. CONCLUSION

ChatGPT and related technologies have the potential to significantly impact academia and scholarly research and publishing. However, it is important to carefully consider the ethical implications of these technologies, particularly in regard to the use of GPT-3 by academics and researchers. While ChatGPT and GPT-3 represent major advancements in artificial intelligence, machine learning, and natural language processing, it is necessary to ensure that they are used ethically and responsibly for scholarly research and publishing. Many questions about the ethics of using GPT in academia and its impact on research productivity remain unanswered. This paper aimed to provide a comprehensive overview of the current state of these discussions and to encourage further exploration of the ethical considerations surrounding the use of GPT and similar technologies in academia.

REFERENCES

Abd-Elaal, E., Gamage, S., & Mills, J. E. (2022). Assisting academics to identify computer generated writing. *European Journal of Engineering Education*, *47*(5), 725–745. doi:10.1080/03043797.2022.2046709

Adamopoulou, E., & Moussiades, L. (2020a). An overview of chatbot technology. In *IFIP International Conference on Artificial Intelligence Applications and Innovations* (pp. 373-383). Springer. 10.1007/978-3-030-49186-4_31

Adamopoulou, E., & Moussiades, L. (2020b). Chatbots: History, technology, and applications. *Machine Learning with Applications*, *2*, 100006. doi:10.1016/j.mlwa.2020.100006

Alutto, J. A. (2008). *Final Report of the AACSB International Impact of Research Task Force*. The Association to Advance Collegiate Schools of Business, Tampa, FL. https://www.aacsb.edu/insights/reports/impact-of-research

American Association of University Professors. (n.d.). *Tenure*. AAUP. https://www.aaup.org/issues/tenure#:~:text=Why% 20is%20tenure%20 important%3F,conduct%20research%20in%20higher%20education.

Anderson, N., Belavy, D. L., Perle, S. M., Hendricks, S., Hespanhol, L., Verhagen, E., & Memon, A. R. (2023). AI did not write this manuscript, or did it? Can we trick the AI text detector into generated texts? The potential future of ChatGPT and AI in Sports & Exercise Medicine manuscript generation. *BMJ Open Sport & Exercise Medicine*, *9*(1), e001568. doi:10.1136/bmjsem-2023-001568 PMID:36816423

Augier, M., March, J. G., & Sullivan, B. N. (2005). Notes on the evolution of a research community: Organization studies in Anglophone North America, 1945–2000. *Organization Science*, *16*(1), 85–95. doi:10.1287/orsc.1040.0108

Basta, C., Costa-jussà, M. R., & Casas, N. (2019). Evaluating the Underlying Gender Bias in Contextualized Word Embeddings. *Proceedings of the Workshop on Gender Bias in Natural Language Processing,* (pp. 33–39). IEEE. 10.18653/v1/W19-3805

Beath, C., Becerra-Fernandez, I., Ross, J., & Short, J. (2012). Finding value in the information explosion. *MIT Sloan Management Review*, *53*(4), 18–20.

Bedeian, A. G. (1996). Thoughts on the making and remaking of the management discipline. *Journal of Management Inquiry*, *5*(4), 311–318. doi:10.1177/105649269654003

Bedeian, A. G. (2004). Peer review and the social construction of knowledge in the management discipline. *Academy of Management Learning & Education*, *3*(2), 198–216. doi:10.5465/amle.2004.13500489

Bender, E. M., Gebru, T., McMillan-Major, A., & Shmitchell, S. (2021). On the Dangers of Stochastic Parrots: Can Language Models Be Too Big? *Proceedings of the ACM Conference on Fairness, Accountability, and Transparency,* (pp. 610–623). ACM. https://doi.org/10.1145/3442188.3445922

Brandtzaeg, P. B., & Følstad, A. (2017). Why people use chatbots. In *International conference on internet science* (pp. 377-392). Springer. 10.1007/978-3-319-70284-1_30

Brockman, G., Cheung, V., Pettersson, L., Schneider, J., Schulman, J., Tang, J., & Zaremba, W. (2016). Openai gym. arXiv. https://doi.org//arXiv.1606.01540 doi:10.48550

Brown, T., Mann, B., Ryder, N., Subbiah, M., Kaplan, J. D., Dhariwal, P., ... Amodei, D. (2020). Language models are few-shot learners. *Advances in Neural Information Processing Systems, 33*, 1877–1901.

Budzianowski, P., & Vulić, I. (2019). Hello, it's GPT-2—how can I help you? towards the use of pretrained language models for task-oriented dialogue systems. /arXiv.1907.05774 doi:10.18653/v1/D19-5602

Caplow, T., & McGee, R. J. (1958). *The Academic Marketplace*. Basic Books.

Chowdhary, K. (2020). Natural language processing. In *Fundamentals of artificial intelligence* (pp. 603–649). Springer. doi:10.1007/978-81-322-3972-7_19

Cox, A. (2022). How artificial intelligence might change academic library work: Applying the competencies literature and the theory of the professions. *Journal of the Association for Information Science and Technology*. doi:10.1002/asi.24635

Dale, R. (2017). NLP in a post-truth world. *Natural Language Engineering, 23*(2), 319–324. doi:10.1017/S1351324917000018

Dale, R. (2021). GPT-3 What's it good for? *Natural Language Engineering, 27*(1), 113–118. doi:10.1017/S1351324920000601

Dehouche, N. (2021). Plagiarism in the age of massive Generative Pre-Trained Transformers (GPT-3). *Ethics in Science and Environmental Politics, 21*, 17–23. doi:10.3354/esep00195

Devlin, J., Chang, M. W., Lee, K., & Toutanova, K. (2018). Bert: Pre-training of deep bidirectional transformers for language understanding. https://doi.org//arXiv.1810.04805 doi:10.48550

Elkins, K., & Chun, J. (2020). Can GPT-3 pass a Writer's turing test? *Journal of Cultural Analytics, 5*(2), 17212. doi:10.22148/001c.17212

Erhan, D., Bengio, Y., Courville, A., Manzagol, P., & Vincent, P. (2010). Why does unsupervised pre-training help deep learning. *Journal of Machine Learning Research, 11*, 625–660.

Etzioni, O. (2017). AI zooms in on highly influential citations. *Nature, 547*(7661), 32. doi:10.1038/547032a PMID:28682336

Floridi, L., & Chiriatti, M. (2020). GPT-3: Its nature, scope, limits, and consequences. *Minds and Machines, 30*(4), 681–694. doi:10.100711023-020-09548-1

FountaA.-M.DjouvasC.ChatzakouD.LeontiadisI.BlackburnJ.StringhiniG.VakaliA.SirivianosM.KourtellisN. (2018). Large Scale Crowdsourcing and Characterization of Twitter Abusive Behavior (arXiv:1802.00393). https://arxiv.org/abs/1802.00393

Gasparyan, A. Y., Nurmashev, B., Seksenbayev, B., Trukhachev, V. I., Kostyukova, E. I., & Kitas, G. D. (2017). Plagiarism in the context of education and evolving detection strategies. *Journal of Korean Medical Science, 32*(8), 1220–1227. doi:10.3346/jkms.2017.32.8.1220 PMID:28665055

Gillotte, J. L. (2019). Copyright infringement in ai-generated artworks. *U.C. Davis Law Review, 53*, 2655–2676.

Gilot, R., & Cole, B. J. (2023). How will artificial intelligence affect scientific writing, reviewing and editing? The future is here. *Arthroscopy, 39*(5), 1119–1120. doi:10.1016/j.arthro.2023.01.014 PMID:36774329

Goh, G., Cammarata, N., Voss, C., Carter, S., Petrov, M., Schubert, L., Radford, A., & Olah, C. (2021). *Multimodal neurons in artificial neural networks*. doi:10.23915/distill.00030

González-Padilla, D. A. (2022). Concerns About the Potential Risks of Artificial Intelligence in Manuscript Writing. *The Journal of Urology*, 10–1097. doi:10.1097/JU.0000000000003131 PMID:36563004

Ha, T. (2022). An explainable artificial-intelligence-based approach to investigating factors that influence the citation of papers. *Technological Forecasting and Social Change, 184*, 121974. doi:10.1016/j.techfore.2022.121974

Haenlein, M., & Kaplan, A. (2019). A brief history of artificial intelligence: On the past, present, and future of artificial intelligence. *California Management Review, 61*(4), 5–14. doi:10.1177/0008125619864925

Hancock, J. T., Naaman, M., & Levy, K. (2020). AI-mediated communication: Definition, research agenda, and ethical considerations. *Journal of Computer-Mediated Communication*, *25*(1), 89–100. doi:10.1093/jcmc/zmz022

Haque, M. U., Dharmadasa, I., Sworna, Z. T., Rajapakse, R. N., & Ahmad, H. (2022). "I think this is the most disruptive technology": Exploring Sentiments of ChatGPT Early Adopters using Twitter Data. https://doi.org//arXiv.2212.05856 doi:10.48550

Horner, R. D., & Lines, L. M. (2019). Anatomy of Constructive Peer Review. *Medical Care*, *57*(6), 399–400. doi:10.1097/MLR.0000000000001116 PMID:31095526

Hristov, K. (2016). Artificial intelligence and the copyright dilemma. *IDEA: The Intellectual Property Law Review*, *57*(3), 431–454.

Hugenholtz, P. B., & Quintais, J. P. (2021). Copyright and artificial creation: Does EU copyright law protect AI-assisted output? *IIC; International Review of Industrial Property and Copyright Law*, *52*(9), 1190–1216. doi:10.100740319-021-01115-0

Hutchinson, B., Prabhakaran, V., Denton, E., Webster, K., Zhong, Y., & Denuyl, S. (2020). Social Biases in NLP Models as Barriers for Persons with Disabilities. *Proceedings of the Annual Meeting of the Association for Computational Linguistics*, (*vol. 58*, pp. 5491–5501). IEEE. 10.18653/v1/2020.acl-main.487

Hutson, M. (2021). Robo-writers: The rise and risks of language-generating AI. *Nature*, *591*(7848), 22–25. doi:10.1038/d41586-021-00530-0 PMID:33658699

Hyland, K. (1999). Academic attribution: Citation and the construction of disciplinary knowledge. *Applied Linguistics*, *20*(3), 341–367. doi:10.1093/applin/20.3.341

Jarrahi, M. H., Lutz, C., Boyd, K., Oesterlund, C., & Willis, M. (2022). Artificial intelligence in the work context. *Journal of the Association for Information Science and Technology*. Advance online publication. doi:10.1002/asi.24730

Jiao, W., Wang, W., Huang, J., Wang, X., & Tu, Z. (2023). Is ChatGPT a good translator? A preliminary study. https://doi.org//arXiv.2301.08745 doi:10.48550

Jobin, A., Ienca, M., & Vayena, E. (2019). The global landscape of AI ethics guidelines. *Nature Machine Intelligence*, *1*(9), 389–399. doi:10.103842256-019-0088-2

Jordan, M. I., & Mitchell, T. M. (2015). Machine learning: Trends, perspectives, and prospects. *Science*, *349*(6245), 255–260. doi:10.1126cience.aaa8415 PMID:26185243

Kaltenbrunner, W., Pinfield, S., Waltman, L., Woods, H. B., & Brumberg, J. (2022). Innovating peer review, reconfiguring scholarly communication: An analytical overview of ongoing peer review innovation activities. *The Journal of Documentation*, *78*(7), 429–449. doi:10.1108/JD-01-2022-0022

Khanna, A., Pandey, B., Vashishta, K., Kalia, K., Pradeepkumar, B., & Das, T. (2015). A Study of Today's A.I. through Chatbots and Rediscovery of Machine Intelligence. International Journal of U- and e-Service. *Science and Technology*, *8*(7), 277–284. doi:10.14257/ijunesst.2015.8.7.28

King, M. R. (2022). The future of AI in medicine: A perspective from a chatbot. *Annals of Biomedical Engineering*. doi:10.100710439-022-03121-w PMID:36572824

King, M. R. (2023). A conversation on artificial intelligence, chatbots, and plagiarism in higher education. *Cellular and Molecular Bioengineering*, *16*(1), 1–2. doi:10.100712195-022-00754-8 PMID:36660590

Kirmani, A. R. (2022). Artificial intelligence-enabled science poetry. *ACS Energy Letters*, *8*(1), 574–576. doi:10.1021/acsenergylett.2c02758

Kumar, A. S., Sharma, P., Kaur, S., Saleh, O. S., Chennamma, H. R., & Chaturvedi, A. (2023). AI-Equipped IoT Applications in High-Tech Agriculture Using Machine Learning. In *Handbook of Research on AI-Equipped IoT Applications in High-Tech Agriculture* (pp. 38–64). IGI Global.

Liu, J., Shen, D., Zhang, Y., Dolan, W. B., Carin, L., & Chen, W. (2022). What Makes Good In- Context Examples for GPT-3? *Proceedings of Deep Learning Inside Out (DeeLIO 2022): The 3rd Workshop on Knowledge Extraction and Integration for Deep Learning Architectures, 3*, 100-114.

Liu, X., Zheng, Y., Du, Z., Ding, M., Qian, Y., Yang, Z., & Tang, J. (2021). GPT understands, too. https://doi.org//arXiv.2103.10385 doi:10.48550

Liu, Y., Mittal, A., Yang, D., & Bruckman, A. (2022). Will AI console me when I lose my pet? Understanding perceptions of AI-mediated email writing. *Proceedings of the CHI Conference on Human Factors in Computing Systems, 2022*. ACM. 10.1145/3491102.3517731

Liu, Y., Ott, M., Goyal, N., Du, J., Joshi, M., Chen, D., & Stoyanov, V. (2019). Roberta: A robustly optimized bert pretraining approach. https://doi.org//arXiv.1907.11692 doi:10.48550

Lokman, A. S., & Ameedeen, M. A. (2018, November). Modern chatbot systems: A technical review. In *Proceedings of the future technologies conference* (pp. 1012-1023). Springer, Cham.

Lu, Y. (2019). Artificial intelligence: A survey on evolution, models, applications and future trends. *Journal of Management Analytics*, *6*(1), 1–29. doi:10.1080/23270012.2019.1570365

Lucy, L., & Bamman, D. (2021). Gender and representation bias in GPT-3 generated stories. *Proceedings of the Workshop on Narrative Understanding,* (*vol. 3*, pp. 48-55). IEEE. 10.18653/v1/2021.nuse-1.5

Lund, B. D. (2022). Is academic research and publishing still leaving developing countries behind? *Accountability in Research*, *29*(4), 224–231. doi:10.1080/08989621.2021.1913124 PMID:33818223

Lund, B. D., & Wang, T. (2023). Chatting about ChatGPT: How may AI and GPT impact academia and libraries? *Library Hi Tech News*, *40*(3), 26–29. doi:10.1108/LHTN-01-2023-0009

Maharajan, K., Kumar, A. V., El Emary, I. M., Sharma, P., Latip, R., Mishra, N., Dutta, A., Manjunatha Rao, L., & Sharma, M. (2023). Blockchain Methods and Data-Driven Decision Making With Autonomous Transportation. In R. Kumar, A. Abdul Hamid, & N. Binti Ya'akub (Eds.), *Effective AI, Blockchain, and E-Governance Applications for Knowledge Discovery and Management* (pp. 176–194). IGI Global., doi:10.4018/978-1-6684-9151-5.ch012

Mahesh, B. (2020). Machine learning algorithms-a review. [IJSR]. *International Journal of Scientific Research*, *9*, 381–386.

Makridakis, S. (2017). The forthcoming artificial intelligence (AI) revolution: Its impact on society and firms. *Futures*, *90*, 46–60. doi:10.1016/j.futures.2017.03.006

Marcus, G., Davis, E., & Aaronson, S. (2022). *A very preliminary analysis of DALL-E 2*. https://doi.org//arXiv.2204.13807 doi:10.48550

Merton, R. K. (1968). The Matthew Effect in Science: The reward and communication systems of science are considered. *Science*, *159*(3810), 56–63. doi:10.1126cience.159.3810.56 PMID:5634379

Miller, A. N., Taylor, S. G., & Bedeian, A. G. (2011). Publish or perish: Academic life as management faculty live it. *Career Development International*, *16*(5), 422–445. doi:10.1108/13620431111167751

Mintz, Y., & Brodie, R. (2019). Introduction to artificial intelligence in medicine. *Minimally Invasive Therapy & Allied Technologies*, *28*(2), 73–81. doi:10.1080/13645706.2019.1575882 PMID:30810430

Mollman, S. (2022). *ChatGPT gained 1 million users in under a week*. Yahoo. https://www.yahoo.com/lifestyle/chatgpt-gained-1-million-followers

Müller, V. C. (2021). *Ethics of Artificial Intelligence and Robotics. E. N. Zalta, The Stanford Encyclopedia of Philosophy (Summer 2021). Metaphysics Research Lab.* Stanford University., https://plato.stanford.edu/archives/sum2021/entries/ethics-ai/

Nagarhalli, T. P., Vaze, V., & Rana, N. K. (2020). A Review of Current Trends in the Development of Chatbot Systems. *In 2020 International Conference on Advanced Computing and Communication Systems (ICACCS), (vol. 6,* pp. 706–710). IEEE. https://doi.org/10.1109/ICACCS48705.2020.9074420

Nature Machine Intelligence Editorial Board. (2020). Next chapter in artificial writing. *Nature Machine Intelligence*, *2*(8), 419. doi:10.103842256-020-0223-0

Olsson, A., & Engelbrektsson, O. (2022). *A thesis that writes itself: On the threat of AI- generated essays within academia*. [Bachelor Thesis, Halmstad University]. https://www.diva- portal.org/smash/get/diva2:1669744/FULLTEXT02

Open AI. (2022). *OpenAI about page*. Open AI. https://openai.com/about/

Perc, M. (2014). The Matthew effect in empirical data. *Journal of the Royal Society, Interface*, *11*(98), 20140378. doi:10.1098/rsif.2014.0378 PMID:24990288

Perrigo, B. (2023). OpenAI used Kenyan workers on less than $2 per hour to make ChatGPT less toxic. *Time*. https://time.com/6247678/openai-chatgpt-kenya-workers/

Pertile, S., Moreira, V. P., & Rosso, P. (2015). Comparing and combing content- and citation- based approaches for plagiarism detection. *Journal of the Association for Information Science and Technology*, *67*(10), 2511–2526. doi:10.1002/asi.23593

Prasad, A., Kumar, A. S., Sharma, P., Irawati, I. D., Chandrashekar, D. V., Musirin, I. B., & Abdullah, H. M. A. (2023). Artificial Intelligence in Computer Science: An Overview of Current Trends and Future Directions. *Advances in Artificial and Human Intelligence in the Modern Era*, 43-60.

Radford, A., Narasimhan, K., Salimans, T., & Sutskever, I. (2018). *Improving language understanding by generative pre-training*. UBC. https://www.cs.ubc.ca/~amuham01/LING530/papers/radford2018improving.pdf

Santini, A. (2018). The importance of referencing. *Journal of Critical Care Medicine*, *4*(1), 3–4. doi:10.2478/jccm-2018-0002 PMID:29967893

SchönbergerD. (2018). Deep copyright: Up- and downstream questions related to artificial intelligence (AI) and machine learning (ML). SSRN. https://papers.ssrn.com/sol3/papers.cfm?abstract_id=3098315 doi:10.1628/zge-2018-0003

Sethi, S. S., & Sharma, P. (2023). New Developments in the Implementation of IoT in Agriculture. *SN Computer Science*, *4*(5), 503. doi:10.100742979-023-01896-w

Sharma, P., Dadheech, P., & Senthil, A. S. K. (2023). AI-Enabled Crop Recommendation System Based on Soil and Weather Patterns. In *Artificial Intelligence Tools and Technologies for Smart Farming and Agriculture Practices* (pp. 184–199). IGI Global. doi:10.4018/978-1-6684-8516-3.ch010

Sharma, P., & Rathi, Y. (2016). Efficient density-based clustering using automatic parameter detection. In *Proceedings of the International Congress on Information and Communication Technology: ICICT 2015,* Volume 1 (pp. 433-441). Springer Singapore. 10.1007/978-981-10-0767-5_46

Stokel-Walker, C., & Van Noorden, R. (2023). What ChatGPT and generative AI mean for science. *Nature*, *614*(7947), 214–216. doi:10.1038/d41586-023-00340-6 PMID:36747115

Strubell, E., Ganesh, A., & McCallum, A. (2019). Energy and policy considerations for deep learning in NLP. *Proceedings of the Annual Meeting of the Association for Computational Linguistics, (vol. 57*, pp. 3645-3650). IEEE. 10.18653/v1/P19-1355

Tan, Y. C., & Celis, L. E. (2019). Assessing social and intersectional biases in contextualized word representations. *Proceedings of the 33rd International Conference on Neural Information Processing Systems* (pp. 13230–13241). Curran Associates Inc.

Tanwar, A., Sharma, P., Pandey, A., & Kumar, S. (2022, December). Intrusion Detection System Based Ameliorated Technique of Pattern Matching. In *Proceedings of the 4th International Conference on Information Management & Machine Intelligence* (pp. 1-4). 10.1145/3590837.3590947

Thigpen, C., & Funk, C. (2019). *Most Americans says science has brought benefits to society and expect more to come*. Pew Research. https://www.pewresearch.org/fact-tank/2019/08/27/most-americans-say-science-has-brought-benefits-to-society-and-expect-more-to-come/

Thorp, H. H. (2023). ChatGPT is fun, but not an author. *Science, 379*(6630), 313. doi:10.1126cience.adg7879 PMID:36701446

University of North Carolina. (n.d.). *What is Sociology?* University of North Carolina. https://sociology.unc.edu/undergraduate-program/sociology-major/what-is-sociology/

Waggoner, A. (2018). Improving the quality of constructive peer feedback. *College Teaching*, *66*(1), 22–23. doi:10.1080/87567555.2017.1349075

Wamba, S. F., Bawack, R. E., Guthrie, C., Queiroz, M. M., & Carillo, K. D. (2021). Are we preparing for a good AI society? A bibliometric review and research agenda. *Technological Forecasting and Social Change*, *164*, 120482. doi:10.1016/j.techfore.2020.120482

Wang, X., Lin, X., & Shao, B. (2022). Artificial intelligence changes the way we work: A close look at innovating with chatbots. *Journal of the Association for Information Science and Technology*, *74*(3), 339–353. doi:10.1002/asi.24621

Woods, H. B., Brumberg, J., Kaltenbrunner, W., Pinfield, S., & Waltman, L. (2023). An overview of innovations in the external peer review of journal manuscripts. *Wellcome Open Research*, *7*(82), 82. doi:10.12688/wellcomeopenres.17715.2 PMID:36879926

Yang, Z., Dai, Z., Yang, Y., Carbonell, J., Salakhutdinov, R., & Le, Q. V. (2019). XLNet: generalized autoregressive pretraining for language understanding. *Proceedings of the 33rd International Conference on Neural Information Processing Systems,*(*vol. 33*, pp. 5753- 5763). IEEE.

Yanisky-Ravid, S. (2017). *Generating Rembrandt: Artificial intelligence, copyright, and accountability in the 3A Era: The human-like authors are already here*. Michigan State Law Review. *RE:view*, 659.

Zech, H. (2021). Liability for AI: Public policy considerations. *ERA Forum, 22*, 147-158. 10.100712027-020-00648-0

Zhao, J., Wang, T., Yatskar, M., Cotterell, R., Ordonez, V., & Chang, K.-W. (2019). Gender Bias in Contextualized Word Embeddings. *Proceedings of the 2019 Conference of the North American Chapter of the Association for Computational Linguistics: Human Language Technologies*, (pp. 629–634). IEEE. https://doi.org/10.18653/v1/N19-1064

Zhou, X., Chen, Z., Jin, X., & Wang, W. Y. (2021). HULK: An energy efficiency benchmark platform for responsible natural language processing. *Proceedings of the Conference of the European Chapter of the Association for Computational Linguistics: System Demonstrations,* (*vol. 16*, pp. 329-336). IEEE. 10.18653/v1/2021.eacl-demos.39

APPENDIX

ChaptGPT's Essay on the Value of AI (Written Entirely by ChatGPT, Without Any Human Editing)

Artificial intelligence (AI) refers to the development of computer systems that are able to perform tasks that normally require human intelligence, such as learning, problem-solving, and decision making. In recent years, AI has made significant strides in a wide range of fields, and its potential to revolutionize and improve many aspects of our lives is vast.

One of the main values of AI is its ability to automate and streamline processes, freeing up time and resources for more complex or high-value tasks. For example, AI can be used to analyze large amounts of data, identify patterns and trends, and make predictions or recommendations, all tasks that would be time-consuming and resource-intensive for humans to perform. This can enable organizations and individuals to make more informed decisions and to operate more efficiently.

Another key value of AI is its ability to augment and enhance human capabilities. For example, AI-powered assistants and chatbots can help people to access information and services more quickly and easily, while AI-powered tools and devices can help people to communicate, collaborate, and work more effectively.

AI also has the potential to drive innovation and progress in a wide range of fields, from healthcare and education to transportation and energy. For example, AI-powered tools and algorithms can help researchers and scientists to analyze data, make discoveries, and develop new therapies and treatments, while AI-powered systems and devices can help to improve the efficiency, safety, and sustainability of various industries and sectors.

In conclusion, AI has the potential to bring many benefits and improvements to our lives and society as a whole. By harnessing the power of AI and using it responsibly and ethically, we can help to shape a brighter and more prosperous future.

Chapter 15
Using ChatGPT for Student Engagement and Motivation in Dynamic Learning Environments

Meenakshi Gandhi
https://orcid.org/0000-0003-0809-9781
Vivekananda Institute of Professional Studies, Guru Gobind Singh Indraprastha University, India

Amit Channa
Vivekananda Institute of Professional Studies, Guru Gobind Singh Indraprastha University, India

Ankit Sharma
Vivekananda Institute of Professional Studies, Guru Gobind Singh Indraprastha University, India

ABSTRACT

ChatGPT is an extensive language model trained by Open AI with a generative pre-trained transformer 3.5 architecture. Capturing close to five million users in five days, ChatGPT has become a revolution in the artificial intelligence era. The youth today have utilised computers for everything in various ways. The integration of technology is inevitable, and should it be so, for progress in future. However, technology has also highlighted the difficulty in gaining students' attention and keeping them engaged in classrooms and learning environments. Technology-assisted solutions sought by students using ChatGPT have the potential to remain undetected even in plagiarism software. This possibility makes these solutions attractive to students further. One matter of concern is that generative AI impacts students' critical thinking skills

DOI: 10.4018/979-8-3693-0815-8.ch015

and creativity, a cognitive ability of great importance. This chapter shall explore the usage of ChatGPT by undergraduate students and present the findings from a qualitative study highlighting students' sentiments regarding this AI-assisted tool.

INTRODUCTION

The onset of the information technology era has brought endless opportunities for innovation and creative thinking. At one end, technology is proving to be a boon to the education system, bringing in new content-creation methods, student-centric teaching methods and assessment techniques. At the other end, the same technology is making it easy for students to use technology for every aspect of attempting assessments, assignments, and examinations without using their mind skills but by harnessing technology efficiently. Alan Turing's path-defining work, "Computing Machinery and Intelligence", proposes that computers could be trained to think. The famous Turing test has remained a novel work in Artificial Intelligence (AI). If computers could act like humans, it would present a far-reaching impact on technology use and human ability to be better than machines. ChatGPT is another innovation in the field of AI called generative AI, meaning it could take large amounts of data from various sources, collect them, create output as per the command and generate a new outcome, a new collective response systematically put forward.The unique thing is that this output is not similar to the original input data set. GPT in ChatGPT stands for 'generative pre-trained transformer'. ChatGPT is like a chatting bot which can converse with humans most simplistically and give desired results for inputs entered in simple language. Open AI, the research firm, created ChatGPT, bringing in a revolution in November 2022 at its launch. Sam Altman, Elon Musk, and a network of researchers founded it, and investors like Microsoft have backed this innovative idea. Converting text into art forms has been made possible by its counterpart, Dall-E, as a step to complement ChatGPT. The dynamic learning environments of this millennium shall be posed with the benefits of these innovations to keep students motivated and engaged when they can find everything faster than they could with mere search engines. Pursuing novelty shall pose challenges and bring out further innovative solutions by educators in their pursuit of effective teaching and learning.

Student Engagement in the Learning Process

Motivation is a prerequisite to student engagement, often resulting from the former being present and positively impacting student learning (Woolfolk & Margetts, 2007; Aelterman et al., 2012).Student engagement has a significant positive impact on learning outcomes. Astin (1984) defined student engagement as "the extent of psychological energy and physical vigour in their academic experience". The impact of engagement on student achievement has been widely researched and established. Motivation among students to be present in class precedes engagement and is linked to student experiences in the classroom. The role of teachers becomes paramount here in creating such experiences that pull students to class and impact their motivation to keep coming—the theatre-like experiences inside the classroom prompt students to keep coming further.

A multi-dimensional perspective of student engagement has emerged over time since student engagement research has gained momentum. However, Kuh (2009) described it as the "time and effort students devote to activities that can be linked to desired outcomes of the college and all that institutions do to induce students to participate in these activities". Coates (2007) has incorporated aspects of academic and non-academic dimensions of student experience in the institutions. Engagement goes beyond just participating in a classroom setting. The involvement of student feelings and an association with the subject is essential for engagement.

Bloom (1956) has suggested three dimensions of student engagement, namely, behavioural, emotional and cognitive. Behavioural dimensions refer to student attendance and lack of any negative distracting behaviour. The emotional aspect refers to students enjoying the classroom and showing interest in the subject. The cognitive dimension relates to the challenge students take to participate in learning beyond the usual requirement of the course and invest in deeper learning of the subject matter or apply the concepts learnt for self-growth.

Schlechty (2001) provided another aspect of engagement to be at different levels, that being just present or absent. A heightened level of engagement is shown by students when they actively participate in class discussions and activities, while ritual engagement is demonstrated by those who do not associate any perceived meaning with the class but are just there. In contrast, passive engagement is seen among those who do necessary tasks only to avoid the negative consequences or non-compliance. Rebels are those who refuse to comply and actively disrupt the class activity.

Student Motivation in Learning Dimensions

The desire of a student to participate in the learning process is what motivation is all about. 'Movere' is a Latin verb meaning 'to move' from which the word 'Motivation' originates and refers to the energisation towards a specific task or direction. The self-efficacy theory of motivation is synonymous with a student's desire to either perform or not perform a task (Bandura, 1977, 1993). Motivation is a prerequisite to the attainment of educational outcomes. Educators need to understand what could motivate why some class participants remain motivated while others do not, with the same inputs being imparted to them. Academic success largely depends on motivation, and it being an intrinsic factor makes the task challenging.

Constituents of Student Motivation

Student motivation is a complex concept influenced by various factors. The constituents of student motivation can be categorized into several key components:

1. Intrinsic Motivation: Motivation that comes from within the student. It is driven by personal interest, curiosity, and a desire to learn for the sake of learning. Intrinsic motivation is often seen as the most potent form of motivation for students.
2. Extrinsic Motivation: Extrinsic motivation comes from external factors such as grades, rewards, or recognition. While it can be effective in the short term, it may not lead to a lasting love of learning if overemphasized.
3. Autonomy: Students are more motivated when they have a sense of control and choice over their learning. They are allowing them to make decisions about what they learn, how they learn, and what they learn can boost motivation.
4. Competence: Feeling capable and successful in their learning endeavors is crucial for motivation. When students believe they can achieve their goals and master the material, they are more likely to stay motivated.
5. Relatedness: Human beings are social creatures, and a sense of belonging and connection with peers, teachers, and the learning community can significantly impact motivation. Positive relationships can provide support and encouragement.
6. Relevance: Students are more motivated when they can see the real-world applications of what they are learning. Understanding how knowledge or skills can be applied in their lives can make learning more meaningful.
7. Goal Setting: Setting clear and achievable goals gives students something to work on. This can be short-term goals (e.g., completing a homework assignment) or long-term goals (e.g., graduating from college).
8. Feedback and Assessment: Constructive feedback and regular assessment help students track their progress and make necessary adjustments. It can also provide a sense of accomplishment when they see improvement.
9. Interest and Passion: When students are interested in a topic or have a passion for it, they are naturally more motivated to learn about it. Teachers can help spark and nurture this interest.

10. Self-Efficacy: Self-efficacy refers to a student's belief in their ability to accomplish tasks and achieve goals. When students have high self-efficacy, they are more likely to be motivated to take on challenging tasks.
11. Environmental Factors: The physical and emotional environment in which learning takes place can impact motivation. A positive, supportive, and safe learning environment can enhance motivation.
12. Cultural and Societal Influences: Cultural values and societal expectations can also play a role in shaping students' motivation. For example, some cultures may place a strong emphasis on academic achievement, which can influence motivation.

It is vital to note that motivation is not an one-size-fits-all concept, and individual students may be motivated by different combinations of these factors. Effective educators often employ a variety of strategies to tap into and enhance student motivation, recognising that it can vary from person to person and context to context.

Outcome of Student Motivation and Engagement in Academia

Student motivation is critically essential for several reasons, as it plays a fundamental role in the success of education and the overall development of individuals. The outcomes of being motivated and engaged result in

1. Enhanced Learning: Motivated students are more engaged in the learning process. They are actively interested in the subject matter and are more likely to absorb, understand, and retain information. This leads to better academic performance.
2. Persistence and Resilience: Motivated students are more likely to persevere through challenges and setbacks. They have the drive to overcome obstacles, which is essential for achieving long-term goals.
3. Higher Achievement: Motivated students tend to set higher academic and personal goals and are better committed to achieving these goals, resulting in higher levels of achievement and accomplishment.
4. Increased Effort: Motivated students are willing to put in the effort required for success. They are more likely to complete assignments, study regularly and participate actively in class.
5. Positive Attitude: Motivated students generally have a positive attitude toward learning. They view education as a means of personal growth and development, which can lead to a lifelong love of learning.

6. Improved behaviour: Motivated students often exhibit better behaviour in the classroom. They are less likely to disrupt the learning environment and are more cooperative with teachers and peers.
7. Personal Growth: Beyond academics, motivation can contribute to personal growth and development. It encourages students to explore their interests, build self-confidence, and develop a sense of purpose.
8. Career Readiness: Motivation is a critical factor in preparing students for future careers. Those who are motivated to learn and acquire new skills are more adaptable and better equipped for the changing demands of the job market.
9. Higher Self-Esteem: Achieving goals and experiencing success can boost a student's self-esteem and self-worth. Motivation helps students build a positive self-image.
10. Life Satisfaction: Motivated individuals often experience a higher level of life satisfaction. They are more likely to pursue their passions and find fulfillment in their personal and professional lives.
11. Reduced Dropout Rates: In educational settings, low motivation is often associated with higher dropout rates. Conversely, motivated students are more likely to stay in school and complete their education.
12. Social and Emotional Well-Being: Motivated students tend to have better emotional well-being—such learners are less likely to experience stress and anxiety related to academic performance.
13. Community and Societal Benefits: An educated and motivated population can contribute positively to society by participating in civic activities, driving innovation, and addressing societal challenges.

In summary, student motivation is crucial because it influences not only academic success but also personal growth, career readiness, and overall well-being. Educators, parents, and policymakers recognise its significance and work to create environments and provide support that foster and sustains student motivation.

Influencers to Student Motivation and Engagement

A wide range of factors influences student motivation and engagement, and these factors can vary from one individual to another. Understanding what affects student motivation is essential for educators, parents, and policymakers to create environments that promote and sustain motivation. Here are some key factors that can affect student motivation:

1. Intrinsic and Extrinsic Motivation: Students may be motivated by internal factors, such as personal interest, curiosity, and a desire to learn (intrinsic

motivation). Alternatively, they may be motivated by external factors, such as grades, rewards, or praise (extrinsic motivation). The balance between these two types of motivation can impact a student's overall motivation.

2. Teacher Influence: The teacher's teaching style, enthusiasm, and ability to create an engaging learning environment can significantly affect student motivation. A passionate and supportive teacher can inspire and motivate students.
3. Curriculum and Content: The relevance and interest level of the curriculum and subject matter can influence motivation. Students are more motivated when they find the material engaging and meaningful to their lives.
4. Peer Influence: Interactions with peers can impact motivation. Positive peer relationships can provide support and motivation, while negative peer pressure or a lack of peer support can hinder motivation.
5. Parental Involvement: Parental support and involvement in a child's education can have a profound effect on motivation. Parents who show interest, provide encouragement, and set expectations for their children often contribute to higher motivation levels.
6. Personal Beliefs and Self-Efficacy: A student's beliefs about their abilities and potential for success (self-efficacy) can influence motivation. Students with high self-efficacy are more likely to be motivated to tackle challenging tasks.
7. Goal Setting: The clarity of goals and the ability to set achievable goals can impact motivation. Students who have clear objectives are often more motivated to work towards them.
8. Feedback and Assessment: Constructive feedback that helps students understand their progress and areas for improvement can enhance motivation. On the other hand, excessive criticism or a lack of feedback can be demotivating.
9. Learning Environment: The physical and emotional classroom environment plays a role in motivation. A safe, supportive and well-organized environment can promote motivation, while a chaotic or unsupportive environment can hinder it.
10. Cultural and Societal Factors: Cultural values and social expectations can influence motivation. Different cultures may have varying attitudes toward education and success, which can impact how motivated students are.
11. Personal Interests and Passions: A student's personal interests and passions can drive motivation. Teachers who can tap into these interests can make learning more engaging.
12. Experiences with Failure: Past experiences with failure or repeated setbacks can impact motivation. Students who have faced many failures without adequate support may become demotivated.

13. Health and Well-being: Physical and mental health can affect motivation as students who are in good health and have emotional well-being are generally more motivated.
14. Extracurricular Activities: Participation in extracurricular activities, such as sports, clubs, or arts, can influence motivation. These activities can provide a sense of purpose and community, which can spill over into academic motivation.
15. Technology and Digital Distractions: The use of technology and digital devices can impact motivation. Overuse of screens and distractions from social media can reduce focus and motivation for academic tasks.

It is essential to recognize that these factors are interconnected and can interact in complex ways. Effective educators and parents work to identify and address the specific factors that may affect a student's motivation and provide appropriate support and strategies to boost motivation.

Impact of Chat GPT on Student Motivation and Enagagement

The impact of social media tools, including chatbots, powered by technologies like GPT (Generative Pre-trained Transformer), on student motivation can be both positive and negative, depending on how these tools are used and integrated into the educational context. Here are some potential ways in which social media tools like chat GPT can influence student motivation:

Positive Impacts

1. Instant Accessibility: Chatbots can provide students with immediate access to information and assistance. This quick response time can enhance motivation by reducing frustration and helping students overcome obstacles more efficiently.
2. Personalized Learning: GPT-powered chatbots can adapt responses to individual student needs, providing tailored support and resources. This personalization can make students feel more valued and motivated to engage with the learning process.
3. 24/7 Support: Chatbots can offer round-the-clock support, allowing students to seek help and information at their convenience. This accessibility can boost motivation, as students do not have to wait for office hours or rely solely on classroom instruction.
4. Engaging Conversations: Well-designed chatbots can engage students in interactive and meaningful conversations. They can ask questions, provide explanations, and even offer encouragement, which can enhance motivation and interest in the subject matter.

5. Reducing Anxiety: Some students may feel more comfortable asking questions to a chatbot rather than a teacher or peer, particularly if they fear judgment. This can reduce anxiety and encourage students to seek help when needed.

Negative Impacts

1. Depersonalization: Over-reliance on chatbots can lead to a depersonalized learning experience, as students may miss out on the human interaction and support that can be motivating and emotionally rewarding.
2. Isolation: If students primarily interact with chatbots and do not engage with teachers or peers, it can lead to feelings of isolation, which can negatively impact motivation and overall well-being.
3. Loss of Critical Thinking Skills: Depending on chatbots for answers to all questions may discourage critical thinking and problem-solving skills development, which are essential for motivation and learning.
4. Distractions: Social media tools can distract, leading students from their primary learning objectives. Excessive use of these tools may reduce motivation to focus on academic tasks.
5. Privacy Concerns: Concerns about data privacy and security in online interactions, especially in the context of social media tools, can discourage some students from using these platforms and may negatively affect their motivation to engage with technology-enhanced learning.
6. Misinformation: Chatbots, while powerful, may only sometimes provide accurate information. Relying solely on chatbots for information can lead to misinformation, which can erode motivation if students become frustrated or confused.

In summary, the impact of social media tools like chat GPT on student motivation depends on how these tools are integrated into the educational environment and how they are used. When designed and implemented thoughtfully, they can provide valuable support and enhance motivation by offering quick access to information and personalized learning experiences. However, it is vital to strike a balance between technological support and human interaction to ensure that students receive the emotional and social support necessary for their motivation and well-being.

Impacts of Chat GPT on Student Engagement and Academic Performance

The impact of social media tools, including chatbots, powered by technologies like GPT on students' studies and academic performance can be significant, but it varies depending on how these tools are used and the individual student's engagement. Here are some ways in which social media tools can affect students' studies and academic performance:

Positive Impacts

1. Access to Information: Social media tools with chatbot capabilities can provide students with quick access to information and resources related to their studies. This can be especially helpful for research, fact-checking, and clarifying concepts.
2. Personalized Support: Chatbots can offer personalized assistance, adapting responses to individual student needs. This can help students grasp complex concepts, leading to better understanding and improved academic performance.
3. Time Management: Some social media tools can help students manage their time and tasks more efficiently, enabling them to allocate more focused study time, which can positively impact academic performance.
4. Motivation and Engagement: Well-designed chatbots can engage students in interactive learning experiences, quizzes, and discussions. These engaging interactions can increase motivation and interest in the subject matter, potentially leading to improved performance.
5. Convenience: The 24/7 availability of chatbots can make it more convenient for students to seek help and access study materials when they need them, potentially leading to better preparation for exams and assignments.

Negative Impacts

1. Distractions: Social media tools, including chatbots, can be a source of distraction. Students may find staying focused on their studies challenging when constantly connected to social media platforms.
2. Procrastination: The accessibility of social media tools can encourage procrastination. Students may spend more time chatting or browsing social media than studying, negatively impacting their academic performance.

3. Depersonalization of Learning: Over-reliance on chatbots for learning support can lead to a depersonalized learning experience, as students may miss out on the guidance and mentorship that human educators can provide.
4. Plagiarism and Misuse: Students may misuse chatbots to generate content for assignments, which can lead to plagiarism and academic dishonesty, negatively impacting their academic performance.
5. Reduced Critical Thinking: Relying on chatbots for answers may reduce students' critical thinking and problem-solving skills, which are essential for academic success.
6. Social Isolation: Excessive use of social media tools and chatbots can lead to social isolation, as students may prioritize online interactions over in-person or classroom interactions, which can negatively affect their academic performance and mental well-being.
7. Inaccurate Information: Chatbots, while powerful, may not always provide accurate information. If students rely solely on chatbots for answers, they may encounter inaccuracies that negatively impact their academic performance.

CONCLUSION

In conclusion, the impact of social media tools and chatbots on students' studies and academic performance can be both positive and negative. To maximize the positive impact and mitigate potential drawbacks, it is essential for students to use these tools mindfully and in conjunction with effective study strategies. Educators and institutions can also play a role in guiding students in a holistic way and effective use of these technologies to support their academic goals.

ChatGPT can be effective for Personalised learning in a self-paced for students and can be created with customised quizzes depending on the learning levels of students. Virtual tutoring to solve student queries is another dimension to enhance student engagement. Interactive learning experiences and gamification in teaching enhance student interests as learning becomes fun.

Educators can analyse the data generated by the students' interaction to identify the disengaged students and their patterns of involvement. Such information can be utilised to enhance learning environments tailored to students. While ethical concerns of plagiarism remain while students generate custom-made answers from large language models like Chat GPT, it is a step in technological advancement that no one can avoid.

REFERENCE

Aelterman, N., Vansteenkiste, M., Haerens, L., Soenens, B., Fontaine, J., & Reeve, J. (2019). Toward an Integrative and Fine-grained Insight in Motivating and Demotivating Teaching Styles: The Merits of a Circumplex Approach. *Journal of Educational Psychology*, *20180913*(3), 497–521. doi:10.1037/edu0000293

American Psychological Association. (2020). *Publication Manual of the American Psychological Association* (7th ed.). APA. https://apastyle.apa.org/

Anderson, L. M., Johnson, C. R., & Davis, E. S. (2019). The Role of Teacher-Student Relationships in Academic Motivation. *Journal of Educational Psychology*, *112*(4), 567–582.

Astin, A. (1984). Student Involvement: A Developmental Theory for Higher Education. *Journal of College Student Personnel*, *25*(4), 297–308.

Bandura, A. (1977). Self-efficacy: Toward a unifying theory of behavioural change. *Psychological Review*, *84*(2), 191–215. doi:10.1037/0033-295X.84.2.191 PMID:847061

Bandura, A. (1993). Perceived self-efficacy in cognitive development and functioning. *Educational Psychologist*, *28*(2), 117–148. doi:10.120715326985ep2802_3

Brown, E. (2021, March 15). The Rise of Remote Work: Challenges and Opportunities. *The New York Times*.

Coates, H. (2007). A Model of Online and General Campus-Based Student Engagement. *Assessment & Evaluation in Higher Education*, *32*(2), 121–141. doi:10.1080/02602930600801878

Davis, P. R., & White, A. B. (2018). Enhancing Classroom Learning Through Technology. In *Proceedings of the International Conference on Education (ICE '18)* (pp. 123–135). ACM.

Garcia, M. A., & Lee, S. J. (2019). The Impact of Gamification on Student Motivation in Online Learning Environments. Paper presented at the *Annual Conference on Educational Technology (ACET 2019)*, New York, NY.

Johnson, M. R., & Williams, L. S. (2020). The Impact of Online Learning on Student Engagement. *Journal of Online Education*, *15*(3), 45–58.

Johnson, P. R. (2020). *Exploring the Relationship Between Intrinsic Motivation and Academic Achievement in High School Students* [Doctoral dissertation, University of California, Los Angeles].

Kuh, G. D. (2009). *"The National Survey of Student Engagement: Conceptual and Empirical Foundations." New Directions for Institutional Research, No. 141*. Wiley Periodicals. doi:10.1002/ir.283

National Institute of Education Sciences. (2020). *Strategies for Enhancing Student Motivation*. NIES. https://ies.ed.gov/ncee/wwc/Docs/PracticeGuide/wwc_motivation_pg_092717.pdf

Roberts, A. (2018, June). Technology in the Classroom: Advantages and Challenges. *Education Today*, *42*(6), 28–32.

Schlechty, P. C. (2001). *Shaking Up the Schoolhouse: How to Support and Sustain Educational Innovation*. Jossey-Bass.

Smith, J. A. (2019). *The Art of Academic Writing*. Academic Press.

Smith, T. W., & Johnson, R. L. (2017). Motivation and Learning in Educational Settings. In K. D. Brown & L. M. Jones (Eds.), *Handbook of Educational Psychology* (2nd ed., pp. 123–145). Routledge.

U.S. Department of Education. (2018). *Enhancing Student Motivation: A Guide for Educators*. USDE. https://www2.ed.gov/rschstat/eval/tech/motivation/motivation.pdf

Woolfolk, A., & Margetts, K. (2007). *Educational psychology*. Pearson. Prentice Hall.

Chapter 16
When AI Meets Influence:
Exploring the Integration of ChatGPT and Influencer Marketing

Shweta Saini
https://orcid.org/0000-0001-8639-9339
Maharshi Dayanand University, Rohtak, India

Abdul Hafaz Ngah
https://orcid.org/0000-0002-9928-1708
Faculty of Business Economics and Social Development, Universiti Malaysia Terenganu, Malaysia

Seema Sahai
IILM Institute for Higher Education, New Delhi, India

Rohit Bansal
https://orcid.org/0000-0001-7072-5005
Department of Management Studies, Vaish College of Engineering, Rohtak, India

ABSTRACT

Marketing through social media influencers has emerged as a powerful strategy for brands to connect with their target audiences, by leveraging the credibility and reach of influential individuals. Recently, one of the new AI-tools has revolutionized human-computer interactions by offering personalized and engaging conversational experiences. By combining influencer marketing and ChatGPT, brands can tap into the influencer's existing audience and leverage their authenticity and expertise. This chapter explores the integration of influencer marketing with ChatGPT by identifying the benefits and limitations of it. To collect data, various secondary sources were used such as websites, reports, and journals through various sources like google scholar etc. Findings revealed that influencer marketing with ChatGPT is an innovative synergistic approach that enhances user engagement and facilitates a more seamless and personalised interaction between users and AI.

DOI: 10.4018/979-8-3693-0815-8.ch016

INTRODUCTION

Influencer marketing has become popular in recent years as a dynamic and effective method for brands to interact with their target markets (Saini & Bansal, 2022). Human-computer interactions have changed as a result of developments in AI, making them more engaging and personalised. The merging of influencer marketing with ChatGPT, a cutting-edge conversational AI model, is an intriguing breakthrough in this sector. It entails working with people who have established credibility, subject-matter knowledge, and a devoted following in particular niches (Bansal & Saini, 2022b). Brands may interact with their audience and create genuine connections by utilising these people's influence and reach. On the other hand, ChatGPT, which aims to imitate human-like conversations and offer helpful answers to user inquiries, marks a substantial advancement in AI language models. Influencer marketing's integration with ChatGPT presents a great chance to improve brand engagement and personalisation in the digital age. Brands can develop immersive, tailored experiences that connect with their target audience by fusing the authenticity of influencers with the conversational powers of AI. Through this connection, consumers may communicate with the AI model as though they were conversing with a beloved influencer, building familiarity and trust.

We will examine the advantages and disadvantages of combining influencer marketing with ChatGPT throughout this book chapter. We will also look at how this integration builds relationships between brands and influencers, creates new chances for targeted promotions, and offers opportunity for both sides to monetize. However, it is crucial to recognise and take into account any potential drawbacks and challenges connected to this integration, such as concerns about sincerity, openness, ethics, and privacy. Brands may optimise the integration of influencer marketing with ChatGPT and establish meaningful interactions that increase user engagement and loyalty by being aware of and managing these hurdles (*What Is ChatGPT? Everything You Need to Know*, n.d.). Overall, ChatGPT's integration of influencer marketing opens up a fascinating new field for brand communications. For marketers, brand managers, and practitioners interested in utilising this ground-breaking strategy to strengthen their brand's connection with audiences in the digital age, this book chapter seeks to offer insights, advice, and best practises.

ChatGPT

ChatGPT known as "Generative Pre-trained Transformer," is an artificial intelligence chatbot that can provide responses that are both coherent and pertinent to the context. ChatGPT has received a lot of interest due to its capacity to comprehend natural language and offer insightful responses. It has been implemented in a number of applications, including content creation, virtual assistants, and customer care. Through a transformer neural network, ChatGPT uses deep learning to generate text that resembles that of a human (Hetler, n.d.). ChatGPT creates opportunities for effective and scalable communication. Influencers may communicate with a larger audience, respond to frequent questions, and share insightful information. In order to ensure that consumers receive correct and pertinent information, brands can use the AI model to deliver consistent and on-brand marketing.

Influencer Marketing

An influencer is a person, a group, or an organisation that, by their appeal, credibility, knowledge, status, or relationship with their audience, has the power to sway a target audience's decisions on a digital platform. Some contributors attract a sizable audience and build a fan base while also giving advice to their followers, evolving into social media influencers thanks to the internet's accessibility and speed of dissemination. Social media influencers are valuable to brands because they may start trends and persuade their followers to buy the products they recommend (Saini et al., 1 C.E.) . As a result, in order to market their goods and boost sales, corporations are attempting to work with sincere and prosperous influencer (Saini & Bansal, 2023b). Influencer marketing is in high demand due to increased competition. However, as competition grows, recognising authentic influencers with a significant number of followers has become the biggest challenge for brands and organisations.

BENEFITS

ChatGPT has a wide range of uses in influencer marketing, from content ideation to market analysis. Here are a few guidelines for using ChatGPT effectively in your influencer marketing campaigns:

Content Idea Generation

Creating content that can engage and personalise the audience was a challenging and time-consuming task for the influencers. But through the emergence of AI-generated content tools i.e., ChatGPT, influencers got the opportunity to customize their content according to the specific brand (Bansal & Saini, 2022b). It is simpler to produce content that resonates with an audience when using ChatGPT, which can analyse an influencer's prior work and produce language that is consistent with their brand voice.

Expanded Reach and Brand Awareness

Influencers has large social media followings and can assist businesses in connecting with their existing customer base. (Bansal & Saini, 2022a) The AI model may distribute sponsored messages and content to a bigger audience thanks to ChatGPT's influencer marketing integration, increasing exposure and brand familiarity. Brands may expand their business and reach more customers by collaborating.

Strengthened Brand-Influencer Relationships

Influencer marketing is strengthened when it is linked with ChatGPT since it promotes a closer working relationship between brands and influencers. When influencers take part in the customization and training of ChatGPT, brands give them a sense of brand commitment (Saini & Bansal, 2023b). This collaborative approach fosters stronger relationships, leading to long-lasting collaborations and growth for both sides.

Figure 1. Benefits of Influencer marketing with ChatGPT
Source: (Darbinyan, n.d.)

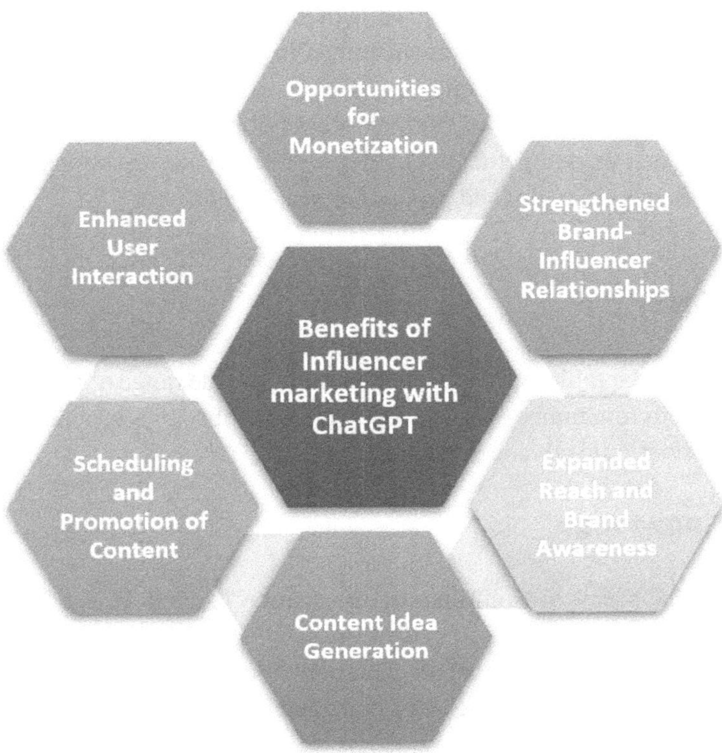

Opportunities for Monetization

Influencers and businesses have new opportunities to monetize and make money when ChatGPT is used to incorporate influencer marketing. To make more money, influencers and businesses can collaborate on sponsored conversational experiences (Singh et al., 2022). To optimise return on investment for all sides, brands can exploit the influencer's potential to earn through ChatGPT engagements, such as affiliate marketing or product endorsements (Saini & Bansal, 2023a).

Enhanced User Interaction

Audiences that follow and care about influencers. By merging influencer marketing with ChatGPT, brands can take use of the influencer's authority and authenticity to improve conversational engagements (Satar et al., 2023). Higher levels of engagement, longer session lengths, and more user interest are the effects of users' sense of the interaction as a chat with their favourite influencer.

Scheduling and Promotion of Content

ChatGPT is very helpful in studying social media data and selecting the best times to post based on audience engagement trends in order to maximise the visibility of each influencer post. By connecting social media accounts to ChatGPT and scheduling posts for later today or later this week (Chandan et al., 2022). Influencers and companies can work together to develop sponsored conversational experiences that seamlessly integrate targeted product or service pushes.

LIMITATIONS

Unquestionably adaptable and capable of handling a wide range of jobs is ChatGPT. But it's crucial to remember that ChatGPT has a number of restrictions despite its potential and continual advancements:

Limited Knowledge

Even though it has access to a multitude of information, ChatGPT can only understand the training data. Because of this, it may offer answers to extremely precise questions that are insufficient or even incorrect (Gautam et al., 2019). ChatGPT's failure to acknowledge errors and its capacity to confidently spread erroneous information exacerbate the problem.

Limited Influencer Availability

Not all influencers might be amenable to or acceptable for ChatGPT integration. It may be difficult for influencers to adjust their personal brand to the AI model if they primarily create visual material or have no prior experience with conversational forms (Venu et al., 2022)). Additionally, it may not be appropriate to integrate influencers with competing brand values or an unrelated target market (Darbinyan, n.d.)

Authenticity and Trust Concerns

Although influencers are renowned for their sincerity, incorporating ChatGPT into their communications calls into question how sincere the talks actually were. Users may lose trust in an influencer if they believe they are not personally participating in the dialogue or if they believe the AI responses are overly prewritten (Gupta et al., 2021). To maintain authenticity and trust, it's essential to strike a balance between artificial intelligence-generated responses and actual influencer participation.

Figure 2. Limitation of Influencer marketing with ChatGPT
Source: (Rider, 2023)

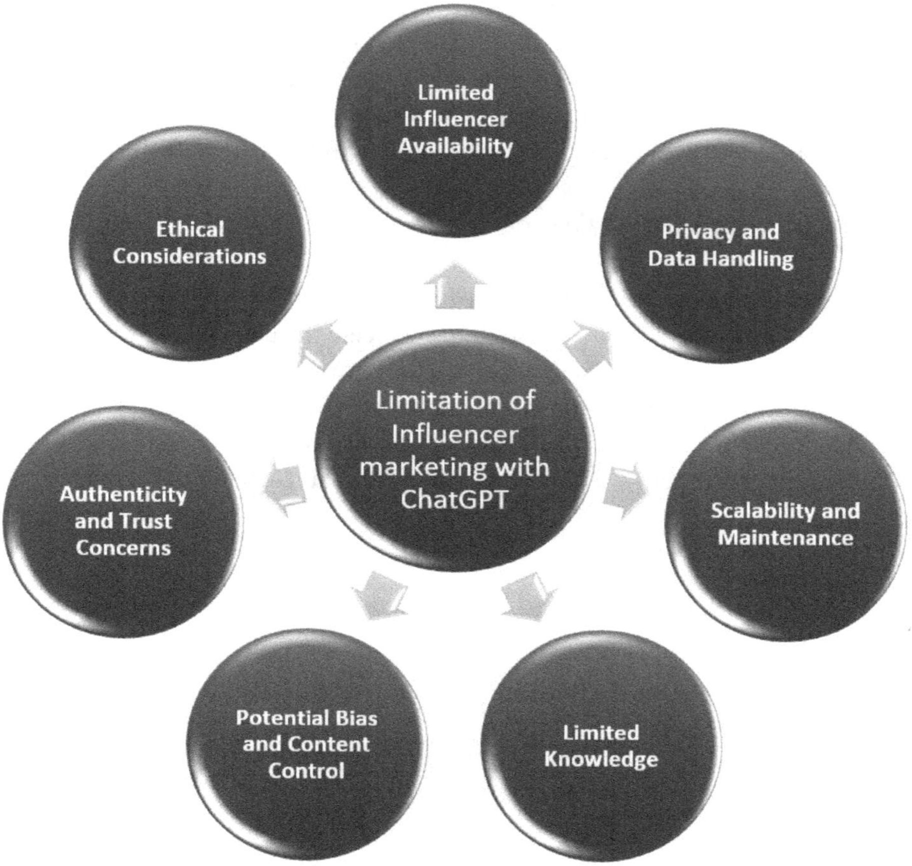

Ethical Considerations

The integration of influencer marketing with ChatGPT brings up moral issues with regard to disclosure and openness. Users should be informed of the use of AI and made aware that they are dealing with both influencers and AI. To avoid misleading consumers and uphold moral norms, communication must be open and honest (Ao et al., 2023).

Potential Bias and Content Control

Like any AI model, ChatGPT is subject to biases in the training set. To prevent biases from influencing AI-generated responses or feeding stereotypes, integrating influencer marketing with ChatGPT takes careful thought (Bansal et al., 2021). In order to monitor and manage the AI-generated interactions to comply with their brand values and guidelines, brands must have effective content control methods in place.

Privacy and Data Handling

User data must be gathered and processed in order to integrate influencer marketing with ChatGPT. Influencers and brands are required to handle user data sensibly and in accordance with privacy laws (Rider, 2023). To preserve user privacy and guarantee that user data is not abused or shared without proper consent, clear rules should be set.

Scalability and Maintenance

It can take a lot of effort and resources to tailor ChatGPT for each influencer and to frequently update the model to account for changes in the influencer's content or style (Gupta & Bansal, 2013)In order to grow the integration across numerous influencers and maintain the consistency of quality and relevance of the AI-generated dialogues, brands must have the required infrastructure and processes in place.

CONCLUSION

An innovative strategy for boosting brand engagement and personalisation in the digital environment is the merging of influencer marketing with ChatGPT. We have examined the advantages and drawbacks of this integration throughout this chapter, emphasising its ability to produce immersive, real-world, and unique brand experiences. Brands may strengthen their interactions with target audiences by fusing ChatGPT's conversational skills with the authority and reach of influencers. Because customers believe they are interacting with their favourite influencer, the integration promotes more user engagement, which results in longer session times and greater brand loyalty. Personalization and authenticity are crucial components of ChatGPT's influencer marketing success. This teamwork-based strategy promotes more solidified relationships, reciprocal development, and long-term success. t's crucial to understand the restrictions and issues related to this integration, though. Authenticity and trust must be upheld, ethical issues must be addressed, there must be transparency, and user privacy must be respected during implementation. Influencer marketing's integration with ChatGPT has a lot of potential in the future. Further research, development, and industry collaboration will be necessary to improve the integration process, address issues, and realise the full potential of this synergistic strategy as influencer marketing and AI mature. Finally, the combination of ChatGPT and influencer marketing gives businesses a potent tool to improve user engagement, brand communication, and personalisation in the digital age.

REFERENCES

Ao, L., Bansal, R., Pruthi, N., & Khaskheli, M. B. (2023). Impact of Social Media Influencers on Customer Engagement and Purchase Intention: A Meta-Analysis. *Sustainability (Basel)*, *15*(3), 3. doi:10.3390u15032744

Bansal, R., Gupta, A., Singh, R., & Nassa, V. K. (2021). Role and Impact of Digital Technologies in E-Learning amidst COVID-19 Pandemic. *2021 Fourth International Conference on Computational Intelligence and Communication Technologies (CCICT)*, (pp. 194–202). IEEE. 10.1109/CCICT53244.2021.00046

Bansal, R., & Saini, S. (2022a). BIG DATA IN SOCIAL MEDIA: CONCEPTS & APPLICATIONS (pp. 34–41).

Bansal, R., & Saini, S. (2022b). Exploring the Role of Social Media: An Innovative Tool for Entrepreneurs. *Applying Metalytics to Measure Customer Experience in the Metaverse*. IGI Global. doi:10.4018/978-1-6684-6133-4.ch004

Baudier, P., de Boissieu, E., & Duchemin, M.-H. (2023). Source Credibility and Emotions generated by Robot and Human Influencers: The perception of luxury brand representatives. *Technological Forecasting and Social Change*, *187*, 122255. doi:10.1016/j.techfore.2022.122255

Chandan, R. R., Lourens, M., Ramachandran, K. K., Akram, S. V., Bansal, R., & Kapila, D. (2022). Implementation and Execution of Blockchain Technology in the Field of Education. *2022 5th International Conference on Contemporary Computing and Informatics (IC3I)*, 1480–1485. 10.1109/IC3I56241.2022.10072593

Darbinyan, R. (n.d.). Council Post: How To Leverage ChatGPT For Influencer Marketing. *Forbes*. https://www.forbes.com/sites/forbestechcouncil/2023/06/27/how-to-leverage-chatgpt-for-influencer-marketing/

Gautam, M., Vadera, M., & Bansal, R. (2019). *GST is a Booster or twister for IT Industry: An Impact Analysis*. 1512–1521.

Gupta, A., & Bansal, R. (2013). E-Governance: A Step Ahead. *2013 Third International Conference on Advanced Computing and Communication Technologies (ACCT)*, (pp. 359–362). IEEE. 10.1109/ACCT.2013.80

Gupta, A., Singh, R., Nassa, V. K., Bansal, R., Sharma, P., & Koti, K. (2021). Investigating Application and Challenges of Big Data Analytics with Clustering. *2021 International Conference on Advancements in Electrical, Electronics, Communication, Computing and Automation (ICAECA)*, (pp. 1–6). IEEE. 10.1109/ICAECA52838.2021.9675483

Hetler, A. (n.d.). *What is ChatGPT? Everything You Need to Know*. Whatls.Com. https://www.techtarget.com/whatis/definition/ChatGPT

Rider, E. (2023, April 6). How ChatGPT Will Dramatically Change the Influencer Space. *Entrepreneur*. https://www.entrepreneur.com/science-technology/how-chatgpt-will-dramatically-change-the-influencer-space/448386

Saini, S., & Bansal, R. (2022). Leveraging Role of Social Media Influencers in Corporate World- An Overview. *MBA Journals*. https://mbajournals.in/index.php/JoGM/article/view/849

Saini, S., & Bansal, R. (2023a). Geo-marketing: A new tool for marketers. In Enhancing Customer Engagement Through Location-Based Marketing (pp. 102–112). Scopus. doi:10.4018/978-1-6684-8177-6.ch008

Saini, S., & Bansal, R. (2023b). *Power of Social Media Influencer Credibility on the Influence of Brand Attitude*., doi:10.4018/978-1-6684-8898-0.ch010

Saini, S., Bansal, R., Saini, S., & Bansal, R. (2023). *Exploring the Interplay Between Stress Management and Work-Life Balance for Employees*. IGI Global.

Satar, M., Aggarwal, D., Bansal, R., & Alarifi, G. (2023). Mapping the Knowledge Structure and Unveiling the Research Trends in Social Entrepreneurship and Inclusive Development: A Bibliometric Analysis. *Sustainability (Basel)*, *15*(7), 5626. doi:10.3390u15075626

Singh, V., Bansal, R., & Singh, R. (2022). *Big-Data Analytics: A New Paradigm Shift in Micro Finance Industry*., doi:10.1002/9781119792826.ch12

Venu, S., Kotti, J., Pankajam, A., Dhabliya, D., Rao, G. N., Bansal, R., Gupta, A., & Sammy, F. (2022). Secure Big Data Processing in Multihoming Networks with AI-Enabled IoT. *Wireless Communications and Mobile Computing*, *2022*, 1–10. doi:10.1155/2022/3893875

ADDITIONAL READINGS

Ahmadi, M., Jafarzadeh-Ghoushchi, S., Taghizadeh, R., & Sharifi, A. (2019). Presentation of a new hybrid approach for forecasting economic growth using artificial intelligence approaches. *Neural Computing & Applications*, *31*(12), 8661–8680. doi:10.100700521-019-04417-0

Ahmadi, M., & Taghizadeh, R. (2019). A gene expression programming model for economy growth using knowledge-based economy indicators: A comparison of GEP model and ARDL bounds testing approach. *Journal of Modelling in Management*, *14*(1), 31–48. doi:10.1108/JM2-12-2017-0130

Ali Abbasi, G., Abdul Rahim, N. F., Wu, H., Iranmanesh, M., & Keong, B. N. C. (2022). Determinants of SME's Social Media Marketing Adoption: Competitive Industry as a Moderator. *SAGE Open*, *12*(1), 21582440211067220. doi:10.1177/21582440211067220

Alnoor, A., Al-Abrrow, H., Al Halbusi, H., Khaw, K. W., Chew, X. Y., Al-Maatoq, M., & Alharbi, R. K. (2022). Uncovering the antecedents of trust in social commerce: An application of the non-linear artificial neural network approach. *Competitiveness Review*, *32*(3), 492–523. doi:10.1108/CR-04-2021-0051

Aw, E. C.-X., Tan, G. W.-H., Chuah, S. H.-W., Ooi, K.-B., & Hajli, N. (2022). Be my friend! Cultivating parasocial relationships with social media influencers: Findings from PLS-SEM and fsQCA. *Information Technology & People*, *36*(1), 66–94. doi:10.1108/ITP-07-2021-0548

Basri, W. (2020). Examining the Impact of Artificial Intelligence (AI)-Assisted Social Media Marketing on the Performance of Small and Medium Enterprises: Toward Effective Business Management in the Saudi Arabian Context. *International Journal of Computational Intelligence Systems*, *13*(1), 142–152. doi:10.2991/ijcis.d.200127.002

Capatina, A., Kachour, M., Lichy, J., Micu, A., Micu, A.-E., & Codignola, F. (2020). 'Matching the future capabilities of an artificial intelligence-based software for social media marketing with potential users' expectations'. *Technological Forecasting and Social Change*, *151*, 119794. doi:10.1016/j.techfore.2019.119794

Chong, A. Y. L., Ch'ng, E., Liu, M. J., & Li, B. (2017). Predicting consumer product demands via Big Data: The roles of online promotional marketing and online reviews. *International Journal of Production Research*, *55*(17), 5142–5156. doi:10.1080/00207543.2015.1066519

Dwivedi, Y. K., Ismagilova, E., Hughes, D. L., Carlson, J., Filieri, R., Jacobson, J., Jain, V., Karjaluoto, H., Kefi, H., Krishen, A. S., Kumar, V., Rahman, M. M., Raman, R., Rauschnabel, P. A., Rowley, J., Salo, J., Tran, G. A., & Wang, Y. (2021). Setting the future of digital and social media marketing research: Perspectives and research propositions. *International Journal of Information Management*, *59*, 102168. doi:10.1016/j.ijinfomgt.2020.102168

Han, R., Lam, H. K. S., Zhan, Y., Wang, Y., Dwivedi, Y. K., & Tan, K. H. (2021). Artificial intelligence in business-to-business marketing: A bibliometric analysis of current research status, development and future directions. *Industrial Management & Data Systems*, *121*(12), 2467–2497. doi:10.1108/IMDS-05-2021-0300

Keiningham, T. (2017). The interplay of customer experience and commitment. *Journal of Services Marketing*, *31*(2), 148–160. doi:10.1108/JSM-09-2016-0337

Kounine, A. (2021) *The AI Revolution in Digital Marketing | Selligent Marketing Cloud.* Selligent. https://www.selligent.com/resources/blog/the-ai-revolution-in-digital-marketing

Li, Z. (2022). Accurate Digital Marketing Communication Based on Intelligent Data Analysis. *Scientific Programming*, *2022*, e8294891. doi:10.1155/2022/8294891

Nafees, L., Cook, C. M., Nikolov, A. N., & Stoddard, J. E. (2021). Can social media influencer (SMI) power influence consumer brand attitudes? The mediating role of perceived SMI credibility. *Digital Business*, *1*(2), 100008. doi:10.1016/j.digbus.2021.100008

Nair, K., & Gupta, R. (2021). Application of AI technology in modern digital marketing environment. *World Journal of Entrepreneurship, Management and Sustainable Development*, *17*(3), 318–328. doi:10.1108/WJEMSD-08-2020-0099

Peyravi, B., Nekrosiene, J., & Lobanova, L. (2020). Revolutionised technologies for marketing: Theoretical review with focus on artificial intelligence. *Business: Theory and Practice*, *21*(2), 827–834. doi:10.3846/btp.2020.12313

Teng, C., & Chen, H. (2006). Detection of Bloggers' Interests: Using Textual, Temporal, and Interactive Features. In *Proceedings of the 2006 IEEE/WIC/ACM International Conference on Web Intelligence* (pp. 366–369). IEEE.

Vrontis, D., Makrides, A., Christofi, M., & Thrassou, A. (2021). Social media influencer marketing: A systematic review, integrative framework and future research agenda. *International Journal of Consumer Studies*, *45*(4), 617–644. doi:10.1111/ijcs.12647

Zhu, Y. (2021) 'BotSpot++: A Hierarchical Deep Ensemble Model for Bots Install Fraud Detection in Mobile Advertising', *ACM Transactions on Information Systems*, *40*(3), 50. . doi:10.1145/3476107

KEY TERMS AND DEFINITIONS

Artificial Intelligence: Artificial intelligence enables machines to replicate cognitive processes like learning and problem-solving that people typically associate with human intelligence.

ChatGPT: ChatGPT, known as "Generative Pre-trained Transformer," is an artificial intelligence chatbot that can provide responses that are both coherent and pertinent to the context.

Influencer Marketing: This is one of the strategy of social media marketing that does endorsements and product mentioning on their social media platform and are viewed as experts within their niche.

Social Media Influencer: SMIs are third party endorsers that attempt to shape consumer attitudes toward a brand.

Chapter 17
Impact of Generative AI in Transforming Higher Education Pedagogy

Arti Gupta
J.C. Bose University of Science and Technology, YMCA, Faridabad, India

ABSTRACT

The purpose of this study is to investigate the impact of generative artificial intelligence in higher education. This study investigates how generative artificial intelligence enhances teaching and learning practices in higher education institutions. Additionally, it also explores applications, advantages, and problems associated with the use of generative artificial intelligence. This study analyses the implementation of Generative AI in higher education institutions employing qualitative methods such as focus groups study and interviews The findings of this study show how significantly generative AI has impacted teaching in higher education. Generative AI solutions can enhance personalized learning experiences, as well as create custom learning resources for students. It also helps in automating administrative processes. However, there are difficulties with adaptability, privacy concerns, and ethical issues in utilizing AI generated applications. The findings of this study have recommendations for teachers, administrators, and policymakers of higher education.

INTRODUCTION

Teachers in higher education have a long history of using traditional pedagogy, which has served as the backbone of academic instruction for decades. Although, traditional methods of teaching have been effective in the past, but they are inadequate in the

DOI: 10.4018/979-8-3693-0815-8.ch017

age of generative artificial intelligence (Generative AI). One of the fundamental limitations of the approach is that it adopts an all-or-nothing approach to teaching, which is a significant flaw. It has been observed that traditional pedagogical methods frequently are unable to suit the great variety of learning styles, speeds, and requirements that students have at present.

In contrast to that, generative AI has the potential to address this issue by offering personalized educational content and pathways based on student background, in so doing student engagement and performance gets improved (Cooper, 2023; Yang, 2022; Tomar & Verma, 2021). Additionally, traditional pedagogy frequently requires teachers to spend a lot of time and resources on mundane administrative tasks like grading and assessment which requires a lot of time and energy.With the help of generative AI, these mundane activities can be taken care of if teachers are able to utilize generative AI application effectively. Thus, teachers will get time for mentoring, engaging in interactive learning, and assisting students in developing the critical thinking and problem-solving abilities that are crucial in the digital age (North et al., 2023; Bygstad et al., 2022; Tomar & Verma, 2021). Thus, it is clear that in a time where generative AI can provide students adaptable, effective, and personalized educational experiences which has ultimate power to transform the landscape of higher education, as the constraints of traditional pedagogy are becoming more evident.

We cannot deny that the landscape of higher education is shifting, and as a result, pedagogy is being transformed significantly (Grassini, 2023; North et al., 2023). Generative AI, a branch of artificial intelligence (AI), has enormous potential for use in higher education institutions (Tomar & Verma, 2021). This study's main objective is to analyse how generative AI has its impact on educationsimultaneously highlighting its uses, advantages, and difficulties.

With the emergence of Generative AIas a revolutionary force, technological developments have led the way in a new era in education (North et al., 2023; Bearman et al., 2022; Yang, 2022). This study's aim is to analyse how generative AI can change the pedagogy in higher education, covering its uses, advantages and challenges. Through quantitative data analysis using interviews and questionnaires, this study explores the adoption of Generative AI in higher education institutions and its implications for teaching and learning.

In this studyqualitative research design is effective in providing thorough investigation of the use of Generative AI in higher education. A standardized survey questionnaire was distributed in higher education institutes located in Faridabad, Haryana. Data was collected from professors and students of higher education institutions in the course of this study. A survey was undertaken on perceived influence of generative AI, its adoption, application and challenges in higher education.Purposive sampling was used to choose institutions from Haryana, India.

With the aim of investigating correlations between the variables, the qualitative data gathered from the survey was evaluated to produce descriptive statistics, such as frequencies and percentages.

APPLICATIONS OF GENERATIVE AI IN HIGHER EDUCATION

This study explores the revolutionary impact of generative AI applications on higher education. The study's findings show how generative AI technologies are revolutionizing pedagogy and learning environments in educational settings, as well as their applications, benefits, and challenges. This study utilizes a qualitative methodology that includes focus group study and interviews. Higher education has been significantly impacted by generative artificial intelligence (GAI), which canimprove classroom engagement, individualized learning, and content production (Dwivedi, Grassini, North et al., 2023; Pitso, 2023; Yang, 2022). Although it also includes some challenges like flexibility, data protection, and ethical concerns (Fullan, 2023).For teachers, administrators, and policy makers, the paper provides guidance on how to the potential of generative AI can be utilized while keeping in view ethical and privacy consideration. It has also been suggested, in order to optimize the benefits of generative AI, faculty development programs can be organized. In this study, the impact of generative AI on higher education is carefully examined. Through literature review, the following artificial intelligence (AI) methods which can be utilized in educational setting are identified:

Virtual Assistants and Chatbots

Chatbots are artificially intelligent virtual assistants that use text or voice to interact with pupils. These chatbots' tasks include providing administrative support, posing questions, and providing information (Ilieva et al., 2023). Additionally, it raises student involvement, provides quick answers to questions, offers 24/7 support, minimizes the administrative burden on teachers, and delivers individualized learning. It also engages users by replying to frequently asked questions, helping students choose courses, providing study tips, and handling administrative tasks.

Adaptive Learning Systems

Systems for adaptive learning use artificial intelligence algorithms to assess a student's abilities and weaknesses. To provide distinctive learning opportunities, they adapt the educational process to the needs of each individual. This also helps to improve student comprehension, retention, and learning outcomes by tailoring instructional content and activities to each student's level of proficiency. Additional features include personalized course materials, assessments, dynamic difficulty adjustment, and real-time feedback.

Creation and Generation of Content

By analyzing existing content, artificial intelligence (AI) techniques can be used to autonomously develop educational materials including textbooks, study materials, and test questions. Additionally, it benefits teachers by saving them time on manual content generation and ensuring uniformity in the information provided. By automatically producing study materials, making quiz questions, and summarizing educational content, one can maximize its potential.

Translation of the Language

Language barriers can be eliminated by using AI-powered language translation systems to translate educational materials and communications into multiple languages. It aids in helping international students, facilitating communication in multilingual contexts, and giving a global audience access to educational resources. For course content, instructional materials, and communications with non-native speakers, these platforms offer translation services.

Recognition of Speech and Natural Language Processing (NLP)

Artificial intelligence is employed in these technologies to comprehend and process spoken words. They can improve the acquisition of foreign languages and automate the grading of essays and oral assignments in the classroom (Alqahtani et al., 2023). Effectively evaluate students' oral work, promote their language learning, and assess their language and pronunciation abilities. These tools can be used by teachers for voice assistant functionality, pronunciation evaluation, automated grading of spoken tasks, and language learning apps.

Anti-Plagiarism Measures

In order to ensure academic integrity, AI-based plagiarism detection tools scan student submissions for possible instances of plagiarism. It helps in maintaining academic honesty, prevent plagiarism, and provide teachers with evidence when academic misconduct is suspected. Such tools help in analyzing essays, reports, and research papers for plagiarism and generating similarity reports.

Learning Analytics

To assist teachers in making data-informed decisions, AI-driven learning analytics collect and analyze data on student performance, engagement, and behavior. Using data to tailor instruction will result in improved teaching strategies, identification of at-risk students, and an overall improvement in learning outcomes. These tools helps in keeping track of student progress, predicting dropouts, recommending interventions, and optimizing the design of curriculums.

Personalized Learning Platforms

By offering information and activities based on students' progress and preferences, AI platforms give pupils individualized learning paths. By customizing educational experiences for each student, you may improve learning results, motivation, and student engagement. Such an application supports individualized course recommendations, adaptive learning platforms, and customized learning experiences.

Systems for Managing Classrooms

Artificial intelligence-powered classroom management software keeps track of student involvement, attendance, and behavior to make sure that teachers maintain a positive learning environment. It assists in supplying in-the-moment insights into the dynamics of the classroom, ensures a focused learning environment, identifies students who require support, and ensures a focused learning environment. These programs are useful for keeping track of attendance, keeping an eye on conduct, and helping troubled students receive early intervention.

System of Tutoring

With the use of AI-driven tutoring programs, students can receive individualized help outside of regular class times. It aids in giving children individualized attention and allows them to understand difficult ideas. The use of this tool helps students understand challenging material better and offers individualized education. Additionally, these resources can be used for virtual tutoring sessions, individualized assignment help, and tutoring sessions that are subject-specific.

Automation of Administrative Tasks

Artificial intelligence can be used to automate administrative chores like scheduling, grading, and data input for the benefit of teachers and administrators. It is useful because it will free up more time for teachers to dedicate to teaching, streamline administrative procedures, and lessen human error in data administration (Dwivedi, 2023; Grassini, 2023). Grading, course scheduling, data entry, and administrative workflow optimization are all automated with the aid of these tools.

Predictive Analytics

In predictive analytics, artificial intelligence is used to analyze data and identify patterns that can help predict which students are at risk of falling behind or dropping out. Enhancing student support services, early intervention for at-risk students, and improved retention rates. This application can provide information such as assessing students at risk, recommending interventions, and optimizing student support programs.

Virtual Reality and Augmented Reality (AR/VR)

Through the use of AR and VR technologies, powered by artificial intelligence, immersive learning experiences can be created (Raja & Priya, 2023). As a result, they enhance understanding and engagement, especially in subjects such as science, history, and geography. These tools encourage active learning, improve comprehension of complex concepts, and create memorable educational experiences. Few examples of such applications are an immersive geography lesson, historical reenactments, and virtual science labs.

Robotics in Education

There is an increasing use of AI-driven robots in education as a means of assisting in the teaching of coding, programming, and STEM subjects (Chen, 2023). Through interactive lessons, they engage students in learning. Engage students in technology and STEM education, provide them with interactive learning experiences, and make learning fun at the same time. Courses on robotics coding, STEM-focused robotics activities, and companions for language learning in conjunction with robotics are the example of such tools.

Content Recommendation Engines

In order to maintain student engagement, artificial intelligence analyzes students' interests and learning patterns in order to suggest relevant educational content, resources, and courses. By providing personalized content recommendations to students, you can increase engagement, motivation, and retention. These application helps in making recommendations for supplementary reading materials, online courses, and other educational resources that are relevant to the course.

Analytics for Emotional Intelligence

AI tools analyze students' facial expressions, tone of voice, and other cues in order to determine their emotional states based on their facial expressions. As a result, teachers will be able to provide emotional support to students and tailor their teaching approach in accordance with this information. It also assists students in improving their emotional well-being, enhance communication between teachers and students, create a supportive learning environment, and enhance their emotional well-being. Support tools, well-being assessments for students, and personalized support strategies for students are all part of the emotional support program.

Accessibility Tools

The inclusion of everyone may be ensured by using artificial intelligence to develop content that is accessible for students with impairments, including text-to-speech, speech-to-text, and screen readers. It is crucial to support diversity, ensure that all students can access educational resources, and adhere to accessibility laws. Speech recognition technologies and accessible document formats are also available, in addition to text-to-speech software.

Security and Monitoring

By identifying and thwarting online dangers, artificial intelligence in educational settings enhances security. It not only secures sensitive information, but it also safeguards the interests of both students and educational institutions (Grassini, 2023). Data about students must be protected, online evaluations must be kept as fair and honest, and the learning environment must be safe. To effectively implement security and monitoring, it is essential to detect and prevent cyber risks, secure online assessments, and safeguard critical educational data.

These AI tools enable educational institutions to better support teachers in their instructional roles, improve administrative procedures inside their institutions, and improve the educational experience for students (Grassini, 2023). These technologies' ongoing development has created fresh chances for innovation in education.

METHODOLOGY

To better understand the experiences, viewpoints, and attitudes of important stakeholders, such as teachers and students, in regards to generative AI in education, a series of in-depth interviews have been performed.

This study's objective is to investigate, through a qualitative approach, the experiences, viewpoints, and attitudes of significant players regarding generative AI in education. In-depth interviews were chosen as the main method of data gathering for the study because they can give comprehensive, context-specific insights into a subject. It was carried out using a purposeful sample of significant educational stakeholders, including teachers, administrators, and students, who were chosen to reflect a range of backgrounds and viewpoints.

A purposeful sample technique was utilized to choose individuals who had direct knowledge of or experience with generative artificial intelligence systems in educational contexts.We were able to make sure that every respondent had pertinent ideas and opinions thanks to this method. A total of 252 people, including 83 teachers and 169 students, participated in the interviews. Combining purposive sampling, in which teachers from educational institutions were contacted, and voluntary participation, in which interested students were encouraged to join, was utilized to choose participants.

DATA COLLECTION AND ANALYSIS

A procedure was created to direct the interview process in order to guide the in-depth interviews. Open-ended questions and prompts were incorporated into the protocol to allow participants to explore their thoughts and experiences while sharing their experiences, viewpoints, and attitudes towards the use of generative AI in education. In-person and online interviews were done in accordance with the participant's preferences and geographic area. The interviews often lasted 25 to 30 minutes, giving participants time to share their perspectives in greater detail.

Before the interviews, the participants received informed consent forms outlining the goals of the study, the confidentiality safeguards, and their rights as study participants. All interviewees were given the assurance that they would remain anonymous, and when the interview results were reported, pseudonyms were used to shield the participants' identity.

To increase the veracity and validity of the findings, a triangulation approach involving interviews with a range of stakeholders (teachers and students) was carried out. The researcher participated in peer debriefing sessions to examine the emergent themes and interpretations in an effort to increase the dependability of the study.

FINDINGS

Based on the findings of the in-depth interviews, separate sections have been arranged thematically to provide a comprehensive understanding of key stakeholders' experiences, perspectives, and attitudes regarding the use of Generative AI in education. Table 1 shows the reliability of the items included in questionnaire.

Table 1. Reliability of questionnaire

Section	No. of Items	Alpha Coefficient Value
Demographic Characteristics	5	
Age		
Gender		
Marital Status		
EducationLevel		
Job Profile		
Impact of Generative AI on in higher education		
Positive Perceptions of Generative AI Adoption	4	0.767
Enhanced Personalization of Learning	4	0.783
Improved Administrative Efficiency	4	0.767
Ethical Concerns and Academic Integrity	4	0.779
Challenges in Adaptation and Training	4	0.799
Mixed Impact on Critical Thinking Skills	4	0.802
Calls for Ethical Guidelines and Training	4	0.770

As part of this research methodology, a series of in-depth interviews was conducted with teachersand students in order to gather rich qualitative data in order to shed light on the intricate nuances of their involvement with Generative AI in educational contexts. This analysis provides valuable insights into the impact and implications of Generative AI in the field of education based on the analysis of these interviews. Table 2 shows the demographic characteristics of respondents participated in the study.

Table 2. Demographic characteristics of respondents

Demographic Characteristics	Frequency(f)	Percentage(%)
Gender		
Male	172	68
Female	80	32
Age		
Lessthan20yearsold	0	0
21to25yearsold	93	37
26to30yearsold	61	24
31to35yearsold	37	15
36to40yearsold	48	19
Morethan40years	13	5
Education Level		
BachelorDegree	94	37
MasterDegree	60	24
Others	98	39

Table 3 shows the descriptive statistics for the impact of Generative AI on higher education based on collected response from teachers and students.

Table 3. Descriptive statistics for impact of generative AI on higher education

Variable	Mean	Standard Deviation
Impact of Generative AI on higher education		
Positive Perceptions of Generative AI Adoption	2.52	0.72
Enhanced Personalization of Learning	3.33	0.52
Improved Administrative Efficiency	3.02	0.85
Ethical Concerns and Academic Integrity	3.33	0.72
Challenges in Adaptation and Training	3.11	0.63
Mixed Impact on Critical Thinking Skills	3.46	0.70
Calls for Ethical Guidelines and Training:	3.13	0.70
Positive Perceptions of Generative AI Adoption	3.24	0.55
Enhanced Personalization of Learning	3.33	0.68

Based on the results of a qualitative analysis conducted the following are some key findings:

Positive Perceptions of Generative AI Adoption

The majority of respondents, both teachers and students, indicated that they were satisfied with the use of Generative AI tools in education, with approximately 26 percent of teachers and 46percent of students expressing satisfaction with the use of these tools and the rest were not aware about Generative AI and its application.

These findings are corroborated by qualitative insights, which highlight the fact that many teachers and students appreciate the ease and efficiency that Generative AI brings in terms of creating and accessing educational content, as well as their learning process.Still a considerable group not aware of Generative AI and its application, these interviews revealed that this lack of awareness might stem from limited exposure about AI tools in their educational environments.

Enhanced Personalization of Learning

Approximately 32 percentage of the surveyed students acknowledge that Generative AI has played a significant role in personalizing their learning experiences, allowing them to access content that is tailored to their learning needs. However, only 12 percent teachers acknowledge that Generative AI has played a significant role in personalizing their learning experiences.

It is concluded that, although students perceive Generative AI as significantly enhancing their learning experiences through personalization, Teachers' perception of its impact is comparatively lower in comparison to students' perceptions of its impact. For teachers to harness the full potential of Generative AI for personalized learning, targeted training, awareness campaigns, and collaborative efforts may be necessary.

Improved Administrative Efficiency

The implementation of Generative AI tools has significantly reduced the administrative workload of administrative staff members and improved the efficiency of tasks such as grading and content generation by reducing the amount of time it takes to perform them.

From interviews with teachers, it was revealed that there were specific instances in which Generative AI tools streamlined administrative processes, allowing time to be allocated to strategic planning and student support.

Ethical Concerns and Academic Integrity

It appears that a significant portion of respondents, including teachers and students (approximately 61 percent), expressed concerns about the potential misuse of Generative AI for academic dishonesty.

It is found that the ethical dilemmas faced by teachers and students regarding the responsible use of generative artificial intelligence tools were reflected while interviews. The need for clear guidelines and ethical education has been highlighted by some teachers.

Challenges in Adaptation and Training

It was reported that more than 52 percent of teachers reported challenges when adapting to Generative AI tools, which were primarily related to technical expertise and integration into existing pedagogical practices.

The interviews conducted indicated that while Generative AI may offer potential benefits, ongoing training and support is necessary in order to integrate it effectively into the teaching process.

Mixed Impact on Critical Thinking Skills

It has been reported that a majority of teachers(approximately 58) believe that the use of Generative AI is having a mixed impact on students' critical thinking skills, with some expressing concerns about the overuse of automated content in the classroom.

In terms of qualitative insights, it seemed that while generative AI does aid in the acquisition of knowledge, some instructors have expressed worries regarding students' capacity for information analysis and synthesis.

Calls for Ethical Guidelines and Training

Approximately 49% of respondents, both teachers and students, felt that in order to promote the ethical use of generative AI in the classroom, explicit ethical rules and training programs are required.

According to the results of the interviews, it is clear that both teachers and students believe that educational institutions should take the initiative to address ethical issues and offer possibilities for professional growth.

These results demonstrate that the pedagogy in higher education is being significantly and complexly impacted by generative AI. In terms of personalization and administrative effectiveness, technology is a significant advancement, but it also raises a number of ethical issues and challenges that call for attention and proactive measures to ensure a responsible and successful integration of the technology into educational practices.

The qualitative analysis of the data offers a thorough understanding of the opinions and experiences of teachers and students with regard to the application of generative artificial intelligence in education.

DISCUSSION

Most teachers and students were found to be content with the employment of generative AI tools in the classroom. The ease and effectiveness these platforms offer for material generation, access, and even the learning experience itself contribute to an increasing sense of happiness. Students embrace the freedom to learn at their own pace, while teachers value the option to adapt the information to each student's specific needs.

The use of generative artificial intelligence has contributed significantly to the personalization of learning experiences. It has been established that qualitative data supports the idea that only 26 percent teachers are using AI. Still a considerable no of teachersare not in support of AI tools and application and has doubt on its credibility.

One of the most notable findings is the widespread concern about the potential misuse of Generative AI for academic dishonesty that has been found. In response to the proposed policy, both teachers and students expressed reservations, emphasizing the importance of maintaining academic integrity in the classroom. In this context, it is evident that there is a need for clear guidelines and ethical education in this context (Chiu, 2023).

Some instructors found it difficult to adopt Generative AI tools due to a lack of technical knowledge and the need to integrate the tools into current teaching methods. The findings of the qualitative study make it clear that continual training and support are required to fully realize these tools' potential to help educational institutes.

The effect of generative AI on critical thinking abilities has been the subject of extensive discussion in recent years. Despite the fact that it aids in knowledge acquisition, questions have been raised regarding pupils' capacity for critical analysis and information synthesis. AI-generated content must be used in a balanced way if its potential is to be fully realized.

There is a widespread desire for unambiguous ethical standards and education initiatives to support the ethical use of artificial intelligence in education. It is generally acknowledged that educational institutions play a significant role in addressing ethical issues and giving stakeholders chances for professional development.

CONCLUSION

This study's findings support the notion that generative AI is indeed altering higher education pedagogy in a variety of ways. This project has unquestionably had a good effect on personalisation, administrative effectiveness, and improved learning experiences. However, these benefits come with drawbacks, including ethical questions, difficulties adjusting to this new technology, and worries about their influence on critical thinking abilities.

Educational institutions must take the initiative to deal with these issues if they want to successfully navigate this transformative terrain. This process includes the creation of precise ethical standards, the execution of thorough training programs, and the provision of continuing support for teachers. In order to fully realize the benefits of generative AI while upholding academic integrity and the standard of instruction in the classroom, proper integration of this technology into educational practices is necessary.

Generative AI has the potential to reshape education, but its success depends on how responsibly and ethically it is used to pursue improved learning outcomes and education experiences in the pursuit of a more personalized curriculum.

REFERENCES

Al Ka'bi, A. (2023). Proposed artificial intelligence algorithm and deep learning techniques for development of higher education. *International Journal of Intelligent Networks*, *4*, 68–73. doi:10.1016/j.ijin.2023.03.002

Bearman, M., Ryan, J., & Ajjawi, R. (2022). Discourses of artificial intelligence in higher education: A critical literature review. *Higher Education*, 1–17.

Bygstad, B., Øvrelid, E., Ludvigsen, S., & Dæhlen, M. (2022). From dual digitalization to digital learning space: Exploring the digital transformation of higher education. *Computers & Education*, *182*, 104463. doi:10.1016/j.compedu.2022.104463

Chen, X., Cheng, G., Zou, D., Zhong, B., & Xie, H. (2023). Artificial Intelligent Robots for Precision Education. *Journal of Educational Technology & Society*, *26*(1), 171–186.

Chiu, T. K. (2023). The impact of Generative AI (GenAI) on practices, policies and research direction in education: A case of ChatGPT and Midjourney. *Interactive Learning Environments*, 1–17. doi:10.1080/10494820.2023.2253861

Cooper, G. (2023). Examining science education in chatgpt: An exploratory study of generative artificial intelligence. *Journal of Science Education and Technology*, *32*(3), 444–452. doi:10.100710956-023-10039-y

Dwivedi, Y. K., Kshetri, N., Hughes, L., Slade, E. L., Jeyaraj, A., Kar, A. K., Baabdullah, A. M., Koohang, A., Raghavan, V., Ahuja, M., Albanna, H., Albashrawi, M. A., Al-Busaidi, A. S., Balakrishnan, J., Barlette, Y., Basu, S., Bose, I., Brooks, L., Buhalis, D., & Wright, R. (2023). "So what if ChatGPT wrote it?" Multidisciplinary perspectives on opportunities, challenges and implications of generative conversational AI for research, practice and policy. *International Journal of Information Management*, *71*, 102642. doi:10.1016/j.ijinfomgt.2023.102642

Fullan, M., Azorin, C., Harris, A., & Jones, M. (2023). Artificial intelligence and school leadership: Challenges, opportunities and implications. *School Leadership & Management*, 1–8. doi:10.1080/13632434.2023.2246856

Grassini, S. (2023). Shaping the future of education: Exploring the potential and consequences of AI and ChatGPT in educational settings. *Education Sciences*, *13*(7), 692. doi:10.3390/educsci13070692

Ilieva, G., Yankova, T., Klisarova-Belcheva, S., Dimitrov, A., Bratkov, M., & Angelov, D. (2023). Effects of Generative Chatbots in Higher Education. *Information (Basel)*, *14*(9), 492. doi:10.3390/info14090492

North, C., Hills, D., Maher, P., Farkić, J., Zeilmann, V., Waite, S., Takano, T., Prince, H., Pedersen Gurholt, K., Muthomi, N., Njenga, D., Karaka-Clarke, T. H., Houge Mackenzie, S., & French, G. (2023). The impact of artificial intelligence on adventure education and outdoor learning: International perspectives. *Journal of Adventure Education and Outdoor Learning*, 1–18. doi:10.1080/14729679.2023.2248302

Pitso, T. (2023). Telagogy: New theorisations about learning and teaching in higher education post-Covid-19 pandemic. *Cogent Education*, *10*(2), 2258278. doi:10.1080/2331186X.2023.2258278

Raja, M., & Priya, G. L. (2023). The Role of Augmented Reality and Virtual Reality in Smart Health Education: State of the Art and Perspectives. Artificial Intelligence for Smart Healthcare, 311-325.

Tomar, P., & Verma, S. (2021). Impact and role of AI technologies in teaching, learning, and research in higher education. In Impact of AI Technologies on Teaching, Learning, and Research in Higher Education (pp. 190-203). IGI Global. doi:10.4018/978-1-7998-4763-2.ch012

Yang, W. (2022). Artificial Intelligence education for young children: Why, what, and how in curriculum design and implementation. *Computers and Education: Artificial Intelligence*, *3*, 100061. doi:10.1016/j.caeai.2022.100061

Compilation of References

Abd-Elaal, E., Gamage, S., & Mills, J. E. (2022). Assisting academics to identify computer generated writing. *European Journal of Engineering Education, 47*(5), 725–745. doi:10.1080/03043797.2022.2046709

AbdelkaderO. A. ChatgGPT's Influence on Customer Experience in Digital Marketing: Investigating the Moderating Roles. SSRN 4441250. doi:10.2139/ssrn.4441250

Accenture. (2019). *Rethinking Customer Engagement with Artificial Intelligence*. Accenture Research.

Adamopoulou, E., & Moussiades, L. (2020a). An overview of chatbot technology. In *IFIP International Conference on Artificial Intelligence Applications and Innovations* (pp. 373-383). Springer. 10.1007/978-3-030-49186-4_31

Adamopoulou, E., & Moussiades, L. (2020b). Chatbots: History, technology, and applications. *Machine Learning with Applications, 2*, 100006. doi:10.1016/j.mlwa.2020.100006

Adewumi, A., Taiwo, A., Misra, S., Maskeliunas, R., Damasevicius, R., Ahuja, R., and Ayeni, F. (2020). A Unified Framework for Outfit Design and Advice. *Advances in Intelligent Systems and Computing, 106*.

Aelterman, N., Vansteenkiste, M., Haerens, L., Soenens, B., Fontaine, J., & Reeve, J. (2019). Toward an Integrative and Fine-grained Insight in Motivating and Demotivating Teaching Styles: The Merits of a Circumplex Approach. *Journal of Educational Psychology, 20180913*(3), 497–521. doi:10.1037/edu0000293

Ahn, C. (2023). Exploring ChatGPT for information of cardiopulmonary resus-citation. *Resuscitation, 185*, 109729. doi:10.1016/j.resuscitation.2023.109729 PMID:36773836

AIMultiple (2023). *ChatGPT for Customer Service: 7 Use Cases & Benefits in 2023*. AIMultiple.

Al Ka'bi, A. (2023). Proposed artificial intelligence algorithm and deep learning techniques for development of higher education. *International Journal of Intelligent Networks, 4*, 68–73. doi:10.1016/j.ijin.2023.03.002

Al Nuaimi, E., Al Neyadi, H., Mohamed, N., & Al-Jaroodi, J. (2015). Applications of big data to smart cities. *Journal of Internet Services and Applications, 6*(1), 25. doi:10.118613174-015-0041-5

Alawida, M., Mejri, S., Mehmood, A., Chikhaoui, B., & Isaac Abiodun, O. (2023). A comprehensive study of chatgpt: Advancements, limitations, and ethical considerations in Natural Language Processing and cybersecurity. *Information (Basel)*, *14*(8), 462. doi:10.3390/info14080462

Albert, B., & Tullis, T. (2013). *Measuring the user experience: collecting, an-alyzing, and presenting usability metrics*. Newnes.

Algharabat, R. S. (2018). The role of telepresence and user engagement in co-creation value and purchase intention: Online retail context. *Journal of Internet Commerce*, *17*(1), 1–25. doi:10.1080/15332861.2017.1422667

Al-Hyari, H. S. A., Al-Smadi, H. M., & Weshah, S. R. (2023). The Impact of Artificial Intelligence (AI) on Guest Satisfaction in Hotel Management: An Empirical Study of Luxury Hotels. *Geo Journal of Tourism and Geosites*, *48*(2 supplement), 810–819. doi:10.30892/gtg.482spl15-1081

Ali, F. (2023). Let the devil speak for itself: Should ChatGPT be allowed or banned in hospitality and tourism schools? *Journal of Global Hospitality and Tourism*, *2*(1), 1–6. doi:10.5038/2771-5957.2.1.1016

Ali, F., Yasar, B., Ali, L., & Dogan, S. (2023). Antecedents and consequences of travelers' trust towards personalized travel recommendations offered by ChatGPT. *International Journal of Hospitality Management*, *114*, 103588. doi:10.1016/j.ijhm.2023.103588

Aljanabi, M., Ghazi, M., Ali, A. H., & Abed, S. A. (2023). ChatGPT: Open Possibilities. *Iraqi Journal For Computer Science and Mathematics*, *4*(1), 62–64.

Allen, N. J. (2023, July 23). *Productive ways to use CHATGPT to turbocharge crypto research*. The Coin Republic. https://www.thecoinrepublic.com/2023/07/23/productive-ways-to-use-chatgpt-to-turbocharge-crypto-research/

Almeida, T., & Haddad, H. (2020). A systematic review of chatbot research in customer service. *Journal of Service Management*, *31*(3), 484–508.

Alnawas, I., & Hemsley-Brown, J. (2019). Examining the key dimensions of customer experience quality in the hotel industry. *Journal of Hospitality Marketing & Management*, *28*(7), 833–861. doi:10.1080/19368623.2019.1568339

AlnuhaitD.WuQ.YuZ. (2023). Facechat: An emotion-aware face-to-face dialogue framework. https://arxiv.org/abs/2303.07316v1

Alshater, M. M. (2022). Exploring the Role of artificial intelligence in enhancing academic performance: a case study of ChatGPT. SSRN *Electron. J.* doi:10.2139/ssrn.4312358

Alutto, J. A. (2008). *Final Report of the AACSB International Impact of Research Task Force*. The Association to Advance Collegiate Schools of Business, Tampa, FL. https://www.aacsb.edu/insights/reports/impact-of-research

American Association of University Professors. (n.d.). *Tenure*. AAUP. https://www.aaup.org/issues/tenure#:~:text=Why% 20is%20tenure%20important%3F,conduct%20research%20in%20higher%20education.

American Psychological Association. (2020). *Publication Manual of the American Psychological Association* (7th ed.). APA. https://apastyle.apa.org/

Anabila, P., Ameyibor, L. E. K., Allan, M. M., & Alomenu, C. (2022). Service quality and customer loyalty in Ghana's hotel industry: The mediation effects of satisfaction and delight. *Journal of Quality Assurance in Hospitality & Tourism*, *23*(3), 748–770. doi:10.1080/1528008X.2021.1913691

Anderson, L. M., Johnson, C. R., & Davis, E. S. (2019). The Role of Teacher-Student Relationships in Academic Motivation. *Journal of Educational Psychology*, *112*(4), 567–582.

Anderson, N., Belavy, D. L., Perle, S. M., Hendricks, S., Hespanhol, L., Verhagen, E., & Memon, A. R. (2023). AI did not write this manuscript, or did it? Can we trick the AI text detector into generated texts? The potential future of ChatGPT and AI in Sports & Exercise Medicine manuscript generation. *BMJ Open Sport & Exercise Medicine*, *9*(1), e001568. doi:10.1136/bmjsem-2023-001568 PMID:36816423

Andry, J. F., Chakir, A., Parlindungan, R. M., Silalahi, L., & Clara, M. (2023). Identification Of Business And Technology Strategies Based On The Ward Peppard-Cassidy Method. *Journal of Theoretical and Applied Information Technology*, *101*(6).

Anshari, M., Almunawar, M. N., Lim, S. A., & Al-Mudimigh, A. (2019). Customer relationship management and big data enabled: Personalization & customization of services. *Applied Computing and Informatics*, *15*(2), 94–101. doi:10.1016/j.aci.2018.05.004

Ao, L., Bansal, R., Pruthi, N., & Khaskheli, M. B. (2023). Impact of Social Media Influencers on Customer Engagement and Purchase Intention: A Meta-Analysis. *Sustainability (Basel)*, *15*(3), 2744. doi:10.3390u15032744

Archibald, M. M., & Clark, A. M. (2023). Chatgtp: What is it and how can nursing and health science education use it? *Journal of Advanced Nursing*, *79*(10), 3648–3651. doi:10.1111/jan.15643 PMID:36942780

Arman, M., & Lamiya, U. R. (2023). Exploring the Implication of ChatGPT AI for Business: Efficiency and Challenges. [JINITA]. *Journal of Innovation Information Technology and Application*, *5*(1), 52–64. doi:10.35970/jinita.v5i1.1828

Arora, A., & Arora, A. (2023). The promise of large language models in health care. *Lancet*, *401*(10377), 641. doi:10.1016/S0140-6736(23)00216-7 PMID:36841609

Astin, A. (1984). Student Involvement: A Developmental Theory for Higher Education. *Journal of College Student Personnel*, *25*(4), 297–308.

Augier, M., March, J. G., & Sullivan, B. N. (2005). Notes on the evolution of a research community: Organization studies in Anglophone North America, 1945–2000. *Organization Science*, *16*(1), 85–95. doi:10.1287/orsc.1040.0108

Ausat, A. M. A., Azzaakiyyah, H. K., Permana, R. M., Riady, Y., & Suherlan, S. (2023). The Role of ChatGPT in Enabling MSMEs to Compete in the Digital Age. Innovative: Journal Of. *Social Science Research*, *3*(2), 622–631.

Ausat, A. M. A., Massang, B., Efendi, M., Nofirman, N., & Riady, Y. (2023). Can chat GPT replace the role of the teacher in the classroom: A fundamental analysis. *Journal of Education*, *5*(4), 16100–16106.

Avila-ChauvetL.MejíaD.Acosta QuirozC. O. (2023). Chatgpt as a support tool for online behavioral task programming. Available At SSRN 4329020.

Aziza, C., & Meriyem, C. (2020). Using Multi-Agent System to Govern the IT Needs of Stakeholders. In *Business Intelligence - New Dimensions in Knowledge and Intelligence Based Society* [WorkingTitle]. IntechOpen. doi:10.5772/intechopen.91440

Baheti, A. R., & Kshirsagar, P. (2021). Chatbot systems for customer service: A review of the literature. *Journal of Enterprise Information Management*, *34*(4), 748–770.

Bahrini, A., Khamoshifar, M., Abbasimehr, H., Riggs, R. J., Esmaeili, M., Mastali Majdabadkohne, R., & Pasehvar, M. (2023). ChatGPT: Applications, Opportunities, and Threats. arXiv preprint arXiv:2304.09103 doi:10.1109/SIEDS58326.2023.10137850

Baidoo-Anu, D., & Owusu Ansah, L. (2023). Education in the era of generative artificial intelligence (AI): understanding the potential benefits of ChatGPT in promoting teaching and learning. SSRN *Electron. J.* doi:10.2139/ssrn.4337484

Balakrishnan, B., Dwivedi, Y., Piercy, N., Akhtar, P., & Clement, M. (2021). Artificial intelligence (AI) in marketing: The role of chatbots in customer experience management (CEM). *Journal of Business Research.*

Bandura, A. (1977). Self-efficacy: Toward a unifying theory of behavioural change. *Psychological Review*, *84*(2), 191–215. doi:10.1037/0033-295X.84.2.191 PMID:847061

Bandura, A. (1993). Perceived self-efficacy in cognitive development and functioning. *Educational Psychologist*, *28*(2), 117–148. doi:10.120715326985ep2802_3

Bansal, R., & Saini, S. (2022a). BIG DATA IN SOCIAL MEDIA: CONCEPTS & APPLICATIONS (pp. 34–41).

Bansal, R., & Saini, S. (2022b). Exploring the Role of Social Media: An Innovative Tool for Entrepreneurs. *Applying Metalytics to Measure Customer Experience in the Metaverse*. IGI Global. doi:10.4018/978-1-6684-6133-4.ch004

Bansal, R., Pruthi, N., & Singh, R. (2022). Developing Customer Engagement Through Artificial Intelligence Tools: Roles and Challenges. In Developing Relationships, Personalization, and Data Herald in Marketing 5.0 (pp. 130-145). IGI Global

Bansal, R., Pruthi, N., & Singh, R. (2022). Developing Customer Engagement Through Artificial Intelligence Tools: Roles and Challenges. In *Developing Relationships, Personalization, and Data Herald in Marketing 5.0* (pp. 130-145). IGI Global.

Bansal, R., Pruthi, N., & Singh, R. (2022). Developing Customer Engagement Through ArtificialIntelligence Tools: Roles and Challenges. In Developing Relationships, Personalization, and Data Heraldin Marketing, 5.0 (pp. 130-145). IGI Global.

Bansal, R., Shukla, G., Gupta, A., Singh, A., & Pruthi, N. (2023). Optimizing Augmented Reality and Virtual Reality for Customer Engagement. In *Promoting Consumer Engagement Through Emotional Branding and Sensory Marketing* (pp. 24-35). IGI Global.

Bansal, R., Gupta, A., Singh, R., & Nassa, V. K. (2021). Role and Impact of Digital Technologies in E-Learning amidst COVID-19 Pandemic. *2021 Fourth International Conference on Computational Intelligence and Communication Technologies (CCICT)*, (pp. 194–202). IEEE. 10.1109/CCICT53244.2021.00046

Bansal, R., Shukla, G., Gupta, A., Singh, A., & Pruthi, N. (2023). Optimizing Augmented Reality and Virtual Reality for Customer Engagement. In *Promoting Consumer Engagement Through Emotional Branding and Sensory Marketing* (pp. 24–35). IGI Global.

Bansal, R., Shukla, G., Gupta, A., Singh, A., & Pruthi, N. (2023). Optimizing Augmented Reality andVirtual Reality for Customer Engagement. In *Promoting Consumer Engagement Through EmotionalBranding and Sensory Marketing* (pp. 24–35). IGI Global.

Basta, C., Costa-jussà, M. R., & Casas, N. (2019). Evaluating the Underlying Gender Bias in Contextualized Word Embeddings. *Proceedings of the Workshop on Gender Bias in Natural Language Processing,* (pp. 33–39). IEEE. 10.18653/v1/W19-3805

Baudier, P., de Boissieu, E., & Duchemin, M.-H. (2023). Source Credibility and Emotions generated by Robot and Human Influencers: The perception of luxury brand representatives. *Technological Forecasting and Social Change*, *187*, 122255. doi:10.1016/j.techfore.2022.122255

Bearman, M., Ryan, J., & Ajjawi, R. (2022). Discourses of artificial intelligence in higher education: A critical literature review. *Higher Education*, 1–17.

Beath, C., Becerra-Fernandez, I., Ross, J., & Short, J. (2012). Finding value in the information explosion. *MIT Sloan Management Review*, *53*(4), 18–20.

Bedeian, A. G. (1996). Thoughts on the making and remaking of the management discipline. *Journal of Management Inquiry*, *5*(4), 311–318. doi:10.1177/105649269654003

Bedeian, A. G. (2004). Peer review and the social construction of knowledge in the management discipline. *Academy of Management Learning & Education*, *3*(2), 198–216. doi:10.5465/amle.2004.13500489

Bender, E. M., Gebru, T., McMillan-Major, A., & Shmitchell, S. (2021). On the Dangers of Stochastic Parrots: Can Language Models Be Too Big? *Proceedings of the ACM Conference on Fairness, Accountability, and Transparency,* (pp. 610–623). ACM. https://doi.org/10.1145/3442188.3445922

Bertaglia, T., Huber, S., Goanta, C., Spanakis, G., & Iamnitchi, A. (2023). Closing the Loop: Testing ChatGPT to Generate Model Explanations to Improve Human Labelling of Sponsored Content on Social Media. *arXiv preprint arXiv:2306.05115.*

Bhandari, R., & Sin, M. V. A. (2023). Optimizing digital marketing in hospitality industries. *Startupreneur Bisnis Digital (SABDA Journal), 2*(1).

Bird, J. J. (2021). Improving customer service chatbots with attention-based transfer learning. arXiv:2111.14621v2, https://arxiv.org/abs/2111. 14621v2.

Bismo, A., & Putra, S. (2019, August). Application of Digital Marketing (social media and email marketing) and its Impact on Customer Engagement in Purchase Intention: a case study at PT. Soltius Indonesia. In *2019 International Conference on Information Management and Technology (ICIMTech)* (Vol. 1, pp. 109-114). IEEE. 10.1109/ICIMTech.2019.8843763

Bist, A. S., Agarwal, V., Aini, Q., & Khofifah, N. (2022). Managing Digital Transformation in Marketing:" Fusion of Traditional Marketing and Digital Marketing. *International Transactions on Artificial Intelligence*, *1*(1), 18–27.

BiswasS. (2023a). The Function of Chat GPT in Social Media: According to Chat GPT. SSRN 4405389. doi:10.2139/ssrn.4405389

Biswas, S. (2023b). *Prospective Role of Chat GPT in the Military: According to ChatGPT.* Qeios.

Bnouachir, H. (n.d.). Intelligent Fleet Management System for Open Pit Mine.

Bogina, V., Hartman, A., Kuflik, T., & Shulner-Tal, A. (2021). Educating software and AI stakeholders about algorithmic fairness, accountability, transparency and ethics. *International Journal of Artificial Intelligence in Education*, *32*(3), 808–833. doi:10.100740593-021-00248-0

Bona, J. D., Powell, A. G., Farrar, E., & Cohen, D. K. (1985). The shopping mall high school: Winners and losers in the educational marketplace. *The Journal of Negro Education*, *56*(1), 122. doi:10.2307/2295389

BorovikovI.HarderJ.SadovskyM.BeiramiA. (2019). Towards inter-active training of non-player characters in video games. arXiv:1906.00535v1, https://arxiv.org/abs/1906.00535v1

Borsci, S., Malizia, A., Schmettow, M., van der Velde, F., Tariverdiyeva, G., Balaji, D., & Chamberlain, A. (2022). The chatbot usability scale: The design and pilot of a usability scale for interaction with ai-based conversational agents. *Personal and Ubiquitous Computing*, *26*(1), 95–119. doi:10.100700779-021-01582-9

Botpress Blog. (2023). ChatGPT: A powerful tool for customer engagement. [Blog post]. *Botpress Blog.*

Bowden, J. L. (2009b). *Customer engagement: A framework for assessing customer-brand relationships*. [Doctoral dissertation, Queensland University of Technology].

Bowden, J. L. (2009a). The process of customer engagement: A conceptual framework. *Journal of Marketing Theory and Practice*, *17*(1), 63–74. doi:10.2753/MTP1069-6679170105

BrandJ.IsraeliA.NgweD. (2023). Using GPT for Market Research. SSRN.

Brandtzaeg, P. B., & Følstad, A. (2017). Why people use chatbots. In *International conference on internet science* (pp. 377-392). Springer. 10.1007/978-3-319-70284-1_30

Brodie, R. J., Hollebeek, L. D., Juric, B., & Ilic, A. (2011). Customer engagement: Conceptual domain, fundamental propositions, and implications for research. *Journal of Service Research*, *14*(3), 252–271. doi:10.1177/1094670511411703

Brodie, R. J., Ilic, A., Juric, B., & Hollebeek, L. (2013). Consumer engagement in a virtual brand community: An exploratory analysis. *Journal of Business Research*, *66*(1), 105–114. doi:10.1016/j.jbusres.2011.07.029

Brown, E. (2021, March 15). The Rise of Remote Work: Challenges and Opportunities. *The New York Times*.

Brown, T. B. (2020). *Language Models are Few-Shot Learners*. arXiv preprint arXiv:2005.14165.

Brown, T. B., Mann, B., Ryder, N., Subbiah, M., Kaplan, J., Dhariwal, P., & Agarwal, S. (2020). Language models are few-shot learners. arXiv preprint arXiv:2005.14165.

Brown, T., Mann, B., Ryder, N., Subbiah, M., Kaplan, J. D., Dhariwal, P., ... Amodei, D. (2020). Language models are few-shot learners. *Advances in Neural Information Processing Systems*, *33*, 1877–1901.

Budzianowski, P., & Vulić, I. (2019). Hello, it's GPT-2—how can I help you? towards the use of pretrained language models for task-oriented dialogue systems. /arXiv.1907.05774 doi:10.18653/v1/D19-5602

Burger, B., Kanbach, D. K., Kraus, S., Breier, M., & Corvello, V. (2023). On the use of ai-based tools like chatgpt to support management research. *European Journal of Innovation Management*, *26*(7), 233–241. doi:10.1108/EJIM-02-2023-0156

BushellC. (2023). ChatGPT for Marketers: Transforming Customer Engagement and Insights. SSRN. https://ssrn.com/abstract=4556644

Bygstad, B., Øvrelid, E., Ludvigsen, S., & Dæhlen, M. (2022). From dual digitalization to digital learning space: Exploring the digital transformation of higher education. *Computers & Education*, *182*, 104463. doi:10.1016/j.compedu.2022.104463

Caplow, T., & McGee, R. J. (1958). *The Academic Marketplace*. Basic Books.

Carvalho, I., & Ivanov, S. (2023). ChatGPT for tourism: Applications, benefits and risks. *Tourism Review*. doi:10.1108/TR-02-2023-0088

Cascella, M., Montomoli, J., Bellini, V., & Bignami, E. (2023). Evaluating the feasibility of chatgpt in healthcare: An analysis of multiple clinical and research scenarios. *Journal of Medical Systems*, *47*(1), 33. doi:10.100710916-023-01925-4 PMID:36869927

Chaffey, D., & Ellis-Chadwick, F. (2019). *Digital Marketing: Strategy, Implementation and Practice*. Pearson.

Chaffey, D., & Smith, P. R. (2022). *Digital marketing excellence: Planning, optimizing and integrating online marketing*. Taylor & Francis. doi:10.4324/9781003009498

ChaidrataA.ShafeeuM. I.ChewS. K.ChenZ.ChamJ. S.YongZ. L.YapU. H.BahrinD. I. K. (2022). Intent matching based customer services chatbot with natural language understanding. http:// arxiv.org/ abs/2202.00480v1

Chakir, A., Chergui, M., & Andry, J. F. (2020). A smart updater itgovernance platform based on artificial intelligence. *Risk (Concord, NH)*, *8*, 9.

Chakir, A., Chergui, M., & Andry, J. F. (2020b). A Smart Updater IT Governance Platform Based on Artificial Intelligence. *Advances in Science. Technology and Engineering Systems*, *5*(5), 47–53. doi:10.25046/aj050507

Chakir, A., Chergui, M., & Andry, J. F. (2021a). A decisional smart approach for the adoption of the IT green. *Environment, Development and Sustainability*, *23*(6), 8857–8871. doi:10.100710668-020-00999-1

Chakir, A., Chergui, M., Elhasnaoui, S., Medromi, H., & Sayouti, A. (2016). Intelligent plateform to select the best IT-GRC framework for treatment the needs of stakeholders. *International Journal of Applied Engineering Research: IJAER*, *11*(12).

Chakir, A., Chergui, M., Elhasnaou, S., Medromi, H., & Sayouti, A. (2016). A decision approach to select the best framework to treat an IT problem by using multi-agent system and expert systems. *Lecture Notes in Electrical Engineering*, *366*, 499–511. doi:10.1007/978-981-287-990-5_40

Chakir, A., Chergui, M., Medromi, H., & Sayouti, A. (2016). An approach to select effectively the best framework IT according to the axes of the governance IT, to handle and to set up an objective IT. *Proceedings of 2015 IEEE World Conference on Complex Systems, WCCS 2015*. IEEE. 10.1109/ICoCS.2015.7483311

Chan, A. (2022). GPT-3 and InstructGPT: Technological dystopianism, utopianism, and "contextual" perspectives in AI ethics and industry. *AI and Ethics*, *3*(1), 53–64. doi:10.100743681-022-00148-6

ChanC. K.HuW. (2023). *Students' voices on generative ai: perceptions, benefits, and challenges in higher education*. arXiv.2305.00290

Chandan, R. R., Lourens, M., Ramachandran, K. K., Akram, S. V., Bansal, R., & Kapila, D. (2022). Implementation and Execution of Blockchain Technology in the Field of Education. *2022 5th International Conference on Contemporary Computing and Informatics (IC3I)*, 1480–1485. 10.1109/IC3I56241.2022.10072593

Chatterjee, J., & Dethlefs, N. (2023). This new conversational AI model can be your friend, philosopher, and guide ... and even your worst enemy. *Patterns (New York, N.Y.)*, *4*(1), 100676. doi:10.1016/j.patter.2022.100676 PMID:36699746

Chen, J., Liu, X., & Zhao, Y. (20233). Conversational Chatbots with GPT-3. 5: A Fine-tuning and Prompting Method. In *Proceedings of the 19th Annual Conference of the North American Chapter of the Association for Computational Linguistics (NAACL-HLT-23),* (pp. 789-796). AAAI.

Chen, Y., Smith, J., & Lee, H. (2023). A Conversational Chatbot with Prompt-based Instructions. (2023). In *Proceedings of the 35th AAAI Conference on Artificial Intelligence (AAAI-23),* (pp. 123-130). AAAI.

Chen, C., & Chen, F. (2021). Chatbots and customer experience: An empirical investigation. *Journal of Interactive Marketing*, *56*, 101–113. doi:10.1016/j.intmar.2021.01.005

Cheng, K., He, Y., Li, C., Xie, R., Lu, Y., Gu, S., & Wu, H. (2023). Talk with ChatGPT about the outbreak of Mpox in 2022: Reflections and suggestions from AI dimensions. *Annals of Biomedical Engineering*, *51*(5), 870–874. doi:10.100710439-023-03196-z PMID:37031289

Chen, H., Chiang, R. H. L., & Storey, V. C. (2012). Business intelligence and analytics: From big data to big impact. *Management Information Systems Quarterly*, *36*(4), 1165–1188. doi:10.2307/41703503

Chen, J., Liu, X., & Zhao, Y. (2020). Chatbot-based customer service in e-commerce: A literature review. *Journal of Electronic Commerce Research*, *21*(1), 1–22. doi:10.100710660-013-9104-5

Chen, X., Cheng, G., Zou, D., Zhong, B., & Xie, H. (2023). Artificial Intelligent Robots for Precision Education. *Journal of Educational Technology & Society*, *26*(1), 171–186.

Chen, Z. (2023). Collaboration amongrecruiters and artificialintelligence:removinghumanpre judices in employment. *Cognition Technology and Work*, *25*(1), 135–149. doi:10.100710111-022-00716-0

Chergui, M., Chakir, A., Medromi, H., & Radoui, M. (2017). A new approach for modeling strategic IT governance workflow. In Lecture Notes in Electrical Engineering (Vol. 397). doi:10.1007/978-981-10-1627-1_22

Chergui, M., Chakir, A., & Medromi, H. (2019). Smart IT governance, risk and compliance semantic model: Business Driven architecture. *Proceedings of the 3rd World Conference on Smart Trends in Systems, Security and Sustainability. WORLD (Oakland, Calif.)*, *S4*, 2019. doi:10.1109/WorldS4.2019.8903997

Chergui, M., Tahiri, A., Chakir, A., & Mansouri, H. (2020). Towards a New Educational Engineering Model for Moroccan University Based on ICT. [IJEP]. *International Journal of Engineering Pedagogy*, *10*(3), 49. doi:10.3991/ijep.v10i3.12421

Chiu, T. K. (2023). The impact of Generative AI (GenAI) on practices, policies and research direction in education: A case of ChatGPT and Midjourney. *Interactive Learning Environments*, ●●●, 1–17. doi:10.1080/10494820.2023.2253861

Chowdhary, K. (2020). Natural language processing. In *Fundamentals of artificial intelligence* (pp. 603–649). Springer. doi:10.1007/978-81-322-3972-7_19

Chowdhury, N. A. (2023). *Unlocking the Power of Chat GPT: An In-Depth Look at ChatAI's Business Model.*

Chowdhury, N. A., Awais, O. A., & Aktar, S. (2023). Improving customer care with ChatGPT: A case study. Retrieved from https://www.researchgate.net/publication/369014417_Improving_Customer_Care_with_ChatGPT_ACase_Study

Christopher, M., & Gaudenzi, B. (2009). Exploiting knowledge across networks through reputation management. *Industrial Marketing Management, 38*(2), 191–197. doi:10.1016/j.indmarman.2008.12.014

Chuma, E., Bang, M., & Alfredson, J. (2023). *Business AI decision-making tools: Case ChatGPT evaluation.*

Coates, H. (2007). A Model of Online and General Campus-Based Student Engagement. *Assessment & Evaluation in Higher Education, 32*(2), 121–141. doi:10.1080/02602930600801878

CoinMarketCap. (2023, June 1). *How to use CHATGPT for crypto research: CoinMarketCap.* CoinMarketCap Academy. https://coinmarketcap.com/alexandria/article/how-to-use-chatgpt-for-crypto-research

Content Marketing Institute. (2021). "What Is Content Marketing?" *Content Marketing Institute.* https://contentmarketinginstitute.com/what-is-content-marketing/

Cooper, G. (2023). Examining science education in chatgpt: An exploratory study of generative artificial intelligence. *Journal of Science Education and Technology, 32*(3), 444–452. doi:10.100710956-023-10039-y

Cortés-Cediel, M. E., Cantador, I., & Rodríguez Bolívar, M. P. (2020). Technological and Human Development of Smart Cities: An Empirical Characterization of EUROCITIES Case Studies. *Proceedings of the 53rd Hawaii International Conference on System Sciences.* IEEE. 10.24251/HICSS.2020.280

Cox, A. (2022). How artificial intelligence might change academic library work: Applying the competencies literature and the theory of the professions. *Journal of the Association for Information Science and Technology.* doi:10.1002/asi.24635

Creswell, J. W. (2013). *Research Design: Qualitative, Quantitative, and Mixed Methods Approaches.* Sage publications.

Cronemberger, F., & Gil-Garcia, J. R. (2019). Big Data and analytics as strategies to generate public value in smart cities: Proposing an integrative framework. In *Setting foundations for the creation of public value in Smart Cities* (pp. 247–267). Springer. doi:10.1007/978-3-319-98953-2_10

Cutler, K. (2023). ChatGPT and search engine optimization: The future is here. *Applied Marketing Analytics, 9*(1), 8–22.

Dale, R. (2017). NLP in a post-truth world. *Natural Language Engineering*, *23*(2), 319–324. doi:10.1017/S1351324917000018

Dale, R. (2021). GPT-3 What's it good for? *Natural Language Engineering*, *27*(1), 113–118. doi:10.1017/S1351324920000601

Darbinyan, R. (n.d.). Council Post: How To Leverage ChatGPT For Influencer Marketing. *Forbes*. https://www.forbes.com/sites/forbestechcouncil/2023/06/27/how-to-leverage-chatgpt-for-influencer-marketing/

Davis, P. R., & White, A. B. (2018). Enhancing Classroom Learning Through Technology. In *Proceedings of the International Conference on Education (ICE '18)* (pp. 123–135). ACM.

De Guimarães, J. C. F., Severo, E. A., Júnior, L. A. F., Da Costa, W. P. L. B., & Salmoria, F. T. (2020). Governance and quality of life in smart cities: Towards sustainable development goals. *Journal of Cleaner Production*, *253*, 119926. doi:10.1016/j.jclepro.2019.119926

De Pelsmacker, P., Van Tilburg, S., & Holthof, C. (2018). Digital marketing strategies, online reviews and hotel performance. *International Journal of Hospitality Management*, *72*, 47–55. doi:10.1016/j.ijhm.2018.01.003

De Veirman, M., Hudders, L., & Nelson, M. R. (2019). What is influencer marketing and how does it target children? A review and direction for future research. *Frontiers in Psychology*, *10*, 2685. doi:10.3389/fpsyg.2019.02685 PMID:31849783

Dehouche, N. (2021). Plagiarism in the age of massive Generative Pre-Trained Transformers (GPT-3). *Ethics in Science and Environmental Politics*, *21*, 17–23. doi:10.3354/esep00195

Demír, Ş. Ş., & Demír, M. (2023). Professionals' perspectives on ChatGPT in the tourism industry: Does it inspire awe or concern? *Journal of Tourism Theory and Research*, *9*(2), 61–76. doi:10.24288/jttr.1313481

Deng, J., & Lin, Y. (2023). The benefits and challenges of ChatGPT: An overview. *Front. Comput. Intell. Syst*, *2*(2), 4465. doi:10.54097/fcis.v2i2.4465

Derner, E., & Batistič, K. (2023). Beyond the Safeguards: Exploring the Security Risks of ChatGPT. *arXiv preprint arXiv:2305.08005*.

Desai, V., & Vidyapeeth, B. (2019). Digital marketing: A review. *International Journal of Trend in Scientific Research and Development*, *5*(5), 196–200. doi:10.31142/ijtsrd23100

DeshpandeA.MurahariV.RajpurohitT.KalyanA.NarasimhanK. (2023). Toxicity inchatgpt: Analyzing persona-assigned language models. https://arxiv.org/abs/2304.05335v1

DeshpandeS.SzeferJ. (2023). Analyzing ChatGPT's aptitude in an introductory computer engineering course. arXiv.2304.06122

Dharma, B. (2023). Analisis Dampak Search Engine Optimation (Seo) Pada. *E-Commerce Yang*, *3*(2).

Dhiraj, A., Kumar, S., Rani, D., Grima, S., & Sood, K. (2023). Blockchain Payment Services in the Hospitality Sector: The Mediating Role of Data Security on Utilisation Efficiency of the Customer. *Data*, *8*(8), 123. doi:10.3390/data8080123

Diez-Martin, F., Blanco-Gonzalez, A., & Prado-Roman, C. (2019). Research challenges in digital marketing: Sustainability. *Sustainability (Basel)*, *11*(10), 2839. doi:10.3390u11102839

Dilmegani, C. (2023a, August 21). *40 chatgpt use cases in 2023*. AIMultiple. https://research.aimultiple.com/chatgpt-use-cases

Dimiduk, D. M., Holm, E. A., & Niezgoda, S. R. (2018). Perspectives on the impact of machine learning, deep learning, and artificial intelligence on materials, processes, and structures engineering. integrating materials and manufacturing innovation. *Integrating Materials and Manufacturing Innovation*, *7*(3), 157–172. doi:10.100740192-018-0117-8

Dogra, J., & Kale, S. S. (2020). Network analysis of destination management organization smart tourism ecosystem (STE) for E-branding and Marketing of Tourism Destinations. In Handbook of Research on Social Media Applications for the Tourism and Hospitality Sector (pp. 1–16). IGI Global.

Doshi, R. H., Bajaj, S. S., & Krumholz, H. M. (2023). ChatGPT: Temptations of progress. *The American Journal of Bioethics*, *23*(4), 6–8. doi:10.1080/15265161.2023.2180110 PMID:36853242

Drexler, N., & Lapré, V. B. (2019). For better or for worse: Shaping the hospitality industry through robotics and artificial intelligence. *Research in Hospitality Management*, *9*(2), 117–120. doi:10.1080/22243534.2019.1689701

Dwivedi, A. (2015). Consumer brand engagement: A framework for assessment and proposition of antecedents. *Journal of Marketing Management*, *31*(9-10), 1053–1079.

Dwivedi, Y. K., Kshetri, N., Hughes, L., Slade, E. L., Jeyaraj, A., Kar, A. K., Baabdullah, A. M., Koohang, A., Raghavan, V., Ahuja, M., Albanna, H., Albashrawi, M. A., Al-Busaidi, A. S., Balakrishnan, J., Barlette, Y., Basu, S., Bose, I., Brooks, L., Buhalis, D., & Wright, R. (2023). "So what if ChatGPT wrote it?" Multidisciplinary perspectives on opportunities, challenges and implications of generative conversational AI for research, practice and policy. *International Journal of Information Management*, *71*, 102642. doi:10.1016/j.ijinfomgt.2023.102642

EASA. (2018). *EASA best practice recommendation on influencer marketing*. EASA. https://www.easa-alliance.org/sites/default/files/EASA_BEST%20PRACTICE%20RECOMMENDATION%20ON%20INFLUENCER%20MARKETING_2.pdf

Elkins, K., & Chun, J. (2020). Can GPT-3 pass a Writer's turing test? *Journal of Cultural Analytics*, *5*(2), 17212. doi:10.22148/001c.17212

Else, H. (2023). Abstracts written by ChatGPT fool scientists. *Nature, 613*(7944). . doi:10.1038/d41586-023-00056-7

Engati Team. (2023). *What are Chatbots? Is ChatGPT a Chatbot?* Engati. https://www.engati.com/blog/what-are-chatbots

Erhan, D., Bengio, Y., Courville, A., Manzagol, P., & Vincent, P. (2010) Why does unsupervised pre-training help deep learning. *Journal of Machine Learning Research*, *11*, 625–660.

Erisher, W., Obert, H. H., & Frank, G. (2014). Brand reputation management within the higher education sector: A literature review on higher education brand reputation management. *International Research Journal of Marketing*, *2*(1), 1–27. doi:10.12966/irjm.02.01.2014

Esmailzadeh, Y. (2023). Potential Risks of ChatGPT: Implications for Counterterrorism and International Security. *International Journal of Multicultural and Multireligious Understanding*, *10*(4), 535–543. doi.org/10.18415/ijmmu.v10i4.4590

Estrada-TorresB.del R'ıo-OrtegaA.ResinasM. (2021). Dialog-based automation of decision making in processes. arXiv:2109.00822v1. http:// arxiv.org/abs/2109.00822v1

Etzioni, A., & Etzioni, O. (2017). Incorporating ethics into artificial intelligence. *The Journal of Ethics*, *21*(4), 403–418. doi:10.100710892-017-9252-2

Etzioni, O. (2017). AI zooms in on highly influential citations. *Nature*, *547*(7661), 32. doi:10.1038/547032a PMID:28682336

Ezenkwu, C. P. (2023, May). Towards expert systems for improved customer services using ChatGPT as an inference engine. *Institute of Electrical and Electronics Engineers*.

Fariborzi, E., & Zahedifard, M. (2012). E-mail marketing: Advantages, disadvantages, and improving techniques. *International Journal of e-Education, e-Business, e-. Management Learning*, *2*(3), 232.

Farook, F. S., & Abeysekara, N. (2016). Influence of social media marketing on customer engagement. *International Journal of Business and Management Invention*, *5*(12), 115–125.

Fernandes, A. J., Hartono, H., & Aziza, C. (2020). Assessment IT governance of humanresources information system using COBIT 5. *International Journal of Open Information Technologies*, *8*(4), 59–63.

Finnie-Ansley, J., Denny, P., Becker, B. A., Luxton-Reilly, A., & Prather, J. (2022). The robots are coming: exploring the implications of OpenAI codex on introductory programming. *Proceedings of the 24th Australasian Computing Education Conference* (New York, NY: ACM). 10.1145/3511861.3511863

Fjell, K. (2009). Online advertising: Pay-per-view versus pay-per-click — A comment. *Journal of Revenue and Pricing Management*, *8*(2–3), 200–206. doi:10.1057/rpm.2008.39

Floridi, L., & Chiriatti, M. (2020). GPT-3: Its nature, scope, limits, and consequences. *Minds and Machines*, *30*(4), 681–694. doi:10.100711023-020-09548-1

FountaA.-M.DjouvasC.ChatzakouD.LeontiadisI.BlackburnJ.StringhiniG.VakaliA.SirivianosM. KourtellisN. (2018). Large Scale Crowdsourcing and Characterization of Twitter Abusive Behavior (arXiv:1802.00393). https://arxiv.org/abs/1802.00393

Fu, H., Manogaran, G., Wu, K., Cao, M., Jiang, S., & Yang, A. (2020). Intelligent decision-making of online shopping behavior based on internet of things. *International Journal of Information Management*, *50*, 515–525. doi:10.1016/j.ijinfomgt.2019.03.010

Fullan, M., Azorin, C., Harris, A., & Jones, M. (2023). Artificial intelligence and school leadership: Challenges, opportunities and implications. *School Leadership & Management*, 1–8. doi:10.1080/13632434.2023.2246856

Fusté-Forné, F., & Orea-Giner, A. (2023). Gastronomy in tourism management and marketing: An interview with ChatGPT. *ROBONOMICS: The Journal of the Automated Economy*, *4*, 42–42.

Fusté-Forné, F., & Orea-Giner, A. (2023). Gastronomy in Tourism Management and Marketing: An Interview with ChatGPT. *ROBONOMICS: The Journal of the Automated Economy*, *4*, 42–42.

Gabrielson, A. T., Odisho, A. Y., & Canes, D. (2023). Harnessing generative artificial intelligence to improve efficiency among urologists: Welcome ChatGPT. *The Journal of Urology*, *209*(5), 827–829. doi:10.1097/JU.0000000000003383 PMID:36795957

Gandhe, A., & Karmore, S. (2020). Artificial Intelligence in Customer Engagement: Opportunities and Challenges. In *Proceedings of the International Conference on Computational Intelligence and Data Science (ICCIDS)* (pp. 1-6). IEEE.

GaoC. A.HowardF. M.MarkovN. S.DyerE. C.RameshS.LuoY. (2022). Comparing scientific abstracts generated by ChatGPT to original abstracts using an artificial intelligence output detector, plagiarism detector, and blinded human reviewers. bioRxiv. doi:10.1101/2022.12.23.521610

Garcia, M. A., & Lee, S. J. (2019). The Impact of Gamification on Student Motivation in Online Learning Environments. Paper presented at the *Annual Conference on Educational Technology (ACET 2019),* New York, NY.

Garvey, C. S. (2019). Artificial intelligence and Japan's fifth generation. *Pacific Historical Review*, *88*(4), 619–658. doi:10.1525/phr.2019.88.4.619

Gasparyan, A. Y., Nurmashev, B., Seksenbayev, B., Trukhachev, V. I., Kostyukova, E. I., & Kitas, G. D. (2017). Plagiarism in the context of education and evolving detection strategies. *Journal of Korean Medical Science*, *32*(8), 1220–1227. doi:10.3346/jkms.2017.32.8.1220 PMID:28665055

Gautam, M., Vadera, M., & Bansal, R. (2019). *GST is a Booster or twister for IT Industry: An Impact Analysis*. 1512–1521.

GeerlingW.MateerG. D.WootenJ.DamodaranN. (2023). Is ChatGPT smarter than a student in principles of economics? Available At SSRN 4356034.

George, T. (2023). What Are the Limitations of ChatGPT? *Scribbr.* https://www.scribbr.com/ai-tools/chatgpt-limitations/

George, A. S., & George, A. H. (2023). A review of ChatGPT AI's impact on several business sectors. *Partners Universal International Innovation Journal*, *1*(1), 9–23.

George, A. S., George, A. H., & Martin, A. G. (2023). A Review of ChatGPT AI's Impact on Several Business Sectors. *Partners Univers. Int. Innov. J.*, *1*, 1.

Gibbs, C., Gretzel, U., & Saltzman, J. (2016). An experience-based taxonomy of branded hotel mobile application features. *Information Technology & Tourism*, *16*(2), 175–199. doi:10.100740558-016-0052-5

Gibson, K. (2023). Revolutionizing Social Content: How Chat GPT Transformed My Business's Marketing Strategy. [LinkedIn Article]. *LinkedIn*. https://shorturl.at/rA569

Gillotte, J. L. (2019). Copyright infringement in ai-generated artworks. *U.C. Davis Law Review*, *53*, 2655–2676.

Gilot, R., & Cole, B. J. (2023). How will artificial intelligence affect scientific writing, reviewing and editing? The future is here. *Arthroscopy*, *39*(5), 1119–1120. doi:10.1016/j.arthro.2023.01.014 PMID:36774329

Gilson, A., Safranek, C. W., Huang, T., Socrates, V., Chi, L., Taylor, R. A., & Chartash, D. (2023). How does chatgpt perform on the united states medical licensing examination? the implications of large language models for medical education and knowledge assessment. *JMIR Medical Education*, *9*, 9. doi:10.2196/45312 PMID:36753318

Goar, V., Yadav, N. S., & Yadav, P. S. (2023). Conversational ai for natural language processing: An review of chatgpt. *International Journal on Recent and Innovation Trends in Computing and Communication*, *11*(3s), 109–117. doi:10.17762/ijritcc.v11i3s.6161

Goh, G., Cammarata, N., Voss, C., Carter, S., Petrov, M., Schubert, L., Radford, A., & Olah, C. (2021). *Multimodal neurons in artificial neural networks*. doi:10.23915/distill.00030

GongT.LyuC.ZhangS.WangY.ZhengM.ZhaoQ. (2023). MultiModal-GPT: a vision and language model for dialogue with humans. arXiv.2305.04790

González-Padilla, D. A. (2022). Concerns About the Potential Risks of Artificial Intelligence in Manuscript Writing. *The Journal of Urology*, 10–1097. doi:10.1097/JU.0000000000003131 PMID:36563004

Gordijn, B., & Have, H. A. (2023). ChatGPT: Evolution or revolution? *Medicine, Health Care, and Philosophy*, *26*(1), 1–2. doi:10.100711019-023-10136-0 PMID:36656495

Gozalo-BrizuelaR.Garrido-MerchánE. (2023). *ChatGPT is not all you need. A state of the art review of large generative AI models*. arXiv.2301.04655

Graham, F. (2022). Daily briefing: Will ChatGPT kill the essay assignment? *Nature*. doi:10.1038/d41586-022-04437-2 PMID:36517680

Grassini, S. (2023). Shaping the future of education: Exploring the potential and consequences of AI and ChatGPT in educational settings. *Education Sciences*, *13*(7), 692. doi:10.3390/educsci13070692

Grbic, D. V., & Dujlovic, I. (2023). Social engineering with chatgpt. In *2023 22nd International Symposium INFOTEH-JAHORINA*. IEEE. 10.1109/INFOTEH57020.2023.10094141

Grewal, D., Hulland, J., Kopalle, P. K., & Karahanna, E. (2020). The future of technology and marketing: A multidisciplinary perspective. *Journal of the Academy of Marketing Science*, *48*(1), 1–8. doi:10.100711747-019-00711-4

Griffith, E. (2023). GPT-4 vs. ChatGPT-3.5: What's the Difference? *PCMag*. https://www.pcmag.com/news/the-new-chatgpt-what-you-get-with-gpt-4-vs-gpt-35

Gruner, K. E., & Homburg, C. (2000). Does customer interaction enhance new product success? *Journal of Business Research*, *49*(1), 1–14. doi:10.1016/S0148-2963(99)00013-2

Gupta, A., & Bansal, R. (2013). E-Governance: A Step Ahead. *2013 Third International Conference on Advanced Computing and Communication Technologies (ACCT)*, (pp. 359–362). IEEE. 10.1109/ACCT.2013.80

Gupta, A., Singh, R., Nassa, V. K., Bansal, R., Sharma, P., & Koti, K. (2021). Investigating Application and Challenges of Big Data Analytics with Clustering. *2021 International Conference on Advancements in Electrical, Electronics, Communication, Computing and Automation (ICAECA)*, (pp. 1–6). IEEE. 10.1109/ICAECA52838.2021.9675483

Gursoy, D., Li, Y., & Song, H. (2023). ChatGPT and the hospitality and tourism industry: An overview of current trends and future research directions. *Journal of Hospitality Marketing & Management*, *32*(5), 579–592. doi:10.1080/19368623.2023.2211993

Haenlein, M., & Kaplan, A. (2019). A brief history of artificial intelligence: On the past, present, and future of artificial intelligence. *California Management Review*, *61*(4), 5–14. doi:10.1177/0008125619864925

Haleem, A., Javaid, M., & Singh, R. P. (2022). An era of ChatGPT as a significant futuristic support tool: A study on features, abilities, and challenges. *BenchCouncil transactions on benchmarks, standards and evaluations,* *2*(4), 100089.

Haleem, A., Javaid, M., & Singh, R. P. (2022). An Era of ChatGPT as a Significant Futuristic Support Tool: A Study on Features, Abilities, and Challenges. *BenchCouncil Transactions on Benchmarks*. *Standards and Evaluations*, *2*(4), 100089.

Hancock, J. T., Naaman, M., & Levy, K. (2020). AI-mediated communication: Definition, research agenda, and ethical considerations. *Journal of Computer-Mediated Communication*, *25*(1), 89–100. doi:10.1093/jcmc/zmz022

Han, H., Shiwakoti, R. K., Jarvis, R., Mordi, C., & Botchie, D. (2023). Accounting and auditingwith blockchain technology and artificialIntelligence: A literaturereview. *International Journal of Accounting Information Systems*, *48*, 100598. doi:10.1016/j.accinf.2022.100598

Harmeling, C. M., Moffett, J. W., Arnold, M. J., & Carlson, B. D. (2016). Toward a theory of customer engagement marketing. *Journal of the Academy of Marketing Science*, *45*(3), 312–335. doi:10.100711747-016-0509-2

Harrigan, P., Evers, U., Miles, M., & Daly, T. (2017). Customer engagement with tourism social media brands. *Tourism Management*, *59*, 597–609. doi:10.1016/j.tourman.2016.09.015

Ha, T. (2022). An explainable artificial-intelligence-based approach to investigating factors that influence the citation of papers. *Technological Forecasting and Social Change*, *184*, 121974. doi:10.1016/j.techfore.2022.121974

Hays, S., Page, S. J., & Buhalis, D. (2013). Social media as a destination marketing tool: Its use by national tourism organizations. *Current Issues in Tourism*, *16*(3), 211–239. doi:10.1080/13683500.2012.662215

Henrickson, L., & Meroño-Peñuela, A. (2022). The hermeneutics of computer-generated texts. *Configurations*, *30*(2), 115–139. doi:10.1353/con.2022.0008

Hermann, I. (2023). Artificial intelligence in fiction:between narratives and metaphors. *AI & Society*, *38*(1), 319–329. doi:10.100700146-021-01299-6

Hess, J., & Kumar, V. (2019). AI in Marketing: A Review and Research Agenda. *Journal of the Academy of Marketing Science*, *48*(1), 4–31.

Hetler, A. (n.d.). *What is ChatGPT? Everything You Need to Know*. WhatIs.Com. https://www.techtarget.com/whatis/definition/ChatGPT

HeumannM.KraschewskiT.BreitnerM. H. (2023). ChatGPT and GPTZero in Research and Social Media: A Sentiment-and Topic-based Analysis. SSRN 4467646. doi:10.2139/ssrn.4467646

Hidayat, A., Nugroho, A., & Nurfaizin, S. (2022). Usability evaluation on educational chatbot using the system usability scale (sus). In *2022 7th Inter-national Conference on Informatics and Computing*. ICIC.

HildebrandC.HoffmanD.NovakT. (2021). Dehumanizing voice tech-nology: Phonetic & experiential consequences of restricted human-machine interaction. arXiv:2111.01934v1, https://arxiv.org/abs/2111.01934v1

Hill-Yardin, E. L., Hutchinson, M. R., Laycock, R., & Spencer, S. (2023). A Chat(GPT) about the future of scientific publishing. *Brain, Behavior, and Immunity*, *110*, 152–154. doi:10.1016/j.bbi.2023.02.022 PMID:36868432

Hoffman, M. (2021). AI and Customer Engagement: A Comprehensive Guide to the Future. *Harvard Business Review*.

Hoge, S., & Cecil, C. (1993). The Electronic Marketing Manual. *ABA Journal*, *22*, 175–185.

Hollebeek, L. D., Srivastava, R. K., & Chen, T. (2019). *S-D logic–informed customer engagement*.

Hollebeek, L. D. (2011). Demystifying customer brand engagement: Exploring the loyalty nexus. *Journal of Marketing Management*, *27*(7-8), 785–807. doi:10.1080/0267257X.2010.500132

Hollebeek, L. D., & Chen, T. (2014). Exploring positively-valenced brand engagement: A model development approach. *Journal of Product and Brand Management*, *23*(1), 62–74. doi:10.1108/JPBM-06-2013-0332

Hollebeek, L. D., Srivastava, R. K., & Chen, T. (2019). S-D logic–informed customer engagement: Integrative framework, revised fundamental propositions, and application to CRM. *Journal of the Academy of Marketing Science*, *47*(1), 161–185. doi:10.100711747-016-0494-5

Holmqvist, M. (2019). Lack of qualified teachers: a global challenge for future knowledge development. In R. B. Monyai (Ed.), *Teacher Education in the 21st Century*., doi:10.5772/intechopen.83417

Horner, R. D., & Lines, L. M. (2019). Anatomy of Constructive Peer Review. *Medical Care*, *57*(6), 399–400. doi:10.1097/MLR.0000000000001116 PMID:31095526

Howell, J. (2023, September 15). *5 ways CHATGPT can help with crypto trading*. 101 Blockchains. https://101blockchains.com/chatgpt-in-crypto-trading/

Hristov, K. (2016). Artificial intelligence and the copyright dilemma. *IDEA: The Intellectual Property Law Review*, *57*(3), 431–454.

Huang, L., & Peissl, W. (2023). Artificial Intelligence—A New Knowledge and Decision-MakingParadigm? In TechnologyAssessment in a GlobalizedWorld:Facing the Challenges of Transnational TechnologyGovernance (pp. 175–201). Springer International Publishing Cham.

Huang, M.-H., & Rust, R. T. (2018). Artificial intelligence in service. *Journal of Service Research*, *21*(2), 155–172. doi:10.1177/1094670517752459

Hugenholtz, P. B., & Quintais, J. P. (2021). Copyright and artificial creation: Does EU copyright law protect AI-assisted output? *IIC; International Review of Industrial Property and Copyright Law*, *52*(9), 1190–1216. doi:10.100740319-021-01115-0

Hussain, I., Mu, S., Mohiuddin, M., Danish, R. Q., & Sair, S. A. (2020). Effects of sustainable brand equity and marketing innovation on market performance in hospitality industry: Mediating effects of sustainable competitive advantage. *Sustainability (Basel)*, *12*(7), 2939. doi:10.3390u12072939

Hutchinson, B., Prabhakaran, V., Denton, E., Webster, K., Zhong, Y., & Denuyl, S. (2020). Social Biases in NLP Models as Barriers for Persons with Disabilities. *Proceedings of the Annual Meeting of the Association for Computational Linguistics,* (*vol. 58*, pp. 5491–5501). IEEE. 10.18653/v1/2020.acl-main.487

Hutson, M. (2021). Robo-writers: The rise and risks of language-generating AI. *Nature*, *591*(7848), 22–25. doi:10.1038/d41586-021-00530-0 PMID:33658699

Hyland, K. (1999). Academic attribution: Citation and the construction of disciplinary knowledge. *Applied Linguistics*, *20*(3), 341–367. doi:10.1093/applin/20.3.341

Ibrahim, B., & Aljarah, A. (2023). The role of social media marketing activities in driving self–brand connection and user engagement behaviour on Instagram: A moderation–mediation approach. *European Journal of Innovation Management*. doi:10.1108/EJIM-08-2022-0452

Ienca, M. (2023). Don't pause giant AI for the wrong reasons. *Nature Machine Intelligence*, *5*(5), 470–471. doi:10.103842256-023-00649-x

Ilieva, G., Yankova, T., Klisarova-Belcheva, S., Dimitrov, A., Bratkov, M., & Angelov, D. (2023). Effects of Generative Chatbots in Higher Education. *Information (Basel)*, *14*(9), 492. doi:10.3390/info14090492

Iqbal, N., Ahmed, H., & Azhar, K. A. (2022). Exploring teachers' attitudes towards using chatgpt. *Glob. J. Manag. Adm. Sci*, *3*(4), 97–111. doi:10.46568/gjmas.v3i4.163

Iskender, A. (2023). Holy or unholy? Interview with open AI's ChatGPT. *European Journal of Tourism Research*, *34*, 3414–3414. doi:10.54055/ejtr.v34i.3169

Ismunandar, I., Andriani, N. Y., Hanis, R., Hamzah, R., & Yusuf, M. (2023). Grand Prand Preanger Bandung Effective Marketing Communication Strategy in the Staycation Program. *Jurnal Ekonomi*, *12*(01), 48–53.

Jabeen, F., Al Zaidi, S., & Al Dhaheri, M. H. (2022). Automation and artificial intelligence in hospitality and tourism. *Tourism Review*, *77*(4), 1043–1061. doi:10.1108/TR-09-2019-0360

Jain, V., Rai, H., Subash, P., & Mogaji, E. (2023). The Prospects and Challenges of ChatGPT on Marketing Research and Practices. *Emmanuel, The Prospects and Challenges of ChatGPT on Marketing Research and Practices*.

Jaiswar, P. S. (2023, April 29). *How CHATGPT benefit crypto investors? experts say "can maximize profits."* Mint. https://www.livemint.com/market/cryptocurrency/how-chatgpt-benefit-crypto-investors-experts-say-can-maximize-profits-11682753323003.html

Jarrahi, M. H., Lutz, C., Boyd, K., Oesterlund, C., & Willis, M. (2022). Artificial intelligence in the work context. *Journal of the Association for Information Science and Technology*. Advance online publication. doi:10.1002/asi.24730

Javaid, M., Haleem, A., & Singh, R. P. (2023). ChatGPT for healthcare services: An emerging stage for an innovative perspective. *Bench Council Transactions on Benchmarks. Standards and Evaluations*, *3*(1), 100105.

Jayaraman, S. (2022). *How AI Tools Make Lead Generation Better and Faster*. CIENCE. https://www.cience.com/blog/ai-for-lead-generation

Jian, M.-S., Hong, W.-C., Tsai, S.-C., Chen, Y.-W., & Fan, C.-L. (2020). Based on Automatic Correlation Keyword Grouping and Combination Based Deep Information Search Corresponding to Specific Language Big Data—Case of Leisure Recreation. *2020 22nd International Conference on Advanced Communication Technology (ICACT)*, 372–377.

Jin, S. V., Muqaddam, A., & Ryu, E. (2019). Instafamous and social media influencer marketing. *Marketing Intelligence & Planning*, *37*(5), 567–579. doi:10.1108/MIP-09-2018-0375

Jobin, A., Ienca, M., & Vayena, E. (2019). The global landscape of AI ethics guidelines. *Nature Machine Intelligence*, *1*(9), 389–399. doi:10.103842256-019-0088-2

Johnson, P. R. (2020). *Exploring the Relationship Between Intrinsic Motivation and Academic Achievement in High School Students* [Doctoral dissertation, University of California, Los Angeles].

Johnson, M. R., & Williams, L. S. (2020). The Impact of Online Learning on Student Engagement. *Journal of Online Education*, *15*(3), 45–58.

Jordan, M. I., & Mitchell, T. M. (2015). Machine learning: Trends, perspectives, and prospects. *Science*, *349*(6245), 255–260. doi:10.1126cience.aaa8415 PMID:26185243

Jungwirth, M. (2023). *Improving customer care with ChatGPT: A case study*. [PDF]

Kaltenbrunner, W., Pinfield, S., Waltman, L., Woods, H. B., & Brumberg, J. (2022). Innovating peer review, reconfiguring scholarly communication: An analytical overview of ongoing peer review innovation activities. *The Journal of Documentation*, *78*(7), 429–449. doi:10.1108/JD-01-2022-0022

Kandampully, J., Zhang, T. C., & Jaakkola, E. (2018). Customer experience management in Hospitality: A literature synthesis, new understanding and research agenda. *International Journal of Contemporary Hospitality Management*, *30*(1), 21–56. doi:10.1108/IJCHM-10-2015-0549

Kapočiute-Dzikiene, J. (2020). A domain-specific generative chatbot trained from little data. *Applied Sciences (Basel, Switzerland)*, *10*(7), 2221. doi:10.3390/app10072221

Kapoor, V., Shah, S. P., Beckman, T., & Gole, G. (2022). Community-based vision screening in preschool children; performance of the Spot Vision Screener and optotype testing. *Ophthalmic Epidemiology*, *29*(4), 417–425. doi:10.1080/09286586.2021.1962918 PMID:34423736

Kasneci, E., Sessler, K., Küchemann, S., Bannert, M., Dementieva, D., Fischer, F., Gasser, U., Groh, G., Günnemann, S., Hüllermeier, E., Krusche, S., Kutyniok, G., Michaeli, T., Nerdel, C., Pfeffer, J., Poquet, O., Sailer, M., Schmidt, A., Seidel, T., & Kasneci, G. (2023). ChatGPT for good? On opportunities and challenges of large language models for education. *Learning and Individual Differences*, *103*, 102274. doi:10.1016/j.lindif.2023.102274

Kaur, U., & Dangwal, A. (2023). A Typology of Digital Marketing Channels with a Special Reference to India. In INDIA'S TECHNOLOGY-LED DEVELOPMENT: Managing Transitions to a Digital Future (pp. 259-268). doi:10.1142/9789811271786_0014

Kaushal, N., Kaurav, R. P. S., Sivathanu, B., & Kaushik, N. (2023). Artificial intelligence and HRM:identifying future research Agenda usingsystematicliteraturereview and bibliometricanalysis. *Management ReviewQuarterly*, *73*(2), 455–493.

Keiper, M. C. (2023). ChatGPT in practice: Increasing event planning efficiency through artificial intelligence. *Journal of Hospitality, Leisure, Sport and Tourism Education*, *33*, 100454. doi:10.1016/j.jhlste.2023.100454

Kersting, K. (2020). Rethinking computer science through AI. *KI - Künstliche Intelligenz*, *34*, 435–437. doi:10.1007/s13218-020-00692-5

Keshvadi, S., Karamollahi, M., & Williamson, C. (2020). *Traffic characterization of instant messaging apps: A campus-level view*. 225–232.

Ke, Z., Sheng, J., Li, Z., Silamu, W., & Guo, Q. (2021). Knowledge-guided sentiment analysis via learning from natural language explanations. *IEEE Access : Practical Innovations, Open Solutions*, *9*, 3570–3578. doi:10.1109/ACCESS.2020.3048088

Khamoshifar, M., Abbasimehr, H., Bahrini, A., & Pasehvar, M. (2022). A Chatbot-Based Customer Support System Using ChatGPT. [IJISSS]. *International Journal of Information Systems in the Service Sector*, *14*(1), 1–16.

Khan, M. S., Mahapatra, S. S., & Sreekumar, N. A. (2009). Service quality evaluation in internet banking: An empirical study in India. *Int. J. Indian Culture and Business Management*, *2*(1), 30–46. doi:10.1504/IJICBM.2009.021596

Khan, M. Y. H., & Abir, T. (2022). The role of social media marketing in the tourism and hospitality industry: A conceptual study on Bangladesh. In *ICT as Innovator between Tourism and Culture* (pp. 213–229). IGI Global. doi:10.4018/978-1-7998-8165-0.ch013

Khanna, A., Pandey, B., Vashishta, K., Kalia, K., Pradeepkumar, B., & Das, T. (2015). A Study of Today's A.I. through Chatbots and Rediscovery of Machine Intelligence. International Journal of U- and e-Service. *Science and Technology*, *8*(7), 277–284. doi:10.14257/ijunesst.2015.8.7.28

Khan, R. A., Jawaid, M., Khan, A. R., & Sajjad, M. (2023). ChatGPT-Reshaping medical education and clinical management. *Pakistan Journal of Medical Sciences*, *39*(2), 605–607. doi:10.12669/pjms.39.2.7653 PMID:36950398

Kim, C., Yang, Z., Park, S. H., Hwang, S. H., Oh, Y.-W., Kang, E.-Y., & Yong, H. S. (2023). Multicentre external validation of a commercial artificial intelligence software to analyse chest radiographs in health screening environments with low disease prevalence. *European Radiology*, 1–9.

Kim, J. J., Lee, M. J., & Han, H. (2020). Smart hotels and sustainable consumer behavior: Testing the effect of perceived performance, attitude, and technology readiness on word-of-mouth. *International Journal of Environmental Research and Public Health*, *17*(20), 7455. doi:10.3390/ijerph17207455 PMID:33066245

Kim, W. G., & Kim, D. J. (2004). Factors affecting online hotel reservation intention between online and non-online customers. *International Journal of Hospitality Management*, *23*(4), 381–395. doi:10.1016/j.ijhm.2004.02.001

Kim, W. H., Lee, S. H., & Kim, K. S. (2020). Effects of sensory marketing on customer satisfaction and revisit intention in the hotel industry: The moderating roles of customers' prior experience and gender. *Anatolia*, *31*(4), 523–535. doi:10.1080/13032917.2020.1783692

King, M. R. (2022). The future of AI in medicine: A perspective from a chatbot. *Annals of Biomedical Engineering*. doi:10.100710439-022-03121-w PMID:36572824

King, M. R. (2023). A conversation on artificial intelligence, chatbots, and plagiarism in higher education. *Cellular and Molecular Bioengineering*, *16*(1), 1–2. doi:10.100712195-022-00754-8 PMID:36660590

Kirmani, A. R. (2022). Artificial intelligence-enabled science poetry. *ACS Energy Letters*, *8*(1), 574–576. doi:10.1021/acsenergylett.2c02758

Kitamura, F. C. (2023). ChatGPT Is Shaping the future of medical writing but still requires human judgment. *Radiology*, *230171*(2), e230171. doi:10.1148/radiol.230171 PMID:36728749

KocońJ.CicheckiI.KaszycaO.KochanekM.SzydloD.BaranJ. (2023). *ChatGPT: Jack of all trades, master of none*. arXiv.2302.10724

KosinskiM. (2023). *Theory of mind may have spontaneously emerged in large language models*. arXiv.2302.02083

Kremer, M. (2022). How to Use ChatGPT in Your Marketing Strategy. *Customer Engagement Blog*. https://onesignal.com/blog/4-ways-to-use-generative-ai-in-your-customer-engagement-strategy/

Krishnamurthy, S. (2006). Introducing E-MARKPLAN: A practical methodology to plan e-marketing activities. *Business Horizons*, *49*(1), 49, 51, 60. doi:10.1016/j.bushor.2005.05.008

Kuhail, M. A., Farooq, S., & Almutairi, S. (2023). *Recent developments in chatbot usability and design methodologies*. Trends, Applications, and Challenges of Chatbot Technology. doi:10.4018/978-1-6684-6234-8.ch001

Kuh, G. D. (2009). *"The National Survey of Student Engagement: Conceptual and Empirical Foundations." New Directions for Institutional Research, No. 141*. Wiley Periodicals. doi:10.1002/ir.283

Kumar, A., Nagarajan, G., Surekha, M., Vijai, C., Mohideen, A. S., Dhinakaran, D. P., & Lakshmi, M. R. (2023). The Impact of chatGPT on E-commerce. *Harbin Gongcheng Daxue Xuebao/ Journal of Harbin Engineering University, 44*(7), 1016-1023.

Kumar, A. S., Sharma, P., Kaur, S., Saleh, O. S., Chennamma, H. R., & Chaturvedi, A. (2023). AI-Equipped IoT Applications in High-Tech Agriculture Using Machine Learning. In *Handbook of Research on AI-Equipped IoT Applications in High-Tech Agriculture* (pp. 38–64). IGI Global.

Kumar, S., Dhiraj, A., Shah, M. A., & Rani, D. (2023). Application of Metaverse in the Hospitality Industry. In R. Bansal, S. A. Qalati, & A. Chakir (Eds.), (pp. 178–194). Advances in Marketing, Customer Relationship Management, and E-Services. IGI Global. doi:10.4018/978-1-6684-8898-0.ch011

Kushcheva, N. (2022). *Monitoring online reputation of tourist destinations in Finland*. 9442–9447.

Kushwaha, A. (2022). *ChatGPT: The Ultimate Tool for Natural Language Processing and Text Generation*. DEV Community.

Kusumawati, N. F., Kusumasari, T. F., & Lubis, M. (2019). *The Effectiveness of Digital Marketing for Show Up Company: Issues and Challenges*. 27–31.

Kuvykaitė, R. and Zailskaite-Jakste, L. (2013). Communication in social media for brand equity building. *Ekonomika ir vadyba, 18*(142-153).

LeadSync. (2023). *7 Ways ChatGPT Can Help with Lead Generation*. LeadSynch. https://leadsync.me/blog/chatgpt-lead-generation/

Lee, F. S., Chakir, A., Nathanael, R., & Andry, J. F. (2020). Architecture information system in electrical distribution company using TOGAF. *International Journal of Advanced Trends in Computer Science and Engineering, 9*(5), 7149–7156. Advance online publication. doi:10.30534/ijatcse/2020/38952020

Leichtmann, B., Humer, C., Hinterreiter, A., Streit, M., & Mara, M. (2023). Effects of ExplainableArtificial Intelligence on trust and humanbehavior in a high-riskdecisiontask. *Computers in Human Behavior, 139*, 107539. doi:10.1016/j.chb.2022.107539

Leite, R. A., & Azevedo, A. (2017). The Role of Digital Marketing: A Perspective from Porto Hotels' Managers. *International Journal of Marketing, Communication and New Media, 2*.

Leung, X. Y., Xue, L., & Bai, B. (2015). Internet marketing research in hospitality and tourism: A review and journal preferences. *International Journal of Contemporary Hospitality Management, 27*(7), 1556–1572. doi:10.1108/IJCHM-05-2014-0268

Li, L. (2017). *Deep Reinforcement Learning for Dialogue Generation*. arXiv preprint arXiv:1606.01541.

Liang, P. P., Roller, S., Stacey, K., Ritter, A., & Smith, N. A. (2021). *Learning from human feedback: Challenges for real-world natural language processing applications*. arXiv preprint arXiv:2106.01269.

Li, J., Monroe, W., Ritter, A., Galley, M., Gao, J., & Jurafsky, D. (2016). Deep reinforcement learning for dialogue generation. In *2016 Conference on Empirical Methods in Natural Language Processing,* pages 1192–1202. 10.18653/v1/D16-1127

Li, J., Monroe, W., Shi, T., Jean, S., Ritter, A., & Jurafsky, D. (2017). Adver-sarial learning for neural dialogue generation. In *2017 Conference on Empirical Methods in Natural Language Processing,* (pp. 2157–2169). ACL. 10.18653/v1/D17-1230

Limna, P. (2022). Artificial Intelligence (AI) in the hospitality industry: A review article. *Int. J. Comput. Sci. Res, 6*, 1–12.

Lim, W. M., Rasul, T., Kumar, S., & Ala, M. (2022). Past, present, and future of customer engagement. *Journal of Business Research*, *140*, 439–458. doi:10.1016/j.jbusres.2021.11.014

Li, S., Da Xu, L. T., & Zhao, S. (2018). The internet of things: A survey. *Information Systems Frontiers*, *17*(2), 243–259. doi:10.100710796-014-9492-7

Liu, B., & Lane, I. (2019). Towards better context-awareness in spoken dialogue systems: Distributional semantics for dialogue context representation. In *20th Annual SIGdial Meeting on Discourse and Dialogue,* 360–369.

Liu, J., Shen, D., Zhang, Y., Dolan, W. B., Carin, L., & Chen, W. (2022). What Makes Good In-Context Examples for GPT-3? *Proceedings of Deep Learning Inside Out (DeeLIO 2022): The 3rd Workshop on Knowledge Extraction and Integration for Deep Learning Architectures, 3*, 100-114.

Liu, Y., Mittal, A., Yang, D., & Bruckman, A. (2022). Will AI console me when I lose my pet? Understanding perceptions of AI-mediated email writing. *Proceedings of the CHI Conference on Human Factors in Computing Systems, 2022.* ACM. 10.1145/3491102.3517731

Li, W., Batty, M., & Goodchild, M. F. (2020). *Real-time GIS for smart cities.* Taylor & Francis. doi:10.1080/13658816.2019.1673397

Lokman, A. S., & Ameedeen, M. A. (2018, November). Modern chatbot systems: A technical review. In *Proceedings of the future technologies conference* (pp. 1012-1023). Springer, Cham.

Lopes, N. V. M., & Rodrigues, J. (2020). Smart Methodologies for Smart Cities: A Comparative Analysis. In Smart Governance for Cities: Perspectives and Experiences (pp. 3–15). Springer. doi:10.1007/978-3-030-22070-9_1

Lucy, L., & Bamman, D. (2021). Gender and representation bias in GPT-3 generated stories. *Proceedings of the Workshop on Narrative Understanding, (vol. 3*, pp. 48-55). IEEE. 10.18653/v1/2021.nuse-1.5

Lund, B. D., & Ting, W. (2023). Chatting about ChatGPT: how may AI and GPT impact academia and libraries? SSRN *Electron. J.* doi:10.2139/ssrn.4333415

Lund, B. D. (2022). Is academic research and publishing still leaving developing countries behind? *Accountability in Research*, *29*(4), 224–231. doi:10.1080/08989621.2021.1913124 PMID:33818223

Lund, B. D., & Wang, T. (2023). Chatting about ChatGPT: How may AI and GPT impact academia and libraries? *Library Hi Tech News*, *40*(3), 26–29. doi:10.1108/LHTN-01-2023-0009

Lu, Y. (2019). Artificial intelligence: A survey on evolution, models, applications and future trends. *Journal of Management Analytics*, *6*(1), 1–29. doi:10.1080/23270012.2019.1570365

Lu, Y., Chen, S., Xu, H., & Yang, J. (2020). Chatbots in customer service: A review and research agenda. *Journal of Service Management*, *31*(4), 642–668.

Lv, Z., Chen, J., Zheng, W., & Gong, Q. (2021, December). Research on Search Engine Optimization Method of Innovation and Entrepreneurship Platform. In *2021 International Conference on Networking, Communications and Information Technology (NetCIT)* (pp. 58-62). IEEE. 10.1109/NetCIT54147.2021.00019

Madakam, S. (2020). Would Be Smart Balinese Cities (Indonesia): An Exploratory Case Study. *Journal of Information Systems and Technology Management*, 17. doi:10.4301/S1807-1775202017005

Maharajan, K., Kumar, A. V., El Emary, I. M., Sharma, P., Latip, R., Mishra, N., Dutta, A., Manjunatha Rao, L., & Sharma, M. (2023). Blockchain Methods and Data-Driven Decision Making With Autonomous Transportation. In R. Kumar, A. Abdul Hamid, & N. Binti Ya'akub (Eds.), *Effective AI, Blockchain, and E-Governance Applications for Knowledge Discovery and Management* (pp. 176–194). IGI Global., doi:10.4018/978-1-6684-9151-5.ch012

Mahesh, B. (2020). Machine learning algorithms-a review. [IJSR]. *International Journal of Scientific Research*, *9*, 381–386.

Makridakis, S. (2017). The forthcoming artificial intelligence (AI) revolution: Its impact on society and firms. *Futures*, *90*, 46–60. doi:10.1016/j.futures.2017.03.006

Ma, L., & Sun, B. (2020). Machine learning and AI in marketing–Connecting computing power to human insights. [CrossRef]. *International Journal of Research in Marketing*, *37*(3), 481–504. doi:10.1016/j.ijresmar.2020.04.005

Manson, K. (2023). Viral ChatGPT Spurs Concerns About Propaganda and Hacking Risks. *Bloomberg*. https://www.bloomberg.com/news/articles/2023-01-11/chatgpt-poses-propaganda-and-hacking-risks-researchers-say?utm_source=website&utm_medium=share&utm_campaign=copy

Marr, B., & Retail, R. (2023). How ChatGPT Is Changing The Shopping Experience. *Forbes*.

McKinsey & Company. (2019). *AI in customer engagement: A primer*. McKinsey Digital.

McLean, G., Al-Nabhani, K., & Wilson, A. (2018). Developing a mobile applications customer experience model (MACE)-implications for retailers. *Journal of Business Research*, *85*, 325–336. doi:10.1016/j.jbusres.2018.01.018

MehrabiN.MorstatterF.SaxenaN.LermanK.GalstyanA. (2019). A survey on bias and fairness in machine learning. arXiv:1908.09635.

Mehralian, M. M., & Khazaee, P. (2022). Effect of digital marketing on the business performance of MSMEs during the Covid-19 pandemic: The mediating role of customer relationship management. *37th Digital Marketing and Customer Behavior Science Conference*. SSRN. 10.2139srn.4195985

Melović, B., Jocović, M., Dabić, M., Vulić, T. B., & Dudic, B. (2020). The impact of digital transformation and digital marketing on brand promotion, positioning and electronic business in Montenegro. *Technology in Society*, *63*, 101425. doi:10.1016/j.techsoc.2020.101425

Mercade Mele, P., Molina Gomez, J., & Garay, L. (2019). To green or not to green: The influence of green marketing on consumer behaviour in the hotel industry. *Sustainability (Basel)*, *11*(17), 4623. doi:10.3390u11174623

Merton, R. K. (1968). The Matthew Effect in Science: The reward and communication systems of science are considered. *Science*, *159*(3810), 56–63. doi:10.1126cience.159.3810.56 PMID:5634379

Michie, J., & Leese, M. (2022). Privacy and the pandemic: A social contract perspective. *Ethics and Information Technology*, 1–14.

Mich, L., & Garigliano, R. (2023). ChatGPT for e-Tourism: A Technological Perspective. *Information Technology & Tourism*, *25*(1), 1–12. doi:10.100740558-023-00248-x

Miller, A. N., Taylor, S. G., & Bedeian, A. G. (2011). Publish or perish: Academic life as management faculty live it. *Career Development International*, *16*(5), 422–445. doi:10.1108/13620431111167751

Minelgaite, I., & Zailskaite-Jakste, L. (2021). Consumer engagement behav-ior perspective in social media: Mediating role and impact on brand equity. [JEECAR]. *Journal of Eastern European and Central Asian Research*, *8*(2).

Mintz, Y., & Brodie, R. (2019). Introduction to artificial intelligence in medicine. *Minimally Invasive Therapy & Allied Technologies*, *28*(2), 73–81. doi:10.1080/13645706.2019.1575882 PMID:30810430

Mishra, A., & Awasthi, S. (2023). Chat GPT: Revolutionizing Communication or Threatening Authenticity? *Management Dynamics*, *23*(1), 8. doi:10.57198/2583-4932.1321

Mittal, G., & Bansal, R. (2023). Driving Force Behind Consumer Brand Engagement: The Metaverse. In Cultural Marketing and Metaverse for Consumer Engagement (pp. 164-181). IGI Global.

Moi, L., & Cabiddu, F. (2021). Leading digital transformation through an Agile Marketing Capability: The case of Spotahome. *The Journal of Management and Governance*, *25*(4), 1145–1177. doi:10.100710997-020-09534-w

Mollen, A., & Wilson, H. (2010). Engagement, telepresence, and interactivity in online consumer experience: Reconciling scholastic and managerial perspectives. *Journal of Business Research*, *63*(9-10), 919–925. doi:10.1016/j.jbusres.2009.05.014

Mollman, S. (2022). *ChatGPT gained 1 million users in under a week.* Yahoo. https://www.yahoo.com/lifestyle/chatgpt-gained-1-million-followers

Mondal, S., Das, S., & Vrana, V. G. (2023). How to bell the cat? A theoretical review of generative artificial intelligence towards digital disruption in all walks of life. *Technologies*, *11*(2), 44. doi:10.3390/technologies11020044

Morgane BINNERT. (2021, September 24). L'intelligence artificielle au service du recrutement : quelles conséquences ? *IP/IT, Propriété Intellectuelle.*

Moro, S., Cortez, P., & Rita, P. (2017). Business intelligence in banking: A literature analysis from 2002 to 2013 using text mining and latent dirichlet allocation. *Expert Systems with Applications*, *42*(3), 1314–1324. doi:10.1016/j.eswa.2014.09.024

Müller, V. C. (2021). *Ethics of Artificial Intelligence and Robotics. E. N. Zalta, The Stanford Encyclopedia of Philosophy (Summer 2021). Metaphysics Research Lab.* Stanford University., https://plato.stanford.edu/archives/sum2021/entries/ethics-ai/

Mustak, M., Salminen, J., Plé, L., & Wirtz, J. (2021). Artificial intelligence in marketing: Topic modeling, scientometric analysis, and research agenda. *Journal of Business Research*, *124*, 389–404. doi:10.1016/j.jbusres.2020.10.044

Mutoffar, M. M., Kuswayati, S., Anggraeny, F. T., & Sumarni, T. (2023). Exploring the Potential of ChatGPT in Improving Online Marketing and Promotion of MSMEs. *Jurnal Minfo Polgan*, *12*(2), 480–489. doi:10.33395/jmp.v12i1.12440

Nagarhalli, T. P., Vaze, V., & Rana, N. K. (2020). A Review of Current Trends in the Development of Chatbot Systems. *In 2020 International Conference on Advanced Computing and Communication Systems (ICACCS)*, (*vol. 6*, pp. 706–710). IEEE. https://doi.org/10.1109/ICACCS48705.2020.9074420

Naim, A. (2022). Mapping Of Social Customer Relationship Management With Electronic Customer Relationship Management. *European Journal of Interdisciplinary Research and Development*, *2*, 14–25.

NaserM. Z.RossB.OgleJ.KodurV.HawilehR.AbdallaJ.ThaiH. T. (2023). Can ai chatbots pass the fundamentals of engineer-ing (fe) and principles and practice of engineering (pe) structural exams? arXiv:2303.18149v2, https://arxiv.org/abs/2303.18149v2

National Institute of Education Sciences. (2020). *Strategies for Enhancing Student Motivation.* NIES. https://ies.ed.gov/ncee/wwc/Docs/PracticeGuide/wwc_motivation_pg_092717.pdf

Nature Machine Intelligence Editorial Board. (2020). Next chapter in artificial writing. *Nature Machine Intelligence*, *2*(8), 419. doi:10.103842256-020-0223-0

Nayyar, A., Mahapatra, B., Le, D., & Suseendran, G. (2018). Virtual Reality (VR) and augmented Reality (AR) technologies for the tourism and hospitality industry. *International Journal of Engineering & Technology*, *7*(2.21), 156–160.

Ngai, E. W., Xiu, L., & Chau, D. C. (2009). Application of data mining tech-niques in customer relationship management: A literature review and classifi-cation. *Expert Systems with Applications*, *36*(2), 2592–2602. doi:10.1016/j.eswa.2008.02.021

Ngo, J., Hwang, B.-G., & Zhang, C. (2020). Factor-based big data and predictive analytics capability assessment tool for the construction industry. *Automation in Construction*, *110*, 103042. doi:10.1016/j.autcon.2019.103042

Nguyen, K. Q., Nguyen, T. H., & Do, B. L. (2023). Narrative attention and related cryptocurrency returns. *Finance Research Letters*, *56*, 104174. doi:10.1016/j.frl.2023.104174

Nielsen, J. (1994). *Usability Engineering*. Elsevier.

NisarS.AslamM. S. (2023). Is ChatGPT a Good Tool for T & CM Students in Studying Pharmacology? SSRN 4324310. doi:10.2139/ssrn.4324310

North, C., Hills, D., Maher, P., Farkić, J., Zeilmann, V., Waite, S., Takano, T., Prince, H., Pedersen Gurholt, K., Muthomi, N., Njenga, D., Karaka-Clarke, T. H., Houge Mackenzie, S., & French, G. (2023). The impact of artificial intelligence on adventure education and outdoor learning: International perspectives. *Journal of Adventure Education and Outdoor Learning*, 1–18. doi:10.1080/14729679.2023.2248302

Novikov, V., Klochko, E., Brizhak, O., & Digtyar, O. (2020). Digital Economy: Human Capital, Technology, Communications. *5th International Conference on Economics, Management, Law and Education (EMLE 2019)*, (pp. 198–204). IEEE.

NovO.SinghN.MannD. (2023). Putting chatgpt's medical advice to the (turing) test. arXiv:2301.10035v1. https://arxiv.org/abs/2301.10035v1

Nunkoo, R., Teeroovengadum, V., Ringle, C. M., & Sunnassee, V. (2020). Service quality and customer satisfaction: The moderating effects of hotel star rating. *International Journal of Hospitality Management*, *91*, 102414. doi:10.1016/j.ijhm.2019.102414

Ochatbot. (2023). *How Do Chatbots Learn - Chatbot Algorithm*. Ochabot. https://ochatbot.com/how-do-chatbots-learn-chatbot-algorithm/

Olsson, A., & Engelbrektsson, O. (2022). *A thesis that writes itself: On the threat of AI- generated essays within academia*. [Bachelor Thesis, Halmstad University]. https://www.diva- portal.org/smash/get/diva2:1669744/FULLTEXT02

Olszak, C., Zurada, J., & Kozanoglu, D. (2020). Introduction to the Minitrack on Business Intelligence and Big Data for Innovative and Sustainable Development of Organizations. *Proceedings of the 53rd Hawaii International Conference on System Sciences*. IEEE. 10.24251/HICSS.2020.021

Open AI. (2022). *OpenAI about page*. Open AI. https://openai.com/about/

Open, A. I. (2020). *ChatGPT: A Large-Scale Generative Language Model*. OpenAI Blog.

OpenAI Blog. (2022). *Introducing ChatGPT: A new way to engage with customers*. [Blog post] OpenAI Blog.

Oviedo-TrespalaciosO.PedenA. E.Cole-HunterT.CostantiniA.HaghaniM.KellyS., & (2023). The Risks of Using ChatGPT to Obtain Common Safety-Related Information and Advice. SSRN 4346827.

Painoli, A. K., Bansal, R., Singh, R., & Kukreti, A. (2021). Impact of Digital Marketing on the Buying Behavior of Youth With Special Reference to Uttarakhand State. In Big Data Analytics for Improved Accuracy, Efficiency, and Decision Making in Digital Marketing (pp. 162-182). IGI Global. doi:10.4018/978-1-7998-7231-3.ch012

Panda, M., & Mishra, A. (2022). *Digital marketing*. Research Gate. https://www.researchgate.net/publication/358646409

Parmar, V., Large, A., Madden, C., & Das, V. (2009). The online outpatient booking system ' Choose and Book ' improves attendance rates at an audiology clinic: A comparative audit. *Journal of Innovation in Health Informatics*, *17*(3), 183–186. doi:10.14236/jhi.v17i3.733 PMID:20074431

Parsons, A. J., Zeisser, M., & Waitman, R. (1996). Organizing for digital marketing. *The McKinsey Quarterly*, (4), 185.

Parvez, S. J., Moyeenudin, H. M., Arun, S., Anandan, R., & Janahan, S. K. (2018). Digital marketing in hotel industry. *International Journal of Engineering & Technology, 7*(2.21), 288-290.

Patel, V. V. (2023). *Revolutionizing Marketing Efficiency with ChatGpt*. GSFC University.

Patterson, P., Yu, T., & de Ruyter, K. (2006). Understanding Customer Engagement in Services. *ANZMAC 2006 Conference*, Brisbane.

Paul, R. (2023). The politics of regulatingartificial intelligence technologies:acompetition state perspective. In R. Paul, E. Carmel, & J Cobbe (eds.) Handbook on Public Policy and Artificial Intelligence. Edward Elgar.

Paul, J., Ueno, A., & Dennis, C. (2023). ChatGPT and consumers: Benefits, pitfalls and future research agenda. *International Journal of Consumer Studies*, *47*(4), 1213–1225. doi:10.1111/ijcs.12928

Perc, M. (2014). The Matthew effect in empirical data. *Journal of the Royal Society, Interface*, *11*(98), 20140378. doi:10.1098/rsif.2014.0378 PMID:24990288

Perera, A. S. (2022). ChatGPT: The Next Level in Conversational AI. Medium. Retrieved from https://medium.com/mlearning-ai/chatgpt-the-next-level-in-conversational-ai-7e4a38dc968a

Perrigo, B. (2023). OpenAI used Kenyan workers on less than $2 per hour to make ChatGPT less toxic. *Time.* https://time.com/6247678/openai-chatgpt-kenya-workers/

Pertile, S., Moreira, V. P., & Rosso, P. (2015). Comparing and combing content- and citation-based approaches for plagiarism detection. *Journal of the Association for Information Science and Technology*, *67*(10), 2511–2526. doi:10.1002/asi.23593

Peters, R. (2023, August 9). *How to use CHATGPT to research crypto in 2023: Ultimate Guide*. CaptainAltcoin. https://captainaltcoin.com/how-to-use-chatgpt-to-research-crypto/

Pieriegud, J., & Zawieska, J. (2019). Mobility-as-a-Service–global trends and implementation potential in urban areas in Poland. *Transport Economics and Logistics*, *79*, 39–51. doi:10.26881/etil.2018.79.03

Piñeiro-Otero, T., & Martínez-Rolán, X. (2016). Understanding digital marketing—Basics and actions. *MBA: Theory and Application of Business and Management Principles*, 37–74.

Pitso, T. (2023). Telagogy: New theorisations about learning and teaching in higher education post-Covid-19 pandemic. *Cogent Education, 10*(2), 2258278. doi:10.1080/2331186X.2023.2258278

Pizzi, G., Scarpi, D., Pichierri, M., & Vannucci, V. (2021). Artificial intelligence and consumer behavior: The case of digital assistants and shopping satisfaction. *Journal of Retailing and Consumer Services.*

Praharaj, S. (2020). Development Challenges for Big Data Command and Control Centres for Smart Cities in India. In *Data-driven Multivalence in the Built Environment* (pp. 75–90). Springer. doi:10.1007/978-3-030-12180-8_4

Prasad, A., Kumar, A. S., Sharma, P., Irawati, I. D., Chandrashekar, D. V., Musirin, I. B., & Abdullah, H. M. A. (2023). Artificial Intelligence in Computer Science: An Overview of Current Trends and Future Directions. *Advances in Artificial and Human Intelligence in the Modern Era*, 43-60.

Priyo, J. S., Mohamad, B., & Adetunji, R. R. (2019). An examination of the effects of service quality and customer satisfaction on customer loyalty in the hotel industry. *International Journal of Supply Chain Management, 8*(1), 653–663.

Proserpio, D., & Zervas, G. (2017). Online reputation management: Estimating the impact of management responses on consumer reviews. *Marketing Science, 36*(5), 645–665. doi:10.1287/mksc.2017.1043

Putri, C. S. (2016). Pengaruh media sosial terhadap keputusan pembelian konsumen cherie melalui minat beli. *Jurnal Performa: Jurnal Manajemen dan Start-up Bisnis, 1*(5), 594-603.

QinC. (2023). Is ChatGPT a General-Purpose Natural Language Processing Task Solver? arXiv:2302.06476

Radford, A., Narasimhan, K., Salimans, T., & Sutskever, I. (2018). *Improving language understanding by generative pre-training*. UBC. https://www.cs.ubc.ca/~amuham01/LING530/papers/radford2018improving.pdf

Radford, A., Wu, J., Child, R., Luan, D., Amodei, D., & Sutskever, I. (2019). Language models are unsupervised multitask learners. *OpenAI blog, 1*(8), 9.

Radziwon, A., & Radziwon, M. (2019). Chatbots in customer service: Current state of the art. In *Proceedings of the International Conference on Business Excellence* (pp. 644-670). CORE.

Rafiq, F., Dogra, N., Adil, M., & Wu, J. Z. (2022). Examining consumer's intention to adopt AI-chatbot in tourism using partial least squares structural equation modeling method. *Mathematics, 10*(13), 2190. doi:10.3390/math10132190

Rahimian, S., ShamiZanjani, M., Manian, A., & Esfidani, M. R. (2021). A framework of customer experience management for the hotel industry. *International Journal of Contemporary Hospitality Management, 33*(5), 1413–1436. doi:10.1108/IJCHM-06-2020-0522

Rahman, M. M., & Watanobe, Y. (2023). Chatgpt for education and research: Opportunities, threats, and strategies. *Applied Sciences (Basel, Switzerland), 13*(9), 5783. doi:10.3390/app13095783

Raja, M., & Priya, G. L. (2023). The Role of Augmented Reality and Virtual Reality in Smart Health Education: State of the Art and Perspectives. Artificial Intelligence for Smart Healthcare, 311-325.

Ralph, D., Li, Y., Wills, G., & Green, N. G. (2020). Recommendations from cold starts in big data. *Computing*, *102*(6), 1–22. doi:10.100700607-020-00792-y

RangapurA.WangH. (2023). Chatgpt-crawler: Find out if chatgpt really knows what it's talking about. https://arxiv.org/abs/2304.03325v1

Ranjan, P., & Patel, P. (2019). Transforming Customer Engagement with AI-Powered Chatbots: A Case Study of Leading E-commerce Company. *International Journal of Artificial Intelligence & Applications*, *10*(5), 45–56.

Rathore, B. (2023). Future of AI & generation alpha: ChatGPT beyond boundaries. *Eduzone: International Peer Reviewed/Refereed Multidisciplinary Journal, 12*(1), 63-68.

RatliffL. J.DongR.OhlssonH.SastryS. S. (2013). Incentive design and utility learning via energy disaggregation. arXiv:1312.1394v2. http:// arxiv.org/abs/1312.1394v2

Rider, E. (2023, April 6). How ChatGPT Will Dramatically Change the Influencer Space. *Entrepreneur*. https://www.entrepreneur.com/science-technology/how-chatgpt-will-dramatically-change-the-influencer-space/448386

Rivas, P., & Zhao, L. (2023). Marketing with chatgpt: Navigating the ethical terrain of gpt-based chatbot technology. *AI, 4*(2), 375-384.

Rivas, P., & Zhao, L. (2023). Marketing with ChatGPT: Navigating the Ethical Terrain of GPT-Based Chatbot Technology. *AI, 4*(2), 375–384. doi:10.3390/ai4020019

Rivas, P., Chelsi, C., Nishit, N., & Ravula, L. (2019). Application-agnostic chatbot deployment considerations: A case study. In *Proceedings of the 2019 International Conference on Computational Science and Computational Intelligence (CSCI)*, Las Vegas, NV, USA. 10.1109/CSCI49370.2019.00070

Roberts, A. (2018, June). Technology in the Classroom: Advantages and Challenges. *Education Today*, *42*(6), 28–32.

Ročkute, K., Minelgaite, I., Zailskaite-Jakšte, L., & Damaševičius, R. (2018). Brand awareness in the context of mistrust The case study of an employment agency. *Sustainability (Basel)*, *10*(3), 695. doi:10.3390u10030695

Rodgers, W., Murray, J. M., Stefanidis, A., Degbey, W. Y., & Tarba, S. Y. (2023). An artificial intelligence algorithmicapproach to ethicaldecision-making in humanresource management processes. *Human Resource Management Review*, *33*(1), 100925. doi:10.1016/j.hrmr.2022.100925

Rowley, J. (2008). Understanding digital content marketing. *Journal of Marketing Management*, *24*(5-6), 517–540. doi:10.1362/026725708X325977

Ruby, M. (2023). How ChatGPT Works: The Model Behind The Bot. *Towards Data Science*. https://towardsdatascience.com/how-chatgpt-works-the-models-behind-the-bot-1ce5fca96286

Saggu, A., & Ante, L. (2023). The influence of CHATGPT on artificial intelligence related crypto assets: Evidence from a synthetic control analysis. *Finance Research Letters*, *55*, 103993. doi:10.1016/j.frl.2023.103993

Saini, S., & Bansal, R. (2022). Leveraging Role of Social Media Influencers in Corporate World-An Overview. *MBA Journals*. https://mbajournals.in/index.php/JoGM/article/view/849

Saini, S., & Bansal, R. (2023a). Geo-marketing: A new tool for marketers. In Enhancing Customer Engagement Through Location-Based Marketing (pp. 102–112). Scopus. doi:10.4018/978-1-6684-8177-6.ch008

Saini, S., Bansal, R., Saini, S., & Bansal, R. (2023). *Exploring the Interplay Between Stress Management and Work-Life Balance for Employees*. IGI Global.

Saini, S., & Bansal, R. (2023b). *Power of Social Media Influencer Credibility on the Influence of Brand Attitude*., doi:10.4018/978-1-6684-8898-0.ch010

Sakas, D. P., Reklitis, D. P., Terzi, M. C., & Vassilakis, C. (2022). Multichannel digital marketing optimizations through Big Data Analytics in the tourism and Hospitality Industry. *Journal of Theoretical and Applied Electronic Commerce Research*, *17*(4), 1383–1408. doi:10.3390/jtaer17040070

Sallam, M., Salim, N. A., Barakat, M., & Al-Tammemi, A. B. (2023). Chat-gpt applications in medical, dental, pharmacy, and public health education: A descriptive study highlighting the advantages and limitations. *Narrative Journal*, *3*(1), e103. doi:10.52225/narra.v3i1.103

Santiago, E. (2023). 190 ChatGPT Prompts Marketers Should Use. *HubSpot Blog*. https://blog.hubspot.com/marketing/chatgpt-prompts

Santini, A. (2018). The importance of referencing. *Journal of Critical Care Medicine*, *4*(1), 3–4. doi:10.2478/jccm-2018-0002 PMID:29967893

Saputra, R., Nasution, M. I. P., & Dharma, B. (2023). The Impact of Using AI Chat GPT on Marketing Effectiveness: A Case Study on Instagram Marketing. *Indonesian Journal of Economics and Management*, *3*(3), 603–617.

Sardianou, E., Kostakis, I., Mitoula, R., Gkaragkani, V., Lalioti, E., & Theodoropoulou, E. (2016). Understanding the entrepreneurs' behavioural intentions towards sustainable tourism: A case study from Greece. *Environment, Development and Sustainability*, *18*(3), 857–879. doi:10.100710668-015-9681-7

Satar, M., Aggarwal, D., Bansal, R., & Alarifi, G. (2023). Mapping the Knowledge Structure and Unveiling the Research Trends in Social Entrepreneurship and Inclusive Development: A Bibliometric Analysis. *Sustainability (Basel)*, *15*(7), 5626. doi:10.3390u15075626

Saura, J. R., Palos-Sanchez, P. R., & Correia, M. B. (2019). Digital marketing strategies based on the e-business model: Literature review and future directions. *Organizational Transformation and Managing Innovation in the Fourth Industrial Revolution*, 86–103.

Schlechty, P. C. (2001). *Shaking Up the Schoolhouse: How to Support and Sustain Educational Innovation*. Jossey-Bass.

SchönbergerD. (2018). Deep copyright: Up- and downstream questions related to artificial intelligence (AI) and machine learning (ML). SSRN. https://papers.ssrn.com/sol3/papers.cfm?abstract_id=3098315 doi:10.1628/zge-2018-0003

Schoop, S. (2023). Digitalization of Corporate Learning. *Digital Management in Covid-19 Pandemic and Post-PandemicTimes:Proceedings of the International Scientific-PracticalConference (ISPC 2021)*, 147–157.

Sciarretta, E., & Alimenti, L. (2021). *Smart speakers for inclusion: How can intelligent virtual assistants assist everybody?* 77–93.

Sedley, R. (2008). Six Theses on Digital Customer Engagement in a Troubled Economy. *Richard Sedley Blog*. http://richard-sedley.iuplog.com/default.asp?item1/4298747

Semrush Team. (2023, January 12). ChatGPT for SEO: The Ultimate Guide to Boost Your SERP Ranking through Blogging. *Semrush Blog*. https://www.semrush.com/blog/chatgpt-seo/

Sethi, S. S., & Sharma, P. (2023). New Developments in the Implementation of IoT in Agriculture. *SN Computer Science*, *4*(5), 503. doi:10.100742979-023-01896-w

ShafieeM. E.ZechmanE. M. (2014). An agent-based modeling frame-work for sociotechnical simulation of water distribution contamination events. arXiv:1405.3342v1, https://arxiv.org/abs/1405.3342v1

Sharida, A., Hamdan, A., & Mukhtar, A.-H. (2020). Smart cities: The next urban evolution in delivering a better quality of life. In Toward Social Internet of Things (SIoT): Enabling Technologies, Architectures and Applications (pp. 287–298). Springer.

Sharma, P., & Rathi, Y. (2016). Efficient density-based clustering using automatic parameter detection. In *Proceedings of the International Congress on Information and Communication Technology: ICICT 2015,* Volume 1 (pp. 433-441). Springer Singapore. 10.1007/978-981-10-0767-5_46

Sharma, P., Dadheech, P., & Senthil, A. S. K. (2023). AI-Enabled Crop Recommendation System Based on Soil and Weather Patterns. In *Artificial Intelligence Tools and Technologies for Smart Farming and Agriculture Practices* (pp. 184–199). IGI Global. doi:10.4018/978-1-6684-8516-3.ch010

Shehan Franciscu. (2022). *ChatGPT: A Natural Language Generation Model for Chatbots*. ResearchGate.

Siggelkow, N., & Terwiesch, C. (2023). Create Winning Customer Experiences with Generative AI. *Harvard Business Review*. https://hbr.org/2023/04/create-winning-customer-experiences-with-generative-ai

Singh, H., Jain, G., Munjal, A., & Rakesh, S. (2019). Blockchain Technology in Corporate Governance: Disrupting Chain Reaction or Not? *Corporate Governance (Bradford)*, *20*(1), 67–86. doi:10.1108/CG-07-2018-0261

Singh, H., & Singh, A. (2023). ChatGPT: Systematic Review, Applications, and Agenda for Multidisciplinary Research. *Journal of Chinese Economic and Business Studies*, *21*(2), 193–212. doi:10.1080/14765284.2023.2210482

Singh, V., Bansal, R., & Singh, R. (2022). *Big-Data Analytics: A New Paradigm Shift in Micro Finance Industry*., doi:10.1002/9781119792826.ch12

Sinha, M. (2023, March 6). Is ChatGPT the future of marketing? - ET brandequity. *ETBrandEquity.com*. https://brandequity.economictimes.indiatimes.com/news/marketing/ischatgpt-the-future-of-marketing/98438927

Şirzad, N. (2022). A review of online reputation management and online reputation components. *Doğuş Üniversitesi Dergisi*, *23*(1), 219–242.

Smith, J. A. (2019). *The Art of Academic Writing*. Academic Press.

Smith, J., & Johnson, L. (2022). Leveraging ChatGPT for Enhanced Customer Support: A Practical Guide. *AI Trends*, *18*(3), 37–48.

Smith, K. T. (2011). Digital marketing strategies that Millennials find appealing, motivating, or just annoying. *Journal of Strategic Marketing*, *19*(6), 489–499. doi:10.1080/0965254X.2011.581383

Smith, T. W., & Johnson, R. L. (2017). Motivation and Learning in Educational Settings. In K. D. Brown & L. M. Jones (Eds.), *Handbook of Educational Psychology* (2nd ed., pp. 123–145). Routledge.

Sohail, S. S., Farhat, F., Himeur, Y., Nadeem, M., Madsen, D. Ø., Singh, Y., Atalla, S., & Mansoor, W. (2023). Decoding CHATGPT: A taxonomy of existing research, current challenges, and possible future directions. *Journal of King Saud University - Computer and Information Sciences, 35*(8), 101675. doi:10.1016/j.jksuci.2023.101675

Sokolova, N. G., & Titova, O. V. (2019, May). Digital marketing as a type: concept, tools, and effects. In *1st International Scientific Conference "Modern Management Trends and the Digital Economy: from Regional Development to Global Economic Growth" (MTDE 2019)* (pp. 508-512). Atlantis Press. 10.2991/mtde-19.2019.101

Sood, K., Singh, S., Behl, A., Sindhwani, R., Kaur, S., & Pereira, V. (2023). Identification and prioritization of the risks in the mass adoption of artificial intelligence-driven stable coins: The quest for optimal resourceutilization. *Resources Policy*, *81*, 103235. doi:10.1016/j.resourpol.2022.103235

Stokel-Walker, C. (2022). AI bot ChatGPT writes smart essays - should professors worry? *Nature*. doi:10.1038/d41586-022-04397-7 PMID:36494443

Stokel-Walker, C., & Van Noorden, R. (2023). What ChatGPT and generative AI mean for science. *Nature*, *614*(7947), 214–216. doi:10.1038/d41586-023-00340-6 PMID:36747115

Stokes, R. (2011). *eMarketing: The essential guide to digital marketing*. Quirk eMarketing.

Strowel, A. M. (2023). ChatGPT and generative ai tools: Theft of intellectual labor? *IIC; International Review of Industrial Property and Copyright Law*, *54*(4), 491–494. doi:10.100740319-023-01321-y

Strubell, E., Ganesh, A., & McCallum, A. (2019). Energy and policy considerations for deep learning in NLP. *Proceedings of the Annual Meeting of the Association for Computational Linguistics*, (*vol. 57*, pp. 3645-3650). IEEE. 10.18653/v1/P19-1355

Sudirjo, F., Diantoro, K., Al-Gasawneh, J. A., Azzaakiyyah, H. K., & Ausat, A. M. A. (2023). Application of ChatGPT in Improving Customer Sentiment Analysis for Businesses. *Jurnal Teknologi Dan Sistem Informasi Bisnis*, *5*(3), 283–288. doi:10.47233/jteksis.v5i3.871

SunnyM. M.BerghoferM.AslanI. (2021). *Towards tool-support for interactive-machine learning applications in the android ecosystem*. arXiv:2103.14852v1, https://arxiv.org/abs/2103.14852v1

Suresh Babu, C. V. (2022). *Artificial Intelligence and Expert Systems*. Anniyappa Publication.

Suresh Babu, C. V., & Adhithya, S. (2023). ChatGPT and Other Generative AI Tools in Education: Transformative Potential and Ethical Considerations. In J. Keengwe (Ed.), *Creative AI Tools and Ethical Implications in Teaching and Learning* (pp. 135–152). IGI Global. doi:10.4018/979-8-3693-0205-7.ch007

Suresh Babu, C. V., & Padma, R. (2023). Technology Transformation Through Skilled Teachers in Teaching Accountancy. In R. González-Lezcano (Ed.), *Advancing STEM Education and Innovation in a Time of Distance Learning* (pp. 211–233). IGI Global. doi:10.4018/978-1-6684-5053-6.ch011

Suresh Babu, C. V., & Rohan, B. (2023). Evaluation and Quality Assurance for Rapid E-Learning and Development of Digital Learning Resources. In M. I. Santally, (Eds.), *Implementing Rapid E-Learning Through Interactive Materials Development* (pp. 139–170). IGI Global. doi:10.4018/978-1-6684-4940-0.ch008

Taecharungroj, P. (2023). *ChatGPT's influence on customer experience in digital marketing: Investigating the moderating roles*. PMC.

Taecharungroj, V. (2023). "What can ChatGPT do?" Analyzing early reactions to the innovative ai chatbot on twitter. *Big Data and Cognitive Computing*, *7*(1).

Talan, T., & Kalinkara, Y. (2023). *The Role of Artificial Intelligence in Higher Education: ChatGPT Evaluation for Anatomy Course*. Research Gate.

Tanwar, A., Sharma, P., Pandey, A., & Kumar, S. (2022, December). Intrusion Detection System Based Ameliorated Technique of Pattern Matching. In *Proceedings of the 4th International Conference on Information Management & Machine Intelligence* (pp. 1-4). 10.1145/3590837.3590947

Tan, Y. C., & Celis, L. E. (2019). Assessing social and intersectional biases in contextualized word representations. *Proceedings of the 33rd International Conference on Neural Information Processing Systems* (pp.13230–13241). Curran Associates Inc.

Taylor, C. R. (2020). There is an urgent need for more research on influencer marketing. *International Journal of Advertising*, *39*(7), 889–891. doi:10.1080/02650487.2020.1822104

Thigpen, C., & Funk, C. (2019). *Most Americans says science has brought benefits to society and expect more to come*. Pew Research. https://www.pewresearch.org/fact-tank/2019/08/27/most-americans-say-science-has-brought-benefits-to-society-and-expect-more-to-come/

Thorp, H. H. (2023). ChatGPT is fun, but not an author. *Science*, *379*(6630), 313. doi:10.1126cience.adg7879 PMID:36701446

Todor, R.D. (2017). Promotion and communication through email marketing campaigns. *Bulletin of the Transilvania University of Brasov. Series V: Economi Sciences,* 61–66.

Tomar, P., & Verma, S. (2021). Impact and role of AI technologies in teaching, learning, and research in higher education. In Impact of AI Technologies on Teaching, Learning, and Research in Higher Education (pp. 190-203). IGI Global. doi:10.4018/978-1-7998-4763-2.ch012

Tosic, D. (2023). *Artificial Intelligence-driven web development and agile project management using OpenAI API and GPT technology: A detailed report on technical integration and implementation of GPT models in CMS with API and agile web development for quality user-centered AI chat service experience.*

Trilling, B., & Fadel, C. (2012). *21st Century Skills: Learning for Life in Our Times*. John Wiley and Sons.

Truly, A. (2023). *Is ChatGPT safe? Here are the risks to consider before using it.* Digital Trends. https://www.digitaltrends.com/computing/is-chatgpt-safe/

TS2 Space. (2023). *ChatGPT: The next generation of customer service chatbots*. [Blog post]. TS2.

U.S. Department of Education. (2018). *Enhancing Student Motivation: A Guide for Educators*. USDE. https://www2.ed.gov/rschstat/eval/tech/motivation/motivation.pdf

Umamaheswari, S., & Valarmathi, A. (2023). Role of Artificial Intelligence in The Banking Sector. *Journal of Survey in Fisheries Sciences*, *10*(4S), 2841–2849.

University of North Carolina. (n.d.). *What is Sociology?* University of North Carolina. https://sociology.unc.edu/undergraduate-program/sociology-major/what-is-sociology/

Vaiciukynaite, E., Zailskaite-Jakste, L., Damasevicius, R., & Gatautis, R. (2018). Does hedonic content of brand posts affect consumer sociability be-haviour on facebook? In *5th European Conference on Social Media, ECSM 2018*, (pp. 325–331). IEEE.

Van Doorn, J., Lemon, K. E., Mittal, V., Nab, S., Dore'en, P., Pirner, P., & Verhoef, P. C. (2010). Customer Engagement Behavior: Theoretical Foundations and Research Directions. *Journal of Service Research*, *13*(3), 253–266. doi:10.1177/1094670510375599

Vaswani, A., Shazeer, N., Parmar, N., Uszkoreit, J., Jones, L., Gomez, A. N., & Polosukhin, I. (2017). Attention is all you need. In Advances in Neural Information Processing Systems. ACL.

Venu, S., Kotti, J., Pankajam, A., Dhabliya, D., Rao, G. N., Bansal, R., Gupta, A., & Sammy, F. (2022). Secure Big Data Processing in Multihoming Networks with AI-Enabled IoT. *Wireless Communications and Mobile Computing*, *2022*, 1–10. doi:10.1155/2022/3893875

Verhoef, P. C., Reinartz, W. J., & Krafft, M. (2010). Customer engagement as a new perspective in customer management. *Journal of Service Research*, *13*(3), 247–252. doi:10.1177/1094670510375461

Victor, A. (2023, September 21). *Top 17 industry applications of chatgpt*. Custom Software Engineering Services. https://insights.daffodilsw.com/blog/top-17-industry-applications-of-chatgpt

Vivek, S. D., Beatty, S. E., & Morgan, R. M. (2012). Customer engagement: Exploring customer relationships beyond purchase. *Journal of Marketing Theory and Practice*, *20*(2), 122–146. doi:10.2753/MTP1069-6679200201

Vujić, M., ĐorĐević, S., & Lakićević, M. (2019). Service quality and customer satisfaction in the hotel industry in Serbia. *Менаџмент у хотелијерству и туризму, 7*(1), 61-70.

Waggoner, A. (2018). Improving the quality of constructive peer feedback. *College Teaching*, *66*(1), 22–23. doi:10.1080/87567555.2017.1349075

Wamba, S. F., Bawack, R. E., Guthrie, C., Queiroz, M. M., & Carillo, K. D. (2021). Are we preparing for a good AI society? A bibliometric review and research agenda. *Technological Forecasting and Social Change*, *164*, 120482. doi:10.1016/j.techfore.2020.120482

Wang, X., Lin, X., & Shao, B. (2022). Artificial intelligence changes the way we work: A close look at innovating with chatbots. *Journal of the Association for Information Science and Technology*, *74*(3), 339–353. doi:10.1002/asi.24621

Wang, Y., Liang, Z., Zhang, Y., & Liang, X. (2023). Enhancing customer engagement with chatbots: An empirical study based on ChatGPT technology. *International Journal of Information Management*.

WenT. H.VandykeD.Mrkši'cN.Gaši'cM.Rojas-BarahonaL. M.SuP. H.YoungS. (2016). A network-based end-to-end trainable task-oriented dialogue system. arXiv:1604.04562.

Wenzlaff, K., & Spaeth, S. (2022). Smarter than humans? validating how OpenAI's CHATGPT model explains crowdfunding, Alternative Finance and Community Finance. SSRN *Electronic Journal*. doi:10.2139/ssrn.4302443

West, C. (2023). *ChatGPT Content Creation: SEO, YouTube, Book Writing & More Made Easy: Become a Better Writer | Make Money Online*. Cea West.

Windelband, L. (2023). Artificial Intelligence and Assistance Systems for TechnicalVocational Education and Training–Opportunities and Risks. In New Digital Work: Digital Sovereignty at the Workplace (pp. 195–213). Springer.

Wong, I. A., Lian, Q. L., & Sun, D. (2023). Autonomous travel decision-making: An early glimpse into ChatGPT and generative AI. *Journal of Hospitality and Tourism Management*, *56*, 253–263. doi:10.1016/j.jhtm.2023.06.022

Woods, H. B., Brumberg, J., Kaltenbrunner, W., Pinfield, S., & Waltman, L. (2023). An overview of innovations in the external peer review of journal manuscripts. *Wellcome Open Research*, *7*(82), 82. doi:10.12688/wellcomeopenres.17715.2 PMID:36879926

Woolfolk, A., & Margetts, K. (2007). *Educational psychology*. Pearson. Prentice Hall.

Xie, Y., Seth, I., Hunter-Smith, D. J., Rozen, W. M., Ross, R., & Lee, M. (2023). Aesthetic surgery advice and counseling from artificial intelligence: A rhinoplasty consultation with chatgpt. *Aesthetic Plastic Surgery*. doi:10.100700266-023-03338-7 PMID:37095384

Yang, K.-C., & Menczer, F. (2023, July 30). *Anatomy of an AI-powered malicious social botnet*. arXiv.org. https://doi.org//arXiv.2307.16336 doi:10.48550

Yang, Z., Dai, Z., Yang, Y., Carbonell, J., Salakhutdinov, R., & Le, Q. V. (2019). XLNet: generalized autoregressive pretraining for language understanding. *Proceedings of the 33rd International Conference on Neural Information Processing Systems,(vol. 33*, pp. 5753- 5763). IEEE.

Yang, W. (2022). Artificial Intelligence education for young children: Why, what, and how in curriculum design and implementation. *Computers and Education: Artificial Intelligence*, *3*, 100061. doi:10.1016/j.caeai.2022.100061

Yanisky-Ravid, S. (2017). *Generating Rembrandt: Artificial intelligence, copyright, and accountability in the 3A Era: The human-like authors are already here*. Michigan State Law Review. *RE:view*, 659.

Yao, X., & Huang, J. (2019). Beyond the hype: A survey of business models in artificial intelligence. *Big Data Analytics*, *4*(1), 1–10.

Yasmin, A., Tasneem, S., & Fatema, K. (2015). Effectiveness of Digital Marketing in the Challenging Age: An Empirical Study. *The International Journal of Management Science and Business Administration*, *1*(5), 69–80. doi:10.18775/ijmsba.1849-5664-5419.2014.15.1006

Yuan, Y., Lu, Y., Chow, T. E., Ye, C., Alyaqout, A., & Liu, Y. (2020). The Missing Parts from Social Media–Enabled Smart Cities: Who, Where, When, and What? *Annals of the American Association of Geographers, 110*(2), 462–475. doi:10.1080/24694452.2019.1631144

YueT.AuD.AuC. C.IuK. Y (2023). Democratising Financial Knowledge with ChatGPT by OpenAI: Unleashing the Power of Technology. SSRN 4346152.

ZarifhonarvarA. (2023). Economics of chatgpt: A labor market view on the occupational impact of artificial intelligence. SSRN. doi:10.2139/ssrn.4350925

Zech, H. (2021). Liability for AI: Public policy considerations. *ERA Forum, 22*, 147-158. 10.100712027-020-00648-0

Zhang, Y., Sun, S., Galley, M., Chen, Y. C., Brockett, C., Gao, X., & Dolan, B. (2020). Dialogpt: Large-scale generative pre-training for conversational response generation. arXiv preprint arXiv:1911.00536. doi:10.18653/v1/2020.acl-demos.30

Zhang, R., Nicholas, J., Knapp, A. A., Graham, A. K., Gray, E., Kwasny, M. J., Reddy, M., & Mohr, D. C. (2019). Clinically meaningful use of mental health apps and its effects on depression: Mixed methods study. *Journal of Medical Internet Research, 21*(12), e15644. doi:10.2196/15644 PMID:31859682

ZhangS.DinanE.UrbanekJ.SzlamA.KielaD.WestonJ. (2018). Personalizing dialogue agents: I have a dog, do you have pets too? arXiv:1801.07243. doi:10.18653/v1/P18-1205

Zhao, J., Wang, T., Yatskar, M., Cotterell, R., Ordonez, V., & Chang, K.-W. (2019). Gender Bias in Contextualized Word Embeddings. *Proceedings of the 2019 Conference of the North American Chapter of the Association for Computational Linguistics: Human Language Technologies*, (pp. 629–634). IEEE. https://doi.org/10.18653/v1/N19-1064

Zhou, X., Chen, Z., Jin, X., & Wang, W. Y. (2021). HULK: An energy efficiency benchmark platform for responsible natural language processing. *Proceedings of the Conference of the European Chapter of the Association for Computational Linguistics: System Demonstrations,* (*vol. 16*, pp. 329-336). IEEE. 10.18653/v1/2021.eacl-demos.39

Zhu, H. (2020). Big data and artificial intelligence modeling for drug discovery. *Annual Review of Pharmacology and Toxicology, 60*(1), 573–589. doi:10.1146/annurev-pharmtox-010919-023324 PMID:31518513

About the Contributors

Rohit Bansal is working as Associate Professor in Department of Management Studies in Vaish College of Engineering, Rohtak. He is a perseverant, passionate academician cum seasoned professional. He obtained Ph.D. in Management from Maharshi Dayanand University, Rohtak. With a rich experience of 15 years, he has achieved growth through robust and proactive academic initiatives. He has authored & edited 28 books with renowned national & international publishers including IGI Global USA, Scrivener-Wiley Publishing, De Gruyter, Weser Books, Scholar's Press, Germany etc. In addition to, Dr. Rohit has published 150 research papers and chapters in journals of repute including Scopus indexed as well as edited books. He has also presented papers in 50 conferences and seminars. His area of interest includes marketing management, organizational behaviour, services marketing, customer engagement, digital marketing, human resource management and organizational development. He is on Editorial Advisory Board as a member in 125 national and international peer reviewed journals. He has acted as session chair in many international conferences.

Abdul Hafaz Ngah is currently a Senior Lecturer at the Faculty of Business, Economy and Social Development, University of Malaysia Terengganu. He received his PhD in technology management (halal supply chain) from Universiti Malaysia Pahang. His research interests are in technology management, halal logistics and supply chain, halal food, pharmaceuticals, cosmetics, technology adoption, consumer behaviour and tourism management. Abdul Hafaz Ngah is the corresponding author and can be contacted at: hafaz.ngah@umt.edu.my.

Aziza Chakir is a Senior Lecturer, Keynote Speaker and currently serve as a HDR professor in the university Hassan II. Her research interests include in the area of Computer Engineering, Information Systems, Digital culture, Software Engineering, Knowledge Transfer Technology, IT Governance, Cloud Computing, Suitable Development (Green IT..), Machine Learning, Big Data, Data mining...

She is currently working on many projects such as "Green computing", "Ecological frameworks"..

Nishita Pruthi is a research scholar at Institute of Management Studies and Research, Maharshi Dayanand University. She has published research articles in Scopus and SCIE indexed journals. She has also contributed chapters in edited books published by IGI Global, Bentham Science and Emerald etc. She participated in various international conferences. She can be contacted at pruthinishita@gmail.com.

***

Sumitha Anantharajah is a lecturer working in the School of Hospitality, Tourism & Events Faculty of Social Sciences & Leisure Management at Taylor's University, Malaysia.

C.V. Suresh Babu is a pioneer in content development. A true entrepreneur, he founded Anniyappa Publications, a company that is highly active in publishing books related to Computer Science and Management. Dr. C.V. Suresh Babu has also ventured into SB Institute, a center for knowledge transfer. He holds a Ph.D. in Engineering Education from the National Institute of Technical Teachers Training & Research in Chennai, along with seven master's degrees in various disciplines such as Engineering, Computer Applications, Management, Commerce, Economics, Psychology, Law, and Education. Additionally, he has UGC-NET/SET qualifications in the fields of Computer Science, Management, Commerce, and Education. Currently, Dr. C.V. Suresh Babu is a Professor in the Department of Information Technology at the School of Computing Science, Hindustan Institute of Technology and Science (Hindustan University) in Padur, Chennai, Tamil Nadu, India. For more information, you can visit his personal blog at .

Amit Channa possesses 25 years of academic and industry experience, spread across electronic media production. At present he is working in Vivekananda School of Journalism & Mass Communication, Vivekananda Institute of Professional Studies-TC, Delhi. He has headed the same department as Dean previously. He guides research scholars for their Ph.D. programme alongside as an academician. Dr. Channa has authored four books and edited two books in mass media studies and management. He has chaired sessions and presented papers in various national and international conferences. Dr. Amit Channa is Ph.D. in Mass Communication and is a trained in Video film production and techniques from NITTR, Chandigarh He has dual master degree in Mass Communication and History. He has also completed PGD in Electronic Media Management and Film Production, Course in

Videography, certificate course in film appreciation from FTII, Pune and a course in Art Appreciation from National Museum, New Delhi.

Arpitam Chatterjee is the associate professor in the department of printing in Jadavpur University. He has completed his PhD from Jadavpur University and produced two PhD scholar.

Omar Durrah is an associate professor and chairperson of management department in the college of commerce and business administration at Dhofar university, Sultanate of Oman. His research interests include human resources, psychology, organizational behavior, leadership styles, and entrepreneurship. Durrah got the National Research Award 2021.

Ruth Sabina Francis, Lecturer & Programme Director, School of Hospitality, Tourism and Events, Taylor's University, has 20 years of both Industry and teaching experience. She is well known in the hospitality Industry for her expertise in Rooms Division Management. She was awarded as the Young Women Achiever in the field of Hospitality for her teaching and learning practices for the year 2016 by the centre for women empowerment in India. As a PSMBB Certified Trainer (TTT) she has conducted various training programmes for the Hospitality Industry personnel in Malaysia. Being in the Industry for seven years she has gained a lot of exposure towards sustained quality management. During her stint as Housekeeper in Chennai she has trained many staff in the area of housekeeping. Her research expertise includes areas such as Human Resources, Emotional intelligence, Organizational Citizenship Behaviour in the Hospitality field.

Meenakshi Gandhi has two decades of experience in teaching, research and academic administration. She has served as Dean Research and Dean of the Business school of VIPS. Prof. Gandhi is an executive alumni of the Oxford University U.K. and successfully completed the Academic Leadership Development Program (LEAP) sponsored by the Ministry of HRD, Govt. of India. She has been recognised for her achievements with the Indira Parekh 50 Women Leaders in Education award in 2018 and the 100 most dedicated professors award in 2019 by the world CSR foundation.Meenakshi Gandhi is a Professor in the School of Business Studies, in Vivekananda Institute of Professional Studies, Guru Gobind Singh Indraprastha University, Delhi. Her research interest covers marketing, entrepreneurship, sustainability and gender. She has been involved in works on sustainable consumption and talent management and retention. She has authored and co-authored several research papers and articles in international and national journals.

Arti Gupta is an Assistant Professor at J. C. Bose University of Science and Technology, YMCA, Faridabad, India. Her research areas include job satisfaction, organisational justice, organisational commitment, and organisational culture. She has published various paper in national and international journals of repute.

A. V. Senthil Kumar is working as a Director & Professor in the Department of Research and PG in Computer Applications, Hindusthan College of Arts and Science, Coimbatore. He has finished is Doctor of Science during February 2023. He has more than 26 years of teaching experience and 5 years of Industry experience. He has to his credit 30 Book Chapters, 220 papers in International and National Journals, 55 papers in International and National Conferences, and 10 edited books and 2 text books. He is an Editor-in-Chief for various journals. Key Member for India, Machine Intelligence Research Lab (MIR Labs).He is Associate Editor of IEEE Access. He is the first person in South India to receive the highest degree in academic field D.Sc in Computer Science.

Sanjeev Kumar is an accomplished expert in Food and Beverage. He currently holds the positions of Professor at the Lovely Professional University, Punjab, India. With over a decade of experience in the field, food Service Industry, his research focuses on Alcoholic beverages, Event management and Sustainable Management Practices, Metaverse and Artificial Intelligence. He has published more than 35 research papers, articles and chapters in Scopus Indexed, UGC Approved and peer reviewed Journals and books. Dr. Sanjeev Kumar participated and acted as resource person in various National and International conferences, seminars, research workshops and industry talks and his work has been widely cited.

Anshit Mukherjee is the BTech student of Computer science at Abacus Institute of Technology, Mogra, Hoogly. He has completed his 10+2 level before starting his education in engineering.

Seema Rathee is currently working as an Assistant Professor at Department of Commerce, Maharshi Dayanand University, Rohtak. She has completed her Ph.D. from the Department of Commerce. Her areas of specialization are Accounting and Finance. She has qualified UGC Net in Commerce. She has approximately 11 years of experience in teaching and research. She has published several research papers in National and International journals. She has presented many research papers at conferences and seminars. She has also organized various academic activities in the form of workshops, seminars, extension lectures, and conferences at the National and International levels. She has attended many workshops and faculty development programs in her academic career.

Sarthak Sengupta is working as a Program Assistant at the Indian Institute of Management, Lucknow and also submitted his Ph.D. thesis at the Indian Institute of Information Technology-Allahabad, Prayagraj. He has completed his Bachelor of Engineering in Computer Science and Masters in Business Administration (IT) in Human Resource & Marketing Management. He has plenty of work experience in academic institutions and industries. His research and teaching interests include organizational behavior, social network analysis, social media analytics, digital marketing, artificial intelligence, cybersecurity, risk management, management information systems, and economics. He has numerous research publications in leading journals, prestigious conferences, book chapters, book, and case study along with patent grants.

Sarabjeet Singh Sethi is working as an Associate Professor in the department of CSE, SKIT, Jaipur, Rajasthan, India. He is a member of many Professional Organizations like the AMIE & LMISTE. His areas of research interests primarily revolve around networking, including topics such as ad hoc networks, wireless sensor networks, Internet of Things (IoT), Cloud Computing and Computer architecture.

Ankit Sharma is a Sr. Assistant Professor at the Vivekananda Institute of Professional Studies (VIPS), Guru Gobind Singh Indraprastha University, New Delhi with two decades of time spent across various media domains: academia, theatre, television, films and Development Sector. A Doctorate in Journalism & Mass Communication and Course in Film Appreciation from Film & Television Institute of India (FTII), Sharma has been recognized for his various award winning documentaries as an independent film maker and number documentaries have been nominated in national and international film festivals. He has directed films for the Directorate of Audio Visual Publicity (DAVP), Doordarshan (DD) and has worked with several Government and non-government organisations and film bodies. He has to his credit various documentaries, serials, features, corporate, AD films and packaging of TV programmes too. He has also worked with Signet Communication Pvt. Ltd., Space TV, Scorpion Media Pvt. Ltd., Mediamen Services and Yuva arts. Dr Sharma is also on the boards of several NGOs and consultant with several bodies.

Priyanka Sharma is born in Jaipur, Rajasthan, India. She Received her B.Tech. degree from Rajasthan Technical University, Kota, Rajasthan India, in 2012 in Information Technology and M.Tech. degree from Rajasthan Technical University, Kota, Rajasthan India, in 2016 in Computer Science. She is working as an Assistant Professor in the department of Computer Science & Engineering (NBA Accredited), Swami Keshvanand Institute of Technology, Management & Gramothan, Jaipur,

Rajasthan, India (NAAC A++ Accredited). She has guided various M.Tech. and UG scholars. She has been the mentor of various NPTEL and Swayam courses. She is member of IEEE, ACM and various professional societies.She has published more than 20 research papers in national and international journals/conferences, book chapters. She has edited one book and She is the editorial member of an American Journal. Also, she has taken part in forums hosted by Infosys, TCS, Oracle, and IBM. Her area of interest are investigating the advancements in machine learning and deep learning applications. She has received accolades on a number of times in a variety of fields, including Designation as an Active Reviewer by some well-known journals. She was also given recognition by Infosys, India, for her remarkable performance in the Campus Link Program.

Amrik Singh is working as Professor in the School of Hotel Management and Tourism at Lovely Professional University, Punjab, India. He obtained his Ph.D. degree in Hotel Management from Kurukshetra University, Kurukshetra. He started his academic career at Lovely Professional University, Punjab, India in the year 2007. He has published more than 40 research papers in UGC and peer-reviewed and Scopus/Web of Science) journals. He has published 12 patents and 01 patent has been granted in the inter-disciplinary domain. Dr. Amrik Singh participated and acted as a resource person in various national and international conferences, seminars, research workshops, and industry talks. His area of research interest is accommodation management, ergonomics, green practices, human resource management in hospitality, waste management, AR VR in hospitality, etc. He is currently guiding 8Ph.D. scholars and 2 Ph.D. scholars have been awarded Ph.D.

Vipin Singh is a distinguished expert in the field of Tourism and Hospitality Management, known for his in-depth knowledge and extensive experience.r. With over a decade of diversified experience, Dr. Vipin Singh has made significant contributions both in the hotel industry and academia. His expertise spans a wide range of areas, making him a valuable asset in the field. In his illustrious career, Dr. Vipin Singh has had the privilege of working with renowned establishments like Taj Hotel and Domino's Pizza. During his time in the hotel industry, he has successfully managed operations, ensuring the seamless functioning of the establishments under his care. His hands-on approach and leadership skills have proven instrumental in enhancing efficiency and guest satisfaction.

Bipan Tudu is the professor in the department of Instrumentation and Electronics, Jadavpur University. He has published many articles of international reputes. He has also produced many PhD scholars.

Arif Ullah working as an Assistant Professor Department of Computer Science at Air University Islamabad Pakistan.

Ligita Zailskaitė-Jakštė is a researcher and lecturer at Kaunas University of Technology (KTU), Faculty of Informatics, Multimedia engineering department. She defended her PhD "Consumer engagement behavior in social media communication impact on brand equity" in social sciences, KTU. Currently, she works in an interdisciplinary area. Ligita has experience in Erasmus+ projects management and in creating new e-learning courses; worked for 10 years as a marketing and communication specialist at KTU. She is a board member of the Lithuanian Communication Association (LTKA) and a member of the National Association of Distance Education (NADE). She upskilled her qualification at KTH Royal Institute of Technology, University of Rostock (Germany), University of Iceland (Iceland) and gave lectures at the University of Ferrara (Italy), the Pontifical University of John Paul (Poland), and others. Her research areas include social media/ technologies online usage for consumer engagement behavior and positive experience creation, consumers' positive acceptance of technologies online, human-computer interaction, project management, and marketing communication.

Index

D

E

G

H

I

L

N

O

P

R

S

T